In Tribute To

Rabbi Newton J. Friedman

**this book is given
Lamar State College of
Technology**

by

Mrs. Newton J. Friedman

DISCARDED

REBECCA GRATZ, FROM A PAINTING BY SULLY

Letters of
Rebecca Gratz

EDITED WITH AN INTRODUCTION AND NOTES
By RABBI DAVID PHILIPSON, D. D.
*Author of "The Reform Movement in Judaism,"
"The Jew in English Fiction," etc., etc.*

PHILADELPHIA
THE JEWISH PUBLICATION SOCIETY OF AMERICA
1929

COPYRIGHT, 1929, BY
THE JEWISH PUBLICATION SOCIETY
PHILADELPHIA, PA.

DEDICATED
TO THE
SISTERHOOD
OF THE
BENE ISRAEL CONGREGATION
CINCINNATI

FOREWORD

As is stated in the essay which introduces this collection of the family letters of the leading American Jewess of her day, these important epistles were placed at my disposal by the niece of Rebecca Gratz, Mrs. Thomas Hart Clay of Lexington, Kentucky. My thanks are due to Mrs. Clay, not only for her ready consent to my request to let me have the letters for publication, but also for the permission to have photographs made of the superb portraits of her father, Benjamin Gratz, and her aunt, Rebecca Gratz, by the great American painter, James Sully, for inclusion in this volume. The picture of the Benjamin Gratz homestead was likewise loaned to me by Mrs. Clay for reproduction in these pages. Mrs. Clay furthermore gave me much interesting information concerning her famous aunt whom she had seen on occasional visits to Philadelphia with her father during her childhood.

My thanks are also due to the Sisterhood of the Bene Israel Congregation (Rockdale Avenue Temple) of Cincinnati, who supplied the funds for the publication of these letters as a memento of the fortieth anniversary of my service as rabbi of the congregation. How beautifully appropriate it is for an organization of Jewish women to be the medium through whom the noble thoughts of a great sister Jewess are given to the world!

I desire to thank my friend, Rabbi Louis I. Egelson of Cincinnati, for his helpfulness in reading the proof and seeing the volume through the press.

D. P.

Cincinnati, Ohio.

February, 1929.

INTRODUCTION

During a brief sojourn at Lexington, Kentucky, several years ago, I had the pleasure of forming the personal acquaintance of Mrs. Thomas Hart Clay, the last surviving child of Benjamin Gratz and a niece of Rebecca Gratz, who is generally supposed to be the original of the famous character, Rebecca, in Sir Walter Scott's novel "Ivanhoe," through the description of the famous American Jewess furnished Scott by Washington Irving, an intimate friend of the Gratz family. In the course of a most interesting and revelatory conversation, Mrs. Clay, whose cultivated mind is a storehouse of valuable historical data and reminiscences, informed me that she had in her possession a large number of letters that had been written by Rebecca Gratz to her brother Benjamin and her two sisters-in-law, the wives of Benjamin Gratz. I sensed at once that here was possibly an unexpected and important discovery that might prove of great value. I urged Mrs. Clay to place these letters at my disposal. She acceded graciously to my request. My supposition as to the value of the letters was more than realized when I had the opportunity to examine the very interesting correspondence.

The letters number hundreds and extend over more than half a century, namely, from the year 1808 to the year 1866. Although being largely family letters still they contain much that transcends the narrow family circle. Events of the day are mentioned and commented upon, books of recent appearance are discussed, men and women in the public eye are referred to. The reader of these epistles feels that he is perusing the outpourings of an unusual personality. The letters are pervaded with a deep religious feeling and a broad humanity, which stamp the writer to have been a noble woman whose charity knew no creed and whose interests were as wide as her heart was warm and her impulses unselfish. These letters verify the traditions that have descended about Rebecca Gratz's loveliness of disposition and elevation of spirit. The famous portrait of Rebecca Gratz by Sully which is in Mrs. Clay's possession shows her to have been beautiful in feature; these letters reveal her to have been beautiful in character as in visage.

In editing the letters I have omitted such portions as are of too intimate a family nature to be paraded before the public eye. I have not edited the language nor the punctuation. The writer of the letters wrote in a flowing manner and employed usually a small dash in place of commas and semicolons. This peculiarity is characteristic and does not at all interfere with the charm and effectiveness of the style.

The letters disclose the very deep affection which existed between Rebecca Gratz and her youngest brother Benjamin. They were the children of Michael Gratz, one of the leading merchants of the country in the eighteenth century and his wife Miriam, the daughter of Joseph Simon, a large landowner of Lancaster, Pennsylvania. Michael Gratz came to the United States in 1755 from Langensdorf, Upper Silesia. He and his brother Barnard, who had arrived in this country one year earlier, became very prominent in mercantile life. These Gratz brothers figure very largely in the commercial activities of Philadelphia and the country during the eighteenth century. They participated in what may be considered the opening remonstrance against the government of Great Britain on the part of the American colonists. For we find the names of Barnard Gratz and Michael Gratz among the signers of the Non-Importation Resolutions adopted on the twenty-fifth of October, 1765, by "the merchants and citizens of Philadelphia." The Non-Importation Resolutions were adopted as a protest against the hateful Stamp Act: the signers agreed not to have any goods shipped from Great Britain until after the repeal of the Stamp Act. When the definite break with the mother country came, the Gratz brothers cast their lot with the revolutionists. A letter written August 14, 1775, by Governor William Franklin of New Jersey to his famous father Benjamin Franklin has been preserved in which Barnard Gratz is mentioned. He took the oath of allegiance to the Commonwealth of Pennsylvania and to the United States as a free nation on November 5, 1777.

The Gratz brothers established connections with merchants and traders in Pennsylvania, Virginia and other colonies. A selection from the voluminous business papers and correspondence of these two brothers extending over many years, was edited in 1916 by William Vincent Byers in a handsome volume, entitled "B. and M. Gratz, Merchants in Philadelphia 1754-1798." In the preface to this volume the Gratz brothers are called significantly "merchant venturers." They were indeed adventurers in the trading and mercantile fields. Theirs is an American mercantile romance. They and other "merchant venturers" with whom they became associated, opened up vast territories to trade and exploration. Their specialty was the fur trade. Their trade routes extended from Lancaster, the Pennsylvania frontier town, to the forks of the Ohio, the present Pittsburgh. From these forks their steamboats plied the river into the then Indian territory which constitutes the present states of West

INTRODUCTION

Virginia, Ohio and Kentucky. Their routes branched out further into what is now Indiana and Illinois. What came to be known as the Illinois and Wabash claim of the Gratz brothers was the subject later of much litigation. Included in these Kentucky holdings was the land wherein was situated the famous Mammoth Cave.

The earlier "merchant venturers" with whom the Gratz brothers became particularly associated were Joseph Simon, William Trent, David Franks, Alexander Lowrey and George Croghan. And it was Michael the younger brother rather than the elder Barnard, who was the venturer. Therefore we find that while Barnard remained stationary in Philadelphia, Michael, after the first few years, left Philadelphia for a time and settled in Lancaster, the frontier Pennsylvania settlement. From here the "merchant venturers" mentioned above directed their trade operations. It was with Joseph Simon, the first named of this group, that young Gratz came into especial relationship. This Joseph Simon, who had settled in Lancaster in 1735 according to one account and in 1740 according to another, was the leading figure in the pioneer Jewish community of Lancaster. Michael Gratz married Miriam, the daughter of Joseph and Rosa (Bunn) Simon in 1769. They founded their home in Philadelphia where twelve children were born to them; seven sons, namely Solomon and Jonathan, who died in childhood, Simon, Hyman, Joseph, Jacob and Benjamin and five daughters, Frances, who married Reuben Etting, Richea, who married Samuel Hays, Rachel, who married Solomon Moses, and two, Sarah and the most famous of them all, Rebecca, who died unmarried.

These brothers and sisters and their children are mentioned so constantly in the letters that it appears advisable to include a statement concerning them in this introduction, notably as they constituted what was doubtless the foremost Jewish family of their day in the United States. Of the sons, Hyman gained the greatest prominence. He participated in large commercial enterprises over and beyond the business he conducted with his brother. He became a director of the Pennsylvania Company for Insurance on Lives and Granting of Annuities in 1817, and in January, 1837, he was elected president of this corporation which honorable office he held until his death. He had interests too other than commercial. Being a man of fine culture he was greatly interested in art and was one of the directors of the Philadelphia Academy of Fine Arts, of which institution he served also as Treasurer and President. Throughout his life he took an active part in all Jewish communal affairs. He was prominently identified with the administration of the affairs of the Mikveh Israel Congregation and one of the leading spirits in the organization of the first Jewish Publication Society in the United States in 1845.

Hyman Gratz never married. He died January 27, 1857. Shortly before his death, namely on December 18, 1856, he executed a deed of trust. After making provision for relatives, in the form of life annuities, he directed that his residuary estate should be used "to establish and maintain a college for the education of Jews residing in the city and county of Philadelphia." The last heir died in 1893, whereupon Gratz College was founded. This institution, situated at York and Broad Streets, is one of the well known Jewish educational institutions of the country.

The brothers Joseph and Jacob Gratz likewise remained unmarried. They too were prominent citizens of the community. Joseph became a member of the First Troop Philadelphia City Cavalry, remaining in active membership until May 1, 1815, and being placed on the honorary roll, March

7, 1853. Jacob was graduated from the University of Pennsylvania in 1807. He was the one brother who had a political career. He was a member both of the lower house of the Pennsylvania legislature and of the Senate, to which he was elected in 1839. Both he and his brother Joseph were elected members of the first Board of Directors of the Philadelphia Institution for Deaf and Dumb, which was established in 1820. Jacob Gratz died December 25, 1856, and Joseph on October 25, 1858.

The youngest son, Benjamin, was the only one of the family who removed from Philadelphia. All the family evinced concern in the extensive land holdings in the western part of the country that had been acquired by the grandfather, Joseph Simon, and the father, Michael Gratz. The brothers, Simon, Hyman and Joseph made frequent trips out of Philadelphia to look after these possessions. In 1818 Benjamin, the youngest, who had graduated from the University of Pennsylvania in 1811 and had been admitted to the Philadelphia bar in 1817, was urged by his brothers to go to the West to look into the landed possessions of the family. He spent that year at Vincennes, Indiana, the western frontier post, and in 1819 he settled in Lexington, Kentucky, to remain there for sixty-five years until his death in 1884.

Benjamin Gratz was one of the first Jews to settle in Kentucky. He was a man of great ability and public spirit and it was not long ere he took his place among the foremost citizens, not only of the town of Lexington but of the state. His portrait, painted by Sully, shows him to have been an exceptionally handsome man. The attractive exterior was a fitting frame for the fine spirit within.

There was no public movement of importance in which Benjamin Gratz did not have a leading place. As early as 1827 he was elected a trustee of Transylvania University,

INTRODUCTION

the leading institution of learning in that entire region. He was one of the incorporators of the first railroad in the west and the second in the entire country, namely the Lexington and Ohio railroad. When Lexington was incorporated as a city in 1832, Benjamin Gratz became a member of the first city council; a branch of the Bank of Kentucky having been established in Lexington in 1834, he was named a member of the first Board of Directors and when the Northern Bank of Kentucky was founded in 1835, he was chosen as a member of the first Board of Directors of this institution. He was one of the incorporators of the Orphan Asylum in 1833.

The foremost citizen of Kentucky was Henry Clay, a resident of Lexington. Benjamin Gratz was one of his most intimate friends; in later years the families became connected by marriage, when Benjamin Gratz' youngest child, Anna, became the wife of Thomas Hart Clay, a grandson of the great statesman. Gratz was an ardent supporter of Clay in his presidential aspirations. When this greatest son of Kentucky died in 1852, Gratz acted as Secretary of the meeting of Lexington citizens which was called to take action on the death. He was one of the committee appointed to go to Washington to accompany the remains to Lexington; he was a pallbearer at the funeral and a member of the Clay Monumental Association that erected the Henry Clay monument in the Lexington cemetery.

The daughters of Michael and Miriam Simon Gratz, as already stated, were five in number. Three of these married and a number of their children and grandchildren rose to prominence. The oldest daughter, Frances, had married Reuben Etting in 1794. Their oldest son, Elijah Gratz, was graduated from the University of Pennsylvania in 1812. He entered the legal profession and served as District Attorney of Cecil County, Maryland. The third son, Henry, served in the United States Navy from 1818, when he became midshipman. When the Civil War broke out he was made Purser and Fiscal Agent of the Navy Department at New York and was placed on the retired list as Pay Director with the rank of Commodore in 1871, at the age of 72.

Three grandsons of Reuben and Frances Etting (great grandsons of Michael and Miriam Gratz) distinguished themselves in the service of the country. Frank Marx Etting, son of Benjamin and Harriet Marx Etting, born in Philadelphia, December 17, 1833, a lawyer by profession, served through the Civil War; he was paymaster with rank of Major in 1861; Brevet Lieutenant Colonel United States Volunteers 1865 and Brevet Lieutenant Colonel United States Army 1868. He held important public offices in Philadelphia, being for a time Director of Public Schools. He wrote the history of Independence Hall and was the chief historian, Department of the Centennial Exposition in 1876. He married a granddaughter of Chief Justice Taney of the United States Supreme Court.

Two other Ettings, great grandsons of Michael and Miriam Gratz, gained military distinction, namely, Charles E. and Theodore M. Etting, both sons of Edward Johnston and Philippa Minis Etting. Charles E. enlisted in the United States Army at the age of eighteen during the Civil War and served from August 4, 1862–June 2, 1865. He was successively Second Lieutenant, First Lieutenant, Captain and Regimental Adjutant on the Staff of the Brigade Commander. He fought in the battles of Fredericksburg, Chancellorsville and Gettysburg and assisted in organizing new Pennsylvania Regiments in 1864. After the war he entered upon a business career in Philadelphia.

His brother, Theodore Minis Etting, was admitted to the United States Naval Academy at Annapolis in 1862 in his

INTRODUCTION

sixteenth year. While on a leave of absence from the Academy, he volunteered his services and was appointed Acting Midshipman in the United States Navy, November 28, 1862. He became successively Midshipman in June 2, 1868, when he was twenty-two years of age; Ensign in 1869, Master in 1870 and Lieutenant in 1874. Several years thereafter he resigned and was honorably discharged July 1, 1877. Two years later he was admitted to the bar and built up a large practice, specialized in shipping, admiralty and corporation law; he wrote a book on "Admiralty Jurisdiction."

Of the children of Richea, the second daughter of Michael Gratz, who had married Samuel Hays, the oldest son, Isaac, rose to eminence as a physician. Graduating from the medical school of the University of Pennsylvania in 1820, four years after his graduation with the degree of Bachelor of Arts, he soon became not only one of the city's but one of the country's leading oculists. He was a prolific writer on medical subjects, being connected in an editorial capacity with the *American Journal of the Medical Sciences* for fifty-two years. He edited likewise *Medical News*. When he died in 1879 at the age of eighty-three he had stood for years in the very forefront of his profession. His son, Isaac Minis Hays, was also an eminent physician.

Of the other nine children of Samuel and Richea Hays distinction was gained through marriage by a daughter, Sara Ann, who espoused in 1836 Captain Alfred Mordecai, a graduate of the United States Military Academy of West Point. Captain Mordecai was one of the distinguished officers of the United States Army. At the time of his marriage he was in command of the United States Arsenal at Frankford, Pennsylvania. He held many positions of high importance and was the recipient of many military honors; among these may be mentioned his promotion to the rank of

Major in 1848 and Major of Ordnance in 1854. In 1855–56 he was sent by the United States Government to Europe as a member of a military commission to the Crimean War; his report on military organization and ordnance in the armies engaged in the Crimean War was published by order of Congress. He wrote many books on military subjects, a number of which became authoritative notably his "Ordnance Manual, for the Use of Officers in the United States Army."

Sara Ann Mordecai published, in 1893, when she was eighty-eight years of age, a small book entitled "Recollections of My Aunt Rebecca Gratz by One of Her Nieces." These intimate recollections constitute a source for the life story of the most famous member of the Gratz family.

A son of Major and Mrs. Alfred Mordecai, Alfred Mordecai, Jr., followed in the footsteps of his father and had a most distinguished military career. He fought through the Civil War holding successively the rank of Acting Assistant Adjutant - General, Assistant Inspector of Ordnance, Inspector of Ordnance, Captain of Ordnance and Chief of Ordnance. He was brevetted Major in 1863 and Lieutenant Colonel in 1865. After the close of the Civil War he was appointed Instructor of Ordnance and Gunnery at the West Point Military Academy, serving till 1869 and again from 1874–1881. In 1882 he rose to the full rank of Lieutenant Colonel. In 1904 he attained the rank of Brigadier General and was retired the following day at the age of 64, the retiring age of the army.

Of the children of Rachel Gratz, the youngest daughter of Michael and Miriam Gratz, who married Solomon Moses and died at the age of forty in 1823, leaving a family of nine children, the oldest of whom was sixteen years of age, one, Dr. Simon Gratz Moses, rose to prominence in his profession. A graduate of the medical college of the University of

INTRODUCTION

Pennsylvania, he removed shortly after graduation to St. Louis, Missouri, where he became a leading physician. He was professor of Obstetrics in the Missouri Medical College; he was elected president of the St. Louis Obstetrical Society and Health Officer of the city of St. Louis.

However, the bright particular star of the family was Rebecca, who stands easily first among native American Jewesses. All accounts agree in praise of this unusual woman. Beautiful in face, aristocratic in bearing, dignified in manner, noble of soul and pure of heart, she is not unworthy of having applied to her the exquisite words used of a rare woman by George Eliot, that, "were all virtue and religion dead, she'd make them newly, being what she was."

Devotedly attached to her family, she was the home-maker for her unmarried brothers and for the orphaned children of her sister, Rachel Moses. She took the mother's place and reared these children to manhood and womanhood. Has mother love ever been more finely delineated than in the words she wrote to one of her correspondents on the death of her mother, "Alas! who can estimate the loss of a mother to a young family ... the training eye of maternal watchfulness not only forms and regulates the character of her offspring but clears their path from unseen and unexpected dangers. There can be no love more pure, more perfect and more enduring than a mothers—what a blissful refuge to the stricken spirit—after the disappointments of life, to be comforted, as a mother comforteth."

Her letters are filled with equally exalted sentiments on all the relations of life. They prove indeed that her niece did not exaggerate when, in her "Recollections of My Aunt Rebecca Gratz," she wrote "nothing could be lovelier than her every day life, which commenced every morning with prayers and thanks to the Creator for support and for protecting her through the night, and ended with renewed thanks for the blessings bestowed during the day, while the record of every day's life was a lesson to everyone around her, fulfilling every duty with patience, kindness, humility and love." How could it be otherwise with one possessed of the trustful faith which was hers and which expressed itself in words like these: "God is so bountiful to us that we have as much cause to be grateful for what He denies as for what is granted - knowing that wisdom and mercy are the attributes of His power, and inconsiderable as we are individually or collectively among the works of His creation, He considers us worthy of His care. It is perhaps easier to conceive that God regulates a Universe, than that every minute being from the least atom that has life and motion is especially His and shares His superintending providence - yet this is His greatness. When Moses asked to be shown the divine Glory, and was told - 'I will cause my goodness to pass before Thee', he must have felt that the whole book of nature was open before him - and every sight and sound and smell proclaimed the glory of God."

This piety was the keynote of her life, both private and public. No woman of her day was more public spirited. As early as 1801, in her twenty-first year, she was secretary of the "Female Association for the Relief of Women and Children in Reduced Circumstances." She was one of the founders of the Philadelphia Orphan Society in 1815 and, being elected secretary in 1819, she served in this capacity for forty years. Upon her retirement, the Board of Managers in an eloquent tribute to her work wrote that to her "much of its prosperity is due, while to her dignity, grace and noble personal qualities the managers have always yielded the tribute of their warm admiration and personal regard."

In 1838 she founded the Hebrew Sunday School Society

and served as its president until 1864, when she resigned in her eighty-third year. In this achievement she found greater satisfaction than in possibly any other. She refers to it frequently in her correspondence. It has become indeed one of her monuments "more enduring than bronze" for during the ninety years of its existence the Society has been instrumental in imparting religious education to thousands of Jewish children in the city of Philadelphia.

This interest in children was ever with her. A letter which appeared in 1850 in the monthly magazine "The Occident" and signed "A Daughter in Israel" has been attributed to her. In this letter the need of a Foster Home for orphaned children was first suggested. This suggestion was realized in 1855 when the Jewish Foster Home was founded largely through her efforts. This institution and the Sunday School Society enlisted her warmest co-operation until the moment of her death.

But the interest in Rebecca Gratz arises chiefly from the quite universally accepted tradition that she was the original of the noble Jewess Rebecca in Scott's "Ivanhoe," declared by so competent a critic as Thackeray to be "the sweetest character in the whole range of fiction."

The story has often been told as to how Rebecca Gratz was brought to the attention of Walter Scott through Washington Irving. Maria Fenno, an intimate friend of Miss Gratz, married Judge J. Ogden Hoffman, of New York. His youngest daughter, Matilda, was the fiancee of Washington Irving, who learned to know the lovely Philadelphia Jewess in the Hoffman home, where she visited frequently. Miss Hoffman died at the early age of eighteen and Irving remained true to her memory. In 1815 he went to Europe and learned to know Scott in 1817. Scott had in mind the writing of a novel with Jews as characters. He must have discussed this project with Irving for in a letter to Irving, written after the appearance of "Ivanhoe," in 1819, he asked, "How do you like your Rebecca? Does the Rebecca I have pictured compare well with the pattern given?" This clearly establishes the connection between the two Rebeccas. It is reported that Miss Gratz, when asked whether she was the original of Scott's Rebecca, answered, "They say so, my dear".

In the letter of April 4, 1820, written to her sister-in-law, Mrs. Maria Gist Gratz, she makes reference to the subject which establishes a connection between her and the famous fictional character. She asks, "Have you received Ivanhoe? when you have read it tell me what you think of my namesake Rebecca." And in the letter of May 10, she reverts to the subject in these words: "I am glad you admire Rebecca for she is just such a representative of a good girl as I think human nature can reach- Ivanhoe's insensibility to her, you must recollect, may be accounted to his previous attachment -his prejudice was a characteristic of the age he lived in-he fought for Rebecca, though he despised her race- the veil that is drawn over his feelings was necessary to the fable, and the beautiful sensibility of her, so regulated yet so intense might show the triumph of faith over human affection. I have dwelt on this character as we sometimes do on an exquisite painting until the canvas seems to breathe and we believe it is life."

It is to this sister-in-law that most of the letters are addressed. Shortly after his arrival in Kentucky in 1819, Benjamin Gratz married Maria Gist, a woman of rare charm and culture, whom he had met during her visit to Philadelphia. The lady was the daughter of Colonel Nathaniel Gist of the Revolutionary Army and a granddaughter of Col. Christopher Gist, an intimate friend of George Washington, whom he had accompanied on his expedition to western Pennsylvania in 1753. He and his sons, Nathaniel and Thomas, were in the British Army in the disastrous battle known as Braddock's defeat. He received for his military service a grant of 12,000 acres of land in Kentucky. Nathaniel was a Colonel of a Virginia regiment during the Revolution. He married Judith Bell. The youngest child of this union was Maria. After the death of Nathaniel Gist his widow married General Charles Scott, who became Governor of Kentucky. Mrs. Scott is mentioned occasionally in these letters. Maria Gist Gratz was one of the leading women of Kentucky. As appears from the letters, a deep affection sprang up between Rebecca Gratz and her sister-in-law. These two unusual women had much in common. Their mutual interests in literature, philanthropy and the common weal find constant expression in the correspondence between them. Maria Gist Gratz died in 1841 leaving four sons, Bernard, Howard, Hyman and Cary. Her portrait by Sully, which is mentioned in several letters, is in the possession of her granddaughter, Mrs. J. R. Morton, of Lexington, Kentucky, who occupies the old Benjamin Gratz homestead on Mill St., facing Gratz Park. Two years after his wife's death, Benjamin Gratz married Mrs. Ann Boswell Shelby, a niece of his first wife. A son, who died in infancy, and two daughters, Miriam and Anna, were the issue of this union. Rebecca Gratz conceived a deep affection also for this new sister-in-law and wrote to her constantly. The latter portion of the correspondence with this lady extending over the Civil War period is of particular interest.

When the war broke out Rebecca Gratz had completed her eightieth year. Her letters to her brother in Lexington dwell on the horror of the fratricidal conflict. An intense lover of the Union, she was greatly concerned for her brother, living as he did in a state where turbulent passions divided the citizens into two camps. Benjamin Gratz himself was one of the staunchest supporters of the Union and contributed greatly towards keeping Kentucky in the Northern column. He freed his slaves. His youngest son Cary, enlisted in the Northern army, and was killed in the battle of Wilson's Creek, Missouri, August 10, 1861. This catastrophe called forth a beautiful letter from Rebecca Gratz, addressed to her sister-in-law, on August 23, 1861. This letter reads:

"Thanks, what grateful thanks My dear Sister I owe you, for your kind letters, over which I have wept again, and again- and prayed for my beloved brother- whose grief I share, but cannot measure even by that which fills my heart- all human sympathy are but drops of comfort in his great sorrow, but God in his mercy will open a fountain of consolation to his mourning spirit- the beloved son, whom "He gave, and hath taken away" will rise in an angel's form to whisper peace- memorials of all his virtues and loveliness- his pure and innocent life, and brave qualities- the noble heart as tender and full of filial love- all perfected and immortal- will in future be to him his very son- his beloved Cary. . . .
Your second letter, which I have also received, gives me great comfort, as it tells me Ben is more composed- I trust the efforts of his friends will be successful in obtaining the dear remains- Frank Blair is now on the spot to aid them- I pray Kentucky will not be involved in this dreadful strife- we live here in constant agitation- every days account of wrongs & outrages perpetrated by kindred on each other- of familiar friends becoming bitter foes, is too appalling to be realized, in our late happy country- even members of the same family warring against each other. . . ."

In the letter written November 14, 1862, Miss Gratz mentions the dismissal of General McClellan whom by a slip of the pen she calls McClennel and adverts to the privations of the Union soldiers. Sadly she writes:

"There is no appearance of light breaking upon the affairs of our country- the dismissal of Genl McClennel has greatly shaken my hopes, and seems to have appalled those who looked upon him with due confidence in his worth & patriotism-Lizzie wrote me that her Father strove with all his might to avert the evil-in vain- she also says every word about the destitution of the noble army is true- their Genl would not move till they were clad- they marched here- barefooted & ragged- so that her mother even on Sunday all day gave needles and thread to mend their rags- where can the fault be that such things exist, when such quantities of clothing and shoes are furnished? We hear the enemies soldiers are well clad- and our brave fellows are suffering- "There seems something is rotten in the state of Denmark"- who can find it out?-"

And in a letter written April 15, 1863 she touches another angle of the war situation:

"I marvel at the apathy of our community- with the knowledge of Fleets of iron clad steamers preparing abroad which might enter our rivers and lay our cities in ashes no movement of defense is made. Phila is as full of idle people- the streets & shops crowded & except in the exorbitant prices asked for commodities- & freely given, the presence of war is unheeded- except indeed in the active works of charity- for the sick & wounded brought to our hospitals. My dear Brother, I am too old to do any good, but feel deep interest in all this & pray for better times."

Rebecca Gratz died August 29, 1869, having attained the ripe age of eighty-eight years. With her passed the foremost Jewess in the United States and one of the noblest women in the country. Her place is secure among the exalted spirits that glorify American womanhood. I like to apply to her the Shakespearean eulogy that I once used in speaking of her namesake Scott's Rebecca,

> "from everyone
> The best she hath, and she, of all compounded
> Outsells them all."

Her last will and testament is a noble document, "I Rebecca Gratz, of Philadelphia, being in sound health of body and mind, advanced in the vale of years, declare this to be my last will and testament. I commit my spirit to the God who gave it, relying on His mercy and redeeming love, and believing with a fine and perfect faith in the religion of my fathers, "Hear, O Israel, the Lord our God is one Lord".[1]

[1] For many of the data of the members of the Gratz family I am indebted to Morais, *The Jews of Philadelphia*, Philadelphia, 1894, *passim:* Byers, *The B. and M. Gratz Papers*, Jefferson City, Mo., 1916, *passim:* and Leach, "Old Families of Philadelphia—Gratz," Supplement to the Philadelphia North American, Dec. 1, 1912. For the life and career of Rebecca Gratz, notably the Ivanhoe incident, see "The Original of Rebecca in Ivanhoe," by Gratz Van Rensselaer, in Century Magazine, Sept. 1882, p. 682: "The Original of Scott's Rebecca," by Joseph Jacobs: Publications A J H S, vol. XXII (1914), pp. 53–60: Morais, *Eminent Israelites of the Nineteenth Century*, pp. 109–112: Byers, *The B. and M. Gratz Papers*, pp. 259–262, and Mary M. Cohen, *An Old Philadelphia Cemetery, the Resting Place of Rebecca Gratz*, Philadelphia, 1920, pp. 76–89.

THE LETTERS

TO BENJAMIN GRATZ

This is the earliest extant letter in this correspondence. It is written on the same sheet as a letter from his mother to her absent son. Although the letter is undated, it is clear from the opening sentence that it was written on August sixteenth, 1808, the day after the mother's letter which is dated August 15, 1808, was penned. The letter is addressed, "Mr. Benjamin Gratz care of N. Schuyler Esqr Troy N. Y." Dr. Nicholas Schuyler, a friend of George Washington, a near relative of General Schuyler and a surgeon in the revolutionary army, had married Shinah Simon of Lancaster, Pa. a sister of the mother of Rebecca and Benjamin Gratz.

Tuesday Morn

My Dear Ben

We just arrived last night as our dear good mother was closing her letter which she gave me the liberty to open again for the purpose of commending you for your attention in writing, and to hint that had you thought proper to have addressed one to me, you should not have had reason to complain of want of punctuality in return. However, I assure you that consideration would not have prevented my writing before, had not my health & spirits both been so low, that my exertions to write would have been badly compensated by the small degree of amusement it would have been in my power to afford you. A few days journeying among the hills and dipping in the waters at the Yellow Springs[1] have greatly recruited me. This place is a miniature resemblance of the scenery around Lebanon[2] where I suppose you are now en-

[1]A watering resort in the Allegheny mountains near Altoona, Pennsylvania.
[2]Lebanon Springs, Massachusetts in the Berkshires.

[1]

joying the luxury of bathing, & the delight of climbing mountains which seem the very abode of health. I am glad you have been so pleased with Boston and my friends there. What progress has Hyman[1] made in the good graces of the ladies? I expect much of your esquireship in his adventures. What route do you take next? If Hyman has any idea of Niagara, he had better proceed immediately there and visit the Springs there, as the autumn is a dangerous season to travel in that country, the Lake-fever is not only to be dreaded for the present inconvenience & danger but is apt to make a winter campaigne.

I have not a word of news to tell you having but returned to town, our family party all well - Aunt Bell[2] just about moving into eighth street, in the house lately occupied by Genl Moylan[3]. We took tea at Bloomfield yesterday on our way home, and found the family there perfectly well. Sally[4] desires me to send her affectionate love to Hyman and yourself.

You must likewise both accept my most cordial and sincere affection with my best wishes for your enjoyment of present pleasure, and long & lasting happiness. If you are at Boston present My love to all the Hays family[5] particularly

[1] An older brother who was accompanying the youngest brother Benjamin on this pleasure tour. Benjamin at this time was sixteen years of age.
[2] Mrs. Solomon M. Cohen (nee Simon) a sister of Mrs. Michael Gratz.
[3] Stephen Moylan, an aide to Washington in the Revolution; he was a member of Washington's staff until he was appointed Colonel of the Fourth Continental Dragoons January 5, 1777 and served to November 3 1783; he became brigadier general September 30, 1783.
[4] Miss Sarah, a sister of Rebecca and Benjamin Gratz.
[5] The Hays family is very prominent in American Jewish annals (see Jewish Encyclopedia. VI 270) The head of the Boston branch that Benjamin Gratz was visiting at this time was Moses Michael Hays, a leading citizen and one of the most prominent figures in Masonry. (Oppenheim, The Jews and Masonry, Publications AJHS XIX 5-8 and passim). A cousin of his, Samuel Hays had married Richea, a sister of Rebecca Gratz. JudahTouro the great philanthropist was a nephew of Moses Michael Hays.

the girls and carry with you to Troy my affectionate remembrance to our Dear Aunt and Uncle Schuyler—to the former say I shall write soon. Adieu, My Dear Ben believe me your friend & affectionate

SISTER REBECCA G

* * *

TO THE SAME

This letter, addressed "Mr Benjamin Gratz Albany N Y" was written doubtless in the year 1812 when Benjamin Gratz made a journey to Boston, Troy, Albany and New York. The reference to the death of the parents Michael and Miriam Gratz brings to mind that the latter died September 12, 1808 and the former September 8, 1811.

Anniversary of parents' death—Day of fasting ordered by the President of the United States—Honors paid an English Captain.

Friday 21st August

We received your letter from New York yesterday, My dear Ben, and are glad to find your journey likely to afford you so much pleasure - the weather has been provokingly unfavorable for travellers, but with so agreeable a party no external circumstance will have power to interrupt the harmony of your feelings - this day we suppose you reach the Springs do not fail to drink deeply of the water, as you will certainly be benefitted by it - I fear you have not been able to visit the curiosities of the country in such a perpetual storm - we have traced you in idea, and participated in the delight of our friends in visiting the highlands &c..

It is scarcely necessary to remind you that the mournful anniversary of our Beloved Parents death is approaching -

on the 27th inst.[1] is our day of Memorial - a day that must ever be overcast by the deepest filial sorrow - doubly mournful as marking the departure of both the Authors of our being - within the little space of three years - pardon me dear Ben, for dwelling on this subject - last month I would have given worlds to have accompanied you to their sacred tomb- on thursday next that duty shall not be neglected -

Yesterday was observed here as a day of fasting and prayer[2] the weather was too bad to admit of Church going - and it seems necessary to exhort the people to abstinence, so I believe cooking was as usual a branch of the daily labour - our neighbour at the corner had a green turtle prepared, and many a servant was dispatched by the surrounding epicures to console themselves under the Presidents ordinance -

There has been a very respectful compliment paid to an unfortunate English Captain, who was captured by an American and wounded in the previous engagement - he was taken to the hospital, attended during his illness, but having died of his wounds, was buried this morning attended by military honours - officers and Marines were also invited to attend the funeral ...

May God prosper you in all your wishes, My dear Ben, prays your most affectionate

Sister R G

---

[1] This was doubtless the Hebrew date of the parents' death.
[2] Owing to the reverses suffered during the beginning of the War of 1812.

TO THE SAME

Undated letter addressed "Mr Benjamin Gratz Washington Barracks Kenneth Square" and written in all likelihood shortly after the beginning of the War of 1812 for service in which Benjamin had volunteered.

My Dear Ben

You can scarcely conceive our surprise and concern at hearing of your departure, or the impatience in which we hastened home, very little better in any respect for our journey. Sallys disease has assumed much the same character it bore last winter and the bustle & continual change of travelling from place to place, crowded steamboats and company increased it to a very distressing degree. I thank God we are at home again - tho hastened to it by alarm and danger. We found Jo here on a short visit but he return'd to camp this morning and we feel forlorn without you and him. I hope it will be in your power to come home for a short visit too - your military zeal is very fine but I hope your wishes will not prevail - an armistice would be more glorious to the country than all the laurels its heroes can gather. Adeline Myers[1] is with us - John departed south this morning to join his General - they do not know where the family has gone but all the female and other useless inhabitants of Norfolk had retired some time. We sit and bewail you much more like women than patriots and turn pale at the thought of a battle. Let us know by Gratz[2] if you are in want of anything more and tell him also when we may hope to see you. Shall

---
[1] An intimate friend of Rebecca Gratz and daughter of Moses Myers a prominent citizen of Norfolk.
[2] Gratz Etting a nephew, oldest son of Reuben and Frances Gratz Etting.

we come down to you or will you be able to come to the city?
. . . .

My dear Brother, amid all the perils & chances of war, may you be shielded by the Omnipotent and return uninjured to your

sincerely Affectionate R G -

* * *

TO BENJAMIN GRATZ ESQR WILMINGTON

Philadelphia in war time—The Day of Atonement.

Philadelphia Sept. 20th 1814

My Dear Ben

We had a mischievous report in town yesterday that an election was held in Camp and your Ensign promoted to the First Lieutenancy of the company. This we did not believe for many reasons, and among them the agreeable letter Jac[1] received from you which was written in such easy spirits that I was sure you had experienced no such mortification during the last few days. . . .

We live rather a dull life without you and Jo[2] in which, however, we share but the common lot. Phila. streets are completely deserted except by the few military companies who parade of an afternoon. Jac bids me tell you he fears their company will fall through- they are dividing it for a marching company - the Capt. will not go - and they have only thirty signatures. He is very anxious to effect its marching - but is less sanguine of success than when I last wrote. For my part, I cannot regret it, he is not very fit for a

[1] Jacob, a brother. [2] Joseph, another brother.

soldier's life tho' I trust in the hour of need would be able to do his duty. Could you not get some business to bring you home for a day or two? say from Saturday to Monday - that you may feast and fast[1] with us on the approaching Great day. We long to see you again and if Sally was well enough should certainly pay you a visit at Wilmington. It seems very tantalizing that you should be so near and conveniently situated but for us in vain. . . .

Jac wishes to add a few lines and I cannot entertain you better than by leaving this place for him.

Adieu believe me always most Affectionately your Sister

R G

* * *

TO LIEUTENANT BENJAMIN GRATZ
CAMP BLOOMFIELD

This letter is undated but was written in all likelihood after the letter of September 20 in which the lieutenancy is mentioned as not yet possessed by Benjamin Gratz.

Rosh Hashanah—the boy Isaac mentioned towards the close of the letter was a nephew, Isaac Hays, later a celebrated physician.

You write, My dear Ben, of marching with as much enthusiasm as if you were a veteran soldier animated by success - while we look with horror on the possibility of such an event- you may easily imagine our trepidation on hearing of the gigantic strides made by the war in the short period of our absence. . . . Jac has become an indefatigable soldier, but found a day's work at the fortification rather too severe.

[1] The Day of Atonement, the most solemn day in the Jewish religious year. It is marked by abstinence from food during the twenty-four hours from eventide to eventide. At the close of the fast an elaborate meal is partaken of.

He has complain'd of burnt arms and shoulders ever since Wednesday. I hope you take the best means to make yourself as comfortable as a camp life will admit of. The clothes you sent home are exchanged - do let us know what else you want. I am afraid to send anything that might encumber you, but would take the greatest pleasure in preparing whatever would contribute to your convenience. I sincerely hope we shall see you ere long but shall not attempt to visit you. Jacob has sent the pistols you wrote for to be repaired - but will send them by the next opportunity if they are not finished in time for this. Gratz will give you all out- doors information and you must accept the love and prayers of all within. Next Thursday & Friday is Roshoshana[1] - we talk of passing it at Bloomfield. . . . All the children send you love. You are their admiration of a soldier but Isaac says he does not think the Major will look well - he criticises his person & face with much severity and winds up with a comparison with his uncle Ben. I congratulate you on the appointment of Cadwallader and hope your intelligent commander will soon make his own countersign from Bloomfield. Adieu, My dear Ben, we pray for you with ardour and trust the God of battles may ever be near you in the hour of danger -, ever affectionately your Sister

R G

TO LIEUTENANT BENJAMIN GRATZ
AT PORT DEPOSIT

First mention of Kentucky in this correspondence—the Gratz holdings in Kentucky.

Oct - 17th 1814

My Dear Ben

If I had been provided with agreeable intelligence you would have heard from me long ago but to repeat the same dull talk could afford you little satisfaction and therefore I have been silent. . . . Hyman left us yesterday morning for Kentucky[1] so that our family party is reduced to four persons. We were greatly shocked on Friday last to hear of the death of old Mrs Cohen who expired without the notice of an hour's illness. She was an excellent woman and perhaps as much prepared to meet death unwarned as any human being could be yet to her survivors it was an awful visitation and has left an impression more deep than that afflicting event would have done under any other circumstances.

The Hayses left Boston this day for Richmond. They will make a few days stay here and Adeline means to accompany them home. Mr H. is going immediately to Europe - he accompanies his Sisters & cousin thus far, and returns to embark at New York. All our dear Sisters and Brothers are well, and send love to you. You will receive the clothes you sent for by this conveyance and I wish you would furnish a list of those you send home also. Mr Rush carried a piece of

[1] Joseph Simon, of Lancaster, Pa., the grandfather, and Michael Gratz, the father of the family, were intinately connected with the beginnings of Kentucky in 1774. Since that date the family had held large holdings there. See Byers, *B. and M. Gratz Papers*, 17.

beef for you on Saturday which I hope was acceptable. We expect Jo tomorrow. God Bless you, my dear Ben with health & every good prays your

        Affectionate Sister RG

* * *

TO BENJAMIN GRATZ ESQR BALTIMORE

First mention in this correspondence of Maria Gist of Kentucky the future wife of Benjamin Gratz. The long gap in the correspondence is due undoubtedly to the fact that Benjamin Gratz was at home during the intervening years.

My dear Ben

I was really surprised to hear of your speedy return to Balt. and have only time to tell you we are all well at home - your letter reached me at dinner time - we had company - who have detained me until the sun is declining - Hyman has just return'd home, quite well - we have had letters from Maria Gist,[1] from Bedford & Pittsburgh. The latter place they expected to leave on the 8th She writes charmingly & sends kind messages to *you* I can not "*bore*" you with long letters this time as the business of the week is to be closed immediately. Give my love to Dr Cousin & family - and believe me always

        Your Affect.te Sister

          RG

Aug. 14 1818

Let us hear from you if you should decide on a longer stay - Adieu

[1] The future wife of Benjamin Gratz.

TO BENJAMIN GRATZ

This is the first letter addressed to Lexington, Kentucky. All subsequent letters in this correspondence are directed to that place where Benjamin Gratz settled in 1818 and where he lived the remainder of his life.

We are now My Dear Ben, in daily expectation of hearing from you. It appears a month since you left home, every hour of which I have missed you, and did I not know that you were much happier in the expedition than I am in thinking of it I should want consolation for your absence but I pray your expectations and wishes may be realized and that after an agreeable and useful tour you will be ready to return home. . . . .

From the continuation of dry weather, we suppose you will not be able to descend the river from Pittsburgh but as you have never travelled thro' the country I suppose it will not be disagreeable to you to continue your journeying by land. We have been reading "The Backwoodsman"[1] and covet such a sail as Basil had down the Ohio for you. You will find him waiting your arrival at Lexington, & I think will be pleased with his acquaintance. There are some fine scenes, fine sentiments & fine sketches in the work- it is characteristic of the author, and I think will gain him an acquisition of reputation. Yet there are some openings for criticism and it is probable the English reviewers will return upon him some of the severities he so liberally bestows upon them. You will have the pleasure of offering Maria Gist this treat as she is an admirer of Paulding. . . . .

[1] A poem by James Kirke Paulding (1778-1860), a prominent American writer.

Poor Fullerton & Mrs. Kemper have "paid the debt of Nature" the latter will be buried tomorrow morning. Fullerton was gathered to his fathers this day - both are much lamented, yet their friends have so long seen them wasting away that they were prepared and reconciled to the event. Letters from Maria,[1] mention that Edward Fenno is going to settle at New Orleans. Mr. P Stone has befriended him, so as to make him to form an establishment there with a young man, a fellow clerk, and he is now making arrangements for his departure - should you have it in your power to introduce him to some of the Kentuckians who are in the habit of going to N. O. I am sure he would be gratified by the favor.

Jo has returned from a meeting of his arbitrators, anticipating a favorable termination to his troublesome business - he unites with our other brothers & sisters in affectionate love to you. Ellen[2] also desires hers she is a little sad today - the loss of Mrs. K has brought many associations & recollections of school day happiness connected with her -

I hope My dear Ben, you will write to us often - nothing but this can reconcile me to the void made by your absence - I feel too stupid to write - but am never tired of thinking of you and somehow anxiety will creep in, in spite of all my endeavors to view through your most favorable medium the object of your journey May health & protection of God attend you -

We had letters from Gratz[3] today - he is well, and the Gentleman who brought them says he is growing quite fat - he is wonderfully well satisfied with his situation considering how few advantages he possesses - remember me affection-

---

[1]Maria Fenno Hoffman, second wife of Judge Ogden Hoffman of New York; she was a close friend of Rebecca Gratz.
[2]Ellen Hays, a niece.
[3]Gratz Etting a nephew who was mentally afflicted and was away from home in an institution.

ately to Mrs. Scott[1] & Maria G. and kindly to my other Kentucky acquaintances I hope that Miss & Mrs. Hunt will like the articles sent them - they are all the fashion here -

Adieu My dear Brother, take care of yourself - for the sake of those to whom your safety is happiness and believe me always most affectionately

Your Sister R G

* * *

TO THE SAME

This letter though undated by the writer is postmarked Phil Nov 12 and the year 1818 is supplied by the recipient of the letter on the back.

I received your few lines from Pittsburg My dear Ben and was rejoiced that you have got that far on your journey so pleasantly. Mr. Peters also told us you had left there in good health and so we must trust you continue until the welcome intelligence of your arrival at Lexington reaches us. There is nothing new from home to communicate Poor Jac has been troubled with another boil which has kept him from the club several days and has confined him to his room - Harry Williams & the Major come occasionally to see him, and play chess. They talk of the metamorphosis now pretty confidently and as there is a new invention of *chess cards* perhaps they may wean themselves from brag thro' this medium.

Ere this you have seen Maria Gist and Canewood[2] and Mrs. Scott and if Mr. Larned was mistaken, you have had some agreeable agitations & no doubt a great deal of pleasure in the society of these charming women. But if Maria has

---

[1] Widow of General Charles Scott, Governor of Kentucky and mother of Maria Gist, later Mrs. Benjamin Gratz.
[2] The estate of Mrs. Scott, the mother of Maria Gist.

really turned Dr. you will be soon ready to return home and I shall be the more obliged to her.

You will certainly not become enamoured of the naked forests in winter, nor of the unsophisticated charms of savage life. Winning under the hardships of this season a rustic maid is very engaging in pastoral poetry - but will not strike the fancy of one bred in the city. I do not think "The Backwoodsman" will help you much in the way of smoothing a path in the wilderness - tho' you will find him rising to distinction by the time your eyes are dim with age. Paulding's reputation is not much encreased by this publication. Thomas has sent you a copy and you will judge for yourself. . . . .

Isaac Hays[1] has had the comfort of abusing two of Dr Hare's[2] lectures which almost reconciles him to his disappointment. Poor Dorsey[3] is very ill - yesterday slight hopes were entertained for his recovery, he was a little better last night. His loss would be a great calamity to the college at this crisis - the medical class this year amounts to four Hundred, last year there were five Hundred students but I should suppose the country must be overstocked with Physicians and who can calculate the injury, if the usual proportion of them are quacks or men of but ordinary capacity.

There are no new engagements spoken of in the beau monde except Willing Francis to his cousin Maria Willing. Mary Lyle is to be married tonight at the Woodlands, her sister's wedding day is not fixed. This is a long idle talk to send so far but, My dear Ben, you must excuse its stupidity,

[1] Isaac Hays graduated as M. D. from the University of Pennsylvania in 1820; he became a celebrated oculist.
[2] Dr. Robert Hare was professor of chemistry at the University of Pennsylvania 1818–1847.
[3] Dr. Philip Swing Dorsey was appointed professor of anatomy at the University of Pennsylvania in 1818. He was attacked by a fatal fever the day he delivered his introductory lecture and died a week later November 12, 1818 as stated in the postscript.

as my object is to keep up the interest of Phila trifles in your recollection. If I were to tell my own thoughts & feelings they would make you sad. I cannot be reconciled to your absence. Your closed office is an eyesore to me and your vacant place a grief of heart, but of this I shall be silent - and only pray for your happiness and success. Jo says he will write tomorrow - and Jac will as soon as he can tell you he is well. God bless you, My dear Brother, it will be a joyful day to me when I hear from you again, that you are well, and as much pleased with your travels as you anticipated - believe me most truly

Your Affectionate R.G.

Thursday Eve'g

Poor Dr Dorsey is no more! he expired at noon this day of a bilious fever, after a few days illness - this is a calamity both private and public, that is felt throughout the city -

* * *

TO THE SAME

This letter is addressed to Benjamin Gratz Esqr., Lexington Ky., via Washington City and is postmarked Phila. 7 Mar. It was forwarded to Vincennes April 29.

Home affection—Disadvantages of a wandering life—Pioneering—The Philadelphia beau monde—The Feast of Passover—The festival of Purim.

I am always delighted My dear Ben, to receive your letters but do not feel any mortification at your silence. When your letters to our brothers assure me of your health I am grateful for the blessing, and am too sensible of the amiable sensibility of your heart to doubt your constant affection for your family. The bond of sympathy will I trust never be broken, which has been such a source of happiness to our family - and you are cherished with the fondest remembrance by all, even the little children of our Sisters enquire with interest for letters & receive your messages with delight. Miriam[1] was much gratified by your flattering notice of her letter and looks forward to the fulfilment of your promise as a thing of great importance. You must not fail to write to her.

I have never been apprehensive of your becoming attached to a wandering life, but that some project of interest would induce you to fix your residence abroad, and I have considered few things in life worth the sacrifice of the society and habits of home, and the cherished associations of early life - at least few that could be obtained in the western wilds. If objects to advance your prospects opened in any city where you could enjoy such advantages as you are accustomed to whether in the new or old world I believe I could submit to separation easier, because I should still believe you surrounded by friends & comforts, but the *ideal good* which of late has been so inticing to our young men of clearing land, building huts - cultivating soil with the sweat of their brows, and waiting till it should grow into a populous city and seeing themselves great proprietors of lots and the wealth of ages is too chimerical for realization, and I could not bear that you should waste the flower of your days - (which can never bloom again) in such vain experiments. You have had a delightful season for your travels, the winter has been like a continued autumn - and spring has returned before we have felt the rigours of a months cold weather. I hope you will be as well pleased with the remainder of your tour. I have written to our friend Maria, and am quite ashamed of having neglected her so long - everybody I see from Ken-

[1]Miriam Moses, a niece.

TO BENJAMIN GRATZ

tucky speaks of her in terms of deserved praise . . . . The amusements of the season have conformed very much to the weather - they have had very little dancing and until lately few parties- the Theatre has been more fashionably attended and as there has been a succession of good actors here- the dramatic taste of the citizens revived- the streets exhibited a great deal more gaiety than usual- fine weather & good walking brought out belles in handsome walking dresses. Your studies in your Chestnut street office would have been constantly interrupted- and what the girls have lost by your windows being shut is hardly to be calculated- but this genial weather does not seem to have quickened the growth of sentiment- there are no new matches on the tapis - at least none that come under this description. . . . .

Jo is still at Washington- Hyman returned last week and I hope to have the remnant of the family collected- it has been very small all winter. The 10th of April is Passover would I might expect you to keep it with us, when you went away I did certainly hope to see you at that time - you must at least let me know where you will be at that period - on Thursday next is Purim[1] no longer a mirthful festival with us - it passes away without celebration - but more solemn feasts are more permanently observed. It is difficult to fix a time to be happy and tho' we feel grateful for the deliverance this feast commemorates as nothing is required of us but to be glad and merry, we are not always able to do so. Accept the affectionate love of all the family, My dearest Ben, and believe me always with the sincerest prayers for your health prosperity and happiness your Most truly Attached Sister RG

March 7th 1819

[1] The feast of Purim is the joyous holiday observed by Jews on the fourteenth day of the month Adar in commemoration of the deliverance of the Jews as recorded in the biblical book of Esther.

TO THE SAME

This letter is addressed to Benjamin Gratz Esqr. Vincennes Indiana, via Washington City and is postmarked Phila. 24 Mar. It was forwarded from Vincennes April 29 to Lexington Ky. Vincennes, the oldest settlement in southern Indiana was even then an outpost on the western frontier. In view of the present situation of Vincennes it is arresting to see it written of in the terms used by Miss Gratz as among "distant regions."
  The Illinois and Wabash claim—Dr. Nathaniel Chapman— The Masonic Hall fire—The Feast of Passover.

March 24 1819

My Dear Ben

    We were quite regaled yesterday by the receipt of your charming letters, and your friend John Biddle came in the evening to boast of his, what can be more grateful to the heart- than news from a friend in a far country? I verified this feeling to excess and return thanks to God for the blessings that attend you in health & cheerfulness- you certainly are a most excellent traveller, and accommodate yourself with much facility to the manners of the people you sojourn among, that I have no doubt you buy favour every where- courtesy is the jewel of life, in every clime, & perhaps none prize it more than the rough independent people of the west- they who acknowledge no superior love to have their pride flattered by the consideration of their more polished friends, and I suspect they do not often meet with citizens so well bred, if we may judge by the anecdotes our Kentucky acquaintances sometimes relate. Vincennes must be a dull place to stay so long in- yet the beauties & richness of the country will compensate you for other deprivations- and it is so interesting to explore those distant regions and still to recognize the same laws & language- and government, that is so dear to us at home- I hope you will succeed in your business- and not be too long detained - The Illinois & Wabash claim,[1] of which I have all my life heard so much, seemed like a romance- I never expected to see anything but maps & pamphlets of the subject, or that it would cost us your society, for so long a time- but since it has proceeded so far- I catch a little of the mania and frame wishes for its success at any rate hope you will not permit it to engage years of toil on an uncertain event & that after satisfying your curiosity with every thing worth visiting you will bend your course homeward.

You are very lenient to Jona^n Guest, people here are more severe in their censures on his conduct. It is probable that he was assailed by temptations, and he was unprepared to resist them- his engagement with Miss P. was hastily concluded after a very short acquaintance, and his attachment must have been of a nature soon to consume itself- the forsaken damsel looks very pensive, but she is pretty & interesting- & may consider herself fortunate in being left with her friends- hardships such as settlers in a new country must encounter, requires at least the steady affection of a kind companion- to make tolerable, and by the bye among the crosses and perplexities of such a situation there should be a solid foundation to ensure domestic comfort- a man would be very apt to feel cross towards those who give him so much additional anxiety, and as Jona^n found the loss of his picture so fatal to his love, what a desperate dilemma he would have been in with a wife who made so slight an impression. . . .

The affairs of gallantry have not thriven this winter, it has

[1] *B & M Gratz Papers* Selected and Edited by Vincent Byers (Jefferson City, Mo., 1916) *passim*, especially 25-26, 177-179, 340-377.

been a dull season in the fashionable world. The weather was so fine during the months of January and February that walking was more agreeable than dancing- and the evening appointed for the last Cotillion party- the Masonic Hall took fire and was entirely destroyed. We were in some peril[1] but thank God were preserved and no other building was injured. The Girls were already dressed for the Ball - indeed some ladies had already arrived in the room when the fire was discovered - you may imagine what a night of consternation it was here. Those who watched the progress of the destroying element say it exhibited a most beautiful spectacle - the most splendid part of it involved too much anxiety to be enjoyed by us, the falling of the cupola on which the safety of our house depended and we were told it would most probably crush our back buildings, but it happened otherwise (do not think I attribute it to chance) it fell in on its own roof and the lodge alone was consumed. "He who walketh in the whirlwind directs the . . . .[2] has an eye to the small concerns of human destiny and even . . . .[3] to avert this evil also. Logan & J. Biddle and many others were here to . . . .[4] the danger. Seeing pretty soon that we should escape, we set about making those comfortable to whose exertion we were indebted and had the house open all night to give refreshments to the firemen. Many a merry fellow whose loquacity was assisted by a dram made enquiries for you - some of the Niagaras[5] I suppose, or your old soldiers who thought to fare better by naming you as their acquaintance.

Jo has just returned from Mrs. Bartley's recitations. You have seen her name in the papers I suppose, a theatrical phe-

[1]The Gratz home was next door to the Masonic Hall on Chestnut Street between Seventh and Eighth.
[2]Paper torn.   [3]Paper torn.   [4]Paper torn.
[5]A volunteer fire company.

nomenon who has been treating our cities. She came highly recommended, and has redeemed her pledges. . . . .

Ellen[1] is reading aloud to amuse Jo who is puffing his last segar - the rest of our brothers have gone to bed. I do not know that I could offer anything to amuse you but the medley of Ellen's book with what I have to say will surely prove tiresome to you. So good night My dear Ben, May the Lord bless & preserve thee and all good journey with you, whithersoever you go. Our Sisters, nieces Aunt Bell and our brothers all send best love to you. I hope you will be at Lexington on Passover - we shall pray for you - believe me with the utmost affection your sincerely

attached Sister R G

* * *

TO MARIA GIST GRATZ

Benjamin Gratz married Maria Cecil Gist on November 24 1819. This is the first letter of Rebecca Gratz to her sister-in-law. A deep affection sprang up between these two unusual women. It is likely that the "difference of opinion" mentioned in the first paragraph refers to the difference in religion. It doubtless pained Rebecca Gratz that her brother married out of the faith but the superior qualities of her new sister-in-law reconciled her to the situation as the many letters which passed between the two amply prove.

Condemnation of the practice of duelling—The Goodwin-Stoughton affair.

You must banish reserve now, My dear Maria for we are Sisters, and with that loved title you have a claim to my warmest affection- and in that title too I look for such love as has been the most fertile source of comfort & happiness to

[1]See page 12, Note 2.

me thro' my life- I thank you most sincerely for your kind letter- Ben should not have made you acquainted with my wishes when it was too late to have them gratified- as it gave you an unnecessary regret- I have every confidence in the integrity of both - may I not say, it was my knowledge of the superiority of your character that induced me to make the request - henceforth we will not remember that there is a difference of opinion on any subject between us- and I trust we shall be sincere friends as well as affectionate Sisters to the end of our lives-

I thank you for withholding any part of my message that would have given pain to your Mother- I have the highest respect for her & would not for the world wound her feelings. You must My dear Maria win her for me if I have offended.

We have had the satisfaction to hear that our dear Hyman is with you- he left home so thin that I was apprehensive the fatigue of a winter journey would be too severe for him- but now that he is in his favorite Kentucky with friends, shall expect to hear of his regaining his health & good looks- Tell my brothers, the most extraordinary things continue to take place on this side the mountains- my last letters told the melancholy tale of Miss Coleman's dying for love and now I have to recount an act of violence, which has thrown young Goodwin (Robert) into prison to wait his trial for Murder- the New York papers relate all the circumstances particularly- it seems however, that his intentions were not murderous- an accidental stroke on the spring of his case exposed the dagger, on which in their scuffle Mr Stoughton fell, & it penetrated his heart- the rencountre took place at mid-day in the most public part of the city- and of course very considerable irritation is excited against the survivor- they had a public funeral at which 10000 persons were collected- of all places I know, New York appears to me the worst, for such an offence to occur in- so many fatal duels have desolated the higher ranks of society- so many families have been plunged in distress by that detested practice, that every act of violence renews the recollection and engages the sympathy and the vengeance of the public mind.

Mr Goodwins family have been peculiarly unfortunate- his brothers have all shared in the troubles of Baltimore and are reduced in fortune- one of his Sisters recently became a widow- and now this calamity, which worse than all, brings guilt & disgrace upon them- is a climax in the history of their woes. . . . .

If Ellen were here she would have some thing affectionate to say for her-self- but she has gone to pass a few days at her Mothers - her little Sister is sick with the Measles which prevails almost universally thro' our city, and Maria being absent she has gone to supply her place as assistant nurse- we have had 25 sick at one time at the Orphan Asylum[1] with that disease-

Your little favorites Becky & Gratz Moses[2] talk of you with great animation and send a deal of love to you and Uncle Ben- I have so much love and congratulation from all quarters to send you both, that it would take a page to give a catalogue of names only- Ben must tell you of all your new relations, and then you will please to bow your head & say thank ye, to each of them- but as for our Sisters bid him salute you for each, and say what ever he thinks will be most agreeable-

Present me affectionately to your dear Mother- tell My dearest Brothers I depend on hearing from them frequently- and you, Maria, I must have you confess that you no longer

---

[1] Rebecca Gratz was one of the founders of the Philadelphia Orphan Society, and its secretary for many years.
[2] Children of Solomon and Rachel Gratz Moses.

feel diffident towards one who loves you sincerely- and who is too simple hearted to cause such a feeling in you- I hope soon to receive such an assurance, and am My dear girl with sincerity yr affectionate

Sister R G-

Saturday Eveg. Decr 25th 1819-

* * *

TO THE SAME

Chess—Hyman Gratz on his travels and in Lexington—Canewood—The decrees of Providence—Children's insight—The Orphan Asylum election.

You will conclude My dear Maria, by my speedy replys, that frequent letters will not be troublesome to me, on the contrary, I shall exact them, as the only means of establishing a sisterly intercourse between us, while at such a distance from each other- I know you are to be very busy in your new avocation of house-keeper- and will have a thousand interesting subjects to engage your thoughts- so much the better, I shall have the more agreeable correspondent- and it is impossible for you to be too minute- for every thing will be full of My dear Bens & your happiness and will find its way direct to my heart-

I am not enough of a chess player to answer your question, but soon after your letter arrived, Miss Rush & Mr Williams came to pay me a morning visit, and I stated the case to them- "tell her to play, by all means" said Julia, and beat him if she can- Why, said Harry, I think she may venture with Ben, if she can win a game without shewing too much triumph in the victory- but continued he Mr & Mrs C will not play chess together- You may tell Ben however- that his friend, seems very earnest in his game with the fair Julia and she plays very skilfully- a looker on may discover that she has the issue in her own hand, but whether she means to stake her heart does not appear so plain.

By letters received today I find our Brother Hyman has left Lexington. I am rejoiced to hear he has regained his good looks- traveling is a charming remedy- and it has the good effect of relaxing the mind from the toils of business which no doubt has its salutary influence on his appearance. I am glad your first interview was at Canewood, as I am sure it gratified him to pay his respects to your Mother at her own house-

And so you approve my taste, in selecting fashions for you? I should like to see how beautiful you look in them, you have received them so kindly that they must be becoming and My brother shall thank you for your gracious acceptance- our winter has just set in, Christmas day was the first cold weather we had, since which we have a covering of snow, and every prospect of hard weather- rain would have been very acceptable to the country in this neighbourhood first as the springs have given out pretty generally- however, I do not join in the murmurs people usually indulge in, when the clouds discharge too much or too little for their convenience- the records of time bear witness, that providence orders all things for the best- and the elements obey its decrees.

I told your little favorite Beck,[1] the other day that I had been writing to you, have you, said she, did you give my love to her? "I loved her dearly, before she was My Aunt and I suppose I must love her better now"- children argue well Maria, when they feel naturally- our family have the happiness of cherishing affection for each other- you will have

[1] Rebecca Gratz Moses, aged nine at this time.

many young relations whose hearts are open to receive you when you make their acquaintance-

Ellen is very busy writing tickets for the Orphan Society, who hold an election on Tuesday- I became weary of writing over the names of 24 ladies, whose features have nothing remarkable in them, and induced her to release me for a while - have you ever amused yourself by writing the name of a person whose image is agreeable - and found their countenance appear at the nib of your pen? but a list of names of indifferent persons might rival the ingenious device of counting to bring on drowsiness - pardon me, My dear, this stupid conclusion to a dull letter - I offer small inducement to the correspondence I invite you to - tell my dear Brother, I shall expect sometimes a letter from him, and to both, if Hyman has returned, present my affectionate love -
. . . .

Adieu, My dear Maria. May God Bless you with a continuance of your present happiness, and realize all your anticipations of the future - believe me Sincerely your Sister

R Gratz

present My affectionate regards to your Mother -
January 2nd 1820

* * *

TO THE SAME

Col. James Morrison—The Barron Decatur duel—The City of "brotherly love" - David G. Seixas and the institution for the deaf and dumb - Ivanhoe - "My namesake Rebecca."

I take a long sheet of paper My dear Maria without being able to promise my self that I shall fill it agreeably, but I have delayed answering your letter so long, and have thought of it so often that I fancy I have a great deal to say, tho' as you will not introduce me into your domestic repositories, I should in like manner treat you as a parlour visitor but I am getting tired of ceremony, and as the spring advances we may venture to linger on a corner sofa and feel perfectly at our ease-

We have been expecting our friend Col. Morrison[1] for a week past but he has not yet made his appearance- the sad occurrence at Washington must have changed the whole gay circle there into a groupe of Mourners, indeed it has produced much sorrow here. Decatur was a Philadelphian and much beloved- the manner of his death was so shocking- that one can scarcely be reconciled to it, so glorious a life as his should have come to a better end. I wish we were a less barbarous people- and could count among us heroes who would not stain their hands with human blood, unless in the field of battle, for their country's honor and safety. Decatur surely had no need to fight a duel- he could never have been deemed a coward, and the example of such a man's declining to fight- might have done much to abolish the practice- his poor wife is now one of the most desolate of human beings- she is alone in the world- her husband was her idol- his glory the pride of her heart She had no children to divide her love- and is of course more wretched in her present bereavement- what a contrast does a few weeks make in her fate & her feelings- perhaps no two human beings could be more different than Mrs Decatur in Jany and at this moment- but you have already had enough of this melancholy theme the newspapers are filled with it-[2]

[1] Col. James Morrison, a business partner of Benjamin Gratz, founded Morrison College and was chairman of the Board of Trustees of Transylvania University. See Ranck, History of Lexington, 151–152.
[2] The duel between the famous naval commander, Captain Stephen Decatur and Commodore James Barron in which Decatur was killed was fought at Bladensburg, Maryland, March 20, 1820.

And what do you think they are doing here? all sorts of wicked things- this city of "brotherly love" has become a den of thieves- there have been prison insurrections, and incendiary conflagations, one beautiful Theatre was last night reduced to ashes- and the whole neighbourhood endangered- the adjoining houses were unroofed- & much property destroyed- this was unquestionably the work of design- our citizens patrole the streets from early in the evening till sun rise, but have not yet succeeded in detecting the gang. . . .

I have sent you a bonnet which I hope will please you - it is fashionable - you will agree with me that these are not the times to indulge in the luxury of fine leghorns. I divided one with you- and had them made exactly alike except in the colour of the trimming- mine is white.

Tell Ben. his old acquaintance David Seixas[1] is distinguishing himself among the benefactors of mankind, and is likely to reap the reward due to his talents and humanity- he has been privately engaged six or seven months teaching a class of indigent Deaf & Dumb children- and has succeeded so well as to atrract the notice of our humane & scientific citizens to whom he has recently exhibited his school- they approve his system, which the Abbe Corree who has visited the European Schools, says is on a truly philosophical plan- they are about establishing an Institution- of which this ingenious and philanthropic young man will be the principal-

It is impossible My dear Maria, to conceive a more interesting sight than these unfortunates exhibit- he has eleven, who write exceedingly well, communicate with their hands very intelligibly- read, spell and cypher and appear cheerful & happy- I hope ere long you will have an opportunity of witnessing their achievements-

[1] David G. Seixas, a son of the Reverend Gershom Mendes Seixas See Morais, *The Jews of Philadelphia*, pp. 296-298.

By a Mr Jones of Virginia Jac has sent the life of Napoleon to you, have you received Ivanhoe? when you read it tell me what you think of my namesake Rebecca - tell my dear brothers they are most fondly cherished in the affection of their family- and that I have thought and wished for them incessently this week- to celebrate the Passover at home. Tell me dear Maria when we may expect you here, Hyman says he sees nothing to prevent your coming- ask Ben & your self whether there be any impediment in the way of our wishes.

Jac is very impatient that I should get to the end of my letter, as he has some ready for the office and he is fearful his post-boy will be taken up by the patrole if I detain him later- this is a fortunate interruption for you, as I feel very much disposed to go to the end of my paper. not having got thro' one half of what I intended to write- but I dare not stay another minute So My dear, you must take a great deal of love from us all in as few words as possible and believe me with great truth your affectionate RG-

My best love to my dear Brothers-

April 4th 1820

TO THE SAME

The year of this letter is omitted from the date but the mention of the visit of Colonel Morrison and the further reference to Scott's Ivanhoe both of which were mentioned in the letter of April 4th, 1820 make it quite certain that this letter was written shortly thereafter, viz. May 10, 1820.

Large families a blessing—Dr. Caldwell's difficulties at Transylvania University—Mr. Carter of Virginia—Scott's Rebecca.

I am afraid your good resolutions of writing to me often, My dear Maria, will give out, when you come to consider what a stupid correspondent you gain by it. Ever since the arrival of your request that a letter should greet your return from Canewood I have intended to write- but intentions travel much faster than actions with us all I believe, and among the most faulty in that particular (I am sorry to say) you will find your Sister- but I am not so insensible as to disregard favors, and if you are not discouraged by what you have already experienced, I hope to improve by your example.

I am glad to hear you have recovered from the first inconvenience of your indisposition, tho' from some hints that have reached us, suppose you are not yet done with the "apothecary-shop," you must not expect more than half my sympathy on this occasion, as our Sister Rachel has bespoke the other half, and indeed I have such old fashioned notions on the subject, that I look upon the patriarchal blessing as a blessing still, and think Mothers do not pay too dear for their treasures, even thro' their period of personal inconvenience. I hope you were not Dr Caldwells patient in his failure of a first attempt as physician-his other discomfitures are quite laughable. Mrs. C. who is all attention to Col Morrison furnished him with the Drs defence and his valedictory address. They have not added much to his literary fame in this quarter, and I think the Kentuckians must have adopted him for their own, before they can patronize such rodomontade- I have no doubt the T.[1] University will draw together literary men, and induce a taste for literature & science. Your society will eventually be improved by it and Dr C. may be a very useful man, but you must have greater than he, to give it such a character as the great western nation will aspire to. Your poets are complimentary. Miss Hunt must be accomplished indeed to extract poetry from the Latin & Greek

We have a neighbour who courts the muses, and every few weeks issues from the press a neat pamphlet on hot press letter paper, beautifully printed, and bearing classical titles. These he sends to the ladies whom he visits, and very modestly denies the authorship, or affects great surprise how he could be detected- no one attempts to criticise his poetry, for no one understands it, the wits read it up & down the page and declare it has the advantage of being equally fine either way- I hope he is not a relation of yours, Maria, he is a Virginian- his name Carter- was married to a Daughter of Genl Lee, from whom he unsuccessfully petitioned our legislature to be unmarried, last winter- he has four daughters at school here- is very rich- a great admirer of beauty and our compassionate ladies have sympathized in his unhappiness on account of his domestic inquietude- but his poetry has dissolved the spell- indeed some of the fair, now take pity on his wife & think had she petitioned for a devorce, she might be justified on the score of his false pretensions to inspira-

[1]Transylvania.

tion- they think his flirtation with the Muses cause sufficient to disgust a woman of sound understanding- . . . .

There is another novel just out by the Author of Ivanhoe, if it is as good, you shall see it- I am glad you admire Rebecca, for she is just such a representation of a good girl as I think human nature can reach- Ivanhoes insensibility to her, you must recollect, may be accounted to his previous attachment- his prejudice was a characteristic of the age he lived in- he fought for Rebecca, tho' he despised her race- the veil that is drawn over his feelings was necessary to the fable, and the beautiful sensibility of hers, so regulated, yet so intense might show the triumph of faith over human affection. I have dwelt on this character as we sometimes do on an exquisite painting until the canvass seems to breathe and we believe it is life-

Jo & Jac are managers of the Deaf & Dumb Institution- we are all much interested, you will be so too when you witness the expression of countenance every new idea lightens up in these poor little blanks- the Col. will tell you how capable they are of improvement and how happy they appear while receiving instruction- he & our Brothers have gone to take a ride this afternoon along the new canal at the Schuykill-

Give my best love to Dear Ben & Hyman, pray Maria give Hyman charges in all his Sisters names not to expose himself to an unhealthy climate in the approaching warm season- I have many apprehensions of his long journey & wish he was back again- Your husband is very much spoiled as a correspondent- do you require all his spare time- that he cannot give me any? Adieu, My dear Maria, May God bless You and him, prays your Most affectionate RG

. . . .

May 10th

TO BENJAMIN GRATZ

Business letters and family correspondence—proposed visit of Mrs. Benjamin Gratz to her Philadelphia relatives—Dr. Caldwell.

June 12 1820

Tho' you are engaged in business and have little time to spare to female correspondents, My dear Ben, I cannot forbear now and then intruding myself upon you. Your dear Maria it is true sometimes kindly and with a welcome pen pleads your excuse and I will not say that any man could have a better substitute but I am not willing to indulge you in the habit of always employing another hand, lest you should altogether forget that it is your business to write to me at all and then by a very natural process in the course of time you will consider me as Maria's correspondent only and perhaps cease to think of me in any other light - and I shall never be blessed with the sight of your handwriting expressing a single kind thought but in the general message at the conclusion of one of the boys letters which like the winding up of an argument will be written after having your head full of India goods, produce and groceries - instead of coming fresh from the heart as all your tenderness does when you take a sheet of white paper, seat yourself in your family circle and express to each of your delighted auditors the fullness of your happiness and your reliance on their constant love. One wishes to write sometimes too but have no particular communication to make and the being a letter in debt is a most satisfactory excuse to one's vanity, for indulging the desire unprovided with sufficient matter. Our brothers keep you so well informed of everything passing here among those you are interested for, that I am sure there is little for me to do, but to indulge myself in the pleasure of calling your attention to the domestic circle in which you are cherished with a Benjamin's portion of love and tender recollections. . . . .

Maria tells me she is anxious to make us a visit but never answers directly to my several solicitations to come, so that I do not know whether to blame you, your business or her for such tantalizing conduct, but I look forward to Hyman's return as offering an inducement you will neither of you resist if circumstances permit you to accompany him. You will come into a community of newly married or engaged acquaintances, and as your own happiness has put you in such a benevolent wishing-mood with all the world, you will have ample field of indulging your sympathy with Hyman's votaries.

Dr Caldwell[1] has arrived here from N. Orleans. We have been in some apprehension respecting the state of that city and some reports of its having been destroyed by fire he has happily been able to contradict. The Dr's defense and valedictory address will not encrease his literary reputation here, nor should I suppose it could anywhere. Mrs. Caldwell provided Col. Morrison with a copy when here, and also presented him with the life of Green that he might judge for himself. . . . .

My friend Maria[2] has as usual been employed in kind offices to the family - her health is moderately good but her husband's circumstances not so favorable. He has realized the truth of Shakespeare's assertion that "unhappy is the

---

[1] Dr. Charles Caldwell was a professor in the medical department of the Transylvania University at Lexington 1819–1835. He was interested greatly in phrenology.
[2] See page 12, Note 2.

man who waits on princes favors" for any man in power is a prince in that respect. Hoffman has too long been pursuing the same shadow. . . . .

Our sisters families are in good health - the Hays' have been a good deal in society this winter - they appear to be favorites but not belles. . . . .

Isaac[1] has just opened an office. . . . . Reuben[2] enjoys better health than he did in town - he gardens successfully and if he had a little money would be very happy at least comparatively so - but so many children unprovided for must be sources of great anxiety to an old man. Edward[3] is trying for a commission in the navy, failing that he will become a sailor.

Give my love to our dear Maria, tell her I look with hope to the post's arrival, as her goodness is my pledge that she will not long be a debtor. May God bless you both, My dearest Brother believe me most truly your and her affectionate

R Gratz

* * *

TO MARIA GIST GRATZ

"The untranslatable language of the soul"—Yellow fever epidemic—Preventive measures.

My dear Maria,

By letters from our brothers you are informed that Rachel is happily over her troubles and is rejoicing in the acquisition of another son,[4] she is in fine health and really looks

[1]See page 14, Note 1.
[2]Reuben Etting, a brother-in-law.
[3]Edward Etting, son of Reuben.
[4]Horace, youngest son of Solomon and Rachel Moses, born Aug. 9, 1820.

beautifully proud of her numerous treasures, and they do her both credit & honor- for they are really good, as well as lovely children, I have seen her almost every day since her confinement and should have lost the opportunity of now addressing you, had not a very timely rain disappointed me of an engagment to pass the afternoon with her, but as I am to have the honor of being God-Mother to-morrow I gladly relinquish this days visit for the pleasure of answering your letter-

In the very first place I beg leave to differ from you, My dear Sister in regard to the superior advantage of cultivating an acquaintance by letter rather than by conversation altho' I admit we may confer as familiarly on paper, and perhaps even express our feelings more fully on some subjects - yet the pleasure of looking into each others eyes, and reading that untranslateable language of the soul which can only be conveyed thro' them is more than an equivalent for the finest epistle - I am not however so forward a child, as to disparage the good within my power, because there might be a greater - and except the charm of your quick bright glances, have no second choice above your letters, which are so easy and characteristic, that they bring you before "My minds eye" and are ever welcome visitors- indeed I am very glad, you were prevented coming here this summer for we are threaten'd with the Yellow fever - several persons have already died within the last week & considerable alarm exists among the citizens - the board of health have reported to-day, and promise a daily bulletin, the infection is confined to the street facing the Delaware on the east of the city and several squares are fenced up to prevent communication - These rigorous measures will I trust arrest the disease - we do not consider ourselves in any danger at present in any part of the city and as dull times have long weaned our Merchants from their shipping I feel much easier on our Brothers accounts than on any previous occasion. Jac & Simon will soon be all who are left at home as Jo will be going on his travels as soon as Simon returns from the Springs. . . . .

We shall send newspapers that you may know the situation of the city from time to time - be ye of good cheer, the Arm of providence is our shield thro' every danger, "the pestilence that stalketh at mid-day shall not come nigh us", if He who gave us life will its preservation. Adieu My sweet Maria, may you and all you love be happy - believe me every truly and affectionately

Your RG

Aug 17th 1820

* * *

TO THE SAME

New Orleans and the South—Yellow fever—The curse of slavery.

Novr 11th 1820

Yes indeed My dear Maria, I acknowledge with much gratitude that I am your debtor for two letters. and tho' sufficient time elapsed between their dates, to have replied to the first, I hope you are too tenacious of the privilege this gives you - to chide me too keenly for following your example- Your interesting acknowledgement affords a plea which is irresistible but I know you are too rational a woman- to take such advantage of it as I have seen done by some ingenious dames- who contrived to make the period of their probation, one of extensive power- you certainly have learned the art of keeping a secret- and tho' you have confessed to the main point- leave us still in suspense as to the age of the charming visitor you will bring us in the spring- we needed some fair promise to reconcile us to the prospect of Hyman's protracted absence, I find you are supplanting me with him- and have made yourself so agreeable that he allows a little business to be sufficient excuse for another winter's residence with you- will you be pleased, when you send him home, to let me know by "what conjuration and mighty magic you have used" as I am resolved to practice any gentle arts you have found so successful, to keep him stationary, when I am once again blest with the sight of him- our brother Jo returned home last week after an absence of two months- he just escaped the winter-journey for it has been snowing here all day- in those cities which were afflicted with yellow fever- this early winter will be hailed with joy- but we are not always grateful for rough blessings and I fear are often discontented even with the seasons.

I rejoice that the pestilence is stayed- at New Orleans & Savannah, I lamented poor Mr Larned very much, and find he is considered a great public loss. Edward Fenno, a young friend of ours, had the fever & recovered- he speaks in the highest terms of the humanity of the coloured women, who attended, and provided him with every comfort during his illness- but for all that I wonder, that persons who know the difference between that climate and the more salubrious north, can for the lure of gain, sacrifice such advantages for the uncertainties of a few fleeting months- when the chances are so much against them. The natives may grow rich and flourish being enured to the climate- and they should have some privileges to compensate them for the evils of their situation- Pray do you know a widow Sargeant, who removed from Natches to our city last summer? she has purchased a fine house in Chestnut St- and set up an equipage- she has a pretty large family, and from appearances is very wealthy-but I do not think she is calculated to make a dash here - she is an active managing woman, and her daughter a gentle creature, forming an entire contrast as they appeared to me, on a visit I made them,-I should suppose Mrs S would superintend her own plantation- while Mrs Thompson would scarcely be able to manage a nursery- but I was much taken with the pretty feeble Mrs Thompson, and as she is very young think she may acquire energy of character- where she finds every Lady must take the trouble of thinking for themselves- aye and sometimes help themselves too. One of the curses of slavery is the entire dependence the poor mistress is reduced to- when she is rich enough to have all her wants supplied by numerous servants- . . . .

Our Sisters & brothers My dear Maria, send you most affectionate love we all long for the spring when we shall have the happiness of seeing you . . . . Tell my dear Ben how rejoiced I am to hear of his happiness which is proclaimed by all who return from Kentucky- and say to dr Hyman that I will write him soon, to both make my love accepted- and to your self Dear Maria, say that your Sister prays to almighty God that all your fond anticipations may be happily realized- that you may be protected in the hour of peril- and blest according to the wishes of your own heart, and when you bring your treasures I will join in your thanksgiving Adieu dear Maria, ever

your affectionate R G-

TO THE SAME

The British Court scandal—George IV and Queen Charlotte—Characterization of George IV—Blue Stockings—Aunt Hetty Simon's death.

Well, My dear Maria, I have given you time enough to anticipate a letter, and I hope you will give it at last a welcome reception - but do not believe me guilty of such affectation as to have waited merely to enhance its value by the length of time it was due. Indeed I have been very busy as I always am at the close of the Year and until my business was accomplished did not feel at ease to sit down to write letters - but this evening I have spread all my dear correspondents claims upon my desk and resolved my sister's should be the first answered. You are quite a riddle Maria, and as I am not very ingenuous in solving such matters, I shall wait patiently until you disclose your own secrets. In the meantime you may assure yourself of the tenderest interest, and best wishes of my heart.

I am very glad to hear our old friend Col. Morrison is recovering- from your letter I apprehended we should never see him again, and I always feel so much indebted to him for the friendship he shews my brothers in Kentucky - besides liking him for his own agreeable qualities, that his loss would be much lamented.

Pray what part have you espoused in the British altercation? will you be pleased to hear that the Queen is acquitted, and the city of London been illuminated three nights in honor of her triumph? this is the latest news we have - and moreover what concerns us more, the Spanish treaty is ratified - a short arrival brings this account so that the New

Year will be joyfully hailed by some of our citizens who have old claims on the Spanish nation.[1] As to the termination of the Queen's trial, I can not say that I feel much satisfaction in it - she is not sufficiently interesting in her own character to make one rejoice for her, altho it is hard that a woman should have been discarded on such a plea as that first adopted by her husband. I suppose we shall now hear of a coronation and wonderfully loyal pagentries. I have lately read a history of Geo: the 3rd - his court and family - a collection of domestic anecdotes which were quite interesting & agreeable - the old king's parents were excellent characters and his bringing up such as was likely to produce a virtuous prince - but his sons did not follow his example - and his successor cannot boast much of his subjects love - some of the caricatures of this trial are the boldest censures on the king that I have ever seen, and might be considered treasonable in any government -

It is a great pity that your Lexington ladies are so perverse as not to be instructed by Mrs Caldwell - is she not their own Professor's wife and come all the way from Phila? Of course she must know better than they, and if they would but allow her to set the fashions for them, she would treat them with an endless variety from her own fertile genius, and might even import an annual supply from . . . . but you western people are too proud to learn and so you must take the consequence and be governed by reason and common sense as long as you live. The learned and elegant Mrs Russel in one of her visits to Saratoga was extremely anxious to form an acquaintance with some Indians - she has a passion for everything Savage and was particularly desirous

[1] The treaty of 1819 between Spain and the United States in which Spain ceded eastern and western Florida to the United States, was ratified in 1821 when the United States took formal possession of the peninsula.

of painting the portrait of an Indian, but could not find one handsome enough - she heard that there was one of great beauty and magnificent stature in the vicinity and sent a messenger in pursuit of him but could not obtain a visit from him - she proposed to the ladies to adopt the fashion of the Aborigines fair & wear ear-rings in their noses, but was not more successful than Mrs. C. Her auditors had as much of Mother Eve in them as the Lexington women and would not be led by the nose, altho Mrs Russel was a real blue-stocking, had been studying costumes in foreign courts, and ventured to exhibit in her own fair person the most grotesque absurdities possible. Thus you see My dear Maria how tyrant custom fetters us and makes us blind to the improvement held out to our invitation.

Assure My dear brothers of My ardent affection- tell Ben he has totally neglected me these six months and more- our Aunt Hetty Simon[1] was buried this morning - she had been ill for five weeks- she suffered patiently and was resigned to the will of providence- to regret the departure of one, whose life was brighten'd by few joys and blest with little usefulness would be vain - for in fulfilling the lot assigned her, she had not many opportunities of conferring benefits- but she was humble & affectionate & departed in peace. Our Sisters and their families desire me to mention them affectionately to you and Ben and Hyman - our brothers write they are all well- do let me hear from you often, my dear Maria, or if you cannot write, plead for me with your husband for a favor which he sometimes used to bestow unsolicited for, I do not think I shall so long be your debtor again, for like you I love to anticipate the pleasure of a letter. Adieu, may the new

---

[1] A sister of Mrs. Michael Gratz.

Year bring you nothing but good and an increase of happiness prays your affectionate Sister

R Gratz

Decr 31st 1820

* * *

TO THE SAME

This letter which is undated is postmarked Jan. 21. The year in which the letter was written is fixed by the reference to the forthcoming birth of Mrs. Benjamin Gratz' first child. This child was born April 8, 1821.
Francis Preston Blair—Edmund Kean the English actor—Jacob Gratz obtains charter for the Deaf and Dumb Institute from the Pennsylvania legislature—trip from Philadelphia to Baltimore takes a night and part of a day.

Several days after the receipt of your letter of introduction my dear Maria, your brother Mr Blair[1] made his appearance and got a very good footing in the good graces of the family at his first visit. The frankness of his manner and friendly address aided by the claims he derived from you were sufficient to ensure him a most welcome reception and if it had not been for Kean the great actor and a little other business, we should have made much greater advances in our acquaintance as he promised to come of evenings and at all times, freely to see us but four times a week the Theatre is irresistible and so our brother Jo & Mr Blair are drawn to it. Next week this attraction will cease and I hope the weather will moderate and then we will try to make ourselves agree-

[1] Francis Preston Blair, who married a sister of Mrs. Benjamin Gratz. He was later the editor of the Globe, Washington D.C. the organ of the Jackson administration. His son Montgomery Blair was Postmaster General in Lincoln's cabinet. Another son Francis Preston Blair Jr. was the vice presidential candidate on the Democratic ticket in 1868, the ticket being Seymour and Blair.

able. Jac too will be at home to add his portion of attention to the stranger. He has been for almost three weeks pleading the cause of charity to our wise ones at Harrisburg - his object to obtain a charter & endowment for the Deaf & Dumb Institution and has a prospect of succeeding - the bill now proposed gives $8000 pr year for five years, by which time we hope the good resulting will induce future legislators to continue it. Mr Blair told us he was an invalid when he left but had so far lost the character of one that after travelling all night and part of a day from Baltimore to Phila he went to the theatre the second night without having any rest - and the weather was colder than any we have had in my memory before, and such as you probably never experienced. I find you have given him some directions about seeing the L . . . here, and he is determined not to forget anything you recommended, but as there are some additions to our stock of public shows I mean to take up the parable after he has gone thro your catalogue. . . . .

I do not like your plan of keeping Hyman to escort you in the spring - we are very much in want of him at home. Brother Simon is going to Washington next week and will be absent perhaps a month. I have been losing & losing, each in turn of the three that remain - and have rarely more than one at a time at home - now Hyman has been so long in Kentucky that I begin to fear he will forget it is not his home - or if he does not forget will learn to like it best, which would be adding less to your happiness than it would be taking from mine - and therefore without giving a less selfish motive, I must again repeat do not make your country and yourself so agreeable as to entice him -

We have not yet been able to shew our Sisters children to your brother, as they are confined with bad colds, but as he expresses himself with great sensibility about children and seems to have a longing after his own, shall take an early opportunity. I always consider it a sign of good heartedness to see a man interested for children - and he will certainly admire our pets. Pray my dear Sister, be good enough to ask your Mother, if she will do me the favor to add a postscript to your next letter informing me when I may look for certain intelligence about a certain event in which you are interested - and then you know (as you do not like to ask questions) you can read it and get the information yourself. I hope my dear Mrs Scott will be in Lexington when this arrives, as I know of no other expedient to serve you in this business. Give my affectionate love to my Dear Brothers, and present my regards to Mrs Blair and your other sisters[1] if you please. . . . . Our sisters and brothers send you their love, and I beg my dear Maria, that you will accept the constant affection and the best wishes of your attached Sister

R G

* * *

TO THE SAME

Francis Preston Blair's return to Kentucky—Mrs. Scott's postscript—Sir Walter Scott's Kenilworth—Novel reading—Hyman Gratz in Kentucky.

If the return of your brother has not dressed your countenance with smiles, My dear Maria, I fear this tardy greeting from your lazy Sister, will not be very graciously received- but indeed you have daily been in my mind & heart and if I had not been very busy, and very stupid and some-

---

[1] These sisters, five in number, all married prominent men. They were, besides Mrs. Benjamin Gratz and Mrs. Francis P. Blair, Mrs. Jesse Bledsoe, Mrs. Nathaniel G. S. Hart (Mrs. Henry Clay was a sister of Col. Nathaniel G. S. Hart) and Mrs. Joseph Boswell.

times very sad too- I should long since have presented myself before you- but I suspect you knew, long before I did that our brother Jo was going to leave me, and have sympathized in my loneliness, and if so, why have you not urged Hyman to hasten home? and will you not hasten yourself too to perform your promise, and realize my long & anxious anticipations? Mr Blair will tell you how much I calculate on your visit and I believe he is so well pleased with Phila that he will give his vote in our behalf- he has gained the esteem of our whole family circle and we shall be very sorry to miss his agreeable society. I have a great desire to see Mrs Blair of whom he speaks with as much animation, as Romeo might have done of his lady-love. He has even given us hopes that he will some day bring her across the mountains and we yesterday planned a charming summer party to the Seaside, which I fear he will quite forget, when he sets foot in Kentucky again.

Will you thank your Mother, My dear Maria, for her interesting P. S. and will you forgive me for reading it first? but how could I help turning to it, with a grateful sense of her goodness and something like triumph in the success of my strategem to learn something about you? It would be presumption in me to attempt giving you any Phila news, as Mr Blair will do it in so much more agreeable manner he has collected or rather culled everything worth transporting for his wifes amusement, and I find is very apt to associate you in them all. "Kenilworth" is the latest literary favorite, and as you have it before this, it has no doubt "beguiled you of your tears", and gratified your imagination- the splendour of Elizabeth's court is finely represented- and her character admirably drawn- but the sweet little unfortunate countess- the ambitious, cruel Leicester, and the noble minded Tressilian are worthy of their renowned author- we have prevailed on your brother to become novel-reader, and have supplied him with Scott- volume after volume, which he takes as eagerly as a boarding-school miss- and I doubt not reads with as much enthusiasm- tho' he rails very learnedly against the practice- and will do penance when he lays them aside, if he returns to the custom of condemning them. . . .

I think of you dearest Maria, with a Sisters solicitude and a sisters hopes and pray the Almighty may bless you with all your heart desires- a little season, and your tribulations will end in joy & gladness which I trust will confirm the happiness of My dear brother & your self and thus delight your affectionate

R G-

March 10th 1821

* * *

TO THE SAME

This letter mentions the first meeting of Mrs. Benjamin Gratz with her husband's family after their marriage. The visit to Philadelphia was paid after the birth of the first child.
The westward trip from Philadelphia to Lexington by stage and steamboat via Bedford, Pittsburgh and the Ohio River— "happiness does not always dwell with riches".

Novr 7th 1821

Hyman told me he would write the first letter to Lexington, & I should write the second, else My dear Maria, I should have thanked you by the last mail for yours dated at Harrisburg. We have been disappointed at not getting further intelligence of your progress, but hope your whole journey will be equally pleasant with its commencement and that we shall soon hear you are safe & happy at home. We daily & hourly regret you- every lovely child reminds me of your darling- and we are continually tantalized by the sight of Mrs Powels little beauties, who have come to town, and inhabit the room immediately opposite our parlour windows- her youngest is an infant not much larger than Gratz, and almost as lovely- I wish they would go back into the country-

I can scarcely realize that you were three months with us- so rapidly do pleasant hours flee away- while the anticipation of three winter months seem to lengthen in the contrast beyond all calculation. We have had several days of rain, which we hope will meet you at Pittsburgh & prepare the river for your accommodation. Why did not our dear Ben send a few lines from Bedford? indeed, Maria, separation from him, is a severe conflict- which the conviction that he is happy, would alone reconcile me to- and that you dearest, make him so is a source of never failing gratitude to your Sisters heart- may you long enjoy every felicity together.
. . . .

I saw Mrs Williams yesterday who gave a long string of regrets & disappointments at not seeing you more frequently- she was sick, and so unfortunate when she did exchange visits- and then she sympathized with me for your loss so kindly and looked so prettily, that I am sure Mr Blair would have admired & excused her if I did not. To day Chestnut Street has been a scene of gaiety- on an occasion which would make a moralist, or an observer of human affairs- quite sad- the splendid furniture of a ruined gentleman, was exhibited for sale, and to-morrow will be distributed under the auctioneers hammer to the four corners of the city- the luxuries which wealth and ambition & taste had combined to render the most beautiful I ever saw, Mrs Walm's drawing-room was certainly more like an apartment in an eastern fairy tale, than a Phila parlour- I wish you could have seen it for I confess I had no idea of its grandeur- and cannot compare any furniture I had before seen with it- alas alas! her french carpets were this day trodden by many a clownish foot- and her mirrors reflected objects, which it would have shocked her nerves to witness in the retirement of her dressing room- but "fallen from her high estate", she will I believe acknowledge that happiness does not always dwell with riches- she is more sensible of her powers to make comforts, than she formerly was, to enjoy them- activity has restored health, and adversity produced an energy she never called into action before. The family all send affectionate remembrance to you and My dear Ben. and kisses to your son- but pray be merciful, for if you perform all these messages you will devour him with too much love- present me affectionately to your Mother. My regards to Mr Blair- and pray My dear Maria, think of us with interest and pleasure, and try to wish that you may make us another visit soon, which will confer happiness on your affectionate

Sister R G.

* * *

TO THE SAME

Social gaieties in Philadelphia—The Assembly dances—Joseph Gratz in Europe—David Seixas' misfortunes in the Deaf and Dumb Institute—The Orphan Asylum report.

At length My dear Maria, we have the happiness to know that you are at home again, and in health. and I trust your darling boy has not suffered- nor made you suffer during your long and tedious journey- it appears an age since you left us yet we have not ceased to regret you. As the season advances when Phila has most attractions for strangers, we wish your visit had been planned so as to have partaken of its amusements. I called to see Mrs Bayard a few days after a grand ball had been given by Mrs Meade, after enquiring very kindly about you, she lamented that you had not been there- said she could not help thinking what a fine figure you would have made among them. and in her usual style of saying pretty things, passed some of her well timed compliments with so much judgment, that I went away quite charmed with her politeness, and scarcely doubting her sincerity- What a pity thought I, she is a . . . .- one might else have been delighted with such candour- she is very beautiful too, and their house is among the gayest of our fashionables- they have already given one large party and are going to have a dance soon. Mrs John Sargeant has invited us to see the old year out at her house- and the Assembly's commence the first week in the new one- but what is all this to you or me? if you were here I should buckle on my old finery again for the pleasure of accompanying you, but as it is, I do not mean to go anywhere, except to matronize Rosa Hays on her debut, for to tell you the truth such scenes are "stale, flat & unprofitable" to me- the companions of former days have either passed away, or have lost their interest in my heart and the idea has so much of melancholy in it to me, that a ball room seems more like a memorial of lost pleasures than an incitement to new ones.

We have had recent letters from our Brother Jo, who appears much pleased with Gibraltar, and the society- he fears he shall not be able to make a tour thro' Italy as he intended, having been so long detained by business- but he expects to go to France & England.

Ellen has at length lost her friend Ann Lee, who was permitted to return home last week- she was much grieved to part with her- but bids me send love & kisses to you and the darling. I assure you no child was ever more lamented than yours- he is quoted on all occasions as the loveliest, the best, and the prettiest of his age. Poor Horace suffered desperately in the comparison- but he is now taken into favor again- he has regained his beauty- and begins to smile very sweetly- but I dare say your boy will walk and talk as soon as he will. I beg you will not fail to let me know all his accomplishments, his first speech, which will no doubt be a fine specimen of natural eloquence- and the ingenious substitutes by which he already makes himself understood.

I please myself with the idea that there is a letter on the way communicating all these interesting particulars. Our dear Ben's rarely blesses my eyes- we are told they are business letters- tell him when he has leisure he must write to me, as otherwise I derive no benefit from his epistles - I called to see his friend Mrs Meredith[1] this afternoon who desires her love, she told me some time ago that she meant to write to you. She is very much interested in poor Seixas' affairs, and among his best friends. You have no doubt seen his appeal, and felt concerned for him. I hope he will be justified- and if innocent, made to appear so before the public- the legislature will no doubt cause an investigation to be made- at present Mr Cleve is in his place in the institution- both he & his wife are dumb. She is a pretty interesting woman, with very fine manners and intelligent countenance, their child only 20 months old, talks very plainly to her nurse, and makes signs to her parents which are really wonderful- she appears equally intelligible to both - had they come here for any purpose but to supercede Mr Seixas I should have thought them an acquisition to the Institution but after he had devoted himself to establish such a school,

---

[1] During the few years that Benjamin Gratz practised law in Philadelphia he was in the office of Mr. William Meredith, a prominent lawyer.

to be turned off, destitute on the world, I think so cruel, that unless he were guilty, it is unpardonable- . . . .

Embrace your son for me, and give my best love to my dear brother. I cannot apologize for my stupidity in any other way than by saying I am very busy as the closing year demands that my annual accounts for the O. Society should be rendered in- and this gives me a distaste to my pen, for at least a month. I will try to do better when I have had the happiness to hear from you- but believe me My dear sister nothing interrupts the pleasure & affection with which my thoughts ever turn to you. May you be ever blest with health, and every domestic comfort- present My regards to your Mother & sisters- I hope you found your Aunt better and that you may long see all you love around you- Adieu.

believe me your affectionate Sister
R G-

Decr 29th 1821.

* * *

TO THE SAME

A mother's foolish vanity—The Orphan Asylum conflagration.

I am not quite sure, My dear Maria, that you are entitled to an apology, altho I have been so long silent that I am almost ashamed of myself, and long most ardently to hear from you, you owe me a letter I believe notwithstanding- but somehow your conscience is not very sensitive on this subject and you are sure, transgress as much as you may, a letter will always make your peace. I wish you had more curiosity about Phila for then it would urge you to enquire what is going on, and you would oftener be induced to tell me something about yourself & son in return for the news I could tell you. Do you know the dear little fellow is free to make choice of another mate, as the infant beauty, Harriet Bayard is no more? Whether she fell a victim to religion or vanity is not determined- the priest who baptised her threw a large cup of cold water over her head, and her young mother, and doting grandmother could not resist the pleasure of exhibiting her to every visitor- many a gentle slumber was broken, and warm night clothes exchanged for more becoming dress, to elicit hollow praise from evening guests, till at length the babe fell sick and after a few days desperate sufferings expired, to the infinite distress of her parents- it is nearly a month since, the family are just coming out again.

You have heard of the more dreadful calamity we have experienced in the destructive fire of the Orphan Asylum, and I am sure have sympathized with our distress- poor little souls how sad their fate! One would scarcely think it possible such a total destruction could take place in so rapid a manner, there was not an article of any thing saved, except what was round the bodies of those who escaped- we have taken a house in Market Street between Schuylkill and Center Square, until an Asylum can be rebuilt. The whole state takes an interest in our misfortune and as much money is already raised as will completely reinstate every pecuniary loss- but the heart-rending circumstance of so many having perished- will create a new anxiety, in the breast of the managers which while it deepens the interest takes off much from the satisfaction of their labours- they have been much abused- as public feeling rather than judgment operates on the first occurance of a fatal accident- but while sensible they were not neglectful of any duty- they can only write their regrets, and confess that liable to such severe dispensation, their utmost endeavours are insufficient to secure their helpless charges from every danger. . . . . Tell My dear Ben, I love him truly and wish he could spare time to write to me but if you his better part will do this kindness for him, I shall be content to wait his pleasure, our brother Jac wishes room for a few lines, and so I shall only beg to embrace your sweet cherub for me, give My love to your Mother, and share with My beloved Ben the Affection of, My dear Maria,

Your attached Sister RG.

Feby 9th 1822

* * *

TO THE SAME

A stranger in the land—The new fuel, anthracite coal—Sir Walter Scott's "Fortunes of Nigel".

Augt 7th 1822

Do not suppose My dear Maria, that I mean to persecute you with letters- the object of this is to ask you to pay *a little* attention to Mrs Stokes the English Lady of whom you heard me speak last summer - I received a letter from her on Friday mentioning that she had retreated from the climate of St Lewis to Lexington where she should stay until her affairs again demanded her presence at Missouri- She is a singular woman, her manners such as cannot be approved of, but I believe her to be highly respectable- and certainly very unfortunate. As she is an unprotected woman, and a stranger- the countenance of a few persons in your station in society may be of the utmost consequence to her and as her residence will be but transient cannot be much inconvenience to you- nor would I pay so poor a compliment to you, as to suppose there could be any danger in such association. As an apology for her, we must remember, that when separated early in life from a profligate husband she emigrated to France, where it seems to have been the object of her friends to make her forget her situation by introducing her into the society of literary persons and perhaps discussing her own affairs in an abstract manner- she now talks and writes of her husband- of divorce and other matters which on this side the water we consider of too serious a nature to be treated lightly, with as much freedom as if she had no particular concern in them. I know My dear Ben, would not select such a companion for his wife, nor would I make her my own or my sisters friend- but as a stranger in the land, oppressed, and slandered, cast off by her husband for no crime and only meaning to prosecute her rights so far as to enable her to live reputably in her own country- it is desirable she should receive a little protection from the good of her own sex, that she may not be cast away by finding them shutting her out from virtuous society because the singularity of her circumstances makes her amenable to suspision. She tells me that she has taken the liberty of sending to enquire about me, of Mr Benj Gratz- this was no doubt to seek an introduction and I think you heard me say enough about her last summer, to know how far her claims on me go. If you see her, she will soon make you acquainted with her story- a confidence she places in every one with whom she converses- and when you have listened to her, what ever degree of pity or censure you may bestow, I think you will be convinced that she relates facts, and "nothing extenuates".

I hope she may succeed and return to France, where she may be respected & happy. She is not calculated for American habits, manners, or characters- yet I feel interested in her fate, and wish her to be assisted by the hospitable and virtuous community of every place her untoward destiny introduces her to. . . . .

I hope your darling is passing thro' his *second summer* (which mothers consider a difficult epoch) with health- how I long to see him and his parents- can you give us a little encouragement to long for the winter? you have no idea how much confort may be enjoyed in this climate from the new fuel the Lehigh & Schuylkill is pouring into our city- and how delighted we shall be to see your bright countenance before its glowing light, dearest Maria, try to win our Benj to think of it. Brother Simon is still at Lancaster, but he is drawing towards the close of his business and we expect him home in a day or two- he has kept Hyman at home much longer than he expected to be, but I do not think it is any injury to him, indeed I should not have liked him to travel alone before, he was too much indisposed and until after Rachels confinement I could not accompany him- now he will have to go without me, which is only to be regretted on my part - he is able to take care of him self again- if he chuses- but among his bad habits imprudence with regard to health is very eminent, and the pain it imposes on him fails to effect a change- so he is incurable. . . . .

We shall send you the Fortunes of Nigel by the first opportunity- it is not so great a favorite as its brothers & sisters- but you can trace a strong family likeness and some features as beautiful as any- it is a great pity your book sellers are so patient, or you might be inundated with new books not altogether worth filling your own library with but very well worth a leisure hours perusal-

Give my best love to My dear Brother and embrace *the boy* for me- present me also to your Mother & Mr Blair when you see them. and then to your sisters- Judith Ann & your other nieces, say something of my wish to be entitled to love them, for your sake- My dearest Maria, and believe me, truly your attached Sister R G

TO THE SAME

The Bonapartes in the United States—Stephen Girard.

The joyful accounts of your safety My dear Sister fills my heart with gratitude and after returning thanks to the Almighty for your preservation I come to express my gladness to you that you have added another blessing[1] to My dear Brothers position- and to utter my hopes that your Boys may ever be sources of comfort and happiness to their parents. In ancient times you know sons were considered the best of all inheritance for our sex was not so important in society as we are at present- and with all the advantages modern civility gives us I cannot but believe you will allow sons have greatly the preference to daughters, in your family particularly- as your first-born will thereby obtain a name and a companion, whereas had the second been a girl, little sister would not have infringed on his rights in the least- and he might have been Gratz alone till the next appeared. I assure you the stranger took me quite by surprise as I did not expect him for some time- but I hope to profit by his early appearance, as he will be of a good travelling age in the spring. . . . .

We have had a most pleasant winter thus far, very little snow or cold weather, and as our fashionable world is very sober, it is very fortunate they have the comfort of pleasant weather as a substitute for gaiety & dissipation. The only novelty of the season is the Countess . . . . , or "Princess" Charlotte Bonaparte,[2] who makes her first appearance in

[1] The second son Michael Bernard, born December 28 1822.
[2] Daughter of Joseph Bonaparte ex-king of Spain who was living in exile at Bordentown, New Jersey.

society- the Princess is patronized by Miss Keene and Mrs Lenox. The report of La Mere's[1] death is not credited by Joseph, as he had letters from Rome but a few days previous to the date of the account- at which time she was well- and being desirous of presenting his daughter it would be very inconvenient to credit- she is a diminutive personage. but very accomplished- speaks a little english and appears pleased with America- the Count is much admired- for his urbanity of manners- and amiable conduct. . . . .

Tell Ben, Mr Jo Sims has made an assignment of his estate!! this a few years ago would have appeared as improbable as that Stephen Girard would stop payment- there could scarcely be a more striking instance of the instability of fortune- in his old age to be . . . .[2] stripped of wealth- his wife has had a stroke of palsy and is an invalid for life- so that misfortunes are multiplied upon his head-

Our brothers & sisters send you affectionate love- and beg you will embrace your children for them- Adieu My dearest Maria, May you be blest with a perfect restoration to health, and long enjoy every happiness is the constant wish of your

attached Sister R G

January 20th 1823

* * *

TO THE SAME

Illness of Mrs. Ogden Hoffman, the intimate and beloved friend of Rebecca Gratz - the naming of children - Henry Clay's presidential aspirations.

There is very little credit due, My dearest Maria, for compliance with a request which is agreeable to one's own in-

[1]Letitia, the mother of the Bonapartes.   [2]Paper torn.

clination, so I beg you will not consider me the most obliging of correspondents when you see the very first mail brings you an answer to your letter. I began to feel the want of some communication between us, and even before the arrival of yours determined to write indeed had I been at home and happy you would not have had so long a respite but the encreased indisposition of my friend Mrs. Hoffman[1] induced me to make a visit to New York the latter part of May, and I have been but one week home- she still continues ill- but as her situation may not vary much during the summer I have promised to see her again during the season - and came away, leaving her constantly in a condition which admits no hope of a recovery. My dear Ben can tell you how deserving she is of affection - and how long we have known and loved each other.

I do not know anything My dear Maria, that has so general an effect on the countenances of our family circle as one of your letters, we were all so bright and smiling and delighted yesterday that a stranger would have taken us for a set of the best tempered people in the world- and your description of your darling boys charmed us into lavishing such a multitude of kind epithets that had you been present you would have had no difficulty in fixing their titles for life - without searching the Scriptures in imitation of your pious friend - I like your idea of combining an agreeable association with the denomination of a child and that is the reason family names are so constantly perpetuated from one generation to another - but then fashion and fancy are so various and our

[1] The wife of Judge Ogden Hoffman in whose office Washington Irving studied law and to whose daughter Matilda he became affianced. Through Miss Hoffman, Irving learned to know Miss Gratz whom he described to Walter Scott. The great Scottish novelist made the American Jewess the original of his character Rebecca in his novel "Ivanhoe". Matilda Hoffman died in 1809. Irving remained true to her memory and never married.

children not feeling the dignity of bearing a title down to posterity which sounded well to ante deluvian ears and in ancient tongues may not sympathize with our taste and hence the difficulty I have witnessed in other parents before you though I must confess it has continued longer with you than most others - I suppose because yours are boys and are not to change them as girls do. It may be too, that you experience an inconvenience you are willing to save your sons' wives, for Maria is certainly too pretty a name to exchange for Benjamin and yet the prodigality of modern usage gives up all to husbands and unless when personally and familiarly addressed you are as much Mrs. Benjamin Gratz as if you had never received a feminine appellation - I hope my future nieces may not have to make such a sacrifice - pray seek out from among your or our relations some well sounding as well as good name or else let the dear little fellows be the first of the Gratzes to bring a handsome name into the family for their grandchildren to carry forward. I met with a young couple in New York suffering under similar difficulties for their first daughter - they belonged to the enormous family of Ogdens - who have named for mother and grandmother through so many branches that Sarah & Mary are no longer a title by which an individual can be identified they must have their parents name tacked to it - and yet the perplexed lady feared it might be visited on her as a mark of disrespect to those cherished relations should she venture to deviate.

I bless you and My dear Ben, for keeping in mind your promised visit - speak of it still, and bring it as near as possible - notwithstanding your pretty simile of the untameable Pheasant I should like to see you figuring in our brightest circles of fashionable society and think a Winter in Philadelphia would suit your taste full as well as any other season, the climate is not so severe as to exclude comfort, and there are some novelties that would amuse you- but come when you please you will find a joyful reception from your friends. Our Brother Jo has not said a word about the project to which you allude, but I heartily wish he would take unto himself a wife, even if he were obliged to proceed more slowly in the damsels favor, than your partiality predicts. We think it might not have been so difficult a matter to relate your son's smart sayings as you suppose and they would have appeared more astonishing by the contrast his cousin Horace offers, who with a very intelligent face, and bright countenance is obliged to devise some means independent of his tongue to make himself understood- he cannot connect a single sentence yet, altho he articulates certain words. His Sister Gertrude[1] has her sex's promptness and will probably speak first, she is a sweet little infant indeed. I saw Gratzs little sea-shore rival young Master Emmet in New York and thought him a fine smart fellow- he was a neighbour of Mrs Hoffmans, and visited Georges squirrel very often- he interested me particularly because I fancied Gratz was about his size and character, and loved to watch his play from the idea that they were alike.

I cannot regret that My friend Mrs Stokes has transferred her epistolary attentions to you. She sent me a commission which I could not execute- to have diligent search made thro' the church registers & magistrates records for many years back to find out whether her quondam husband was married in Phila to the person who now usurps her rights- this neither my patience nor modesty could undertake nor is there the least probability of such an enquiry being successful- she is indeed an oddity- and if I did not really pity her unhappy situation, should be amused at her extravagance.

[1] The youngest child of Solomon and Rachel Gratz Moses born Aug. 20, 1822, died Sept. 30, 1823.

She strangely imagines that her private wrongs, should engage the public and is Quixotick enough to believe her champion would be immortalized thro' every state in Christendom. No doubt Mr Clay[1] would gain more fame by pleading her cause, than by the office of President for which his friends are so industriously electioneering. Ellen bids me announce her resuscitation, and declares her intention of soon appearing before you in form of a letter- poor girl she has been housekeeping and house cleaning for me during my absence, and has been sick besides so this time she will be able to make a very sufficient excuse. All our Sisters & Brothers send you much love- they are well. Simon is about commencing his summers tour to his town in Penna. Jac talks about his Centre-county journey - but he loves to be at home so much that I know he will not be long gone- he left a message of affection to you as he passed the library door on his way to his chamber, & Jo is waiting till I close this ere he bids me good night. Adieu My beloved Brother & Sister, embrace your boys for me & believe me most affectionately

Your unalterably attached RG

June 23rd 1823-

* * *

TO THE SAME

The Small pox epidemic—vaccination—memories—"sorrow makes us egotists as well as happiness".

March 28 1824

Truly My dear Sister, the arrival of a letter from you is a circumstance of great joy and triumph in your circle of

[1] Henry Clay was an intimate friend of Mr. and Mrs. Benjamin Gratz and is mentioned frequently in this correspondence.

Philadelphia friends and is perused and re-perused with so much interest by all the females of the family (as they chance to visit me after I become possessed of the treasure) that I think could you witness its reception you would in the future be ashamed to offer such disqualifying apologies lest you might impugn our judgment in these matters. . . . . I cannot accept your reason My dear Maria for depriving us of the anticipated pleasure of seeing you and your darlings - that your Boys are bad you did not intend I should believe and if they were, I should urge their coming- as it is generally supposed travelling improves the manners of youth - now as people who are provided with *two reasons* are apt to give the best first if they do not chuse to put forth all their strength I must suppose the one you have withheld is not more difficult to remove than the first - and therefore I do hope you will think better of it, and accompany your husband bringing your whole stock of happiness along. I know you would rather cross the mountains than be separated from your Ben and he would be but half content in coming to his ancient home leaving his most precious gifts behind . . . .

You ask if I feel no apprehensions about the small pox - in the beginning of the winter there was great alarm on that subject and on the opinion of Dr Physick[1] I had all our dear ones vaccinated lest they might not have had the right protection against that disease. Dr Hays performed this operation rather in conformity to our wishes than from an idea of necessity and we have heard of no fatal consequence arising from it where the vaccine was pursued - poor people and blacks who had neglected it were the principal sufferers. I believe I mentioned that I. Hays had found the scab he took from Gratz's arm labeled and pronounces him to have had

[1] Dr. Philip Syng Physick, Professor of Surgery in the University of Pennsylvania.

the genuine so you may be easy on his account. Mrs John Cox's children had the varioloid but she considered it a trifling disease- I am thus particular, as I find the small pox is travelling westward and may soon reach Lexington- it is disappearing here & is said never to last longer as an epidemick than three months- I should say indeed to those who viewed only the dark side of destiny that children were too intensely interesting to be blessings- but the care of them is mingled with so many indearing and sweet responsibilities, that I do not wonder they were by the pious patriarchs considered as the Treasures & blessings by which God rewarded his faithful servants and what earthy possession My dear Sister is held on more secure terms- are not all we love equally liable to be taken from us and if we are not parents, have we not our hearts held by other relations as strongly as the nature of our affections can endure; and when these ties are severed do we not suffer as keenly as if we had lost our children? it is but learning to submit ourselves to the will of God-

Remember that all we have are the gifts of His bounty and that according to their greatness & value are our obligations to love & cherish them- to use them wisely- and when they are withdrawn to remember by whom we are afflicted- these bereavements My dear Maria, have been so often repeated- that I sometimes look back on the days of my fullness with wonder & gratitude- retrace the Years which have taken one after another of My beloved companions- my revered parents- and most cherished sisters & friends and feel how wonderfully the goodness and Mercy of God accompanies his judgments- in leaving me so much to love sustaining me to endure- and directing me to objects who still make life with all its crosses so valuable to me- but I forbear- I fear to lift the veil which hides the griefs of my heart- and seek to

dwell only on the blessings which my beloved Brothers & Sisters- and their precious offspring encircle me with- sorrow makes us egotists Maria as well as happiness- Adieu embrace My beloved Brother & nephews for me. and assure youself of the affection of your sisters heart My sweet Maria- ever your attached R G-
P.S. Your friend Henry Sergeant has finished his pilgrimage- this afternoon he was consigned to his Mother earth- after an illness of a fortnight- he met with an accident some time ago which confined him by a lame foot- but was not considered to be seriously hurt- his death was occasioned by bilious fever. . . . .

* * *

TO THE SAME

Experience should teach wisdom—faith in God—the name sister—the hope of immortality.

June 13th 1824

I suspected from your former letter My dear Sister, that you had more weighty reasons for not coming to see us, than those expressed and was not disappointed that My Brother declined your generous proposal of his favor - indeed, greatly as we desire to behold his beloved face again we would not accept of such a sacrifice. We hope to see his brow unclouded by care & anxiety which would not be if he left his wife and bairns behind - he will require such a solace as their presence when he finds himself at home and the dear one missing[1] whose smile was the brightest and whose heart the most glowing with love & joy of any he left - when he sees all her bereaved little ones- and the traces of sorrow which time

[1] The sister Rachel (Mrs. Solomon Moses) died September 29, 1823.

cannot efface - he will turn to his own sweet treasures for sympathy & consolation You must tarry a little while for strength and then bear him company. I trust the hour you dread will be happily gotten over, and regarded like your former ones as maternal triumphs it is natural to tremble at the approach of pain & danger, but the eye of faith can look steadily on, knowing that the hand of God leads safely through every peril. It is his will we should surmount, and seeing in our own & others destiny how rarely the final messenger is perceived on his approach. The experience of a single year would be sufficient to teach us wisdom, did we know how to apply it - we see the young & the healthful cut down in the fulness of joy- and in the midst of their days - while the emaciated - and the hoary headed continue their course without danger tho' apparently drawing hourly to an end. . . . . Sometimes my dear Sister we are amazed by ill-timed gravity & grow melancholy at forced mirth. I hope such a contrariety will be produced by this letter. Since receiving yours I have wished to write and cheat you out of your sadness - but I no sooner seated myself at my desk than so many tender regrets came over my heart that my eyes overflowed unbidden and I could not discourse of indifferent things. There is something so soft - so heart subduing so exquisitely dear in the name of Sister, that I could not read your address without emotion - it conjured up the shades of so many happy years spent in such society - do you think my dear Maria, this kind of witchcraft could have been included in the divine prohibition? if so, I fear I am more guilty than Saul or the woman of Endor - and verily I have my punishment - when that which has passed away returns to consume the present. I must think of this, the idea never occurred to me before and I have used this faculty as a connecting link between the present & the future - it is a strange association, but seems to justify our hopes that it may be preserved thro' eternity and will enable us to recognize in the world of spirits the individuals we have loved and honored on earth. . . . .

The accounts you give of your dear little boys interest me greatly. My sweet Horace, seems to think he & Gratz are to be fast friends & companions- he continually talks of what they shall do together- he expects to move in quite another element and will bathe & swim when "the little Ben Gratz" comes- he has kept a little piece of money for a long time, and when asked what he means to do with it, says it is to buy for Gratz- whatever he happens to like best at the time- it has of course bought more than ever the like sum produced before- tops & balls, new hats and books & watches- but still it is in his purse till "little Ben Gratz" comes and walks down street with him. . . . .

I pray you My dearest Maria write soon again, if you have time- if not, bid my dear Brother to give us early information of your state, and tho' anything you bring will be truly acceptable, I cannot but think you very proud to covet boys exclusively- this is a slight on our own sex, and I should be glad were you disappointed and this time give me nothing but a niece- our Brothers are all well and send their affectionate love- give mine most fondly to My dearest Ben, and believe Me My dear Maria, you have the tenderest love & most fervent prayers of your attached Sister

R GRATZ

TO THE SAME

Family joys—another man child—Lafayette's visit to the United States—visitors from Lexington—family affection.

Phila Sept 5th 1824

Yesterday was our dear Ben's birthday and as the glass circulated round the board and each one had some affectionate wish to express for his happiness and long life and continuance of merited blessings, I conceived the wish to send him these congratulations and to tell you how grateful I feel to heaven for the restoration of your health, My dear Sister, and the sweet little boy[1] who makes up your trio - from all I hear of his brothers, I can only wish he may resemble them, and tho' I dare say you would have welcomed a girl with equal joy, I am sure for the poor child's sake you should be more happy as in the arrangements of this working-day world the men have honors and glory - while the weaker vessels are most heavily laden'd by care - in your family whatever little girls may succeed will have a brave escort to assist and bless them. I can appreciate such treasures most justly for them, as my experience has proved their value. I wish you were all here just now that your Gratz & Bernard might see the wonders this busy city is working for the reception of La Fayette, they would talk of it through life - it will be a memorable epoch in our annals. Little Horace puzzles his brain with anticipations of the illumination of which he has no distinct idea and as he has a most romantic attachment for his cousin little Ben Gratz he associates him in all his schemes of enjoyment, and never speaks of the

---

[1] Henry Howard the third child born July 12, 1824.

soldiers and music and La Fayette without saying how Ben Gratz and he will act on the occasion -

I suppose having got over the first difficulties of naming your sons your third will not have to wait long for his, let me beg My dear Sister soon to be informed what you call him- and anything else respecting your domestic concerns. We seem immeasurably distant from each other while you do not write- for Ben, My dearly beloved Ben never condescends to dip his pen for My information- and all I hear from Kentucky- is that a business letter has arrived- and as no particular mention is made *we must suppose* his family are well- we nevertheless talk of you very constantly and make up the want of certain information by a great many ingenious supposes. Mr McIlvaine has told us something. Mr Ralston came home charmed with you all- Lexington stands next to Phila in his estimation- and Mr Holly in an evening visit to Mrs Meredith talked more about Ben- so that from various sources we have culled much sweet discourse of late- which I assure you we make good use of and rehearse again & again- but now your boy is old enough to admit of your writing I shall hope for a letter- and if you can prevail on Ben to write also in lieu of the visit of which (I will not say how much he has disappointed me) I shall be greatly delighted.

Our Brother Hyman within the last week has greatly improved in his health and good looks but you would think he still looks ill, for he is much emaciated- Jo is absent, gone up again to . . . .[1] on business, he is generally very tired of his visit to that country before he finishes, the cold weather over takes him in the northern climate and winter being very unfriendly to his feelings- added to the trouble of his tenants giving him, makes him impatient of this annual tour-

[1] Illegible.

Jac is home for the present, but we scarcely begin to feel the pleasure of his return before he talks of going off again- and he leaves us uncertain as to the length of his stay- sometimes he threatens to go on to the West before he returns- I wish it were possible to keep together for the brief time we sojourn here. What a delightful world it would be if all we loved could be collected into a circle, to be seen & visited whenever we desired it- how often would your threshold My dearest Brother & Sister be pressed by friendly feet- how fondly would your boys be caressed daily- but perhaps so many more ties would bind me too powerfully to existence and render the transient scene too alluring- I hope & pray another year will not pass away without my seeing you all- Ben must pay us for this summers disappointment by bringing you here in the next. . . . .

Remember me affectionately & respectfully to your Mother- and believe me My dear Maria Most affectionately
Your Sister RG

* * *

TO THE SAME

The year of this letter, 1824, is omitted in the date but the recipient supplied it on the back of the letter—the responsibility of rearing children.

Your letter My dear Sister, was gratefully received, the sympathy of those we love soothes our sorrows- and when we must weep we are grateful for the tears which mingle with our own, from hearts which bear a part of our grief. and consecrate the virtues of those we honor. I have endeavoured to write to you My dear Maria, before this, but could not for all my thoughts & feelings were unutterable.

Would that Your dear family were with us. I long to see My dear Brother and Sister & their lovely boys- separation is doubly severe when such visitations occur- we talk of you every day. Little Horace has heard so much of Tony, that he seems to think of him incessently- repeats every day that he is coming over the mountains to see us in the spring- and all his infantile projects of pleasure & instruction are associated with *little Ben Gratz* as he styles him- you may suppose My dear Sister, that these precious children are the objects of my constant and tenderest concern[1]- they have given me a deep interest in life- which the many & severe trials it has pleased Heaven to visit upon me, might otherwise have made a weary pilgrimage- but I dare not complain- and feel that I ought not, whilst so many beloved friends are left and so many important duties still remain to be done. . . . .

I beg you My dear Maria to write me when you have leisure- our dear Ben's letters contain so little of domestic news that even when I have the happiness of recognizing his hand writing and the affectionate salutation of continued remembrance with a word assuring of your health I feel the more desirous of further communication. I trust you still cherish the design of visiting us in the spring- should it please Heaven to continue to us the blessing we still possess for alas from the suddenness of our recent affliction I fear to look forward with too earnest a desire to any earthly good- . . . . embrace My dear Ben & your lovely boys for me and believe me My dear Sister most truly

Your affectionate R G.

Decr 13th

---

[1] The children of her deceased sister, Rachel Moses, whom Rebecca Gratz reared.

TO BENJAMIN GRATZ

This letter is of unusual value because of the minute and vivid description of the dedication of the new synagogue of the Mikveh Israel congregation of which the Gratz family were prominent members.

The presidential election of 1824—the Clay - Adams "bargain"—Representative Kremer of Pennsylvania.

Feb'y 27th 1825

I scarcely know how to regret the defection of our brothers My dear Ben, since it has procured me the happiness of receiving a letter from you - I have never the less chid them for their neglect and as speedily as possible sit down to remove the evil of which you complain but I confess now that the pen is in my hand- I am at a loss where to begin. My heart and my eyes overflow at the idea of the long separation from my beloved brother - and a family record would be too full of feelings which have a home in every breast but may not be uttered without realizing what Byron says of "the mirror which dashes to the ground, and looking down on the fragments - sees its reflections multiplied"-

I am not disposed tho' to indulge such sad thoughts in return for the grateful pleasure your letter afforded - lest I "weary you in well doing" - and deprive myself of hearing again particularly as you mention your dear Maria is not well and I shall anxiously desire to hear of her recovery.

I am surprised you have no account of the consecretion except from the newspaper as it was a subject engaging universal attention - the article you mention was written by your old friend Tom Wharton[1] who was a spectator on the

---

[1] Thomas I. Wharton born Philadelphia, May 17, 1791, died April 7, 1856. He was reporter of the Philadelphia Supreme Court and a writer of legal works.

occasion. I have never witnessed a more impressive or solemn ceremony or one more calculated to elevate the mind to religious exercises - the shool[1] is one of the most beautiful specimens of ancient architecture in the city, and finished in the Stricklands best manner- the decorations are neat yet rich and tasteful - and the service commencing just before the Sabbath was performed by lamp light - Mr Keys[2] was assisted in the service by the Hazan[3] from New York Mr Peixotto[4] a venerable learned & pious man who gave great effect to the solemnity - the doors being opened by our brother Simon and the blessing pronounced at the entrance - the processions entered with the two Reverends in their robes followed by nine copies of the Sacred Rolls - they advanced slowly to the Tabah[5] while a choir of five voices chanted the appointed psalms most delightfully when the new Hazan had been inducted into his office and took his place at the desk. Mr P in slow and solemn manner preceded the Sephers[6] in their circuit round the area of the building between the desk and the ark- whilst such strains of sacred songs were chanted as might truly be said to have inspiration in them - between each circuit, the prayers appointed (as you will see in the book our brother sent you) to be performed by the Hazan and the congregation were said and among the most affecting parts of the service- Mr Keys in a fine full voice and the responses by Mr Peixotto in a voice tremulous from agitation and deep feeling. I have no hope of

[1] Traditional Jewish term for synagogue.
[2] The Reverend Abraham Israel Keys, minister of the Mikveh Israel congregation from June, 1824, to his death in October, 1828. See Morais *The Jews of Philadelphia*, 44.
[3] Cantor.
[4] The Reverend Moses Levi Maduro Peixotto minister of the Shearith Israel congregation New York City 1820–1828. See Publications of the American Jewish Historical Society VI 132–133.
[5] The reading desk.
[6] The scrolls of the law or Five Books of Moses.

conveying by description any idea of this ceremony- you must have seen the whole spectacle - the beautiful ark thrown wide open to receive the sacred deposit, with its rich crimson curtains fringed with gold - the perpetual lamp suspended in front with its little constant light like a watchman at his post - and with the humble yet dignified figure of the venerable Mr P. as he conducted the procession in its seven circuits and then deposited the laws- after which Mr Keys recited with an effect amounting almost to eloquence that impressive prayer of King Solomon[1] - the whole audience was most profoundly attentive and tho' few were so happy as to understand the language - those who did - say they have never heard the Hebrew so well delivered as by Mr Keys - the bishop expressed this opinion- and all who were there acknowledge there has never been such church music performed in Phila - you will wonder where "these sweet singers in Israel" were collected from - the leader, teacher and principal performer is Jacob Seixas[2] and his female first voice his sister Miriam,[3] they were fortunately on a visit to their sister Mrs Phillips and induced a class to practice for some weeks - Miriam and Becky Moses[4] contributed very considerably and all in the congregation who Mr S. found teachable assisted - he is now resident here and we hope by his assistance to keep up a very respectable class of singers in the synagogue. The service continues to be finely performed and the congregation behave with the utmost decorum and propriety during the service. I scarcely know how to answer your questions concerning Mr Keys - I do not believe he is a

[1] I Kings VIII, the scriptural passage usually read at the dedication of a synagogue.
[2] Son of Benjamin Mendes Seixas and Zipporah Levy. Publications AJHS IV, 211.
[3] Daughter of ibid and wife of David M. Moses. See ibid.
[4] Daughters of Solomon and Rachel Gratz Moses and nieces of Rebecca Gratz.

TO BENJAMIN GRATZ

learned man- nor indeed a very sensible one - but he is a good Hebrew scholar- an excellent Teacher, and a good man, he is moreover very popular with the congregation and reads the prayers in a manner as to make his hearers feel that he understands and is inspired with their solemnity - perhaps his usefulness is not lessoned by his diffidence - he is modest and unassuming, which suits the proud, the ignorant & presumptuous - these require most reformation and he is so respectable on the Tabah that he gives general satisfaction - Mr P. is such a man as you describe, he was a merchant before the death of Mr Seixas[1] but has since his clerical appointment studied and become as learned as he is intelligent- Mr K. has had a congregation[2] which only required him to perform his shool duties - now that he is among more intelligent people he too will feel the necessity of study - he has a wife and three clever children and when he gets over his West Indian indolence he will shew what he can become - one very important talent he certainly possesses - he is a good Hebrew teacher - yesterday one of his pupils read a barmitzvah portion[3] very handsomely altho' he had only a few weeks instruction. Our brothers have all become very attentive to shool matters - Hyman is Gaboy[4] and they

[1] The Rev. Gershom Mendes Seixas was minister of the Shearith Israel congregation New York 1768–1816 barring a few years when he lived in Philadelphia. Publications AJHS IV 204–208.
[2] Mr. Keys came to Philadelphia from Barbados W. I.
[3] Upon reaching his religious majority at the age of thirteen the Jewish lad reads the weekly Pentateuchal portion. The term Barmitzwah (son of the commandment) designated his status from then on. He was considered an adult and responsible for the performance of all the mitzwoth (religious commandments or duties). This barmitzwah ceremony which was formerly observed universally is now more honored in the breach than in the observance except in orthodox circles. Even in many conservative congregations the barmitzwah lad recites merely the benedictions before and after the reading of the Torah passage by the minister. In most reform congregations the barmitzwah ceremony has been displaced by the confirmation ceremony.
[4] Warden.

rarely omit attending worship. We all go Friday evening as well as on Saturday morning - the gallery[1] is as well filled as the other portion of the house - I think continually of you My dear Brother when I enter that temple and I pray that I may again see you worshipping within its walls - I know your faith is unchangable and will endure even tho' you are alone in a land of strangers.[2] May God be merciful to us all and keep us stedfast to our duties. I love your dear Maria, and admire the forbearance which leaves unmolested the religious opinions she knows are sacred in your estimation. May you both continue to worship according to the dictates of your conscience and your orisons be equally acceptable at the throne of Grace. . . . .

I suppose you have been much interested in the presidential election, and tho' Adams has not been your candidate you must be satisfied since Mr Clay has resigned to him his pretensions - Maria has no doubt been indignant at the treatment Mr C received from the Pennsylvanians and indeed so were we here and were no little scandalized that the state should have sent such a mean spirited fellow as Kremer to represent us[3] . . . .

[1] In the traditional synagogue the women occupied the gallery and the men the main floor. The reform movement introduced the family pew.
[2] Though he married out of the faith twice Benjamin Gratz retained his Jewish allegiance. His request that he be buried according to Jewish rites was honored by his wife and children though not one of his descendants was in the Jewish fold. The Rev. Dr. Isaac M. Wise of Cincinnati officiated at the funeral.
[3] There were four candidates in the presidential campaign in 1824, namely, John Quincy Adams, Andrew Jackson, Henry Clay and William Harris Crawford. No candidate received a majority of the electoral votes. The election was therefore thrown into the House of Representatives. Adams having received a majority of the votes of the representatives was declared elected by the Speaker of the House, Henry Clay. Clay was accused by the Jackson supporters of having used his great influence as Speaker to insure Adams' election. Adams offered Clay the Secretaryship of State which he accepted. This lent color to the charge of the Jacksonians that he had made a bargain with

God Bless you & yours my beloved Brother - accept again my thanks for your letter and believe me always your attached sister

R G

* * *

TO THE SAME

Visit of the Lexingtonians to Philadelphia—the departure for home—children's affections and fancies.

We were much concerned My dear Brother to find your journey was delayed by the indisposition of our darling Gratz. My thoughts have journeyed with you and been anxiously fixed on that dear child ever since your departure but I trust your predictions will be verified and that he has proceeded from Hagerstown better than he left Phila. My dear Sister too I have thought so much of- on account of her encreased fatigue that I have scarcely enjoyed the gratitude I owe her for the happiness of this happy Summer. When I hear that you are all safe home and in possession of your usual comforts she may expect an overflow of those feelings- which a sense of her present toil keeps in check- but you must tell her and your sweet boys- that every body here loves them and talks of them daily- Horace bewails his little companions and refers every thing to Aunt Maria. Julia & Charles Hoffman arrived on thursday - he immediately

Adams. This charge had been preferred publicly in a Philadelphia newspaper, The Columbian Observer. This accusation was promptly denied by Clay who denounced the writer of the article as "an infamous calumniator, dastard and liar". The Kremer mentioned in this letter, a representative from Pennsylvania, revealed himself as the writer of the article. He offered to furnish proofs but when the crucial test came, he weakened. The "bargain" story however would not down and it was used effectively in the campaign of 1828 when Jackson ran against Adams and was elected by a large majority.

adopted Julia for a sweetheart and being asked what he would do with so many he said he would pack them all up & send them to Kentucky for Aunt Maria to chuse three of the best out for Gratz, Bernard & Howard- indeed there are few hours pass without some reference being made to the beloved travellers- sun shine & clouds clear breezes or dumps all are noted and commented as they may affect you- The family are all well except Mr Hays who within some days has been indisposed yesterday he had some symptoms of intermittent but I hope it will soon go off. Ellen has not been home since Friday- our dear little nieces opposite are among your most ardent admirers their eyes sparkle with joy or moisten when ever they speak of you here- or of the happiness we miss since you left us- Becky wonders if a journey across the mountains would make her grow- Julia Hoffman is as tall as I am- and only of her age- Horace bids me tell the boys when he gets big enough to ride he will come to Kentucky to see them- tell the little darlings too that Aunt Becky has sent them little chairs to sit by the fire on when they get home- and that she sends them a great many kisses- and says they must not forget her- My dearest Ben accept and beg Maria to believe in the sincere & devoted affection of my heart- and May the Almighty shower blessings upon you both- ever & for ever

Yours R Gratz

Oct: 17th 1825

TO THE SAME

Alternate joys and fears—ill bestowed wealth—the follies of rich men.

Feby 26th 1826

Thank you My dearest Brother for your kind letter- and a thousand thanks & congratulations for the heart-cheering intelligence it contained. Our dear Maria's communication threw us all into extacies but- with my usual ingenuity in cases of such deep interest- I began to entertain a multitude of fears- lest her exertion in writing might have injured her- and your letter was a most welcome assurance of safety- long may you My dear brother be so happy with your lovely family, and May every addition, prove a new blessing- and May God prosper you in all things- and keep you worthy of all He bestows. My heart overflows with gratitude & affection as the picture of your domestic comforts is presented to it- your admirable wife is greatly beloved by all your family, and the gratitude we owe her for your happiness, brings her daily & hourly nearer to our hearts. The children are quite in amaze that Howard should have a younger brother[1]- and Horace was very much concerned at hearing some one say his "nose was out of joint" and came to enquire of me "if it hurt him"- every day he talks of his little cousins, and is very much afraid as Gratz goes to school he will soon get before him in learning. . . . .

Our Brothers I suppose keep you informed of all that is doing out of doors- and a gloomy record no doubt it is of the

---

[1] The fourth child of Benjamin and Maria Gratz named Hyman, born February 6, 1826.

mercantile world- Two rich men have gone off the Stage last week- paid their last debt- and left large fortunes behind them- Com. Dale & Harry Wikoff- and thus- as Shakespeare's fool says- "The world wags". The latter lived meanly from loving his money too well to enjoy it- and has left it in a manner that reflects no honor to his memory- one is easily reconciled to live without fortune- when such examples shew that riches sometimes fail not only to make ones own life happy & comfortable- but destroys the noble pride of making it serve the purpose of benefiting others- and transmitting an honest fame. What shortsighted fools men are, My dear Ben- who hide their vices from those around them- and blazon them forth to their successors, so that if they have any virtues to redeem their faults they do not take the benefit of them, if another generation hears of Harry Wikoff it may only be to know how badly he bestowed $130,000. . . . . Our little friend Sally Minis[1] begs you & Maria will accept her love, she continues to visit us weekly and becomes still a greater favorite with the family. Mr Moses sends his congratulations & love to you both- It is difficult to vary the expressions of such messages, and I am charged with so many that I must either give you a catalogue of names or trust your family register- and only say all send an abundance of affectionate welcome to the little stranger. God Bless you My dear Brother My sweet nephews- and My well beloved Sister- I embrace all the precious groupe, and beg to live in their affection as they must ever in the heart of Your

Sister R Gratz

[1] Daughter of Isaac and Dinah Cohen Minis of Savannah, Georgia, who later married Dr. Isaac Hays, a nephew of Rebecca Gratz, May 7, 1834.

TO MARIA GIST GRATZ

Presuming and certitude—Tristram Shandy—the famous actors Cooper and Miss Kelly—Panacea Swain—love for children and children's ways.

March 12 1826

I presume long ere this My dear Sister you have recovered your liberty and are permitted to grace your parlour fire-side- but as *presuming* is not more satisfactory to those who possess the faculty, than to others for whom it is exercised I should greatly rejoice to have my presumption in this respect certified- it is probable the late weather has thrown some impediments in the way of punctuality- for I find even counting house letters have not been forthcoming as usual- and therefore I have been wise enough this time, not to fancy any thing wrong- I assure you we are all very proud of this fourth son- and would not exchange him for two daughters . . . . Not only the girls but even the children have had their tastes about your sons name, and at last have come to the conclusion that you have succeeded so well in your other boys that you will after all do best without help- Mrs Meredith insists on its being William, some of the others would add Frederick- then have passed in succession all the most illustrious english names- not perhaps as wisely as the Shandy disquisition- but resembling it in its conclusion- and I hope my nephew will not be so blundered out of the title he is designed to figure in the world by- as was the renowned Tristram. . . . .

Our winter gaiety has all been postponed till March this year. The Theatre now holds out great attractions Cooper[1]

[1] Thomas Apthorp Cooper considered the foremost English actor of

& Miss Kelly- the fashionables- who can afford it will be ashamed to see their unreturned cards of invitation- and make an effort to follow suit- Tell Ben- the renowned Panacea Swain has bought both Moses Levy's and Wm Walm's fine houses- he is to be our neighbour- and will convert a wing of the great house into a cake shop! is not this too bad- worse still- the beautiful garden & pleasure ground will be covered by small tenements- Mr Short purchased the property intending to luxuriate in all the bachelor whims his fancy could form- he would have a boarding-house-keeper under his own control- dine when he pleased at five or six- or even if he pleased (as Tremaine did in the country) at 7- what other whim-whams were in his embrio arrangements did not transpire- but lo! the housekeeper was not to be obtained with out some difficulty and Mr Short does not luxuriate on difficulties- so he cut the matter short- and found Swain's purse a panacea for this new disease. What a pity he had not sought a wife to keep house for him- it might have tormented two people- but then it would have been much more agreeable to the neighborhood- and much prettier for Chestnut street. My children are well and talk of yours from morning till night- Horace is determined to write a letter to Gratz on his birth day- he will write a long letter full and if he cannot do more with his own hand he can certainly sign his name- he has a great deal to tell Gratz and Bernard & dear little Howard already and he will have a great deal more to say next month he wants to learn his multiplication table quite thro' before he writes tho', for he is afraid as Gratz goes to school and was bigger than he when he was here that he will beat him in learning he want to know too if Gratz has been riding on Kate since he got

his time made his first American appearance at the Chestnut St. Theatre, Philadelphia, as Macbeth in 1796. His daughter married a son of President Tyler.

home- if he can shoot his arrows straight and knows any new plays to teach him when they meet again- now Maria, if you do not give me some of your boy's talk I shall think you too proud to descend, or that you are ashamed of my folly- but indeed I love children- & childrens talk - their own words expressing their own thoughts goes quicker to my heart than any thing much wiser that is said for them - Jac imitates Bernards voice and his expression "old man what are we going to have"- after dinner to the delight of the table- old & young and then comes all the little ones remember of their cousins- Uncle Ben & Aunt Maria are the loved theme of each delighted talker- till we live over every scene of the last happy summer. Dear, Dear Maria- if you knew how we all love you- you would think of returning again and again without fear of the journey- every body here embraces you affectionately. Tell my dearest Ben how tenderly I love him, and beg he will write again- Adieu My dear Maria, I am late for the mail- or should perhaps scribble on to please my self

God Bless you all

ever Your attached R G-

* * *

TO THE SAME

Family troubles—"anticipation of evil, the hardest to bear"— the sympathy of the community—"the uses of adversity."

Aug 6th 1826

One misfortune has followed so swiftly on the heels of another My dear Maria in our once happy family that if I had not to tell you of our dear Brother Hyman's safe return in much better health than he left us - I believe I should not have had resolution to address you again so soon altho your affectionate letter reached me yesterday and filled my heart with gratitude. I know too that you will have heard before of the fall of this house[1] and both you and our dear Ben will want to hear how it has been borne by the lesser as well as the greater sufferers- Well then I believe the anticipation of all evils is hardest to bear. It is "the dreadful note of preparation" and the human mind when prepared may sustain the worst that is permitted - for a fortnight before last Saturday poor Simon's distressed countenance almost broke my heart, the more so as I dared not speak a word on the subject of his impending ruin- but when the blow was struck I felt as if the worst was over and if I could afford him no more consolation than even Jobs miserable comforters, it was some relief to speak & be spoken to - they have received too so universal a sympathy - so much respect and consideration from the whole community as well those who might expect to suffer by their misfortune as those who only knew them as enterprising citizens - that their hearts must be steel not to have melted at such kindness - indeed we have shed more tears of gratitude than grief and I begin to philosophize on the subject - and examine the question whether poverty be so great an evil, as it is represented to be - time may enable me to form a judgment, at present I must confess my ignorance - but as I have implicit faith in Scripture and believe as firmly in the integrity of my fathers - I do not fear that we shall

---

[1] The bankruptcy of the brothers Simon and Hyman Gratz. They had been in business at Seventh and Market Sts. There was a tradition in the family that this was the building in which Thomas Jefferson had written the Declaration of Independence while living there during the sessions of the Continental Congress, the house being conducted by a Mrs. Graff. After the Revolution the house was occupied by Judge James Wilson, a signer of the Declaration and an Associate Justice of the Supreme Court (see Leach, Old Philadelphia Families, The Gratz Family, Philadelphia North American Dec. 1 1912). Mr Leach however proves that this tradition rested upon an error and must be abandoned.

be forsaken- moreover My dear Sister there are a goodly proportion of working men & women left to put their hand to plough & distaff if necessary and one of the "uses of adversity" is already manifested in the improved state of My poor Sister Richea and her mourning daughters. While they had no other grief - the loss of dear Maria,[1] threatened to break down all their strength - Sister & Sarah Ann[2] seemed ready to sink & I was afraid would lose their own health - now they are roused to comfort their father - and prepare themselves for such exertions as their altered fortunes may demand.

When you come to see us again My dear Maria (for Alas! I fear we shall only meet now on this side the mountains- however delightful to my imagination a visit to you might appear)- you shall still find us a cheerful & contented race - and I doubt not just *for vanity* we shall consider a humbler house full as pleasant. *You* always loved the quiet little Library where I am now seated and sometimes I have preferred it to every other part of the house, so a snug little parlour will be our Library[3] and the dear boys' merriment will make our hearts glad & our *ears tingle*- Hyman talks delightfully of you all- Howard is now I find the pet- sweet fellow how I should love to hear the music of his voice in articulate sounds. I thank you, for giving your youngest our dear brother's name- may they both bear it unsullied to the skies and leave it as an honored example to your grandchildren- embrace my dear Gratz & Bernard for me and tell Howard Aunt Becky loves him dearly- I am sorry My

---

[1] Maria daughter of Samuel and Richea Gratz Hays, died July 2, 1826.
[2] Sarah Ann Hays married Major Alfred Mordecai June 1, 1827; author of booklet, *Recollections of Rebecca Gratz, by one of her Nieces*, Philadelphia, 1893.
[3] After the financial misfortune the family removed from their spacious home on Chestnut St. near Seventh to the smaller house Number 2 Boston Row on Chestnut St. near Twelfth.

Brother Ben ever feels "sad & gloomy" but it was not on his account he was so- tell him things are not so bad as they appear at a distance- that the worst is over and we now look forward to better times- the commercial world has been terribly rent in pieces- but the fragments are not totally lost- they may be gathered in patches- and used more prudently in future and they will still be fit for service.

God bless you both with every comfort & happiness. May all your affairs prosper- and your sons grow & flourish, and encrease your happiness daily & hourly -

Jac is waiting for my letter- and if you have never seen Jac in a hurry you can have no idea how impossible it would be to write a letter under such circumstances therefore I will release him & you at the same time

Adieu, My best love to My dearest Brother & Sister now and ever - their attached

R G -

* * *

TO THE SAME

The Gratz name—Simon Gratz and Mr. Elkin a creditor— bravery in misfortune.

Sept 10th 1826

You give me credit, My dear Sister for a virtue not yet called into requisition, and I shall be the more ambitious of attaining it, that I may secure your approbation. Our brothers' situation (sad as the reverse must be to them) has been attended with so many alleviating circumstances that we must be the most ungrateful family in the world not to be comforted and thankful. So much confidence & moderation has been exercised, and so much sympathy expressed, that my tears have often flowed from sensibility of generous forbearance - but not once for change of fortune. I need tell you of one act which penetrated us most because it was from a person whose character was before unknown to us. Mr Elkin[1] whom our dear Ben may remember as an emigrant from the West Indies - he married and settled in Phila where he encreases the product of his Island property by lending money on Mortgages and other securities- he was a creditor of our brothers and on the day of their failure Simon sent a message to him begging he would not be alarmed, & the next day he walked out to his place, told him, his visit was not to enquire about his property but to express his sympathy & to offer his services, that he had not much in his power, but had 3 or 4000 in bank which was at his command - that his debt was of no consequence - he would withdraw the note and tear it up and that he might pay when it was convenient - if not for ten years he should not complain - indeed it would gratify the first wish of his heart if he could redeem that beautiful spot (Willington)[2] for him - Poor Simon wept like a child when he related this anecdote to me- Mr Elkin is a Jew, when he first came here he consulted our brothers about the disposition of his affairs and seemed much attached to Hyman, but there has never been any intimacy between them and as he bears the character of a man close to his interests, lives retired & prudent- tho' highly respectable, we had no idea he was so noble & generous-

What the situation of affairs are likely to turn out, I know not- but Ben will no doubt soon be able to inform you. A proposition has been made by our Brothers which will prob-

[1] In all likelihood Abraham Elkin listed in the Philadelphia Directory of 1825 as gent 2 South 10th. See Morais *The Jews of Philadelphia*, 446.
[2] The country seat of Simon Gratz. It comprised the section of Philadelphia extending at present from Broad to Sixteenth Sts, and from Girard to Columbia Ave.

ably be acceded to and when that is decided they will be able to make their arrangements- we continue in our house until it can be sold which I hope will soon be the case, for I feel impatient that some steps should be taken to release them from their difficulties- their spirits & health are thank God better- indeed they are all well- Jac is the most depressed of all- he has less power to resist the ills of life in whatever shape they may approach him - and he takes the very worst method to acquire fortitude, for he shuts himself off - communes with his own gloomy thoughts, and becomes - if I were to say nervous it would offend him - but at any rate unhappy. I hope our dear Ben, has by this time acquired more philosophy - we must not expect always to have the things we wish for in this world but as you say, to make the best of what we have - and I assure you My dear Maria I feel no apprehension that we shall ever want what is really necessary. . . . .

Adieu, My dear Sister - the time will come I trust when we shall have to talk of better things - but can never find me more truly your and my beloved Ben's affectionate Sister

R GRATZ

Embrace the dear boys for me again and pray do not let them forget me -

* * *

TO THE SAME

The natural beauties of Kentucky—"carking care clips imagination's wings"—city and country—the vicissitudes of life—a society scandal.

May 4th 1828

I am astonished My dear Sister to find that I have been so long your debtor- and for a letter too so full of interesting description- that I have been enamoured of the Kentucky river and its picturesque scenery ever since- it is hard to be so encompassed with cares and dull realities- that the very wings of imagination are clipped short off, and one cannot even fancy such a delightful possibility as feasting their natural vision with such a prospect. Well I must be content to adopt My friend Mrs Merediths idea- who means to cast a downward glance on the wonders & beauties of this excellent globe- during her passage to a higher sphere, when she "has shaken off this mortal coil"- and in the meantime My sweet Sister let me profit by a transcript of your journeyings and as you are directing your attention to the fine arts I may even have the pencils aid, when that instrument can better display your taste- and yet, to tell truth I wish nothing more graphic than your pen in cases of that nature. There is nothing that I can send you from the bustling city which can compare with it- the important vibrations of a compact community - where every day casualties alarm agitate or change the destiny of some portion, and afford subject of brief interest to all- is a fertile subject for the moralist- but one sickens with the oft repeated tale- and it all ends in the stale truism that we are all to take our turns in the ups and downs of life. . . . .

This seems quite an era of strange events in our community- but I dare say Hyman or Jo has told Ben all of the gossip, and of course you have heard of Mr Tilghman's ill timed gallantry and its unhappy result- he is a light-headed & perhaps light principled character tho' past 40 and the father of a large family- two of his daughters were belles this winter and his wife accompanied them to all fashionable parties- entertained at home, and seemed to renew her own youth in her daughters pleasures- which are now at an end. One of Mr T's professional proteges a youth of about 22 married a young lady from the country and on bringing her to town introduced her to his patron, as one of his best friends- the gentleman received her very kindly and endeavoured to make himself so agreeable, that she requested her husband not to invite him as she felt no disposition to entertain or be entertained by Mr T. However supposing it was only Mr Tilghman's manners that Mrs Browne objected to, he told her, that she would like him better when they were more acquainted- in a very short time after, she related their interviews & Mr Browne thought proper to chastize the freedom of Mr Tilghmans conduct- and took occasion to give him a public horse whipping at mid-day in front of the state house in Chesnut Street this was followed by a challenge from T- which not being accepted he prosecuted Browne for an assault- and in this trial such excitement and evidence appeared- that the award for damages was one cent. Mr Tilghman totally subdued- disgraced and humbled left the city to recover his composure- when his magnanimous wife followed him into his retirement- consoled forgave and I hope will reclaim him- as for the Brownes they are victorious, but the notoriety of the whole affair- the appearance of the Lady at court to prove that she had been insulted and the variety of reports respecting them- are so at variance with the delicacy of a young female- and a bride too- that I think I would rather the offender had been privately avoided than publicly punished. I hope however good, will come out of it- if there be one spark of virtue in the nature of Ben Tilghman, his wife's conduct must fan it into light- which may purify his heart, and his innocent daughters- make him respect other women's fame. . . . . our Brothers & Sisters are all well. Hyman received Bens letter by Mr. Christie yesterday- present my best love to My dearest Ben- tell him we find that "enduring patience makes the burden light"- it is a year since he laboured so hard to commence the business, which Heaven only knows when time will finish- Adieu My beloved Maria- believe me always your sincerely affectionate

Sister R G

* * *

TO THE SAME

Removal of the Gratz family to the new home in Boston Row— the summer in Philadelphia—the sea shore—Lexington friends.

August 3rd 1828

My dear Sister I must introduce you to our new habitation in Boston-row, for so Mr Brooke denominates the stone buildings he was erecting opposite our Sister Hays' residence in Chestnut Street, when you were last here- ours is No. 2 from 12th Street, the house is small compared with the one we left our two parlours being nearly covered by the mat taken from the floor of the back room but then there is a small dining room besides- a Library & bathroom above it- and very comfortable chambers - we were a little at a loss where to place all our conveniences & accommodations at first, but being now accustomed to the appearance, begin to feel quite at home and should be delighted to welcome you all here within its compact walls- we have as many sleeping rooms tho' not so large as those we left and I am sure we shall be as happy and contented as we could be in a palace under existing circumstances. . . . .

Hyman in about 10 days will go to Pittsburgh - it will be very tantalizing to have crossed the mountains and not be able to pay you a visit- but he cannot be away now long enough. I hope in the Autumn all our troublesome business will have an end- and our brothers be able to get at something more profitable- I saw Mrs Hunt & Catharine on their way to Jersey they & the girls were to have traveled together to the branch but she was detained a few days and the houses were so full- that she determined not to stay there and put up with the inconvenience of a crowd and bad accommodations - the girls laughed when they could not sleep & made light of all difficulties for the sake of bathing until the company separated and left them a room to live in.

. . . .

Mrs Hunt told me your next visit would be to spend the winter, now My dear Sister, if such happiness is in store for this year you do not know how gratefully it will be received- indeed we have room enough, altho I told you the house is small- we have two excellent rooms convertable into chambers. I had fixed your accommodations before we took possession of the house, and I know you love us well enough to put up with the best we can give you, and be content-

I expect the Miss Hays' from Richmond next week, to spend a few days on their way to Boston- the weather last week was melting- and as we were engaged in the exercise of moving had the full force of it- now it is become pleasant, but the city is empty- every body that is any body have gone to the shore, or the falls or the springs- and the nobodys left at home are as dull as my letter- God Bless you My dear Maria, make my most affectionate love acceptable to My dearest Ben, and embrace the sweet boys for me- believe me most sincerely and devotedly your affectionate Sister R G-

Persevere My dear sister, in your labours in the fine arts and you will no doubt succeed- I wish you had better originals that your skill may produce more beautiful pictures, and if you please will send you some- let me know whether you prefer Landscapes or heads- ever yrs

TO THE SAME

This letter is addressed to Mrs. Benjamin Gratz, New Orleans—Dr. Benjamin Rush's theory of will control—a matrimonial triangle.

Feby 1st 1829

I was charmed My dear Sister not more by the intelligence than by the tone of your last delightful letter, and feel my confidence in your constitution restored by the very natural cause of your late indisposition, and trust your lungs will now become as sound as your liver did on a former occasion. You are somewhat more indebted to Dr Dudley for sending you on a pleasant tour to winter in the mild climate of N Orleans- than to Chapman for covering your side with those blood thirsty reptiles . . . . I have been very much amused this morning by an old medical essay of Dr Rush's[1] in which he lays such stress on the powerful influence of *will* over the diseases of the body, that I do not wonder women so frequently long for indulgences in the restless state they are doomed for so many months to endure and that their wills obtain such importance in the eyes of their anxious friends- If it had not been recently decided by the enlightened college that this opinion is erroneous I would just give you a hint to long for a Philadelphian, and then My dear brother would bring you here and let his native city have the honour of being hers also . . . .

You will see My sweet little interesting friend Mrs Erwin[2]

---

[1] Dr. Benjamin Rush (1745-1813) was one of the most famous physicians of his day. He was one of the signers of the Declaration of Independence and a member of the Pennsylvania Convention which adopted the Federal Constitution in 1787. In 1796 he was appointed professor of the theory and practice of medicine in the University of Pennsylvania.

[2] A daughter of Henry Clay, residing in New Orleans.

present My love to her dear Maria, and tell her I often think with much regard of her & desire to know that her hopes are realized and that her health is restored-

Ben Etting has not yet returned from Richmond. the sister of his mistress is to be married in a few weeks to Mr Mayo and I suppose he will await that event, unless it should be postponed by the death of . . . . who is in a very precarious state of health- poor fellow! he has been long languishing with that incurable disease "the memory of a rooted sorrow"- his life has been marked by sadness ever since the rash committal of a crime, from which there is no refuge- and perhaps it is wise & merciful that his life is called thus early for in the eye of heaven it is not length of years, but sincere repentance that must expiate offences- I trust his has been accepted, and that pardon awaits him at the throne of grace.

Mr. Marxs[1] family presents an instructive picture of human life at this moment - one of his daughters - attending the death bed of her husband- another preparing for bridal festivities- and a third in that state full of hope & fears which preceeds the change most important to happiness in all that is to come of after life. I have been lately a good deal interested in quite a different scene of conjugal affairs- a neighbour of mine had a matrimonial fracas, which producing an alarming indisposition, I sent to offer services to the invalid- was accepted and have become quite a party in the fair sufferers cause. It was a love match between a couple reared in the country and perhaps had not fortune played a blind vagary in their behalf, might have been as happy in obscurity as they anticipated- but an Irish entailed estate fell

---

[1] Mr. Joseph Marx of Richmond who had married Richea Myers, a cousin of Rebecca Gratz; their daughters Harriet and Frances married the brothers Benjamin and Horatio Etting, nephews of Rebecca Gratz.

upon the head of the gentleman's father, who being very old, and he heir apparent they came up to town- furnished a house elegantly- the lady dressed tastefully and they set up for the fashionable sports- dinner parties the Theatre & taverns with the dissipation of idle young men, carried benedict so continually from home- that the lady grew jealous of her husbands company- having no children to occupy her lonely hours she became nervous & unreasonable- and perhaps complained that she was not first & last in his dear thought- she pouted instead of smiled, when he condescended to return after a weeks absence- and solaced her solitude by bemoaning to her friends how much she suffered- they echoed her wrongs- and it became a gossip among the fireside circle of her friends - at last a spark fell on these combustibles so imprudently spread and the angry husband proposed a separation- the wife wounded in pride & affection acceded to the proposition- and then repented & has been miserable & sick ever since- lawyers are engaged & the business proceeds- he is frolicking with his friends who strengthen his resolution, by keeping up his resentment and ridiculing her extatics- she is in bed kept under the effects of laudanum to prevent spasms or fluctuating between hope & fear- a sense of having misused power when she had it and a conviction that she has it no longer- when it is all terminated I will let you know the result- and you may make it up into a novel with proper reflections & morals for the foolish wives & dissipated husbands of the west, if there are any such to be found- in the mean time present me most tenderly to my Beloved brother, and accept dearest Maria, the best wishes and affectionate greetings of Brothers sisters nieces and cousins here . . . . let me hear from you again- and if you tell me you are getting well- or as well as you expect, you will most sincerely rejoice the heart of My dear Sisters most affectionately attached R G-

TO THE SAME

A voyage on the Mississippi—Henry Clay's disappointment—the inauguration of Andrew Jackson as president—a "young Jewish legislator" in Kentucky—fallacy of the "good old times"—

March 22nd 1829

My Dear Sister

It is but two days since I received your letter dated the 5th of Feby describing your voyage to N Orleans and we had been long wondering - and anxiously waiting for some accounts of your travels, fortunately the papers announced your arrival and so we were freed from any apprehension of your having uprooted the snags or been swamped in shoal water on the great river, but then we did not know what you have so delightfully told, that your health is much improved and the charming account of your peregrinations had the most happy effect on the physiognomy of our circle, that you could desire- it was pretty late dinner hour too, before I came home, and our brothers were collected, and growing impatient - Jac told me I had been keeping them long for the inside of the letter, and while Hyman rang the bell for dinner, I opened it and read aloud - when we had been twice summoned to the dining room, I looked up, and found my auditors smiling with so much satisfaction that I ventured to give them the sequel before moving to the manifest injury of a smoking beef steak - the perfume of which would intrude from the cellar kitchen and gave notice "that if it were to be eaten it were better to be quickly eaten"-

We have had a short visit from Ellen[1] and it would do your

---

[1] Ellen Hays, a niece who had married Samuel Etting of Baltimore, November 5, 1828.

heart good to see how well and happy she looks her husband had a little business here which required his presence and he brought her & Isabella home to the surprise of all their friends who had no notice of their intention until the carriage stopped at the door - Ellen staid with us five days and had hardly time altho all talked fast - to tell and hear all that had been doing during four months separation - however she is to spend the Passover with us and is going to her own house in the beginning of May when some of the girls are to pay her a visit - they are anticipating a great deal of pleasure from these events. Ellen received your messages with much pleasure and says she shall certainly write to you as soon as she hears of your return home and I have just sent word by Etting Myers that we hope soon for that information. You must not forget that every thing from N Orleans will be new & strange to me - except dear Mrs. Erwin and of her I shall be more glad to hear than any thing else for she took fast hold of my affections - and I often think of her sweetness and her sorrows with an interest which brings her still nearer to my heart, I hope she has another daughter to heal the wounds poor little Julia's death inflicted on her happiness - I am glad to see by Mr Clay's letter to the Baltimoreans that his health is better - that will be a consolation at least to his family, for any political disappointment[1] - we have had very amusing account of the great babel Washington - on the day of inauguration - scenes on the portico - the Senate chamber - the palace - drawn by various eye witnesses but I would rather read Ann Boswells[2] account of her southern winter - than twenty such pictures of intrigues successful & unsuccessful- where selfishness and all other ugly deformities are

[1] Henry Clay had been Secretary of State during the administration of John Quincy Adams and was Adams' chief supporter for re-election to the presidency in 1828 when Jackson was elected.
[2] Later the second wife of Benjamin Gratz.

brought to light - instead of the natural wonderment and delight of a lively & innocent mind imbibing first impressions of the world on her debut into new scenes - and among strange people - by the bye I have just had the honor of selecting a dress & cap for your sister - and as my order was for that which was fashionable, had the good luck to find at Mad^e Pratts a sample of French taste in silk of which but a few pieces were imported - your friend E Fisher took one & Mrs. . . . . has the other - butterflies, and every colour which adorns the wing of that beautiful insect is the tone at Paris - and our ladies are nothing loath to adorn themselves as gaily as the airy tenant of the spring - I hope they will not be deemed too gaudy in Lexington - we have heard before of your young Jewish legislator[1]- himself and a brother married two of David Seixas sisters they resided at Cincinnati - and were both so unfortunate as to lose their wives within a year or two after marriage - they were but a short time in Phila - I never saw them, but they visited at Aunt Bell's and were much liked by the family . . . .

It snowed last night - and since the beginning of March we have had nothing but winter continued - we old folks are consoled under all this severity by recollecting it used to be so in our young days, and are stopped for once in our reference to old fashioned things - now unless the spring comes on as bright as the poets glowing lays we shall still proclaim that times are changed for the worse - embrace your dear

---

[1] Abraham Jonas and his brother Joseph married sisters the daughters of the Reverend Gershom Mendes Seixas of New York. Joseph Jonas was the pioneer of the Jewish community of Cincinnati (see Philipson, Jewish Pioneers of the Ohio Valley, Publications of the American Jewish Historical Society, VIII 43). Both sisters died shortly after marriage. Abraham Jonas removed to Willianstown Grant County Kentucky and is the "young Jewish legislator" referred to. His son by a second marriage was Benjamin Franklin Jonas, United States Senator from Lousiana, 1879–1885.

boys for me - you cannot imagine how I long to hear something about them - I wrote to your dear Mother more to enjoy the pleasure of talking about them & you than from any hope of gaining information, I hope she excuses me - give my affectionate & respectful love to her - tell My dear Brother how delighted we shall be to hear from him at home - and believe me dearest Maria your & his most affectionate Sister RG -

* * *

TO THE SAME

Although the writer neglected to place the year in the date of this letter, this was supplied by the recipient who wrote on the back July 28th 1829—R Gratz answered.
Nature studies—Aesop's fables—fire at Transylvania University—a matrimonial reconciliation.

It is true My dear Maria, that nothing delights me more than your charming letters and whether it is because you always choose agreeable subjects or grace your subjects by the manner of treating them I shall not attempt to determine but take them all in all, your letters are like the magic glass of the good fairy and present to my view such a complete picture of your family, that I seem to be in the midst of the dear group, and flatter myself I shall soon be able to become quite sociable with all the boys by means of the key you have given to their different dispositions - tell them I wish they could see Horace's silk worms which have been quite a business and an amusement to Uncle Jac and him - and for some weeks no small annoyance to the chamber maid who could never keep the library in order while they were feeding - but then there was such pleasure in seeing them grow, that he scarcely minded the trouble of supplying them with food - and the beautiful operation of spinning amply reconciled him - then he wound off the silk leaving them but a transparent covering for their chrysalis - and now they are about leaving the inanimate shells and coming out butterflys to the delight of their attentive nurse - he expects to be amply supplied with eggs for the next season, and will reserve them for the boys to cultivate if they are so disposed - how wonderful My dear Maria are the most minute operations - these little insects and a collection of beautiful shells sent to me by a friend in the West Indies have made me ashamed of my ignorance on the most interesting of all studies and sad to think how much of life is wasted on unworthy objects, when by proper direction every moment might be employed to make us wiser, and better and happier than we are - yet what must have been Aesop's feelings when he wrote the fable entitled the trial of Aesop - had he studied the habits and propensities of animals only to find all their most cruel & destructive qualities prototyped in man - and did he only point out the evil under the persuasion that his readers would discover a likeness in better qualities readily enough? - however that may be I am sure we do not find the moral - or understand half the wisdom of his work till long after we are familiar with and laid aside his book-

You must have been quite a heroine on the memorable night of the fire at your University[1] - and I am glad little Bernards affectionate apprehensions for your safety stood in the place of prudence on that occasion - for had you acted by the impulse of your own inclination, you might have undone all the good of your winter journey, thus the care of providence is sometimes manifested by means that seem totally distinct from the object - the timidity of your child may

[1] The disastrous fire May 29, 1829, destroyed the college and library building.

have been your safe-guard - I bless him for it my dear Sister and hope in the Autumn to have the happiness of embracing him and all of you into the bargain . . . .

Hyman has not looked so well for years, the girls all call him handsome in spite of his white head and indeed his fresh complexion, and well filled cheeks would allow him to pass for a young man if it were not for his frosty pate- he is quite proud of his name sake,[1] whose bright eyes have made an impression on his vanity. . . . .

We have the family of Urquharts from N Orleans to pass the summer- they regretted very much not having seen you last winter & Mrs U reproached Sister Hays, who knew her before, for not writing to inform her of your visit - the girls spoke of Mrs Erwin as I suppose everybody who knew her should speak, if she is in your vicinity pray present my best regards to her, and as you have introduced the story of Mrs Gaskill to her- tell her this little anecdote of their reconciliation, the woman who washed Mr Gs clothes happened to be employed by some lodger in the same house in which Mrs G resided she questioned her respecting his clothes - and asked who repaired them, on hearing that no body took care of them, she desired the woman to bring them to her - accordingly for several weeks she darned his stockings &c and returned them to the washer woman - this little act of kindness was afterwards discovered by her husband, and he immediately visited her and they became reunited . . . . Your friend Mde d'Orval spent an evening with me last week, fortunately there were several who could talk french with her - she is very pretty & interesting & is likely to succeed very well. Mr Walch patronizes her- will you have the goodness to present my kind regards to Mrs Bodley and say how much I feel indebted to her- I wrote to her sometime

---

[1] Hyman, the fourth son of Benjamin Gratz.

ago. Hyman gave the letter to some gentleman going to Lexington if she has not received it - she must think me very ungrateful as well as ungracious - do you My sister undertake my justification . . . .

Adieu dearest & best, present me to My beloved brother & nephews and believe me ever most tenderly & truly

Your sister RG

June 28th

* * *

TO THE SAME

The Anniversary of the destruction of Jerusalem—Jeremiah and Job—Dr. Dudley, professor at Transylvania University visiting in Philadelphia—blue stockings.

I should be very stupid My dear Sister, and very ungrateful too if I did not answer your delightful letters promptly for then I should not be entitled to hope for more - and would deprive myself of the pleasure of telling you how rapidly the report of them circulates through the family, and brings me visitors from every house, that they may all share my pleasure . . . . Mr Erwin has not yet appeared and as the Postmark indicates that he has stopped at the Sulphur Springs suppose we shall not see him this season, which I regret on his own account - as well as for the love I bear his sweet little wife -

I thank you My dear Sister for the pleasure you have procured me in Smallie's interesting book- I laid it aside today for the lamentations of Jeremiah & the book of Job,[1] but

[1]The reading for Tisha b'Ab, the anniversary of the destruction of Jerusalem. This day was observed as a day of fasting and lamentation by the Jews generally up to the nineteenth century when the reform movement gave a different interpretation to the significance of the anniversary. The day is not observed by reform congregations as a season of mourning. (See Philipson *The Reform Movement in Judaism*, 353 note)·

shall resume it tomorrow with no diminished relish, from having communed with these holy men. I always feel a keener interest in Jeremiah on the anniversary of the calamity he so eloquently mourns- and Jobs admonitions are never out of season nor his example unprofitable - poor Mad^e D'Orval is just now called to the exercise of patience on a subject so singular, that I think you will sympathize with her - she is succeeding very well here, and intends making Phila her permanent residence, but being very lonely has determined to adopt a little Orphan girl, to educate & bring up as a daughter- she went out to the Asylum and fixed her affections on a child of about seven years old, supposing it would be gladly relinquished by the matron without further trouble - but the age at which they are bound out is twelve - and the authority is vested in the board of managers alone to make an exception in her favor- Mr Vaughan accordingly undertook her business, called on several of the ladies, and brought a letter to be laid before the board- but on the day of meeting it rained- many were out of town- and Mrs Williams fearful of a failure- requested that it might be postponed until next month -

Mad. D'O. called on me the day after to hear the decision - and poured out her disappointment so eloquently that her interpreter (Miriam) caught the spirit of her complaint, and has made quite a party in her cause - she piteously bemoans her hard fate, that she has nothing to love - nothing to bestow her affections on in her lonely exile. She is passionately fond of children but never had one of her own, and wishes to bestow a mothers love on a poor little creature who has lost the tender care of her parent - and really she is so pretty & so earnest that I wish most heartily she could have been indulged without delay. Mrs Fisher who is the president is at the shore, ...

Your friend Dr Dudley[1] dined with us on Wednesday- he is so much engaged with professional men & philosophers that we have seen but little of him. Jac dined with him at N Williams- but there too he had a Dr at his elbow - when he next makes me a visit I will try to find out whether he would like to become acquainted with some ladies - for we have a score of belles in the neighbourhood - and one or two who have some pretensions to science & the arts - I paid a visit the other day and was immediately presented with a portfolio of drawings, where bugs & caterpillars & butterflies crept over the paper in perfection- they were the product of a young artist - and his lady patron descanted so learnedly that I was astonished at her cleverness in all the technical terms appropriate to the occasion - and should have thought I had made a profitable acquaintance, had she stopped there- but finding her equally voluble in botony, music, engraving &c the idea struck me that being in the wave of youth she was setting out as a Savant- I became alarmed at my own ignorance and made my escape determining the next time to take someone who might give me a little credit with the Lady, and if I can produce Dr Dudley I may go on the weight of his reputation for at least a dozen visits - you see the Dr has been mentioned by the Essayist on silk worms in Walsh, and I hope he will be pleased with his travels in this quarter and carry a favorable report to the west . . . .

Dr Dudley has just called to bid adieu- I am glad My dear Sister, he will be at home to amuse & comfort you when you require his presence, and as My dear Ben encourages the hope of seeing you all here before winter, I shall cherish it with as much confidence as we are permitted to indulge our wishes in this uncertain state- the children are claiming my

---

[1] Dr. B. W. Dudley, Professor of Anatomy and Surgery at Transylvania University. See *Transylvania University, Its Decline and Fall*, by Robert Peter M. D. 96 (Filson Club Publications No. 11).

promise to take them to see the Solar Microscope- when they expect to see squirrels skipping from branch to branch on the frieze of a peach- and performing evolutions on the surface of a fig- Adieu My beloved Sister . . . .
your affectionate R Gratz

Aug 10th 1829

* * *

TO THE SAME

The beauties of November—love can always find room—James Brown ex-Minister to France and United States Senator from Louisiana—the White House—rabbinic wisdom.

Novr 4th 1829

I have not answered your letter before My dear Sister because of the disappointment it gave me, and I had no arguments at hand to oppose to your difficulties- for I was detained at Bellefonte nursing poor Gratz through another severe attack of the same dreadful disease he had last year and Hyman had gone also to look after his affairs in the country, but he told me he had written to our dear Ben, and as he threw out some hints not indeed so plain as to give me a clue to his designs, but they were accompanied with an encouraging shake of the head- which if it did not restore my confidence did certainly revive my hopes and I waited until I could tell you that Gratz was better (which good news arrived last night) and that our Brothers had gone forth on their journeyings before I again speak to you of Phila and the way to get here - your boy[1] is now three months old, and better able to bear travel than he would have been earlier- and almost any time in this delightful month that the river

[1] Cary the youngest child.

will afford you a passage will be quite reasonable- I think the poets on this side the Atlantic (when we get them) will give a new character to November for it is a thousand times more lovely than May except that the parting songs of the birds are not so joyful- and the brilliant colours of the forest give one the melancholy thought- that their beauty is passing away! but then you will say "When I come over you again Majestic Mountains, your trees will be dressed in your verdure - and tho' the many coloured leaves which now adorn your branches, will be spread as a warm carpet at their feet- as you display the varied beauties of the changeful year- your autumnal, and spring charmes are both lovely to an eye like mine" Dear Sister what a delightful winter, would your & our dear Bens society give us- you know too how I love children, and that the additional business it would give me as housekeeper, would be both salutary & agreeable, indeed I am in danger of losing all my talents in that art for Jo and the two children[1] are my whole household and I shall grow fat & lazy without some such motive for activity so I beg you discard all the *cons* relating to that part of your cogitations and let the *pros* have their due preponderance- My next door neighbour has a family of eight children- her Mother & two sisters bringing a little girl or two are coming here to spend the winter with them- and as Mr Rutledge is a clergyman some brethren of the clothe are ever and anon increasing his family- yet his house has no more accomodation than ours- and they are the most charming cheerful family in the Row- so you see altho the house is exactly half as large as the one down Chestnut street, I have not the least apprehension of being too crowded- your husband's business is indeed an obstacle I cannot approach, *he* will, I know do what is wisest, kindest best- and our wishes

[1] Sarah and Horace Moses.

must not outstrip his better judgment- nor expose you to difficulties beyond your strength-

The girls are all going to spend the last week in this month with Ellen, Rosa has been there a fortnight, and will return home with the Moses' leaving Sarah in her place- they have never been to Balt[re] and anticipate a great deal of pleasure from the visit- Miriam said yesterday to crown all, if they could but meet you there, and all come home together it would really be incomparable and if you can obtain so great a favor from your kind Sister, pray bring one of your nieces with you. I was exceedingly gratified by the attention of Mrs Brown of Frankfort in making her visit in Phila known to me, tho I only had the opportunity of seeing her once, but she spoke so affectionately of you and My brother, and of all my nephews that she won my heart- I have not heard in what state of health Mrs James Brown has returned they are still in N. York and Susan's friends have received no letters from her yet- but as the papers talk of a public Dinner to the Ex-minister[1] suppose she is not too ill to receive the attentions of her country folks- I have not seen Mr Hunt yet, he called one day when I was not at home. and you know how difficult it is to get the gentlemen through a course of etiquette visits- so I do not know whether he will again make his appearance in Boston Row- for the last week I have been at the mercy of an upholsterer - my carpets were to be fitted- but President Jackson is now furnishing his east room- and every hand in Christie's shop was employed with curtains, carpets and damask sofas- for the great man's great room- but the vessel is freighted- and what future display of grandeur or grace- may reward the labour, will probably reach us through a public channel

[1] James Brown of Frankfort Ky. Minister to France 1823-1829; later United States Senator from Louisiana to which state he had removed from Frankfort.

Our *domestic hospitals* are broken up, thank heaven! Ben and Isabella Etting are out again and well- and Henry Hays walks abroad on his stick and is exchanging the pale yellow of his complexion for its natural brown. our sisters deserve patents for the art of sustaining life without the aid of sleep or food, for they both look well after a campaigne of watching few sentinels could sustain- The Cohens are delighted with your kind messages and I am never so welcome a visitor as when I carry your letters to read what you say of them. Rachel is still unable to walk more than a square or two, she rode down to Mr Phillips last month that she might go to Synagogue during the holydays but it is not probable will be so far from home again this winter - her spirits are good- she was always an enthusiast, and having survived the object of her youthful devotion is now not so exclusively- but still with zeal attached to other considerations- she patronizes our young pastor[1] who is certainly more attractive to those who are indifferent to the *outer Man* - there is a witticism on record of a mean looking sage, who in reply to a high born damsels remark on the freak of nature in placing so much wisdom in so ugly a creature, demanded what kind of vessel her father kept his wine in- she said a common earthen, for wine kept in precious metal became sour- he observed wisdom is safest with ugliness- for there are fewer provokatives to *vanity*- which is an enemy to wisdom- this anecdote is most aptly applied to Mr Leeser- who is ugly & awkward- but so sensible & pleasant as well as pious- that all the old ladies are charmed, while the girls are obliged to persuade themselves to be pleasant- we have another of Coopers novels for next week- there are three Theatres open- concerts & lectures- and all kinds of exercises for the mind &

---

[1] The Reverend Isaac Leeser who had assumed the post of minister of the congregation a few months previously.

taste inviting to our improvement and yet if you do not come to partake of them I believe I shall not listen to the charmers - "charm they ever so wisely" I beg your pardon, My dear Maria, (if you object to quotations)- for I so often find the language of others superior to my own that I have not resolution enough to repel it. I shall take care not to let Miriam read my letters and may pilfer expressions which run in the course of my ideas without any qualms of conscience knowing you are so well read that you can easily give every one his due- to My dear Ben present my affectionate love- and embrace your children for me- you hold a large portion of my heart which I beg you will dispose of in a manner to yield fair interest in your love- and it shall be my treasure till we meet- God Bless you, My dear Sister- Your RG-

* * *

TO THE SAME

A street encounter and a duel—Baltimore society—Miss Sedgwick and Philadelphia society—Indian lands in Georgia.

Jany 14th 1830

It is a long time My dear Sister since I have written to you, and I feel the ill consequences of it - for I have no right to expect a letter and greatly as I love them, believe I should be ashamed to receive one, until I have told you that my heart thanks you for the last and has many times feasted on it- in fact when I received it a foolish affair which having terminated without mischief need not have given so much trouble entirely engrossed my concern - a young German, whom you may remember as sister Hays' neighbor named Bohlen with whose Sister the girls were all intimate set out with the romantic determination of making himself noted as the champion of national customs, and as his Sister gave waltzing parties - threw down the gauntlet to all who disapproved of that dance - he singled out Isaac Moses[1] to begin the fray, and wrote him a very insolent letter - accusing him of having spoken disapprovingly of *his national* Dance, and forbidding him on penalty of chastisement to ask any lady of his (Bohlens) acquaintance to waltz with him - Isaac, not desiring to accept him as a censor of his conduct, nor relishing his impertinent threats, gave him a cowskinning in the public street which produced a challenge (after a day or twos deliberation, during which a great noise was made, so that the whole town knew what was going on) Isaac accepted the challenge and on his way to the encountre was arrested - his antagonist managed to keep out of the way of the police- and again issued his invitation for the fight, offering to *pay* the amount of his cognizance for breach of peace & his parole of honor - this was received as an additional insult, and rejected by Isaacs friend - who declined all further communication until the period had expired for which he was bound - the girls were all prepared for their Baltimore visit before this occurence took place - and believing they should be unmolested and moreover desirous of withdrawing Isaac from the chance of meeting Bohlen, they departed and in the hospitalities and gaieties of that city began to lose sight of their troubles (for they were acquainted with every step taken in the affair and were miserable every time their brother was out of the house) When lo Mr B. and his Second arrived at Baltimore and again proffered his claims to satisfaction- Isaac's friends in B. were very indignant at this conduct and replied for him that he was not at liberty to meet him there - he was the protector of

---

[1] Son of Solomon and Rachel Gratz Moses, born April 14, 1807, graduated as M. A. from University of Pennsylvania, 1827.

several ladies, and moreover in a few days would be at home, and released from legal restraint - the same evening Bohlen "posted" him in the public reading room - and departed next morning - a card in the newspaper of the next day proclaimed in Baltimore that Mr B. had been whipped in the street here - and it was decided that he was no longer entitled to the honourable privilege of being killed or killing in a duel - for which My dear Maria, I most heartily thank him - and as he is but 19 years old I hope he may grow wiser and better by the time he becomes a man - . . . .

Gratz Etting has been extremely ill, of a similar disease to that he was afflicted with last winter, he had recovered and was journeying home under the care of Edward, when he was seized with a relapse more severe than the first attack, which has detained him in Harrisburg nearly four weeks- he is now convalescent again and we are extremely anxious to see him under his mothers care- who tho so continually schooled in affliction, is perhaps more keenly tried in her separation from him during his illness than all the charge of him would inflict, ... we have had a delightful season thus far, My dear Maria, I can hardly yet cease to regret that you did not come to us this winter- I wish so much that you should know a little of the society of Pa and I want too that you should be known (forgive my vanity) - it is not very gay this winter but very sociable- we have had the charming Miss Sedgwick[1] for a few weeks, and everybody was delighted to honor her with such kind of intellectual parties as they thought would suit her taste- the old beaux- literati- philosophers- all turned out, and to the great amusement of young girls and men, they brought the high flown compliments & flattery of the last century on the tapis- old **Mr D**

---

[1] Catherine Maria Sedgwick (1789-1867) a well known American novelist of that period.

.... whose sight is none of the clearest- and whose mind is never present addressed himself to the corner where he had left Miss Sedgwick- then occupied by Mrs Hughes- telling the Lady he had never seen so much genius in a person possessing such youth, and beauty & cheerfulness- he could see Hope Leslie in her countenance- they talked of her works till the eloquent blood mounted to her forehead- she is a modest, diffident woman, with as much good sense, as good taste, and would much rather converse & listen in turn, on agreeable general topics than be the Lion in any society- My dear Ben must remember her when here before and knows she is quite free from pretensions- she came to town with Mrs Griffith & staid at F I Wharton's where the distinguished Author of a new boreing invention had the gratification of receiving court, on his own & Miss S—s celebrity- ....

We have been anxiously expecting letters from Ben, his last is a month old- I accuse myself for not daring to expect one from you My dear Maria, and sometimes the fear that all are not well sends a more reproachful pang to my heart, that I have so long forborn to enquire

God Grant that this fear may only be the punishment I deserve, and have no ground in reality- but dearest pray assure us in your own sweet words that you are all well & happy- and accept an abundant share of love from all your brothers & sisters here- we have just had another meeting of the Orphan Society- my neighbour Rutledge prepared a beautiful address on the occasion, which I will send you when printed- have the Ladies of Hartford requested your aid, to "supplicate justice & mercy" for the Indians?- they have sent circulars to various cities- and if their charity crosses the mountains, you have no doubt heard of them- but alas, the poor Indians have good lands- and the Georgians are savage enough to covet & if they can get will have them - embrace your darling boys for me My dearest Maria, how I long to embrace you all myself- tell My beloved Ben I am his & your most devoted & affectionate RG

* * *

TO THE SAME

Easter fashion parade—the rearing of children—mothers.

April 13th 1830

I am quite perplexed My dear Maria, about your Sister's things and must apply to you again for instructions - I do not know whether my letter ever reached Mrs Boswell, or whether she thinks me very impertinent and does not mean to answer it- but the beautiful dresses are still lying on the shelf in my wardrobe which should have been adorning the graceful figures of the fair ladies for whom they were intended long before this. If I had only known of what dimensions they were required. I am sadly afraid of the changeable goddess in the west tho' I doubt whether hers will not eclipse them- as I procured a paris silk imported by a lady who being obliged to put on mourning, sent it to MMe Pratt- the lengths of the skirts & arms & width on the waists is all that is required to be told, or if she prefers it I can procure a Paris print of fashions and send her the materials to be made at home- do not let your sister suppose I have had any trouble about the matter, except my fears of her disappointment in the delay and should my letter or her answer have miscarried, you can convey to her this apology for the detention- assuring her at the same time that I shall always be much gratified to execute her commissions if I am so fortunate as to suit her taste- You know My dear Sister that there is no difficulty in doing what I offer, as my avocations so frequently take me into Second Street, where every thing that is fashionable and beautiful are displayed and look so inviting that one would be tempted to go into the shops to admire if they even did not want to purchase - our streets now are quite a show since the spring weather has made our ladies throw aside their cloaks- and the spring ships have brought out the varied coloured wares for female apparel- I wish you could have been seated at the front window in Boston Row on Easter Monday, just to have let me look at you- while you looked at the world of light and bright objects passing by- the only thing wanting in your last letter dearest, to make it delightful was some intimation of an intended visit, but tho a little disappointed, I attributed it to forgetfulness, among the many animated subjects of discussion- I wish your steam car[1] had a road to run on, from Lexington to Philadelphia, that you might put your children in it, and come at once . . . . The essay on children which you admired so much, has been greatly commended here- every one having a heart, and being in the habit of seeing children may realize all that is said of them. I heard a lady say she was only surprised that a man should have felt & written so much like a mother. I believe mothers are only laughed at for talking of children, when they are so silly as to be exclusive - it is not the love of children- but the fears for or the admiration of *My* children whether they be clever or not that we are apt to be annoyed with- and it generally happens to be the faults entailed on children by over indulgence, which are the subjects of this annoyance . . . . Sarah's visit to Washington was quite a domestic one, but

---

[1] The Lexington and Ohio Railroad running from Lexington to Portland opened in 1829 was the first railroad in the Middle West and the second in the United States; Benjamin Gratz was one of the incorporators. See Ranck *History of Lexington, Kentucky*, 319.

her friends are dispersing from the city. Capt Dallas[1] is ordered to Pensacola. Mrs Meade came with her daughter to bid her friends here farewell, and this is perhaps the severest trial she could be put to as Henrietta & her husband were the most efficient friends left to her, and have been her support & advisers since the death of her Husband- they sail in the Natchez to which ship Henry Etting[2] is attached. . . . . Our brothers are all well - Jac was absent when your message arrived but I think I am doing him a favor to encourage you to put your threat in execution, and open a correspondence with him- I must however stipulate that it is not to be at my expense, as I would not give up your letters to me, to the highest dignitary in church or state, and therefore shall be very jealous if he being the most agreeable correspondent you do not scrupulously give me at least my due notwithstanding- every body here sends love to you and our dear Ben ------ Adieu My dear Sister, embrace your Beloved husband & children for me and believe me always your affectionate R G

---

[1]Alexander James Dallas, son of Alexander James Dallas, Secretary of the Treasury in Madison's Cabinet. The son who was born in Philadelphia was appointed captain in the United States Navy in 1828. He had served in the War of 1812.

[2]Son of Solomon and Rachel Gratz Etting of Baltimore. His mother was a daughter of Barnard Gratz and a cousin of Rebecca Gratz. Henry Etting was born in Baltimore May 20, 1799, became a midshipman in the U. S. navy in January 1, 1818, was advanced to paymaster with the rank of commodore in 1830 and retired with the rank of captain in 1861. See Morais, *The Jews of Philadelphia*, 470.

TO THE SAME

The first-born child of Mr. and Mrs. Benjamin Gratz, referred to constantly in this correspondence as Gratz, died September 16, 1830. It is this affliction to which this letter refers - Rebecca Gratz' deep piety finds expression in this communication as so frequently in these letters.

My heart & thoughts have been with you My dearest Maria in all your afflictions- and tho my pen has been silent, day after day longing to express my feelings- I have found it easier to weep than to utter them- now my anxiety can hold out no longer and I must beg either you or My dear Brother to write. I know the God you trust in will not desert you in your affliction and that as you suffer by his will- he will visit you with consolation, I pray most earnestly that your health may not suffer and that the lovely children who are left to you may be spared to requite you for all the cares and tenderness- bring them to us, My dearest Sister and let me this winter share with you the comfort of attending to their little wants. I have so long anticipated the approach of November, as a season of rejoicing that I feel sufficiently admonished of the tenour of all earthly expectations, but if we are not permitted to enjoy according to our own calculations there is still enough Mercy extended towards us to fill our hearts with gratitude and it is in this chastened sense I look forward to the period when I shall fold you and my beloved brother to my heart participating in your blended feelings of regret and love and saying with Job, Blessed be God who giveth & taketh away . . . .

Ben Etting[1] has gone for his wife - he took the two Miriams[2] with him to escort her back - they are to be married on

[1] See page 94, Note 1.
[2] Miriam Moses and Miriam Etting.

Wednesday next, and will probably be home on the first of Novr.

Our Brothers Hyman & Joe send affectionate love to you, they are as anxious as possible to hear that you will come, and Jac promises to spend the winter at home if such an inducement as your society & dear Ben's is added to the family- at present he is in Bellefonte- he has been so much away during the last year that I fear unless you come he will not be contented in Phila

Embrace your dear children for me. and accept our Sisters & nieces best love . . . . poor Gratz has had another relapse, during his intervals of health he is as affectionately interested about all his friends as he ever was and frequently enquiring about you all, he was distressed to hear of your misfortune- the day he was last taken ill, his father had promised to take me to see him and in a few days more he would have been at home! - alas- is life desirable on such terms? his afflicted Father, who is the only one of his family permitted to visit him says not- I have never seen the old gentleman so subdued by affliction as on this occasion- his spirit seems bowed down and inaccessable to comfort- our Sister too is wasted to a mere shadow, by the continual pressure of this living sorrow- "here is a noble mind overthrown" indeed, and every attack seems to put the hope of recovery more distant and weaker-

Adieu My dear Brother & Sister let us soon hear from you, that we may hope you are coming to us and believe ever in the affection of your attached

R Gratz

Oct: 11th - 1820

TO THE SAME

First letter written after death of the child—the "mercies of God" even in affliction—the country in winter—home scenes—"separation is a formidable bar to happiness when those we love are in sorrow".

I thank you My dear Sister, for the kind effort to relieve my anxiety which dictated your last letter, My heart is with you in all your sorrows and your pious elevation of soul to Him who is the fountain of comfort gives me assurance, that you will be comforted - May his Mercies be already manifested by the restoration of your sweet Howard, and may the residue of your Beloved children be registered in the book of life - and grow like "olive plants around your table"- and the memory of your departed angel living in the hearts of his brothers lead their young minds to think of everlasting life! I have sometimes been edified and surprised to hear my little Horace, express his feelings for his Mother, and the place where she dwells - he connects her idea with future rewards, and makes his heaven her home. I thank God, that My dear Brother, in this affliction as well as in all the trials that have yet visited your married life is enabled to be your support and consoler, and I trust you may long share together through weal & woe that which the world cannot give or take away

We had letters from Richmond yesterday announcing Ben's marriage. Miriam is much pleased with the Bride and the whole Marx family. . . . . Our brother Jac returned home yesterday, in very good health - it will depend on you whether we retain him for the winter, for I find he has become such a rover that he requires more excitement than my dull society to fix his thoughts at home- and yet from his account of Pine Grove, it must be a dreary place for a gentleman's residence- one may manage very well when the fields are green, and the cheering notes of populated nature invite abroad- to sleep & feed in a country tavern- but in dull winter scenes with nothing better than coarse uncultured men- My dear Ben will not reminiscenses of early days cheat you of present sadness, and our Maria smile by the winter fire, at the pleasant tales you can conjure up from almost forgotten pastimes? I have so long lived in the hope of seeing you, that I shall ill brook a disappointment- yet feel what an effort it will cost to gratify us- let me hear from you soon My dear Sister, we are more anxious for frequent letters because we think of you constantly, and the time seems longer than when we imagine you happy and engaged in cheerful occupations- separation is a formidable bar to ones happiness when those we love are in sorrow- Adieu, May God bless you all- this is the sweetest hope, and in it every wish of My heart is satisfied- God bless you My beloved Sister

ever Yours
R Gratz

Oct 19th 1830

TO BENJAMIN GRATZ

Montgomery Blair—Visit of Mr. and Mrs. Benjamin Gratz to Philadelphia—the new Transylvania College—the Hoffman family.

I have just received your letter My dearest Ben, and am so delighted at the thought of your wishing to write more frequently that I cannot resist the pleasure of expressing my thanks. I believe an aversion to writing is only the effect of habit, and if you desire to overcome it you will not find it very difficult to do so. I trust long before this your home has changed its aspect, and become bright with the smiles of your beloved Maria, and vocal with the merry tones of the dear boys- how can I express my gratitude to you, my own dear Ben, for the happiness of the last six months, when I hear that you are surrounded by your family and your circle is again complete. I shall perhaps be better able to speak of all I owe you, but while an anxious doubt is yet to be removed I feel that words are feeble- our brother Jac will do it for me, and his presence will in some degree reward you too.

. . . .

Your favorite Montgomery Blair,[1] was delighted with Phila. Gratz[2] took him everywhere that he could go in two days, and gave him letters to his friend Stockton at West point- & I believe he made rapid progress in the girls good graces for he continued with them the greatest part of Sunday and did not leave them till late at night, and he invited *cousin* Becky[3] to pay him a visit when his mother went to see

---
[1] See page 43, Note 1.
[2] Gratz Moses.
[3] Becky Moses, a cousin of Montgomery Blair's cousins, the children of Mrs. Benjamin Gratz.

him. I am very glad to hear of the improvements going on at Lexington, which will conduce to your advantage & pleasure and hope some day to witness them- Maria will take such interest in the New College[1] - and I hope you will be efficient & popular. Have you any prospect of one for the next session?

I believe there is nothing new in our city to amaze you with and in the unfinished affairs Maria left there appears slow progress making . . . . One of the agreeable recollections of your visit must be the benefits you bestowed, and really it would delight you to hear how often the collected girls talk of the good they have derived from Uncle Ben & Aunt Maria- you exhibited such a picture of rational & perfect happiness that you have elevated their ideals of married life- Maria's conversation has improved them- has taught them to think- and My dear little Sarah, owes so much love & happiness to you all, that she does not know where to begin or end her praise- at breakfast this morning she said - I wonder if Cary remembers me- Yes said I, he will remember you for a month- a month! she exclaimed with tearful eyes- but all the other dear boys will remember you, even little Hyman will not forget, this consoled her, and she said she was going to write to them all today- give our love to them all, and tell them Aunt Becky misses her dear little boys so much and is so lonesome & sad sometimes that she would gladly travel to Kentucky to enjoy their loving and amusing talk.

I received a letter yesterday from Julia Hoffman, mentioning the sudden & distressing death of Ogden's wife- she had the scarlet fever, but not badly- on Thursday morning

---

[1] Transylvania College, rebuilt after the fire of May, 1829. Benjamin Gratz was a trustee of the college.

they gave her an anodyne- she never awoke- she was a very lovely woman, and has left five children.

Tell My dear Jac, that I wish very much to hear from him. It is almost three weeks since he left home and not a word written by his hand has reached us- if he has no business to write about, let him tell us of his pleasures- tell My dear Maria I was going to trouble her today- to complain of my want of her society- and of my ever present, & ever enduring love- but she shall escape with this- accept for her & yourself the best love of all our Sisters, Brothers & nieces- and believe me My dear Ben most fondly & truly your

Affectionate Sister
R Gratz

June 19th 1831

* * *

TO MARIA GIST GRATZ

Messengers of glad tidings—return of Mrs. Benjamin Gratz to Lexington—the Washington Globe—troubles in Jackson's cabinet—Philadelphia as a medical center—Reich's invention—Paulding's book "The Dutchman's Fireside".

Blessed be they who send glad tidings- tidings of safety and joy from distant friends- and blessed are they who receive it too, My dear Maria, as I did in your letter from Lexington, announcing your arrival at home- where you had journeyed in pleasantness and peace- excuse me for using scripture phraseology (not profanely) for my heart is lifted up in gratitude to the Most Holy whose presence guarded you and your little ones on the way- now my Sister I can thank you with a free and grateful spirit- for all the pleasure your affectionate society procured me- since you are again restored to your happy home and domestic comforts. while here the thoughts of a fatiguing journey you had to encounter, tied up my tongue, and perhaps we are not so well able to express our value of a blessing while in its full enjoyment- as when it is withdrawn, and the contrast places it in the strongest light- the dear boys loudest merriment would be music to my solitary morning occupations- but Jac will soon be home again and will give his glowing accounts of great Kentucky.

I wrote to Mr Blair last week and sent him your message from Pittsburgh but have seen no puff in the Globe.[1] The fragments of the old cabinet are such perfect Hydras that the more it is cut in pieces the more heads rise up against the old Genl and the strength of Atlas can scarcely support the Globe in his defence. He has gone on a visit to old point Comfort- and verily he must need it, after the perplexities of such a season- I find Henry Hart[2] has gone to Norfolk also, and shall send him his shirts next week. Saml Marx is in town and will take charge of them, he says. . . . .

I was at the Academy on Friday with Miss Peters- O if you could hear her speak of you! I believe My dear Maria, I seek her society for the selfish pleasure of hearing her praise you, because I know she sincerely regards you, and appreciates your society. . . . . Dear Bernard is moving about at home & well!! his splint shall be sent with your bonnets- as a model for your medical or rather surgical school. I hear Dr Physick attributes the reputation Phila obtained for the care of complaints to which it may be applied, entirely to its invention- unfortunately since they no longer would employ

---

[1] The Washington Globe, edited by Francis Preston Blair, brother in law of Mrs. Benjamin Gratz. This was the organ of the Jackson administration.

[2] Son of Col. Nathaniel G. S. Hart, brother of Mrs. Henry Clay and Ann Gist, sister of Mrs. Benjamin Gratz.

Mr Reich's talents in carving heads for ships he could not continue here, and no one else has taken up the trade- so if your clever mechanics are taught this art Lexington may through Bernard fall heir to this important discovery.

I went to Mr Griggs and procured "the Dutchman's Fireside" for you which waits an opportunity. No other new work of merit has appeared, and this is not the best of Pauldings writing- he seems as much opposed to internal improvement- steamboats & rail roads as his friend Jo- and he does not bear out the superiority of the olden times in this country over the new- his characters are modern enough in their caprices - faults - & feelings . . . . give my best love to my dear Ben & Jac if with you- and believe dearest you have left an impression which can never be effaced on the hearts of your relations here- and are most tenderly & devotedly beloved by your own true

sister R GRATZ

June 26th 1831

* * *

TO THE SAME

Dissensions in President Jackson's cabinet—Henry Clay's candidacy for the presidency—Sir Walter Scott's Robert of Paris—Sully's portrait of Mrs. Benjamin Gratz.

Philadelphia July 31st 1831

There are some happy influences my Dear Sister, that can extract good from everything, and you seem to possess them - this is a moral alchemy far more valuable than changing baser metals into gold, in as much as you have more subtle materials to work on- and the result is certainly more conducive to human happiness, for if you put iron in the crucible you may spoil a plough-share to make an idol - whereas when you put poor old Jackson in the way of doing a kindness to the emigrant Prince[1] - and advance the fortunes of an orphan youth you give him an act of kindness which "twice blesseth"- and verily it must be a comfort to him in the turmoils and vexations by which he is surrounded to do one little deed which may "bless him that gives" for what with the disclosures of his old cabinet, and the interference of the new one - he may be tempted to doubt his own identity and exclaim, am I the President, am I the honored Chief? do you not feel mortified, My dear Sister, at all these disgraceful scenes exhibited so near the place of highest honor in our country. I do- and I wish you were near enough to exercise your influence at court - and give council to friend Preston[2] who holds the ear of Majesty - by the bye a change of dynasty will not destroy your power, and I shall be so happy to see you at the right hand of the next president- that I am determined to accompany you to Washington at the inauguration of Mr Clay[3] at which occasion Hyman has always promised I should be a witness - it is rather long to be sure to wait - but then if I go to Kentucky in the summer and help you to bring in the boys at Autumn, we shall be able to exe-

[1] In all likelihood, the "emigrant prince" here referred to was one of the sons of Joachim Murat king of Naples. After the fall of this kingdom the two sons emigrated successively to the United States. The younger Prince Murat was a friend of Rebecca Gratz and is mentioned later on in this correspondence.

[2] See correspondence between Francis Preston Blair, editor of the Washington Globe and the Jackson Organ, and his sister-in-law, Mrs. Benjamin Gratz, during the years 1830–1833, in which the tumultuous events in Jackson's first administration are described in detail. *B & M Gratz Papers*, 290–292.

[3] Henry Clay was defeated in the presidential campaign in 1832, when he ran against Andrew Jackson.

cute all our plans- provided the people are wise enough to do as we wish them[1]

Miss Peters is charmed with your letter but she has not had the civility to shew it to me. She has been working on a cravat which is very pretty, and continues to be kind to me for your sake- we went together to hear Judge Hopkinson's oration on Friday - the citizens have deserted for watering places which makes the streets very dull- and gives us fine opportunities for home pleasures - I am sorry I cannot send you "Robert De Paris" - Sir Walter is not so prompt as usual - but the Young Duke is highly spoken of and will accompany the Dutchman[2] . . . .

I wish you could hear the colloquy addressed to your portrait[3] when any of the girls come to pass the day with me - your little Sarah[4] has grown quite eloquent and apostrophizes Dear Aunt Maria in every Key and measure her young imagination can suggest - I came in at the end of an oration she was making to Sarah Hays the other day which concluded by comparing you to a full blown rose- perfection! she thinks she should be perfectly happy to live with you always- she is reading very diligently and I hope when

[1] Alas for the vanity of human wishes! The hope expressed here by Rebecca Gratz was entertained by thousands throughout the country who were devoted adherents of Henry Clay. He was the most popular statesman in the country and although he was a candidate for the presidency several times he never succeeded in his ambition to occupy the White House.

[2] Paulding's novel "The Dutchman's Fireside" mentioned in the preceding letter.

[3] Sully the famous portrait painter (1783–1872) was a friend of Rebecca Gratz. He painted the portraits of Miss Gratz and of Mr. and Mrs. Benjamin Gratz. The portrait of Mrs. Gratz mentioned here is in the possession of her granddaughter Mrs. J. R. Morton of Lexington. The portraits of Benjamin and Rebecca Gratz by this artist are among the most prized treasures of Mrs. Thomas Hart Clay, the daughter of Benjamin Gratz. Reproductions of these portraits appear in this volume.

[4] Sarah Gratz Moses, a niece, who later married Mr. Jacob Henry Joseph of Montreal, Canada.

you see her again you will find her mind ripening into intelligence, and improved by knowledge - she is becoming my most interesting companion - our Brothers send you a great deal of love- Hyman was much pleased with your letter- and went to Griggs immediately - but could not get what you want - Mr Griggs told me he wished your opinion on the vol of "Forsaken"[1] you took out - the work is not yet completed, but as the bookseller is greatly interested, and may be more liberal to the Author if your report it fairly, pray gratify him with your opinion - you see Madam, your consequence is not confined to court, the literature of your country looks to you for patronage - little Emmeline[2] came to me the other day at the Asylum, to enquire when I heard from Mrs Gratz, if she was well - how the little boys were - and said she had read the book you gave her and found it very pretty - I am very busy hunting teachers, one of ours thinks of emigrating to the neighborhood of Lexington, where she has a brother residing, if she does, I shall give her a letter to you, for she is a very valuable character & if she opens a school there, you may be of service to her . . . .

Jo had a line from dear Ben, since his return home. I hope you are all well, how I long to see the dear children again - do tell me something of each when you next write - the boys must remember Phila and try to love their friends here - that they may be glad to come again - for I hope never to be so long separated from them again - or you either My dear Brother and Sister, I feel now that what remains of life is too precious when in the society of those I love to be measured out in such long intervals between - Adieu May God forever bless you

ever your affectionate RG

[1] The Forsaken, A Tale, 2 Vol. Philadelphia, 1831.
[2] Undoubtedly an orphan child in the asylum in which Rebecca Gratz was so greatly interested.

TO THE SAME

Masonic signs—stoicism of boys—a medical controversy—the Lord a present help in time of trouble—mother love.

August 9th 1831

Our sweet Carys birth day and the arrival of your charming letter, My dear Sister draws me so irresistably to my desk with a thousand tender and grateful feelings that I am quite at a loss how to express them- but I am sure you will understand them, even if I fail in words to do them justice- for we have so often exchanged thoughts without the aid of words when together, that I think a hint even at this distance will like a masonic sign, communicate what is passing in my heart- I do not know tho' since Masonry has become a venal thing, or made to serve venal purposes that I should use it as a symbol- yet what is there within human reach, that may not be liable to perversion? our forefathers called Masonry a holy & honorable institution and for the good it has done we may regard it notwithstanding its being a sealed book to all of our sex. Ben's letter yesterday & yours to day speak of our dear little Hymans broken arm, but when & how it happened we have not yet heard, bless the sweet boy! I could not but weep at the accident altho you say he does not mind it- with all your intensity of feeling how is it, My dear Sister that you have been able to make your children so courageous in bearing pain- I never saw them in the least alarmed at accidents- or yielding to fear whilst suffering- Howard broke his head- & Bernard was laid on the sofa & Hyman had many a fall, but there never was any exaggerated complaint nor fuss- Hyman's brimful eye would over flow in an appeal for pity, the boon received, and a kiss would dry it again- and the little fellow was quite a hero. I suppose some tardy traveller, will bring us accounts of his arm- our brothers are anxiously looking for news of the Kentucky election- they know Ben is so much interested that he will write immediately. Jac is more engaged than I have ever known him he even said the other day, that he would write to Mr Clay upon some occurrence that he thought might give him pleasure- I do not believe he did so, but I mentioned this to shew what a journey to Lexington has achieved- he has got quite well again, but was in his chamber the greater part of a fortnight with a sore face after his return home- whether poisoned at Pittsburg as he suspected, or by good living previously it matters not now, he is well- . . . .

Gratz[1] is well at present, and as interesting as he is unfortunate - to see him thus- and know what he is liable to be in a few weeks is too hard indeed! it is only by throwing ourselves on the mercy and wisdom of divine Providence that we can be reconciled to such a dispensation - in *his* wisdom & goodness alone repose our hopes for what so ever purpose *he* has so afflicted our Sister through her suffering children, will be accomplished - if to prepare her for their removal alas! she will be resigned- if to reward her patience & long watching- she will be admonished- and so shall we all, dear Maria who have witnessed the hard struggle- Ben & his amiable wife, are the happy mixture on which she loves to dwell- Henry is very kind & generous & affectionate, and is able to assist his parents- indeed all the boys do what they are able to contribute to their comfort but still as you know, a parents heart is open at every pore and each object of maternal love, has its particular chord whose vibration no other

[1]See page 12, Note 3.

touch can still, or make respond- it is sacred to the one for whom Nature implanted it- and does not lose its object through time or through eternity- memory hallows it with sorrowing love, and it becomes a link uniting us by faith to God- thus dearest Maria a child seeks her Mother & thus a Mother still dotes on her child. I have often seen you thus, silently mourning, and My heart has silently sympathized- May God Comfort you, with a Mothers comfort. and May you & My dearest Ben, leave sorrowing, and in all that parents can desire long live the happiest & the best, among the lovely children who are blooming around you- Kiss My darling Cary for me on his birth day- Jacob has brought me a note for him to inclose- Give my best love to the dear Boys- and tell Hyman how sorry I am for his broken arm, and how I should like to tell him pretty stories now he cannot go to school- our Sisters & brothers & nieces all send a great deal of love to you- Adieu My dear Sister, believe me always most truly your own

R G--

. . . . . .

What are you studying? if we may judge of the tree by its fruit- or an argument by its result, you will convince your opponent that you are right- let us suppose the mind a soil on which our own efforts are to do this part of the cultivator- and adapt improvement suited to its capacity- every soil is capable of producing something- Newton might never have made a poet- nor Byron an astonomer- yet they came not into life with all their light about them- nor can we suppose the most intense labour would make Isaac Moses or Edward Etting either poets or philosophers- therefore we believe study necessary to develop the powers of mind and produce ideas, but minds are as different in human bodies, as soils on the bosom of mother earth- and happy are they whose judgment is directed to the proper culture, or whose taste like yours ranging through the wide fields of nature & of science, every where finds something to fill & improve the mind- Cowper says "the earth was made thus various that the mind of man studious of change & fond of novelty might be indulged"- adieu dearest.

Sept 4th 1831

* * *

TO THE SAME

The Sully portraits—the Eaton Lewis scandal in the Jackson administration—the Reverend William H. Furness, the celebrated Unitarian preacher.

It would be in vain My dear Sister to attempt expressing the delight your letter afforded and therefore I had as well say nothing about it- "come then expressive silence make her praise"- this is a very pretty idea of the poet's, but it is so liable to misconstruction that there is scarcely in the whole range of poetry a line more difficult to be made a reasonable use of- and therefore must be kept as it was originally intended for devotional purposes, but then I can give you good reasons for the extraordinary pleasure your letter produced- in the first place it was excellent in itself, written with great spirit and so characteristic that the very expression of countenance & play of features were conveyed to the paper- we had not heard from you for a long time and began to be a little worried and- but what signifies- I never yet received a letter from you that I could not find many reasons for admiring nor one that did not send a thrill of affectionate gratitude through my heart- The day before this arrived Mr Gildermeister & Professor Keating dined here, & I raised the green veil from your & Ben's portraits, that they might see what Sully could do when he had subjects that pleased him, you would have been amused to see Jo's extacy as he directed attention to the perfection of each. I could scarcely bear to cover them again they look so bright & true- even the Dr laid aside his criticising acumen- and did nothing but approve.

If I had time I should like to go and spend a day with Mrs Blair[1] - we never hear a word about her- you must tell me something all the way from Lexington, for I do not like to lose sight of her altogether- I take up the Globe to look for some little selection of elegant literature or poetry which I may attribute to her taste- for politicks no longer interest me- I am offended at seeing Mrs Eatons name in every print- What ever she may deserve- the decencies of domestic life ought not be violated as they have been- & Miss Lewis, with the young ladies of the ex secretaries' families dragged before the public. Major L's letter will do little good to the cause, when it is known that his daughter is not permitted to return to Washington- her tour to Europe has been abandoned she is probably about forming an establishment here- at least it is reported that Pierce Butler is her adviser . . . .

Your favorable opinion of Mr Furness[2] will be confirmed by a fact which has raised him in the estimation of his congregation, so much that they are at a loss how to express their admiration. He had permission to accompany his family to New England and pass July & August away. He

---

[1] Mrs. Francis Preston Blair, a sister of Mrs. Benjamin Gratz, and the wife of the editor of the Washington Globe, mentioned in a former letter.
[2] The Reverend William H. Furness pastor of the Unitarian church of Philadelphia and father of the famous Shakespeare student, H. H. Furness.

preached at Boston, and had a unanimous call to a church in that city, at a salary of $2500- and an allowance of $200 more for fuel, and the perquisites which would add considerably to the richness of the living- he receives here but $1500- yet his love for his own congregation, and sense of duty to them was put in the balance, and out weighed the tempting offer- he returned home last week- I will go this evening & hear him preach, that I may see how the people appreciate such a rare instance of disinterestedness- John Vaughan goes about like a messenger bringing glad tidings- and the swiftness of his feet through the streets, are remarkable considering his age- that no one lacks the beauty which is spoken of by the prophet[1]-

To sweet Ann Erwin,[2] you must say how I rejoice that she remembers & loves me- tell her too that I shall never forget her loveliness nor the interest she made in my affection- and my dear Maria do not assail my humility in your own, & her home again, lest I should forget myself - and like the foolish bird in the fable, grow vain, and lose my hold on your regard . . . . God Bless you My dearest Maria believe me always your own R G.

* * *

TO THE SAME

Visit of Col. Leslie Combs of Lexington to Philadelphia— death of Mrs. Reuben Etting of Baltimore—Stephen Girard's will.

Jan'y 12th 1832

It is well My dear Sister, that in all the causes which occurred to my mind as keeping you so long silent I did not think of your being sick- (I suppose because that thought

[1] Isaiah LII:7.
[2] See page 93, Note 2.

would have been the most painful of all) or I should not have suffered you to remain quiet, and in the irritable state you *pretend* to have been thrown by your fever, there is no torment so irritating as repeated enquiries concerning your health- this I have learned by experience of our brother Jo's case. When he is sick (and he had the influenza very badly for a few days) I am afraid to propose a remedy- or ask a question- and have only to sit still and observe what he is in want of, or make John enquire if he will be attended to- but I am glad your husband is not quite so much afraid of you, and did venture to plead for a letter for me, for which I thank the dear fellow in my own behalf and besides think it creditable to himself, and albeit fortunate, as it sometimes happens that your diseases take a long term- for various symptoms, liver complaint- consumption- or fever, are thank God all curable and come to a happy issue- and I pray that whether your recent sickness be of that character- or the prevailing epidemic- its uncomfortable effects have all disappeared by this time, and left my beloved & charming sister herself again . . . . Col Combs[1] brought letters from the Barrys, and was entertained according to the gratitude felt for Kentucky hospitality by their family here- he was continually walking with their beautiful cousin Jane- and playing the beau much as he did last winter. I intended to send you some books by him, but he did not let us know of his departure until late the evening before he started- if this weather continues for it is very mild to day- you may stand a chance to receive all your articles except the looking glasses which have not yet left Phila the river being closed before they were ready to pack, but Mr Doggart told me

---

[1] Col. Leslie Combs, a prominent citizen of Lexington, who gave a brick house to be used for Transylvania university after the fire of May, 1829. See Peter, *Transylvania University* 103 n.

BENJAMIN GRATZ, FROM A PAINTING BY SULLY

yesterday that he should soon send them on their journey as he thought travelling would do them no harm

I wish you could hear the witticism passing on the affair of Mr Brown & Miss Peters- it will hardly do to call it a flirtation between two such proper & sage personages but there is certainly an uncommon intimacy- and interest- he derives pleasure & consolation from her society and she is delighted & enlightened by the conversation of distinguished men- but she protests against ever changing her situation- Miss Peters will always retain her consistency- and she certainly does in her attachment to you- she laughed at your message- and said "that is so like her! but remember you always tell her how much I think of her, and still more how much I talk of her" . . . .

The death of our well beloved cousin[1] threw a gloom over our family circle- she was the companion of our Sisters youthful days- and associated with all our recollections of early life- her departure was sudden too- after an illness of only two days- her constitution was broken up and yielded to an attack of the prevailing disease- Sam[2] went immediately to Balt. and tried to console his father- but left the family in great affliction Sister Hays has had her hands full they are all getting well- It is nearly two months since our Sister has been in Boston Row- fortunately for me Julia Hoffman was detained by the bad travelling and has consented to tarry all winter, so that I am not alone, and I am more pleased too on Sarah's account, for she is now becoming more in want of rational companions than play fellows, and Julia is well educated & sensible. Sarah is fond of her- and talks about Aunt Maria & the dear little boys so con-

---

[1] Mrs. Reuben Henry Etting of Baltimore, daughter of Barnard Gratz and cousin of Rebecca Gratz.
[2] Samuel Etting, her son, who had married Ellen Hays, a niece of Rebecca Gratz.

stantly- that Julia's interest is as much awakened as if she had made one of the last winters party-

There is nothing talked about here but Girards Will- Jac sent a copy to Ben, but if he had not - the newspapers would have carried it to you before this- it is well that it was not opened before his funeral or perhaps the Catholicks would not have given him a grave- as it was they said no prayer- no mass, a requiem was chanted in the chapel- and then he was deposited- but he has made all Phila a monument of gratitude- and his Orphan College will sing his praise through untold ages- nobody objects to his excluding the clergy from its walls, and we may hope that religion purer than that of the Sunday School Union will grow up and flourish there. . . . . The newspaper last week gave an account of a clergyman who told his congregation- that he had left the side of the corpse of a beloved child to administer the sacrament to them!! I did not pity that man- for I thought if he had felt like a father- he would have either have staid home- or have performed his service, without telling of his loss- when people can be eloquent on their own sufferings they greatly console themselves by the effort, or else they argue on what they should feel rather than on what they do-

A dull winter in the city makes one very stupid- almost all my friends are in black, and so I hear nothing of style & high fashion to amuse you with- even the weddings are in mourning- here is Mr Cadwallader brought his New York bride to town- and his most intimate friends cannot entertain her- and Mr Willing has brought his charming little wife home just when she must keep her foreign acquirements up until they are out of date, but I really believe they will all make more rational wives for at least three months adulation and public spoiling will be spared- and then Mrs Blight & Mrs Swift will have to divide the town between them, their

Equipages- and furniture- & palaces are quite rivals- in magnificence . . . .

Our Brothers are constantly scolding Ben for not writing- but I do not know whether they deserve that he should- Jac never looked better than he does now- and the girls make him play chess & gallant them about most successfully- Hyman goes to whist parties now & then- & Jo complains of the climate- and again regrets that he was caught another winter in our frozen city- but they console themselves with a game of dummy every night- and manage to keep a good appetite- and enjoy a late breakfast- John has come to your relief My dear Sister- he reminds me that my writing table must give place to the dinner preparations. I have passed a delightful morning with you- and at your expense perhaps- but all things have an end- and this timely interruption will save your patience- God Bless you, Dearest- May this New Year and many succeeding ones- shine their brightest on you, and always find you happy, ever

your own Sister R G--

* * *

TO BENJAMIN GRATZ

Charming letters—loving family circle—death of Adeline Myers—demise of James Craig philanthropist—death of Levi Phillips—Sir Walter Scott's tales.

January 31st- 1832

I am so continually receiving favors & kindnesses from My Dear Brothers that I have scarcely words left to express My gratitude, yet believe Me My Dearest Ben My heart registers every new instance of their love & bounty, and your recent gift was received with feelings- which I may not utter- but would not for the world repress-

I sincerely hope before this your dear little Hyman has recovered- and all the rest are well- I am looking anxiously for one of Maria's charming letters- she manages to give us such living pictures of all her dear household that we see you in the very mode & expression she pleases to place you- you would be quite amazed at the sensation the arrival of such a letter produces in Boston row- each one picks up the sketch that pleases them most- and descants on the perfection of that art which makes time & distance subservient- and brings us into the presence of absent friends- we have had rather a dull winter- cold weather & influenza have made great ravages among our friends- and in our community- the most recent & unexpected was the death of my friend Adeline,[1] who was only sick three days- poor Mr Myers seems doomed to realize the mournful apprehension of his wife- that of surviving all her children- in little more than a year the two eldest, and most important members of his family have been hastily snatched away- Adeline apparently from perfect health- and in the very prime of her usefulness- her father & brother seemed to depend upon her powerful mind, as the adviser & prop of their fallen fortunes- her cheerfulness & exertions kept the old man from sinking into despondency- I do not know what will become of them now they have lost her-

I suppose the Barrys are afflicted at the death of James Craig- it was so sudden- that every one was shocked- he was thought to be but slightly indisposed, and having taken an anodyne was left to sleep- at dinner time they found his door fastened- and broke it open, when he was found dead- it is said he has left no will- which is unfortunate for his poor

[1] Adeline Myers of Norfolk, Va.

relations- as his brother & Sister have wealth enough and there are many he cared for whom it is probable- had he thought of dying so soon he would have provided for- it has been reported since his death that he was engaged to be married to his beautiful young cousin- he will be greatly missed by a number of needy men who lived at his table, and fared sumptuously every day-

Levi Phillips' death has left his poor blind wife[1] entirely destitute, indeed he was so impoverished as to be supported by his nephews for several years previous to his death . . .

Tell Maria- Sir Walters last tales have just issued from the press this morning, and are only waiting a conveyance to Lexington with a book that Hyman tried some time ago to get smuggled into the baggage of a traveller- who unfortunately had packed his trunk so tight that he could not get in a novel- and whose head was so full of speculations- that he would not break the web of his golden dreams- by mixing them with the no less romantic imaginings of the author- so she will have Count Robert- and the Countess Jacqueline to entertain her together- I hope the Ohio will not be so impassable, as our Delaware again- and then she may get her looking glasses- for the first party she gives in February- as they have been several weeks on their journey- present my most affectionate love to her and the dear boys- . . . .

God Bless you- with all you & your beloved Maria can desire to make life happy and preserve it so, and believe me dear Ben most affectionately & gratefully
your attached Sister RG

[1] Leah, daughter of Joseph Simon of Lancaster and sister of Mrs. Michael Gratz, the mother of Rebecca Gratz.

TO MARIA GIST GRATZ

The wisdom of experience—"God metes out good and evil as seems good unto Him, and is most merciful and just, although we know it not"—Mrs. Child's "The Mother's Book"—Jacob Mordecai's writings—Sir Walter Scott's "Tales of My Landlord".

February 16th 1832

I have thought My dear Maria for the last two days that I would not write to you, until I had refreshed myself with a good long walk, and got rid of the stupefying effects of dull weather & dyspepsia - stocking darning & ennui- but alternate rain & snow holds dominion in the atmosphere- my basket, (your beautiful basket, which accompanies me in all my journeys up and down stairs) is almost empty and shews your dear letter, unanswered at the bottom, and my conscience is more troublesome than my other ailments- and so I shall bestow myself with all these imperfections on your clemency and try if I cannot brighten by the good company I force myself into - my blessed little Hyman was just getting well when you last wrote, I hope you have had no more sickness in your family since - but hear that all the Barry household have had measles. I hope your new city will not go after the fashion of old ones and send such evils abroad into all houses in the corporation- here we have had scarlet fever of which many children have died very suddenly and the Measles is coming after it- but a little experience in the ways of this world teach us, that it is wise never to anticipate evils- many here are dreading the arrival of the Cholera- in whom the breath of life appears to be flickering like the last light of an expiring taper and here too was my much loved friend Adeline Myers in the full glow of health - the prime of life & usefulness - cut down like a young tree in a summer storm! alas, alas! how unable are we to judge according to the wisdom of Him who governs the creation he has made and metes out good & evil as seems good unto him, and is most merciful & just, although we know it not - . . . .

Your admirer Mrs Furness has been enquiring about you with much interest, she sent me "The Mothers Book" to read, which is highly recommended written by Mrs Child of Boston- the 1st Edition is all sold off or I would send you one it is very good and practicable, but I dare say you can bring up your children as well without it- Julia & I have criticised some positions she holds, altho we do not doubt the wisdom of them- her theory of the manner we ought to feel and consider the visitation of Death, is the most difficult lesson she would inculcate and I think to the extent she recommends, would require us to remodel our human affections on a more sublime nature- I have recently seen a fond Mother resign a little suffering child with as much composure as I should wish or approve, and yet she parted with more agony than Mrs Childs thinks consistant with religion or reason- Mrs Rutledge lost that pretty little girl she sent in to see you last spring- she was just one year old and died from the effects of influenza, which attacked her when she was weakened by previous indisposition- Mr R.[1] is in Carolina for his health- his wife has better hopes of his recovering than his other friends and I pray sincerely that they may be fully realized, misfortune brings us close to one another, and during a weeks visits to her nursery I saw more into the character of my neighbour than in our whole previous acquaintance of three years-

[1] The Reverend Mr. Rutledge next door neighbor to the Gratz family.

I am so much in the habit of telling you every thing that interests me, when I write, that I dare say I mentioned old Mr Mordecai's[1] visit in the fall- and how much delighted we were with the patriarchal manner and wisdom of his conversation- since his return he has twice written to me, and sent me valuable papers of his own writing which I consider quite a treasure, the last was a character of "David King of Israel"- "the man after Gods own heart"- and he has said that he would occasionally send "the outpourings of a mind long devoted to important researches after truth"- I shall hoard them all up My dear Sister for your perusal- he has the advantage of understanding the language in which the scriptures were written- and has a large learned library a liberal spirit- and leisure to devote to his favorite study- he has never printed a book, but desires to make his own children & grand children well acquainted with the religion they profess and there are so few Jews in this country that he has frequent applications from Christian divines on scriptural texts which leads him into extensive examinations & they are conducted with good feeling and good taste . . . .

Hyman has paid your bill at Griggs and will send it out, that you may see whether you have received all your books- I shall in future keep a list, and put it in a letter, for we sometimes send them by persons who have no letter with them- the latest were "Tales of My Landlord" among the next will be "Forsaken" if I do not find the 2 Vol. too stupid to export. My dear little Cary's frocks are ready for the next conveyance.

19*th* I am quite concerned My Dear Sister that I left my letter unfinished, for Hyman came in last Evening, when our

---

[1]Jacob Mordecai of Warrenton N. C., the father of Major Alfred Mordecai, who married Sarah, daughter of Samuel and Richea Hays and niece of Rebecca Gratz.

TO MARIA GIST GRATZ

Sister Hays was here, and said he knew of an opportunity- she urged me to go write- and then our party was encreased and I could not obey- so I fear you will have to pay more for this sheet than it is worth- what a humiliating thought to come in at the third page- do you remember the oriental tale, of putting gold into a scale to weigh a scull and it was too light for the metal- and then they heaped more in, and put in the opposite scale a human Eye- which alone changed the balance?- now dearest, just place my love before your minds eye, and let it cover all these pages which would be dross without it- and then I know your kind heart will accept is as full weight of the postage - present My Dear Brother with my affectionate love, and tell your boys, how proud I am to hear of their improvement - I shall look out for some improving books for their entertainment, embrace them for me - we sit talking of them for hours - and at every anecdote each recollects, the general smile of recognition illumines the whole circle. Julia Hoffman, is so well acquainted with you all- that she fancies she has seen you, and desires that she may be considered entitled to the privilege of sending her regards . . . .

Our next door nieces & nephews, and a few straggling individuals not already named- are desirous to have their stations in your kind thoughts perserved- and send you their love- and so dearest, & best beloved- does your own loving and ever grateful Sister - God Bless you all, now & ever more

RG

TO THE SAME

This letter (the only incomplete one in the series) is undated, but the date may be fixed approximately by the mention in this letter and in the letter of April 18, 1832 of a review of Bulwer's novel, Eugene Aram; this letter must have been the earlier of the two as is clear from the reference to this review.

Religious controversies—proscription of the Unitarians by orthodox Christians—the misfortunes of "single ladies."

I wrote a long letter to you last week My Dear Maria, but did not get it closed in time for Mr Leary and thought it not worth the postage, and so commended it to the grate- and should not now rake up its ashes, but to let you know that I have thought of and answered your charming letter before this, altho you have been spared the trouble of reading all that a very anxious state of mind might have suggested on that occasion . . . . I am going to send you by this conveyance a review of Eugene Aram from the New York American written by Charles Hoffman - if you are in the habit of seeing that paper, perhaps you will know his pieces by the mark of a star, and as I think he writes well, I would commend him to your notice- he likes to get Julias approbation and sometimes sends her the paper, we were all pleased with this novel except Sarah Hays- and I believe she heard it too much criticized before she read it- the real Eugene seems to have borne little resemblance to Bulwers, except in scholarship- but the extreme refinement of the novel hero is a strong contrast to the personage whose wife & accomplices are more on a level with himself- than the angelic being he is associated with in this interesting book . . . .

That which you call the misfortune of single ladies, My dear Sister, is in my case converted into a blessing- for by sharing the troubles I gain admittance into the affections of my friends- and what should I do with the heart nature has given me if all its warm pulsations were to beat against closed bosoms? that pretty tale of "Second best" made me weep in very sadness- at the cold picture of a perfect character- too perfect for any one to love- and it seemed lifted out of the reach of love as a passion- tho' full of benevolence for all human beings with whom she was associated- I never sat for such a picture My dear Maria and would not exchange the memory of keener pangs for the beautiful & placid mirror of a life spent as we might imagine the angel of pity would pass on earth- I am satisfied dearest- nay, grateful for the place I hold in the hearts of my brothers & sisters, and to tell you the truth am often afraid I shall grow vain of such praises as you bestow upon me. So if you spoil & then cease to love me, because spoilt, I shall be unhappy & you unjust. I warn you therefore, that you must take heed of your words, knowing as you must how every word of yours is treasured and in future say no better of me than I deserve.

I had my philosophy a little tried the other day by some good Christians, and as I dare not complain about it to anybody else (for I hate to set the subject in its true light at home)- I must make you my confidante- You know I promised our friend Mrs Furness to apply for a little girl out of the Asylum for her- well there is a good little girl I have kept my eye on and she is ready for a place- and my application is rejected because it is for a Unitarian- but "Ladies, said I, there are many children under my special direction- you all know my creed - suppose I should want one to bring up in my family?"- "you may have one, said a church woman- because the Jews do not think it a duty to convert"- but said a presbyterian "I should not consent to her being put under the influence of a Unitarian"- and so my dear after putting

the question to vote- I could get nothing- and when the meeting broke up, had a mischievous pleasure in telling one of the most blue of the board that I construed their silence into consent- for only one lady voted in the affirmative- and they were all ashamed to vote no- but I do not mean to let Mrs F know how she is proscribed, because notwithstanding my own position, I am ashamed of such an illiberal spirit- I got into a long discussion on the subject of religion, with a lady after the meeting and though we have been more than twenty years acquainted- I expect she will look shy on me for the rest of our lives- what a pity that the best and holiest gift of God, to his most favoured creatures, should be perverted into a subject of strife- and that to seek to know and love the most High should not be the end and aim of all- without a jealous or persecuting feeling towards each other-
. . . .

* * *

TO THE SAME

Byron's poetry—"Pope, Milton and others"—Bulwer's Eugene Aram—Gouverneur Morris' Life.

I do not know My Dear Sister, whether to sympathize with you or rejoice- if you are over your sickness- let me be glad, for verily the more I have to love belonging to you the better- and since the days of the patriarchs children have been called an inheritance of the lord- and of all the happy families I have ever known- those are the happiest where sisters & Brothers have dwelt together in love & society- you & Ben agree so well in bringing them up, that you may look forward to their being a blessing to you in your old age, and so welcome, a glad welcome to all who come- our brothers have got the very bad habit of reading your letters- and so when I want to keep a secret, it is as certainly betrayed by my concealing your letter, as if it were open before them- I dare say Jac will count for you from the time your last arrived, just because it was not in my basket, and I could not make it convenient to bring it downstairs. I was sorry not to let them see some of the agreeable sprightly remarks but it would not satisfy them to have parts read- when they are used to read the whole, and so they must abide by the loss- there are others tho in the family who profit by all you do- our dear Sarah, begins to find delight in poetry- Byron has been her great favorite, until I shewed what you say of the older poets- since which I have given her selections from Pope, Milton & others- to chastise her taste, and give her other standards of excellence- she assisted at Mrs Sigorgnes annual concert last Thursday- she has improved very much- indeed plays delightfully- she gained much credit from ama- tures & her teachers on this occasion- her manners and mind become more womanly- Julia Hoffman's society has been an advantage, she is highly cultivated cheerful & amiable- and very much attached to Sarah- she left us last week. I observe my dear Sister you mistook the object of my sending you the newspaper- there was a review of Eugene Aram, I wished to shew you- Halleck's lines I did not read, but no matter - I like your own criticism of the novel, tho think it less offen- sive to good morals than either of Bulwers other novels- the crime of Eugene was followed by such signal punishment- even from the day of its commission (as his confession proves) that I do not think with every perfection that adorns his character, you ever feel on easy or equal terms with him- and would always rather the lovely Madelina should fall a sacrifice than be united to a murderer. We shall soon have Irving's & Paulding's books to send you - the life of Gouverneur Morris[1] is so expensive a work that I thought you might think the price more than it is worth, tho the letters are very fine, it is probable some copies have already reached you- if not would you be willing to risk $7 on the chance of the librarys taking it? .... I have no little children near me now - for poor Mrs Rutledge has sent all hers away to Connecticut - and to morrow she follows them- I went to bid her farewell last evening- her husbands brother, came to wind up his affairs and to take the family to Carolina- but she could not so soon make up her mind to go, her own mother wished her to pass the summer in retirement with her, she is an invalid, and said she could not survive the separation at present so Mrs R. acquiesced- and will not go to Charleston until the Autumn- he has left no property- and she must depend on his Mother-

Every body here My dearest Sister sends you messages of love- say the fondest & the kindest words to my beloved brother to express my feelings for him- and assure yourself that you are constantly in the mind & heart of your affectionate sister R GRATZ-

April 18th 1832

* * *

TO THE SAME

The tedium of illness relieved—the uses of adversity—the cholera epidemic.

It is a long time My dear Sister since I have been able to write to you- and few deprivations have been more impatiently borne- I cannot say that I have suffered a great deal- but felt that so much time was wasted in darkness, without

[1] *Life of Gouverneur Morris* by Jared Sparks (Boston, 1832, 3 vol.)

occupation, that weariness would have been even a greater evil than pain- had not my amiable & affectionate nieces devoted themselves to My care and amusement- they read to me several hours every day- and then would return from their visits or walks to tell the anecdotes or gossip they picked up- so that I must have been totally ungrateful, not to be penetrated by their kindness- our good Sister Hays too came every day, and brought word of poor Isabella,[1] and her Martyr Mother, and if these were not motives "voluble of thanks" for all the benefits I possessed over those worthier than myself, I must have lived long, in all the plenitude of health, to little advantage- There are few conditions in life, My dear Sister, which may not I believe afford occasions for improvement- "sweet are the uses of adversity" Shakespeare says- and dull must be that heart- which in solitude & darkness- does not meditate on brighter things than those which occupy the senses in the outer world- my eyes are now perfectly free from disease or inflammation- but are still too weak for constant use, I can only employ myself for a few hours- and then must rest- I cannot read at night at all- nor always in the day time- but I hope they will be getting stronger by & bye- your letters to the girls are written in such agreeable spirits that I fancy you well, tho' you do not say much about yourself. . . . . You have heard I suppose how rapidly the Cholera is approaching us- it has been some 10 days at New York- and is increasing in its ravages- our Physicians have returned from Canada- their accounts have induced such preparations, as will be likely to ameliorate the distresses & sufferings of the poor, when it makes its appearance in Phila - hospitals are provided but it is a frightful pestilence to meet with - people here, do not seem disposed to leave their homes, lest they should encounter it at a dis-

[1] Isabella Etting, an invalid niece.

advantage without medical aid, or other comforts they can have at home, it has traversed the globe so generally that climate seems no barrier or stay - and with all that experience can furnish - there seems no system adopted with the usual success as in most other diseases - we are therefore like David, in a great strait, and with his faith may say - "let us fall into the hands of God for his Mercies are great" &c . . . . Montgomery Blair is at Washington - we hear the highest praises bestowed on him by a West Point Cadet - he is much beloved - very industrious - & distinguished in his class - he is chosen corporal an office bestowed on the best looking person in the corps -

Henry Hart too you see has been commanding a boat in the fight- I hope he had not to encounter the heroines on that occasion- for My own part, I do not like the manner that attack was made- it is not on the town and its inhabitants indiscriminately that vengence should be taken- but I have no doubt your Nephew acted nobly- and he might justly draw his sword on savage murderers - making the cause his own- we did not see Montgomery on his way through, but expect he will call on his return- your Sister promised me last Autumn that she would come to Phila this summer but before congress breaks up- people will be afraid to approach our city- and Mr B would not be able to leave his office earlier- whatever old Hickory may think of rotation in office, in his own case- he seems to practice it vehemently in his cabinet & ministers abroad- I think My dear, if he had a place in his gift for a woman, you might be sure of gaining it- pray would you like to have a lithographe made from your picture- to return his compliment? do not say yes- for I should not like to send it as a companion to Van Buren . . . . our brothers are home again and all unite with Sisters & the girls in affectionate remembrances- embrace the

The Benjamin Gratz Homestead, Mill Street, Lexington, Ky.

darlings for me- and accept for dearest Ben and your self the best wishes and truest affection of your own attached Sister

RG

July 8th 1832

* * *

TO THE SAME

Henry Clay's speech containing allusion to "Moses Myers the Jew"—"The more difficult the duty faithfully performed the greater the reward"—contemplated visit to Kentucky.

July 22nd 1832

I was rejoiced My dear Sister to receive a letter from you again and written in sweet fine spirits too- I am now willing to sail around the world- or through your drawing room- you shall be pilot and if I lack knowledge of a single phrase nautical or blue you shall enlighten me with one of your own illustrations- your friend Miss Peters says her criterion of good society is made by reflecting on her return home whether she has carried any thing worth remembering away- I am very sensible that your letters always put to this test satisfies my heart & my understanding that I have been in good company- and I am happier and more agreeable for days after their perusal. . . . .

At present our city is very healthy- we enjoy this blessing with fear & trembling - as the mediciners tell us the Cholera will certainly be here, and the daily reports from New York are so distressing, ... Do Maria, when you see Mr Clay ask what was meant by an allusion to "Moses Myers the jew"[1] in one of his speeches- I read it without understanding it, and several persons equally dull here asked for an explanation- our respectable old friend from Norfolk dined with us yesterday and made the same enquiry- he had no suspicion that he is the object of remark- poor old man! affliction has almost riven his heart in pieces- I never have seen such a monument of parental grief. He has but one Son left and two daughters out of a family of nine and they all grew up to maturity- and were the pride as well as the staff of his age- Mrs Myers died of grief after the loss of her two youngest sons in rapid succession- she was under the apprehension that she should be left childless- such an idea might prove fatal to her husband, did he entertain it with equal force- but Sterne was right- "God tempers the wind to the shorn lamb"- and He does not leave the Mourner without consolation- Myer is going to Norfolk to reside- and thus fill the gap- and cherish his aged Father- and this has given him something to look forward to- & to Bless the name of him "who giveth & taketh away"- I received a very affecting letter from my neighbour Mrs Rutledge the other day- she is now with her Mother in Middletown- and is going in Oct. to Charleston to reside with her husband's- Mr Rutledge died poor- and if the climate is unfriendly to her children- she will have nothing but her own exertions to depend on- The old lady is a noble spirited affectionate woman, and I hope they will be happily situated in Carolina- for her relations in Connecticut are not able to assist her.

[1] In a speech in the United States Senate Henry Clay had made what was considered a derogatory reference to "Moses Myers the Jew". Solomon Etting of Baltimore wrote the eminent statesman on the subject. This letter called forth an answer in which Clay referred to his friendship with Benjamin Gratz as a proof of his friendliness to Jews. See "Correspondence between Solomon Etting and Henry Clay" by Walter Liebman. Proceedings American Jewish Historical Society XVII 81–88.

Gratz[1] has finished his College studies and is preparing for the commencement- he has chosen the character of Lawrence for the subject of his oration, and written a very pretty little sketch- which he is reciting he says to the fishes in the Delaware, from whose shores the echoes are very flattering- he is with Campbell at Devon . . . .

I heard a lady (an old maid) say that the worst husbands always had the best & most loving wives- and she cites Mrs. R. and Mrs B- we disputed the point, and I had contrary instances in abundance but in very sadness was obliged to own that those ladies had keen trials- yet the bright and cheerful countenances of both at the moment came to my recollection, and I concluded, the more difficult the duty faithfully performed, the greater was the intellectual reward, and therefore these ladies were gifted by providence with an inspiration, which enabled them to extract the bitter from the poisoned chalice - and enjoy a happiness - one from the best of children- and the other from a mothers love- whilst they retained charity & affection with the memory of what they had enjoyed- as you have not a bad husband, Maria, and my opponent had none at all- pray let my argument stand- even if you do not approve. . . . . How I should love to come to you if I had not so many immovable ties in this quarter- but now danger surrounds them I cannot get away- I hope another year will make up for the disappointments of this- 'tis thus dear Maria, we cheat ourselves, and grow old without accomplishing our desires- but I hope to see Kentucky and all the beloved ones there- God Bless you all- believe me most fervently your attached R G-

I shall not send you the books you can have from your bookseller, unless you wish to possess them- the bearer will

[1]Simon Gratz Moses a nephew who graduated from the medical department of the University of Pennsylvania in 1832.

carry one or two vol. not named in your letter- adieu My Sister

The children desire their best love to you & the boys- we talk of you every day our Sisters & their girls also embrace you, tell dearest Ben his portrait has been feasting the eyes of his friends abroad- and arrived safe home last week to its most welcome place-

* * *

TO THE SAME

Lessons in self denial—precautions against cholera—the Arch Street prison—"of all laws imprisonment for debt is most abhorrent to reason and justice."

August 19th 1832

After the cloth was removed yesterday and all the girls were assembled around the dinner table, I thought how long it was since I had heard from you My dear Maria, and expressed my desire to get a letter, when our brother Jo, drew one from his pocket which he had been in possession of for some days and because you said so many flattering and agreeable things to him he had been too modest to shew it- well, was he not rightly served for keeping it so long a secret for there was Sarah Hays- and our three Moses girls as veritable daughters of Eve in such matters as could be found, and so your excellent epistle was handed round, and Mr Joseph had to hear your praises, praised in good earnest- we admired the ingenuity & grace by which just praise can be rendered grateful and when it flatters must not appear exaggerated. I hope My dear you will often have occasion to exercise your pretty talent on like occasions- there was a notice in it of your dear little Boys, which pleased me so much that I cannot help expressing my satisfaction- you say they gave up eating unripe fruit because you told them "it would make you uneasy" and you must tell them, that this proof of their obedience, makes me love them better than ever, and that their example shall be recommended to all the children I know- it is very well to begin such lessons of self denial- for here are we in the midst of a luxuriant season, with abundance of fine fruit & vegetables which are *all forbidden* - our bill of fare, consists of meat- bread rice & potatos- desert, a pudding- by special favor Dr Chapman allows one peach a day- at first it was very hard, and I was afraid to look into Hyman's market basket particularly when corn came in season- he did bring it home daily for one week, but finding no one but himself transgressed in that favorite article- he left off buying it- we moreover, sleep with our windows shut- wear flannel and keep out of damp night air- these are sanitary measures- we have remedies at hand for premonitory indications and thank God have been thus far free from the "foul fiend"- and cheerfully keep the even tenor of our way "hoping that the pestilence will pass by & we remain untouched" except by a deeper sense of dependence on the guardian who neither "slumbereth nor sleepeth!"

A very small proportion of the citizens have removed, and I believe it is better so- in every direction the villages and towns have been afflicted in some degree with the Cholera and at New York & Montreal, it has been prolonged by the return of the inhabitants who are said to be more liable coming from purer air- There was but one day of panic in Phila and that was occasioned by the mortality in Arch Street Prison- the only place that was totally unprepared for it- this is a receptacle for vagrants, and the police so defective that nothing less might have been expected- now all the poor prisoners are released (a large number by death) I hope the stain will be wiped off by appointing more efficient & humane officers- of all laws imprisonment for debt is most abhorent to reason & justice

I will never again attempt to write you a letter on such paper- for I find it will blot, but it was my poverty and not my will- I had no other, and a rainy day- well, dear, I am afraid you will find me out- my poverty is not only of paper but on it- if I could cover it sensibly- you would not mind its texture, and perhaps I should have forgot to apologize- thus we deceive ourselves in attempting to deceive others- I have seen many a good letter, badly written on coarse paper but I doubt whether I could make one on fine vellum. . . . .

God Bless you My dearest embrace all you love for me, and believe me most truly

yours R G--

* * *

TO THE SAME

Habits easily formed and difficult to discard—the Stark Minis duel.

Sept 2nd 1832

As the board of health have done reporting, I shall no longer have a plea for writing to you every week on account of the Cholera, but My dear Maria, there is some danger in forming habits, if they are not agreeable at first they become so- but when we set about indulging a favorite propensity and fancy it an act of kindness there is no knowing how long we may continue the self deception, unless our friends admonish us of the fact- now I have been writing so continually upon trust that I think it is time to tell you this is the last

Cholera bulletin you will receive- and that in future I shall expect answers to my letters- the people are returning from the country in all directions- watering places are shut up, and the city is again full of inhabitants- and those who have been away seem to lay it so little to heart, that pestilence & death follows in the training of feasting & indulgence- that I fear there will be many victims to plumbs & watermelons- among those who fled in July and apprehend no danger in Sept.

Mrs McAlister's bridal visit, has brought her to the house of mourning- the family all went to Willow Grove to avoid the epidemic, and the old Gentleman took cold by being caught in a rain, and died in consequence- it may be a consolation to her husband to have been here at this period, but poor Elinor's introduction into the family will leave a sad impression on her memory- is it because the sacred writings are so full of beautiful similes of bridal honors & bridal ornaments that we look with such intense interest on one bearing that title, and consider them entitled to exemption from sorrow, or is it experience which showing us the shortness of human happiness- makes us sympathize more with those who in a little period, set apart for joy unmixed- should have scenes of sorrow intruded upon them?

I received a letter- a heart-rending letter, a few days ago from our dear Sally Minis[1]- giving an account of the situation of the family, in consequence of that unfortunate affair of Philips, and at his request stating the particulars, by which he is exonerated from the stigma the newspaper account left on his character-

"he was consulting some of his friends at the races in April about naming a horse, when Mr Stark passing by said

[1] See page 80, Note 1.

"Name him Shylock" and afterwards called him a "D--d Jew"- Minis challenged him then- he apologized, and the affair slumbered- until some of Starks friends induced him to retract his apology, and another challenge was sent & accepted- a difference about the hour of fighting arose between the seconds. Mr S--s friend wished them to meet on the same day- Minis's insisted that a sufficient time was not allowed to settle his affairs, and proposed the dawn of the next morning or any hour after that they would prefer- the seconds parted without coming to any agreement and Mr Stark with his friend went to the ground at 5 o'clock that afternoon, although assured that the other party would not meet them then- they returned and publicly pronounced Minis a coward- the next morning they met accidentally at the city Hotel- Minis reproached Stark for his conduct- he drew a pistol and advanced. Minis did the same, and fired instantly- Stark fell mortally wounded- and Minis immediately expressed his determination to give himself up to the civil authorities- and is now in close confinement- where he must continue until January- as his father is a judge in the inferior Court, and Mr S's nearest relation is judge in the Superior Court, and so a new election must take place before he can be tried-"

Sally says her poor Mothers health is so bad- and her father's spirit so broken down that she sometimes fears, they will not be able to support this long season of anxiety & suffering, her own misery is acute indeed- yet she feels so much depends on her, that she strives to bear the burden of all their griefs- Sweet pious, child- the God of Mercy will be her stay, and not suffer her to fall when she calls on him for support-

Henry Etting too has had a fight at the navy yard in Boston but no serious consequence is likely to result- our Sister had a few sleepless nights to endure on his account, as a

Mother's fears have so many objects- but the Capt and other officers have sent testimonials of his good conduct in the affair- that we have every reason to rejoice he has come off so well- Dr Hays has returned home cured, and now acknowledges that his illness was Cholera- Dr Chapman's letter will give you as accurate an idea of its character here, as any I suppose- & will prevent your feeling as much alarm, should it cross the mountains- as was experienced by those who witnessed its first ravages as a devouring unknown scourge- but I pray you may never encounter it- present My best love to My dear Ben and the darling boys . . . . God Bless you my precious Sister believe me always Yours RG-

* * *

TO THE SAME

Although the year of the date of this letter is omitted it was written, in all likelihood, in 1832. This appears from the mention of the fatalities resulting from the cholera epidemic which took place in that year and also from the mention of an election in which the administration of Andrew Jackson was an issue; Jackson was re-elected to the presidency in 1832.
  "Westward Ho" by James Paulding—Miss Harriet Martineau's Tales.

A new novel and an opportunity to read it- then "Westward ho!" shall hie to thee My dear Maria, before a critic has the chance to forestall your relish, and taking for granted that our old favorite will not be less agreeable when he aspires to entertain you in your own regions- I hope he will meet with a kind reception, and brighten the hours you devote to his labours. I have been reading Miss Martineau's tales or illustrations of political economy, and should be very glad to send you a copy, but find they are not to be had- they came out in numbers, and but few copies have been sent to subscribers, but suppose they will be more common when better known in America, for they would be useful to young readers, and make a dry subject very easily understood, and quite interesting- I was introduced yesterday to a boy whom I could have hugged for being so like our dear Bernard, but he was smaller and 12 years old- he was so affectionate, and watchful of his father that I fancied his heart was as much like your sons as his face- poor little fellow he & his father were saved from a wreck in which his mother and two younger children perished and they passed through this city on their way home overland- fearful of again trusting the element that had been so fatal to their happiness . . . .

Tell Ben, Philadelphia has done wonders at the Election on Tuesday- the Anti-Jacksons are triumphant- and Jo bids me say, there is great possibility- nay almost a certainty that Pennsylvania will give an Anti Jackson vote- they are all up & doing here- Hyman was as busy with ward and general Election as he could be- I believe Mr C[1]- has not a warmer friend- they wanted to send Jac to the Legislature- but he refused to stand as a candidate- I was very sorry- for I wanted him to get some employment that would interest him and I think from his knowledge of state politics- and state interests that he would have been a very useful member- I wish our brothers had a little more public spirit- or at least would take some of the burdens of public affairs on themselves- they have time enough to spare- and in spite of all experience, if I were a man, I would like to have some share in public concerns- that is if I had money enough to be sure that I did not seek honors for the lucre of gain!

God Bless you dearest Sister, I think of you- and pray for you daily- embrace all your darlings for me- tell the boys they must never forget us- Horace goes to Mr Sanderson's

[1] Henry Clay.

school again- and is quite happy- Sarah has taken a long holiday- all her companions have left school, and the classes have not formed, as cholera took a great many away who have not yet returned she recommences in a week more- Mr Furness & Mrs Sully enquired for you when I saw them a few days ago . . . . Adieu My dear Maria, tell Ben I hope we shall hear from him soon- ever Your & his affectionate

RG

12th Oct-

* * *

TO THE SAME

Death of infant child of Benjamin Gratz—future bliss—the contemplation of God—the love of life by the aged.

Novr 26th 1832

Why My Beloved Sister is it impossible that you should all spend this winter in Phila? the season is still mild and pleasant for travelling and I hope by this time your own precious health is sufficiently restored- the wish has long since sped from my heart- and been reiterated by all around us ever since the pestilence has taken its course west & south. I have not mentioned it until last week to our dear Ben, because I thought so many difficulties presented, that you would not listen to me but since it has pleased God to take away the blessing he lent to your arms for a few days and your other treasures would not suffer in a journey why might ye not come to us and make us so happy? Oh dear Maria, do think of it not as an impossibility but as easily accomplished- take the shortest and most travelled route and forget the hardships and accidents of your former jaunt- and do not stay until the evil spreads in your city- and the fear of it fills the country through which you are to pass- come dearest Sister, and make our hearts glad- we share your anxiety for our darling Brother- and for you all, yet trust in Heaven's Mercy for your preservation- you have been stricken, & I have wept for the sweet blossom that faded & fell[1] before my eyes beheld it- you will think of it with love & with resignation, but do not aggravate the trial- by imagining any other cause than the will of Him who gave it for its removal and pray, remember how much the joy of all you love depends on you- strive to be cheerful that your health may be more perfect- the children around you command your love & duty- those treasured in heaven & dwelling in your secret thoughts are not less dear- they form the strong mysterious link between you & your God- they & those who preceeded them- bind one "Nature fast in faith"- is it not dear Maria the memory of such that people the heaven of our wishes?- we cannot believe that the "souls of even the righteous made perfect" can be fit to associate with God- therefore our highest conception of future bliss- must be to commune with spirits thus purified in the beatitude of contemplating *his* goodness- & constantly do my thoughts commune with My own dear Parents & sisters that I sometimes am on the point of calling those I speak to by their names- particularly the children of my Sister Rachel- and I have learned to love them more & regret them less from that circumstance- I saw Aunt Bell on Saturday & told her of you, she expressed great tenderness for both you & Ben and begged I would send you her love- she is very feeble & infirm, but cheerful, and tries to persuade herself that she shall be stronger- the love or life or rather the unconsciousness of these warnings that her frame is wearing out astonishes me and yet good woman! she must be bettered by the change for she has trod a rugged

[1] The sixth child of Benjamin and Maria Gratz died in infancy.

path, in the long years of widowhood & poverty- except the constant attention of affectionate children, she has no outward signs of comfort to love this world for . . . .

. . . . God Bless you, My Sister, I embrace you all. I pray that you may be preserved from all danger & distress & hope that we may soon meet & embrace indeed

always your RG

* * *

TO THE SAME

The Francis Preston Blairs—Jackson's second election to the presidency—the southern nullifiers—Henry Clay's friendship for Benjamin Gratz—Washington Irving in Charleston—Fanny Kemble's acting.

Decr 18th 1832

It is so easy to believe what we wish Dearest Maria that I thot I went more than half way to cater for my own disappointment, and out of merely a hint that you wished to be here I set about thinking it might really be accomplished, and see too how the same bright idea spread- I had a letter from Mr Blair suggesting the plan of our uniting our endeavours to draw you over the mountains again, as likely not only to afford us all much pleasure- but tending to advantage to your health- *that* argument would indeed balance all others, and make My dear Ben of our party, and I have been scrutinizing your letter to see if I could find anything that indicated disease of either mind or body- now I perceive nothing but that chastened sense, which recent events might have left on your sensitive mind- a sort of moon light pensiveness, which is more interesting if less brilliant than the mood in which you sometimes write- but so far from either weakness or lassitude that I will not believe you have any remains of indisposition, and suppose our friend Preston wants you to see his comfortable new house in the spring- which he has hospitably invited me to visit this winter. Henry Etting has just returned from there and gives most agreeable accounts of the whole family, Mrs Blair is one of the most popular Ladys at Court, and I suppose this winter will take a fashionable lead- if she does I am sure, she will improve the style of conversation & society in her circle- and as the grand political question of presidential election is decided she will have a better chance- Mrs Johnston does not go to Washington this winter- and I suppose few of the opposition members will take their wives- for they had very little comfort last session- Mr Clay passed through Phila yesterday Jac saw him at Mr Browns- he took a young son to Jersey. I wanted to see him, that I might talk of my dear Mrs . . . . and also hear him talk of whom I have heard so much and know My dear Ben loves so well-

Self-examinations My dear Maria are very edifying and seldom fail to bring us nearer to the light of truth- but I give little credit to the recorded self abasement of sactified per- sons and think their example would be much more useful if they would call things by their right names. We feel and acknowledge the liability of our nature to fall into errors and that we require continual watchfulness to resist temptations- but to sink into the slough of despondency because we are placed a little lower than the angels seems taxing the designs of providence, and instead of being acceptable humility, is down right presumption- the beautiful admonition we find in Scripture "commune with your own heart and be still" seems to express all we desire to feel- and there is no sentence strikes me more forcibly or solemnly on this important sub- ject-

There is little danger My Sister, of your being spoild by your husbands indulgence, while you accept the offerings his love so freely brings, with such gratified affection. I really think you are a happy woman, not only in possessing the treasures most desirable to a rational being, but in feeling their value, I do not know why married life affords so few such examples it must surely be their own faults who choose their destiny when it is otherwise- such silly matches as are begun in the romance of Childhood and postponed until they are no longer the same persons that made them, are hardly to be expected to succeed, ...

The girls brought a charming little girl from New York, who staid a fortnight with them, and stirred up the gallantry of our Youths, we had fine serenades in Boston Row- but there it will probably end, for they are all enough of political economists to provide cages before they catch birds- and thus are likely to sing a solitary lament within the gilded wires, when it is too late to be mated. Let Hyman practice medicine if he will- there is no state in human life where a tender heart is free from trials, and Drs have a good right to be cheerful, when they arrest the hand of death, or cheer a suffering patient under mortal disease- and I know you are so fond of administering, that it would be quite a convenience in your practice to have a son with M. D. attached to his name- as to Howard- he is to be a hero of some sort, he has Mothers own genius- and I think was born to high destinies[1]- God Bless them all, Maria, you have the training of a goodly race, May you be spared to witness & enjoy the glory of their well doing

I hope these southern Nullifiers will not break down the beautiful edifice their fathers have erected to freedom, and

---

[1] For career of Henry Howard Gratz, editor of the Kentucky Gazette see *B & M Gratz Papers*, 308–328.

oh how I tremble lest american blood should be spilt by american hands[1]- our young Carolina students are deeply affected and talk of breaking up their class to go home, and defend their rights—Washington Irving I hear gives a fearful account of the state in which he found society in Charleston- while Miss Kemble[2] is in town I spend a great many lone evenings- Hyman & Jo go to the theatre- she is really charming. I have seen her three times and more wonderful still Jac went once- Adieu Dearest ever & for ever Your own RG

* * *

TO THE SAME

Cholera epidemic prevents visit to Lexington which had been planned—Young's "Night Thoughts"—President Jackson and the Indian chieftain Black Hawk—

Our arrangements were all made My dear Sister, and we were to have commenced our journey next week- but the increasing alarm of Cholera which every days report is spreading through the country has induced us to defer the happiness we were anticipating in your society until this afflicting impediment has passed away- the accounts from Wheeling & Maysville are so appalling that we dare not risk approaching them- God Grant that the pestilence may not spread further- Dr Caldwell says there is little chance of its finding lurking places in your city- I cannot tell you what fallen countenances our deferred party wear- your letter greatly aggravated our disappointment by the animated picture you draw of your lovely familys intended

---

[1] Reference is made here to the South Carolina Ordinance of Nullification passed November 24, 1832, which caused the most intense excitement throughout the country. See Beveridge, *Abraham Lincoln*, I, pages 128–132.
[2] Fanny Kemble. the famous actress.

reception, but My dear Sister we shall hope on, until the season passes- or brighter prospects dawn- yesterday's mail brought the distressing accounts of Judge Johnstons death, by the blowing up of the steam boat in which he & his son were on the Red river- poor Mrs J is plunged in the deepest grief- a few days ago she was the happiest & the gayest- now the most forlorn of widows. her only son maimed- perhaps a lingering victim to the same sad accident- my first impulse was to have gone to her- but remembering how little entitled I am to offer attentions at such a period I have desisted- she has lived so much in the gay world- that we have seldom met & I do not know whether she has cultivated intimacy with any one disposed to bestow the consolations of friendship in her extremest need- as soon as I have closed this letter I will go to enquire about her, for as she has no kinsfolk near- perhaps the "velvet friends" of happy hours may be too fine for use now- alas! what a picture of human happiness! Young was right, as every days experience proves- Mans hold upon it is as frail, as attenuated as a spiders thread-

The Barrys friends were all wishing that they too could go to Kentucky, and promised many letters- were *they* not surprised at their cousins' union, what would have been thought of such a contract had not immense wealth been in the scale- with a dissipated heartless young man- to balance against a lovely blooming & innocent creature just entering life, with every quality most attractice and capable of ensuring happiness- she has been journeying from city to city to attend the races in which her husband is running horses- sacrificing delicacy & refinement- to pursuits where a man of common feeling would be ashamed to introduce his wife-
. . . .

The president arrived in town yesterday & Black Hawk is expected to morrow- quere- which of the chiefs will excite more attention- interest is divided- the most generous will certainly be bestowed on the Savage- but self is most powerful- and that interest will surround the president where ever he moves-

God Bless you My beloved friends and may it be his will that we meet in joy & happiness. when the visitation has passed away, leaving all we love unscathed- believe me ever most sincerely & affectionately

Your Sister R G--

June 9th 1833

* * *

TO THE SAME

The mention of the cholera epidemic which raged in Kentucky in 1833 fixes the year of this letter omitted from the dating— Adam and Eve—forbidden fruit.

A thousand thanks My dearest Sister for your considerate kindness in writing- it is impossible for me to express my anxiety about you all- may God shield you from surrounding dangers and keep you & my beloved brother & your darling boys all safe from the pestilence- and may all your household & your friends be preserved from its ravages- such heart rending accounts as arrive from the afflicted cities of the west, make us tremble for those exposed to the scourge. I pray it may soon pass from your vicinity and that none you love may suffer. I thank God that you and My dear Ben possess so much courage, and are enabled to sustain yourselves in the trying duties you are called on to perform- remember dearest Maria, that fatigue and anxiety are to be avoided if possible- and do not overtask your strength- I commend the prudence of dear Howard- and the obedience of my Bernard- they must resist all temptations of forbidden fruit and remember the original penalty for such offense brought death into the world- I should like them to see two beautiful pictures- illustrating the temptation of Adam & Eve- and their expulsion from Paradise for disobedience- tell them when they travel into Kentucky and are exhibited they will be able to compare the cherries & Mulberries they refuse to eat with the apple in Eves hand which changed her bright and innocent beauty into the blighted- and bowed down figure, the dark picture represents- but the love your boys bear their mother, will prevent their doing any thing to trouble her- and will keep them safe-

I am grateful to you dear Sister for saying you will keep us informed daily of your condition we shall think of nothing but you while you are beset with cholera . . . . My heart would sink with fears were it not that my confidence in an all Merciful God sustains the hope that He will protect you- a week which must pass before your letters reach me- appears like an age to my anxiety- but I will strive to be patient- I hope your next will be more favorable- take care of yourself My dear Sister & May God bless you- our disappointment is aggravated by the idea of your situation but I trust we shall meet again in happier times, and have nothing to regret- but the delay- when I wrote on Sunday the idea of the cholera's reaching Lexington never occured to me- and the shock was greater to hear it was actually there than it would have been had I heard it was again in our own city- it has been a fatal visitor wherever it has appeared- the news paper of this evening announces 16 cases to have occured in Lexington - I hope the needed and worthy may be spared - and if it must have victims, none suffer but the . . . . . - pardon the presumption- I dare not name a victim of any sort- He who sends, best knows how to direct its course- Adieu dearest I cannot write coherently- but will pray for the preservation of my beloved Brothers family and send them the warmest affection of a Sisters heart

RG

June 11th

* * *

TO THE SAME

Joseph Gratz, a brother, finished the sheet as stated in Miss Gratz' letter—the letter is dated June 16th without the year but on the back the words "Rebecca Gratz, Joseph Gratz June 16 1833" were written by the recipient; this fixes the year.

Death of Mrs. Scott, the mother of Mrs. Benjamin Gratz - a mother's love- words of consolation.

Your grief My dear Sister has entered my heart and I weep for what you suffer and suffer more than I can tell for the danger & desolation by which you & My beloved brother are surrounded- no human reason- nor human aid can avail to speak of comfort or relief- but *he* the great and Merciful God- whose power & glory is manifested in the terrors of far spreading pestilence- and in the succoring love which even in wrath remembers mercy- to him you have poured out your sorrows and I trust his peace has entered your soul- yes My dear Sister, if ye all are spared to each other to rear your tender offspring and imitate the excellent being to whom you have performed the last duty of affection, your hearts will still glow with gratitude, and be comforted - the keenness of that pang which has separated you from a mothers' arms, will make you cling more fondly to your tender children, and guard your life for their sakes. O nothing in this hard world is like a Mothers love! you & I, dearest grew under its shelter and felt all its worth, before we were called on to resign the blessing. You have indeed been suddenly bereaved- but you had the consolation of receiving her blessing- and seeing her depart in peace- in a good old age "removed from evil to come" - Oh My Sister, grieve not for the few years which might have been added to your dear parents life, in the course of nature- since it has pleased God that she should "rest her labours," before her strength yielded to infirmities or the energy of her mind diminished- how dear to memory will all your recollections of her be- her last residence on earth was with you- and your husband administered to her latest wishes the duties of a son- for ever blessed My dear Sister, may you both be here & hereafter- in the love & virtues which unite your hearts to do good wherever the power is given-

My dear Ben's exertions to relieve the afflicted will I hope be visited on him for a blessing, may good angels guard him -

. . . .

I hope tomorrow will bring me a letter from you written in more composure of mind- endeavor to attain composure as a preservation of health- I trust the cholera is abating- it is now two weeks since its dreadful ravages began- and as so many fled, it can have nothing to feed its fury- in thickly populated places its continuance has not been longer than a few weeks.

The post mark of dear Ben's letter was dated 10th and we received it on the 15th - this would have appeared in ordinary times very quick- but five days seems an age when every hour is marked by anxiety- the family are all well- all eagerly anticipating the mail hour- and they send love & loving wishes to you- God bless you, my Sister & Brother, sleeping

& waking my thoughts are with you, I reserve the other page for Jo- embrace your dear children for me and believe me ever your devoted sister

RG-

June 16th-

* * *

TO MR. & MRS. BENJAMIN GRATZ

The cholera—the prophet's appalling vision—physicians the prophets of these degenerate days.

June 26th 1833

Your letters, My beloved sister & brother are such comforts to us, that I cannot too often or too warmly express my thankfulness for your thoughtful kindness- amidst all your sufferings you have still remembered us- and daily when the mail arrives we are collected to receive your greeting and pour out our grateful feelings in silent tears- your preservation through such scenes of havoc, must be alone ascribed to the goodness of God, and that you are enabled to assist the suffering- and bear the deprivations it has pleased *Him* to inflict are further proofs that *He* will not desert you in your hours of trial - before this I hope the dread pestilence has passed away and the air you breathe no longer tainted with its baleful influence. It grieves me to see by the papers that Cholera has appeared at the Springs where many of your citizens sought refuge. I hope their return to their deserted homes will not bring the "Monster" back again.

It has been such an awful far spreading scourge borne on the wings of the wind to all the country of the earth, that one is reminded of the prophet's appalling vision of the "cities without inhabitants & the houses without man, and the land utterly desolate". We shall have an anxious summer for our physicians (the only prophets of these degenerate days) are of opinion that we shall not escape, however as they make no pretensions to inspiration it is wise not to anticipate evil- and thereby mar the blessing that is still in our possession- you will of course be very cautious how & when you return to your own house, use the chloride of lime plentifully, and endeavour to accustom your thoughts to bear the services of strangers- where you have been used to receive the duty of affectionate dependents- I can imagine how severe a trial this will be, tho I have only known the interested and cold hearted exchange of hired servants. . . . .

Pour out all your sorrows to me My dearest Sister, my heart sincerely sympathizes in them all, you have consolations which few daughters can claim- and when you recollect how the few added years of protracted life are burdened by infirmities and shorn of powers both mental & bodily, you can hardly repine that she you loved so dearly departed before her eyes became dim- or her excellent mind decayed- when I think of poor Aunt Bell, and the change that a year, a dying year made in her whole being- how tremblingly the cup of life was held to her lips till she had drained the last drop, I cannot but marvel that her children still mourn- still appear unreconciled to the dispensation which freed her spirit from its worn out tenement.

God bless you, dearest Maria, present my truest, best love to my dear brother and believe me always

Your R G

TO MARIA GIST GRATZ

Year not given in date but the mention of the cholera fixes the year 1833—prediction of medical conquest of the scourge—help in distress.

Your last letter My dear Sister was comforting indeed- the Cholera has disappeared from your city and peace and hope beginning to take up their abode among you- I reiterate your prayer, May you never again witness such a season of desolation and trial and may new sources of comfort and joy spring up around you to recompense the path and shew you the loving kindness of that Heavenly Father who preserved you, your husband and children when the angel of death was mowing down hundreds nay thousands around you- thus far thank God! we have escaped, tho it has been the general opinion that we should be re-visited by the scourge this Summer- I hope good may be derived from this apprehension in using such precautions as conduce to the health of the city- yet from your experience in the west- the wisdom of the wise- has proved folly- perhaps to shew that the will of God rules all things- and the visitations of his power falls on all alike- but dearest your salubrious Lexington will again return to its former character- we do fear that the air will continue poisoned by this pestilence longer than while its commission lasts- altho some of our medical theorists say the Cholera will take its place among other diseases which "flesh is heir to" when it ceases to rage as an epidemic-

On Friday Morning a young woman came to me in great distress, she had a brother living in Lexington of whom they had never heard since the plague began altho they had written several times- he was a mechanic named Byrnes, the person to whose care his letters were directed was dead and they did not know how to get information- she discovered thru the post man, that we had received the latest letters and she came to see if I could in any way relieve the anxiety of her distrest Mother- I was delighted to dry her tears with the news that the disease was disappearing and gave her permission to direct her letters to the care of our dear Ben, promising that I would acquaint him of the reason she had taken that liberty- the person who employed her brother was named Jones- and he was known to Mr Hunt- this was all the poor thing could tell me- but my own feelings made out a case of deepest grief, when I compared our sufferings notwithstanding your daily kindness My beloved sister and brother in writing with what they must have been, had ignorance of your condition been added- I think she said Byrnes was a silver- plater . . . .

Of our journey[1] My dearest Sister- with all its delightful anticipations I have scarcely thought yet you have never been more constantly the objects of love and wishes- if we might securely anticipate an exemption from disease- I should say come to us My dear Sister with your treasures - and in change of scene, strengthen your spirits and health after so many trials- Ben must require repose too and some relaxation from painful excitement- present our tenderest love to him, and embrace the dear boys for me- Hyman is waiting to take my letter to the office- which is so distant that old John makes it a journey

God Bless you my well beloved, with the most heart felt gratitude I return thanks for your health and pray for your continued happiness- ever your own attached

June 30th   RG-

[1] Proposed visit of Rebecca Gratz to Lexington. This took place in the year 1835.

TO THE SAME

Year of letter omitted from date but the reference to the cholera in Lexington fixes the year 1833.
Visit to Saratoga Springs—Montgomery Blair in Philadelphia.

I was greatly in hopes My beloved Sister that we should have heard from you again, before I left home- but tomorrow we start for Saratoga- Miriam Moses Sarah, Horace & Hyman make the party and we shall probably be absent during August- it was long before I could make up my mind to go so far- but the waters of that spring are always of great use to me- and two days journey takes us there- Sister & Ellen are still at the branch- greatly benefited- and Sister Etting looks better since she has walked abroad-

Mrs Stoll is at present at the sea shore, when she returns home I will procure the cap you wrote for- she is one of the most actively benevolent women we have in our community- early last winter she made exertions to establish a repository for work done by reduced gentlewomen[1]- she has placed a respectable family in the shop- and gives her patronage & attention to its concerns- as soon as she arrives, the young woman says she will procure the pattern and have it exactly copied- should it be done before I return our brothers will forward it- The papers give us the comfortable tidings that the Cholera has departed from your land- and I fancy you engrossed by your new scheme of benevolence[2] and prevented from writing- I will not suppose any less agreeable cause for your silence- Montgomery Blair passed a day with

[1] Predecessor of Women's Exchange.
[2] Mrs. Benjamin Gratz founded the Orphan Asylum Society of Lexington.

us on his way to Washington- your pictures were unveiled for his gratification and I promised he should see the letter I expected by that days mail- he looks very well- and the character he bears at the Point would gratify you to hear- military descipline has not spoiled his native sympathy of manner & joyous hilarity- tho the tears glistened in his eyes- when he recurred to all you have suffered- and the dangers you have passed through- tell me dearest Sister if I can give you any further useful information respecting your orphan society- when I return I will collect as many of the early reports as I can find- which may shew how ours was governed in its infancy- if you are fortunate in getting a good matron one half the difficulty will be avoided- . . . . farewell My dear- dear Sister the tenderest love- and the warmest wishes for your happiness fill the heart of your affectionate

R Gratz.

July 28th

* * *

TO THE SAME

A delightful journey—a visit to West Point—social life among the cadets—fortitude in adversity.

Sept 1st 1833-

We arrived home My dear Maria on Wednesday and found your two delightful letters- for which I hardly know how to express my thanks- we found Sally Minis[1] and her father[2] in New York who accompanied us home- and continued here until this morning, when they proceeded to

[1] See page 80, Note 1.
[2] Isaac Minis of Savannah, Ga.

Baltimore where the Dr is stationed, he received orders at Washington, which prevented his delivering your letter in person- Sally has become a lovely woman and seems to have laid the lessons of adversity to heart, she is intelligent pious, & amiable, yet cheerful, still idolizing her brother- and dwelling on his unfortunate plight- which had nearly destroyed them all- we took a very pleasant journey from Saratoga proceeding to Lake George & Champlaine as high as Burlington thence following the courses of the Green- White-& Connecticut Rivers through a beautiful country along the Valley of Connecticut the scenery along the whole distance is beautified- sometimes wild & uncultivated- with majestic woodland mountains, then varied by all the luxuriance of successful husbandry and the teeming fields alive with busy mowers- and the bright clear rivers branching off in fertilizing streams in so many curvings & windings till you are quite puzzled to trace its entire paths- on Mount Holyoke we met some travellers who were concerned to see how *much trouble* the Connecticut River took in its crooked course- and had a mind to cut a passage straight from one point to another, and let the water through- the extensive prospect of 160 miles suggesting no more magnificent simile to their well furnished imagination than that of a handsome carpet of various colours- yes said Miriam an in grain carpet- and then was vexed, that she had been so common place as to make a pun when the clouds were beneath her feet- and her admiration ready to soar with Eagles in their upward flight. When we reached New York, she & Becky could not resist the temptation to a Ball at West Point- to which *Cousin* Montgomery[1] had invited them. and their Uncle Moses offered his escort so I left them behind, and they have

[1] See page 43, Note 1.

written that nothing could be more charming than the moonlight scene- the grey coated gallants and the tasteful brilliancy of the ball-room- at home I found quite a different scene. Jac was alone- Jo had been a fortnight absent- and my servants were sick- Elizabeth had just under gone the operation of cupping- and my frequent visits to her chamber have broken up many associations that were on the nib of my pen- and are now dying on the ink-rag- no matter, a freer home will bring me to you again, My beloved Sister to tell of my wanderings and to wish - Oh how vainly wish they could have been directed Westward- to be with you at Canewood My own dear Maria, has long very long been the wish of my heart- I venerated your sainted parent, and in the scene of her benevolent influence- where I always imagined her in the sphere of active duties- and where you grew so near the perfection of her fondest wishes- would be worth all the journeys I could make on this side the Mountains. Would to God! your example My dear Sister, were written on the hearts of some of our relations & friends who have lost parents dear to them indeed- but not more loved- more missed- than she you cherished with such filial devotion- and mourn with such true & chastened sorrow- would our poor cousins permit religion & reason to speak- they would hear a voice of condemnation for self abandonment- and rebellion against Almighty wisdom and fear to incur the judgment of some other sacrifice to their persevering grief, ... if they would go into the country- and see in the face of nature, how much there is to love in the works of God, to feel the sweet breath impregnated with odours from a thousand fields visit their cheeks with health & a living sense of enjoyment, they would not pine in silence- that He who created such a world, had been pleased to recall the virtuous spirit of their Mother- to a still better & higher state of happiness, surely it is only necessary to love and confide in God, to render us submissive to his laws & when the weary find repose after the toil of a well spent day - . . . .

Susan has fortunately returned from W. Point where she had been on a visit during August- I am glad you have heard from Jo Hart[1]- every body speaks well of him- who have seen him abroad- I do not doubt he will take advantage of his opportunities of improvement- Montgomery is a credit to your bringing up- the girls are quite proud of his superiority to the rest of his class- we found our sisters well- . . . . Adieu My dear Maria, I have been so often interrupted that I do not know what connection there may be between the pages of my letter- but I have determined not to select Sunday morning in future for writing- May God bless you all, with the choicest of his good gifts- and keep you ever in his care- ever your sister R G-

* * *

TO THE SAME

The Day of Atonement—boarding school an epitome of fashionable life.

Sept 21st 1833

It is three weeks my own dear Sister since I have written to you- but my thoughts have visited you every day- and my love accompanies you every hour and dwells with you all unceasingly- since my return home my household has been damaged for the want of servants and the duties of nurse superceded to that of overseer has kept me busy and made me stupid- so I had compassion on you, and kept silence-

[1] See page 123, Note 2.

perhaps too, I was not willing to appear before you under such disadvantages for you have said so much to raise my vanity- that I could not more effectually prove how I had profited by your commendations than by keeping my dullness out of view- but there are times, dear, when the veil must be dropped and our real characters be seen in all their deformities- such a period for self examination approaches. To morrow will be the day of Atonement- and tho' I believe the Eye of God is upon us every day with the same unerring judgment- the same pardoning Mercy- it is well when we search our own hearts, and desire to acknowledge our sins- that we look for motives as well as actions, and when I thought of offering an apology to you, the truth came so straight before me that I could not help telling you, your praise was so sweet to my heart, that knowing it was undeserved was hardly enough to make me relinquish it- and I rather chose not to write at all- than to do it in a manner to tire you quite-

Now my home anxiety has abated I begin to feel a little concerned for the want of your accustomed letter and tho' Dear Bens letter to Hyman informed that you were still at Canewood- and I can realize how fully & engrossingly your mind is occupied in scenes so hallowed to tender recollections- so full of the tenderest and dearest thoughts & memories- yet My Beloved Sister I must covet a little very little of your attention- just to say that your mind is recovering its equanimity and that your dear boys & yourself are well -

Jo returned about 10 days ago and Jac, this afternoon- so our family party is complete- & Sally Minis is still our guest- her brother was charmed with his visit to you, and brought away such impressions, as you never fail to make on your visitors- I am ashamed to confess that I have seen little of your country woman Mrs McIlvaine, for in truth Elizabeths illness has prevented my receiving any company & I have not sought her again- I received a letter from Mr Blair the other day, and expect to have your niece in Phila this winter as a pupil to Mrs Sigorgnes. Sarah is delighted with the anticipation of having her as a companion- tho' I believe she will not return to school again- there seems to be so much required at home to complete her education- that a year or two is necessary to devote to study before a young lady makes her debut, and all Sarah's class mates left her last winter- she is full of vivacity & enthusiasm & I believe a boarding school is too much an epitome of fashionable life to be the safest place for regulating the taste & feelings of a girl approaching womanhood- God Grant I may be successful in this arduous task with my sweet Sarah she resembles her mother in so many points that I am constantly reminded of my promise & my loss- . . . . how comes on your Orphan Society? a Young Woman several years Teacher in ours (Miss Haydock) who was everyway qualified to take charge of an institution is somewhere in your state- she went to visit a Brother living in Smithland or Smithton Ky- and just when we were expecting her back- received intelligence that she was going to be married- should she be in Lexington, she might be induced to accept a situation in your asylum & would be very valuable- I did not hear the name of her intended husband- and mention her because if she visits your city she will probably make herself known to you- and may suggest some useful hints in the way of her profession- tell My beloved brother & your children how devotedly I love them- and accept dearest Maria the warm affections of your Sisters heart Adieu Yr RG

TO THE SAME

The year omitted from date of this letter, but the reference to the tour of Black Hawk the Indian chieftain establishes the year 1833 as the date of the letter. After the defeat of Black Hawk and his warriors by General Henry Atkinson on August 2, 1832 a treaty was signed on September 21. Black Hawk was sent to Fortress Monroe where he was confined a short time. In June, 1833 he was conducted by the Government through some of the Eastern cities, to which tour reference is made in the letter.

Reception to Henry Clay—Fondness of Americans for parades and shows—Washington Irving—"a life of usefulness is a life of enjoyment".

Philadelphia

Oct 12th

It is long My dearest Maria since I have written to you- or to any one- I am ashamed of Myself for such a defection of duty- and if I were not conscious that I suffer more than anyone else from it should not be able to offer any apology- but sins of this kind bring their own punishment- and I know you will pardon me when you hear that my mind has been so engrossed with common place affairs that you would not have been able to extract an idea from a whole sheet full had I even traced the impressions or related the events of a whole month- to you My Sister this will appear incredible- for you can find "books in the running brooks sermons in stones & good in everything"- and I doubt not teaching a dull irish servant & fixing carpets would have suggested some amusement to lighten the toil, but I will not put your patience to the trial, of following me through this drudgery- I have now a better prospect in My household, Elizabeth has recovered & gone into the country to recruit.

. . . . . .

I this morning met Mrs Barry, who told me she had recently seen our dear Ben, and that you were still at Canewood- Mr Blair wrote to me some days ago that he thought we might hope for a visit from you this Autumn, pray dearest Sister confirm this good news- if you can bring all and spend the winter with us we should indeed be happy- we will go to visit your Sister in Washington during the season- and try each of us to beguile you of your cares- do not postpone the journey (if you can come) until the roads become bad & the river falls. We have talked of it so often lately that we do not like to think there are any obstacles in the way of its accomplishment- do not think us selfish or unreasonable to subject you to so long a journey for our gratification, if your husband & children are with you, you can be at home here, and you know how devotedly we all love you, change of scene will be of benefit to your spirits too- your charming little niece Elizabeth Blair[1] has been here nearly a fortnight and is quite a favorite at school- Sarah goes there frequently, as a visitor- but ceased with the August vacation to attend as a scholar- She will study at home this winter, and thinks your society & counsel would make a woman of her- Your renowned Country man Mr Clay is expected here immediately and all honors are preparing for his reception- I think Hamilton is right- we are certainly too fond of parades, & exaggerated praise- the Presidents tour last Summer, was comparable to Queen Elizabeth's progress through her dominions as described in Kenilworth- Black Hawk had as many in his train- and when ever a political character ap-

[1] The daughter of Mr. and Mrs. Francis Preston Blair and niece of Mrs. Benjamin Gratz, a sister of Mrs. Blair.

pears he is to be followed & fed and the trumpet sounded throughout the land- you ask me who Kennedy[1] is, that he should be classed with the honored & observed- he is the author of a tale cailed "Swallow-Barn"- and is preparing for another & he says a better work for the press- he is moreover a very gentlemanly personage, and is blest with an intelligent & interesting wife- Washington Irving appeared too happy & too much engaged with the great ones of the land to write much at present- he has gone to Washington again- if his old spirit of inspiration comes on him there- he might find subjects for sketches as piquant as any in Salmagundi- but I rather think his chastened judgment will view them more in sadness, than in mirth . . . .

I wish I could send you some of Mrs Stoll's beautiful flowers- she has a perfect paradise of fruits & flowers growing around her- and her house is the palace of taste and neatness- and herself the beautifying genius, who plans & directs the whole- Mrs S-- is a bright example that a life of usefulness is a life of enjoyment- she is a widow- that name gives an idea of sadness & suffering- but when you look on her placid countenance, see her ever employed for the poor, or in some elegant work of art- and know that her ample fortune is made a blessing to thousands you cannot help respecting her, and rejoicing that her liberal hands are strengthened in such a good cause- she told me yesterday how much she had heard of our dear Ben's good works last summer- and drew tears from my eyes by her just praise- it is a luxury to weep such tears- all who come from Kentucky tell the same tale- . . . . dearest & beloved Sister & Brother accept my warmest love & best wishes for your happiness ever your own RG

[1] John P. Kennedy (1795-1870) Secretary of the Navy in Fillmore's Cabinet. He was a native of Maryland, of whose house of delegates he was a member 1820-23. In 1832 he published his novel, Swallow-Barn, whose scene is laid in Virginia in the eighteenth century.

TO THE SAME

Anticipations—"it is hard trusting to wishes that have no sure foothold"—Hamilton's "Men and Manners"—English travellers and America—Mrs. Henry Clay in Philadelphia—Charles Hoffman's western tour.

I have been very patient My dear Sister and waited at least ten days longer than I might reasonably . . . .[1] a letter from you, but none has yet arrived . . . .[1] begin to grow uneasy at the unusual silence- dear Ben has not written either- Sarah whose hopes are most buoyant, conjectures that you may be on the road, and are going to give us an agreeable surprise, she & Elizabeth Blair have so many bright visions afloat in which you are always conspicuous that they talk themselves into the belief that they will be realized- and I almost regret that I cannot cheat myself into the same persuasion- but when one has trodden so long the beaten path of life, it is hard trusting to wishes that have no sure foothold, so pray you, give me a little leg of hope to step on, and be sure I shall meet you half way- and not give place even to our glad nieces in happy anticipations-

I have been reading Hamiltons "Men & Manners" and am quite provoked that he should have lent his talents to such an unfair purpose as that of misrepresenting America for political Views- because it seems as if no English traveller can speak the truth of us. Trelawney[1] has been entertained here too, and will no doubt issue a book of caricatures as soon as he crosses the Atlantic- it is quite amusing to hear our young ladies from the sea shore & Saratoga, talk of the foreigners they met with in their summer excursions- one

---
[1] Paper torn.
[2] Edward John Trelawney, the friend of Byron and Shelley.

told me of a Young Irishman just arrived in July and went down to Long branch, where a large party were collected who enjoyed themselves in their own way- and were as merry as good health good spirits and freedom from all restraint could make them- until he arrived- but he eyed them with such inquisitive glances- was so observant, & sinister, that they felt whenever his attention was directed towards them, as if an invisible note book was . . . .[1]

I went to see Mrs Clay when she was in town, and was very kindly received by her, she spoke affectionately of you all, and there was such genuine frankness in her manner, that I felt drawn towards her, and if she had not been surrounded by the great folks of our great city should have been pleased to keep my seat, as long as decorum permitted- however, I suppose Mr C- will sojourn longer on his return from the north, and then hope to see her again-

Should our young friend Charles Hoffman find his way to Lexington this winter let me bespeak your kind offices for him, he is on a western tour for literary pursuits that is, he is going to write letters for publication in the American of which he is a Junior editor- he goes through Ohio into Michigan- and return to the Ohio river- thence down to N. Orleans, but his sketches will be incomplete if he omits Lexington and other towns in Kentucky, not immediately in his course & I think he has too much taste to pass them by- you will find him so agreeable & clever that I do not hesitate to put you to the trouble of entertaining him- poor Julia has not only to part with him, her chief companion, but is kept at home to nurse George, who in a deer hunt, deposited the contents of a gun in his own arm- tell Bernard when he teaches Howard to shoot, he must manage things better-
. . . .

[1] Paper torn.

The girls at Sigorgnes had a fancy party last Saturday Even'g- Jacob was invited, and put on the dress of a french peasant- Elizabeth personated a sailor boy, Miss Cass a gipsey, and little D'Orval an old gentleman- this was a school room frolick, which ended at 10 o'clock- your niece has already found her way to Mrs S-s heart, and is a general favorite at school & at home, for she is permitted to pass two days with Sarah every week- and sleeps with her Saturday night- . . . . Pray My dear Sister let me hear from you soon. I long for some sayings & doings of the sweet boys- some account of my brother & yourself- your intentions for the winter- give us the blessed hope of seeing you all here- at any rate My own dear Maria, let me hear that you are well and happy- present My best respects to Mrs Bledsoe[1]- are you still at Canewood? to my dear Ben give my best love embrace Your children for me, and believe in the entire affection of your attached Sister RG

Oct:28th 1833.

* * *

TO THE SAME

Thoughts penned in the shadow of the closing year—New Year wishes—"Sweet sixteen"—happiness and content—this world and the future life—efforts at conversion—eulogies—freeing slaves—noble spirits under a sable skin.

You have taught me one thing My dear Sister and it is right you should profit by it- to scan my letters before I send them, and if they will not bear a second perusal at home not to send them on their destined course- and so with a sheet full of idle thoughts which I penned in the shadow of a closing Year- When my Dove had gone forth and could find

[1] Mrs. Jesse Bledsoe, a sister of Mrs. Benjamin Gratz.

no rest for the sole of its foot- and a flood of anticipated evils were overwhelming my (what you call regulated) mind- I have taken counsel by your example and condemned the paper to the fire- How many out pourings of the heart are thus devoted! traced "in tears that coursed down the writers cheek fast as the periods from their fluent pens" - but this I cannot withhold because I experienced its power that writing to you acted like the harp of David on the vexed spirit of the King- and by the time my paper was full- I looked for the grief of which I complained and found it not- but I remember that your affection and My dear Brothers sometimes construes silence into causes for anxiety, and so as I do not know that any one has written since the year commenced, I just come to greet you with warm wishes for your continued happiness through many circles of revolving time- and to tell you that all you love here, love you most truly & devotedly- that you are the theme of every days discourse- and cited as the point to which all our Young folks direct their ambition! Sarah said the other night- that Aunt Maria was the only being she would be willing to change herself into- now when you take into consideration the bright visions which float in the enthusiastic brain at sweet Sixteen- the aspirations after unattainable bliss & perfections of all kind you will appreciate how highly you & yours are held- I think you will be delighted in the improvement of your little favorite- she has so much brightness- so much joy in her heart that one can scarcely wish to see with other eyes than hers the map she sketches for her lifes journey yet what says experience? you will answer, nothing to pluck one feather from the wing of hope for- and I- My Sister- with the memory of many sorrows and disappointments may still encourage her thus far, that if she misses the favorite path to happiness she may find another leading to content. I can never realize the picture some moralists draw of this good world- calling it by such hard names- that one would think God had withdrawn his favor from the beautiful planet he created in love- and bestowed all *his* treasures on another State in which the beings he has placed in this must centre all their joys- and how can we mixed creatures of clay be fitted for celestial transports if in this our probationary sphere no glimpse of heaven can be made visible, no touch of happiness enter into our hearts- the soul that is within us would not be imprisoned during all our natural lives in such a world and after be fitted for such a heaven, as we can conceive of- if this blessed earth were such a den of care & sorrow-

I received a note from one of my neighbours a few days ago, requesting the loan of *my* bible, as she found according to *hers* the time was *near at hand* when the Jews would be gathered to their own land- on returning it she expressed in another note her joy at finding my bible the same she used- she begged me not to let the light that was in me be darkness - but daily to examine myself- and have regard to my soul - by studying the scriptures etc- and she is so earnest that I cannot help being obliged to her- tho she sent me more books than I can read- and should try to canonize herself by my conversion- thank God I have the law & the prophets and am willing to hear them

I do not know how long My dear Sister, I should continue to write on, if I were not very disagreeably interrupted by some ladies of the Orphan Society- who wish me to add something to the annual report- before tomorrows meeting- a manager died last summer and alas! I had forgotten her- now her friends come to me for an epitaph, do not begin my dear Sister secretary or you establish a precedent- we have lost some members, whom I loved- and whose services deserved commemorating- but to be obliged to say something for every one of the twenty four- to whom perhaps belonged no further notice than that they lived- was a member & died- is too hard a task, particularly when you have congratulated yourself that the board had accepted your work, and it was done- I beg you will send me your book of laws- of which acknowledge the authorship to Miriam- we are about to revise our school regulations and should be glad to borrow such as would suit us from you-

And now I am mentioning your letter to M- let me tell you how I wept for joy that I had such a brother as your dear Husband to buy that afflicted Mother & daughter from the base servitude to which they were doomed, and my knowledge of his feelings & character made me anticipate the issue before I turned the page on which with such sweet words you record the act- I hope the poor blacks will prove worthy of his mercy and fit to supply some of your losses- If God did not allow of some noble spirits inhabiting a sable skin her husband & old master would have changed complexions- . . . .

God Bless you my own dear Sister- may a long life of happiness be yours- and every New Year find you loving & beloved, as you are at this present time- our Sisters & brothers greet you- and the young folks send love & respect- again accept the benediction of your attached

R Gratz

Jany 6th 1834

TO THE SAME

Young people's capers - the wealth of contentedness - an ideal woman—Southern ladies—the Reverend Isaac Leeser—Mrs. Mary Woolstonecraft Shelley's "The Last Man".

Feb 2nd 1834

I cannot tell you My dear Sister, how I have longed for a letter from you until the desire absolutely begot such an anxiety that I fancied a thousand untoward causes for your silence- yesterday brought a letter to Miriam and I know you will soon again take up your pen- but you speak of langour, or drooping spirits- and I feel as if I should love to be with & cheer you- I wish you could have seen our merry nieces at the breakfast table this morning, enjoying the fruits of their own tricks- it seems they had planned their mischief some days before at Mrs Sigorgnes- and last nights storm gave peculiar effect to their design- they deranged their Uncles & Horaces & Rosas beds, and then crept quietly to their own- this morning the affair was discussed with great glee, and while they were triumphing its complete success- Horace slipped out of the room and requested the cook to suspend the operation of the griddle and the girls sat waiting very patiently after all had finished their breakfast but themselves until they discovered a counter trick had been played on them- they have now gone to church to hear Mr Furness & I hope they will be sobered by dinner time & mentioning Mr F reminds me of a visit I paid his interesting wife lately and the affectionate enquiries she made for you, the poor Lady has her patience & other virtues tried by a tedious disease her only daughter is suffering under- white swelling on her ancle which will probably make her lame for life- she is one of those persons whose contentedness sheds an influence over all that approach her- the elements are so blended "in her character & disposition as to produce a perfect harmony"- if Cowper had given such a wife to his clergyman the picture would have been complete. Dr Hays is one of her favorites and she seems very much interested in his approaching happiness- it is yet to be proved what kind of a husband he will make- I think Sally will require a great deal of attention- she has been accustomed to much devotion from her family & friends, southern ladies are treated with much gallantry by all their male associates, and she has been a favorite abroad & eldest sister at home- she has much dignity with sweetness of manner- and as the Dr enjoys but a written courtship, I expect his bride will be a little divinity in his sight- .... There is another evil under the sun that has been making havoc in our city varioloid- poor Mr Leeser is one of its present subjects, his attack has been unmitigated small pox, and tho his life & eye sight have been spared I am told his countenance will bear many marks of its ravages- he has always been so sensitive on the subject of personal disadvantages- that his former humility will appear like vanity to his present state- and unless some Desdemona shall arise to see his visage in his mind- all his future expectations must be confined to solitary studies[1] - .... Gratz brought me a list of Morrison College[2] students the other day, to shew me dear Bernard & Howards names- and he was very proud of his cousins- could hardly believe that Howard was learning Latin already- I had a letter from Mr Blair last week, and E heard from Montgomery- he is a most attentive correspondent to his sister- you should have seen how her face bright-

---

[1] Isaac Leeser remained a bachelor.
[2] A Lexington boys' academy.

ened when she told his standing at the Point- in a few weeks Henry Hart will be in too, and I am sure you will rejoice again to see this favorite youth with all the improvements his travel has bestowed. I hope our beloved Ben enjoys health, thru all the labours of his various duties- and I am sure the more important his public services[1] are in the land of his adoption, the better you will be pleased. Thank God, whereever his virtues are tested they are found sufficient May he be successful in all he undertakes with such pure motives, and ever as happy as he deserves to be- with some people this would be such niggard justice that it might be doubted whether it were a friendly wish- but with your husband My dear Maria it makes him as blest as mortal can desire to be- . . . . We have been reading Mrs Shelleys "Last Man" it is worth more than her other book- but still her genius runs wild of good principles- God Bless you, My dear Sister believe in the love of your own RG

* * *

TO THE SAME

Spurzheim's "Phrenology"—phrenology as applied to education—"Nature is our first and last love"—the imitation of God—fashionable society—a fancy dress party.

When we suffer under any unusual deprivation or anxiety, we are apt to look into ourselves for a cause- it is now full two months, since my eyes have been gladdened My Dear

---

[1] Benjamin Gratz held many offices of public trust in Lexington; he was a trustee of Transylvania University; one of the incorporators of the first railroad west of the Allegheny mountains and the second in the United States, namely the Lexington and Ohio, running from Lexington to Portland; he was a member of the first city council, Lexington having been incorporated as a city in 1832; he was a director of the branch of the Bank of Kentucky established in Lexington in 1834; a member of the first Board of Directors of the Northern Bank of Kentucky founded in 1835; etc.; etc.

Maria with the sight of a letter from you, and I have wearied myself with conjectures, could I have offended you? No, for not a thought has entered my mind- not a feeling lodged in my heart that could have given utterance to an offensive word- are you sick? no, thank God, of that we are assured by persons who have seen our dear Ben, within two or three weeks- .... are you tired of a dull correspondent? then why do Montgomery & Mr B complain likewise of your silence? - I will ask no more harassing questions- but believing you must have good reasons which in time will be told shall go on My dear Sister to prate of other things in which I hope you may be interested- I am reading a delightful book which if you have not seen already, I will send you "Spurzheim's Phrenology". I was rather prejudiced against this science some years ago from hearing it treated philosophically by persons who used it as a cant word of which they understood very little- but happening to meet with a work on education by this same author- and the interesting account of his character- his visit to this country & his death- gave me a keener relish to enjoy his great work and if the study of this theory can be applied to the purpose of education every parent and teacher ought to be a phrenologist- then if perfectibility cannot be attained in human nature- still many evil propensities may be repressed and good ones applied to their most useful results- how many difficulties too might be saved in choosing professions for boys when the whole map of the mind is drawn in legible marks on the skull- one must however be well skilled before they determine- for my part I can only see developments where I know characters- The spring has opened here in the most beautiful appearances- vegetation is prematurely advanced I fear, our rose-bushes are in leaf & the willows quite green already. I always loved the spring- but now as I advance in years it appears still more lovely- nature is our first & last love, for we outgrow taste for every pleasure less enduring and less pure- or rather we have a portion in our selves which harmonizes with all the work of the creators hands - the green earth- our mother & our tomb- the air we breathe- the heavens to which we aspire- all commune with our affections and draw us to the worship of God- would that we amazed at the wonders we witness in creation- and the all enduring benevolence manifested in the care with which every creature is provided for- honored the image we bear by making ourselves more perfect- and imitate his mercy in our intercourse with our fellow creatures-

We hear of nothing but hard times among merchants & politicans whilst the fashionable circles make the most of the few opportunities they have for frolicks- where you used to admire forest trees on Girards lot- stately edifices are now erected, and inhabited by some who are fortunately out of the chances of trade and can give parties. Mrs C. . . . .'s fancy ball was one of the rarities of the season, and admirably adapted to the times, for the sanction of its title was given to any costume, caprice might adopt- Becky chose a gypsy. She looked very pretty in her black and yellow cotton dress- blue apron- red cloak & chip hat- while her fingers were covered with borrowed (or stolen) jewels. Sarah had the dress of a real Squaw- presented by Col Craighan to Mrs Campbell- it was scarlet cloth very richly ornamented and she was painted & acted quite in character- many of the company wore the brocades of their grandmothers and every other grotesque conceit was introduced to give variety & effect- I was not there but saw some of the masquerade and have been amused by the detail of some well sustained parts and other failures- . . . .

The Hays' are anticipating a new scene of happiness for the

Dr who I believe will bring us his bride in May- poor Sally has had another domestic calamity to mourn- her Uncle was killed in a duel- he was a young man brought up in the navy rather wild, and as it proved reckless of good counsel, and religious obligation- his antagonist was a relation of amiable character & engaged to be married- so that the whole weight of this dreadful affair falls on his own family-

I pray you My dear Sister, return to your good habits, and let us again be cheered by your charming letters- the children are sure it is all the post offices fault they are sure your letters are lost- because you never were so long silent before- they all send love & pleading to you- . . . . tell my dearest Ben, how painfully anxious we are to hear from him when you do not write- and accept for both the truest affection of your devoted Sister RG

March 9th 1834

* * *

TO THE SAME

Year of letter omitted from date but the mention of the introduction of Sally Minis, the bride of Dr. Isaac Hays, to the family, fixes the year of the letter as of 1834. The marriage had taken place May 7th of that year. The mention of an early romance in Washington's life, namely, his betrothal to Miss Gist, an aunt of Mrs. Benjamin Gratz, lends an especial interest to this letter.

Criticism of "fairs" in the interest of charity - interpretation of Scripture "prophecies" - an abandoned visit to Lexington - Charles Hoffman's book "A Winter in the West" - Washington the man - Colonel Gist, the father of Mrs. Benjamin Gratz - a forgotten romance in the life of Washington - American biography - Gouverneur Morris' Letters.

I am vexed with myself Dearest Maria, when I leave your letters unanswered- and yet ashamed of the unworthy returns I make to them- I had just dispatched my last when yours arrived- the heads of the family were collected to do honor to the new member, and she claimed the privilege of sharing Aunt Maria's love, as she intends to be a very dutiful niece- she has obtained universal suffrage, even Aunt Reyne[1] has been invited to a place of honor in the Drs household, and the old lady with her most insinuating manner declared it the happiest day of her life, that she prepared "the fatted calf" for the feast of welcome to the bride. Sally[2] possesses a good deal of discrimination and frankness- which gives her influence exactly where it will produce the happiest results- already she has drawn her husband more into the bosom of his own family- and our sister realizes that she has gained a daughter & regained a son by this union- nearly all her family are at present in Phila so that she has not even a regret for familiar faces in the change she has made, she is quite in love with her neat little establishment and promises herself a great deal of pleasure in becoming a good housekeeper, which for the indulged daughter of a southern family is an entire new character- however a poor mans wife must take a part of his burden, and as he is travelling upward, the hardship & privations are light to young shoulders while a fair prospect is in view and affectionate encouraging friends bear them company-

You really My dear Sister have been suffering in a good cause, and illustrated most emphatically that the offices of Charity are not all engrossed by the Church & fancy Fair gossiping so much in fashion throughout our country- I am

[1] Mrs. Solomon Etting, a sister of Mrs. Michael Gratz, and daughter of Joseph Simon of Lancaster, Pa.
[2] Mrs. Isaac Hays.

glad that our opinions are the same of that subject- It appears a very exceptionable service which employs the rich to do work for "fairs" - which might be so much more useful to the poor - many ingenious ladies in very reduced circumstances supply our shops with fancy articles the proceeds of which maintain their families- a "Fair" is advertised to forward a scholarship for some church, or pay for an asylum attached to a religious institution- and all the weak minded, and pious females for miles round & in the city spend months in manufacturing trifles. Music & confectionery, are introduced, some complimentary verses or popular oration is recited, and vanity supplies the further incitements to complete success- a whole week was consumed in the public business of one of these Fairs last spring at Washington Hall - a large sum of money received - and many just complaints murmured by regular vendors- while Mothers & prudes were shocked that young & Innocent girls should be bartering pin cushions & smiles at these sanctified tables at an expense of modesty far beyond the price of gold-

Your friends will remember the Fair- not for the charity that brought them to it- but for that which they received at your hands- and if they do not apply it to more extensive use than building a church- they have not yet caught a speck of that divine spirit, of which religion is composed-

I admire your ingenious interpretations of the prophesies which tho' too free for theologians, are practically good and while acting on such principles you have a right to draw authority from the Scriptures- if every one would follow your example the reign of peace would indeed be universal, and tho the Lion & Lamb should retain their dispositions in the natural world- the human family would derive all the happiness a union of strength & gentleness could obtain in the moral one- Cadet C Fry has been to see the girls and offers to carry letters direct to Lexington, so I shall give him a packet for our Dear Ben that has been sometime waiting- shall I acknowledge it My Dear Sister- I have been cherishing the hope for a whole month that I should be its bearer myself but Hyman could not leave home, and thus, week after week of the summer has gone- until I have been obliged to relinquish the idea altogether - I could not trust myself to write for fear my wishes should escape me, and you share my disappointment- now My Sister I must hang my hopes on a more distant period- but still shall look for their realization in Kentucky- Elizabeth is in high spirits at the thought of seeing her brother and accompanying him home, we shall miss her greatly- she is so general a favorite, Henry Hart is still at Washington - he is much improved in ease of manner, and was in fine spirits the day he returned here- his eyes sparkled on recognizing your likeness in Sullys best work- Charles Hoffman too was overflowing with gratitude for your kindness- you made him feel as if he was indeed with old friends- he spoke of your boys- your house- and all the elegance & hospitality exercised towards him- he is so much pleased- that he has talked of making a home for his family in the west at some future period- he is now compiling a book from his letters- a "Winter in the West" which I hope will enable him to make another tour- his health was certainly improved- we are reading "Spark's Washington"- the 2 & 3 vols only are out- the first will contain his Life- pray My dear, furnish him with that interesting portion of Washingtons biography which relates to your Aunt for I fear he has slender materials of exhibiting the sentiment of his character- Mrs Washington having destroyed all his letters addressed to her, shortly before her death- now everything great and noble, in the Soldier & Statesman may be presented to our respect & veneration- but it requires some touches of human affections and passions to complete the man, and give him a place in our hearts- he writes most affectionately to Col Gist[1]- and my imagination constantly runs on his fair Sister,[2] tho Mr Sparks is evidently ignorant of this attachment- he speaks of a humble attachment, which prevented his being endangered by the attractions of some inmates of the Fairfax family- and the letters which relate to his Marriage are so passionless that I am sure there was a corner of his heart locked up to the memory of his first betrothed- that generous self devoted being whose very rejection was a proof of superiority which could not have been lost on such a heart as Washingtons- now Maria, if among old family papers you could find but a single note of his to your Aunt, or any record of their engagement- it would give such interest to the Editors task- that you ought not withhold it- The mass of American biography now collecting will be a valuable addition to our literature- If you have not read "Gouverneur Morris" I would recommend it as finely written & excellent letters- present My best love, to our dear Ben, and your lovely boys- charge a rainy afternoon with all this scribble- and believe I would not have been so unreasonable if a private conveyance had not offered- the sun now appears and an engagement abroad saves you from further tediousness which this fair sheet might invite- God bless you My beloved- . . . .

[1] Col. Christopher Gist, the grandfather of Mrs. Benjamin Gratz, who served with Washington in "Braddock's War" in 1755.
[2] There was a tradition in the Gist family that a sister of Col. Christopher Gist, who was an intimate friend and companion-in-arms of Washington, was his early sweetheart. Was she possibly the mysterious "Lowland beauty" who is spoken of by biographers of Washington as having won his attachment in his youth? Mary Bland, Lucy Grimes and Betsy Fauntleroy and others have been mentioned in this connection. See *George Washington, the Image and the Man*, by W. E. Woodward, New York, 1926, p. 39

I embrace you all with my whole heart and am devotedly
your Sister RG

June 29th

* * *

TO THE SAME

Shakespeare, the interpreter of the human heart—"the commonplace actions of men in city life"—marriage of Fanny Kemble, the famous English actress.

It is three weeks this day My dear Maria since the last dispatches were sent from Boston Row to you and then we were anxiously expecting letters from Kentucky for whether our Brother was at home or still dragged from your side by business we were ignorant- and various conjectures have been hazarded where to locate you during this long suspension of intercourse- Montgomery paid his visit to Washington, and could not instruct us from any recent dates- and so I have resolved this morning that you shall be retaliated on- and as "a fellow feeling makes us wondrous kind" sit down to let you see "the goods & ills that chequer our every day life" cannot exclude you from a participation of my thoughts & society- verily dear Sister it would take a nice casuist to decide whether this be kindness or not, for one is so apt to do (without reflecting) what is agreeable to themselves that they should wait till the result is known before they take credit for any act thus performed, and if I proceed in this style shall rather exercise your patience, than satisfy your judgement- still you will say the practice of virtue is beneficial- and what woman can deny from her own experience that patience is a virtue?- and so you have helped me to the conclusion that even this letter may be made profitable-

Shakespeare has beautifully expressed the powers of meditation "to find books in the running brooks, sermons in stones & good in everything" and few of us (tho less inspired) but may trace back in our minds that spark of divinity which may be kindled to our own edification, where no visible object has been present to illuminate our faculties- does not this encourage us to believe that nature has done greatly for us? when we feel, what others have power to express the cultivation and improvement of faculties prove they are blessings not only to their possessors, but to their species- as long as language is understood Shakespeare will commune with the human heart, and will reach out a fellowship, which no distance of time can change, for nature is always the same- . . . .

If the July thermometer has been in less extremes with you, I shall hardly make you understand the complaints of your Georgia friends, who complain of our sunshine, as if that planet removed his night cap during the summer for their accomodation to the south- but they have gone to Saratoga, and will hardly credit that we are so cool & pleasant here, that we shut out the night air, and even add another garment to our wardrobe for the last 2 or 3 days- I have rarely seen a more lovely family of girls than Mrs Minis' she has left two with Sally who are very interesting & intelligent and my little namesake is a beauty- they make me think of your darling boys whose independent spirits would contrast finely with these females of their own age- do dear Sister let me hear something of them soon- in asking this I put you on your generosity- for I have nothing in return to offer you- the common place actions of men & women in city life offer nothing in interest to be compared to the developements of young minds- they are in pursuit of amusement or gain- and the excitement of political or professional pursuits are so involved in prejudices & passions of personal natures on one side, or flirtations & gallantry on the other, that they must be witnessed to be partaken- . . . .

The marriage of Fanny Kemble made some talk for a few days- she went to church, and the ceremony was performed on a Saturday morning just before the steamboat started in which the party embarked for New York, at which place her performance was announced for Monday evening- some passengers said she wept all the way up to Bristol- her marriage was inserted in the papers- and it was thought indecorous that the bride should appear on the stage by her former name, Mr Butler accompanying her on her journey- but these incongruities were thus explained- she had consented to another years labours for her father, and was to have accompanied him to England- when the time arrived, her lover, who was prevented by a law suit from leaving the country, could not bear to part with her, without first securing her hand- and when married, would not consent to the separation or to her continuing on the stage- her Father was angry at losing the aid of her professional talents, considered himself wronged & deceived and made the poor girl very sad, after all the good already done for him & his family- she wrote to him a letter imploring that he would consent to her remaining with her husband, after fulfiling her engagement here- he consented, angrily- because he hoped to have retired with eclat on a good fortune, but embarked without her- since which it is reported that the Miss Butlers, have granted an annuity to her Mother, which secures her from any disappointment her daughters retirement might occasion and thus the good and talented Miss K is rewarded for her filial piety, and it is believed she will be a very happy wife, if so she may employ her leisure in writing moral tales from her own experience- or if she should be disappointed in this dear & rational expectation- she may devote her genius to writing & acting another tragedy- the Butler family receive her very cordially so for the love of nature & romance we will suppose she is to be happy[1]- tell my beloved brother how tenderly I love him embrace the dear children for me and believe me my dearest Maria devotedly your attached

Sister R GRATZ.

July 20th 1834

* * *

TO THE SAME

The year of this letter is omitted from the date but is fixed by the mention of the recent marriage of Dr. Isaac Hays to Sally Minis which took place May 7, 1834.
Henry Hart's travels—John Randolph's eccentricities and kindnesses—woman's blessed influence—a romance in real life.

I thank you most sincerely My Dear Maria for your kind letter -- you are always so good in writing when there is no cause for silence- that you must not wonder at my importunity after every long interval- besides I felt that you were sad- sympathy has its signs as well as free masonry. When I took Henry Hart by the hand I could have wept at the thoughts of your meeting with him- but now My Sister, you must be happy in his society- he loves you so warmly- and you are of so much consequence to him- that you must recover your spirits, to teach him how to regulate his feelings- He must have wonders to relate of his various travels by field & flood and the beautiful testimonials of his remem-

[1] Fanny Kemble's marriage to Pierce Butler, a southern aristocrat, proved most unhappy.

brance from every shore round the world's surface will afford histories to win your pliant ear. It will be worth while to arrange & class these shells so as to afford a kind of map for the circumnavigator and his young cousins- while to you they will have a value beyond their scientific worth in the recollection that they were gathered for you- have you seen John Randolphs letters? Sarah is reading them aloud to her Sisters & me, as an hour's exercise of a morning- and we are much pleased with them- there is much affection, and rational domestic kindness for which we never gave that eccentric genius credit- the nephew to whom they are addressed was a frequent visitor at our house, and was warmly attached to his Uncle- it is a pity subsequent caprice should have separated them- I am glad these letters are published- for they vindicate Randolphs character from the charge of heartlessness- he was so deeply interested for his sisters children and took upon him to provide for so many young destitute boys that he must have been by nature tender, & generous- compare the character of his mind during this period- with that exhibited in public later in life- and just before his death & I think there can be no doubt that he laboured under occasional aberrations of mind, which were as decidedly a disease as any that afflicted his body. If he had been blest with a tender wife, how different might have been the colour of his destiny!- Whatever the lords of creation may imagine they are infinitely the most helpless beings in the decline of life unconnected by the ties of family- the sedentary habits of women keep them only dependent for a few comforts on their friends- but the man who has no one to influence and console him, when vehement passions, painful diseases and disappointed pride cross his vexed spirits- is a sad spectacle of suffering & helplessness- I should be frightened for our own single brothers when such a picture is presented to my mind- if it were not for the hope that I may be able to repay all their goodness to me- by keeping up a domestic home with those charities alive, which may rescue them from the worst effects of bachelorship- a care-for-nobody independence-

This is giving a new turn to self-importance is it not? My dear Sister? and if you did not know that the spirit of humility had set her stamp on my character I would not venture to take such a view of my situation- but indeed, we who have neither fortune to support, nor other right to an establishment must endeavour to set up a claim to usefulness in some subordinate way to reconcile us to the idea of not being a burden to our relations- You will remember I have six single nieces besides, for whom to think forward- . . . . Do you remember Elizabeth Kappell? if you do not Ben will remind you of her- you will find her marriage announced to John R Latimer, about a fortnight ago. This gentleman an old beau of hers, went 10 years ago to Canton to seek his fortune, and continued there all that time- a few weeks after his return, he told his mother that if he found Elizabeth unchanged- he would address her- and in three weeks more they were married- this is "the romance of real life"! exclaimed our friend Miss Peters with her usual enthusiasm- "such a long attachment"- but if we look into the romance- & long attachment- we shall find that had her mother consented, she might have married a widower during Mr Ls absence, and had that been the case- the old attachment would not have been remembered by John Latimer- it is however a most agreeable match to all parties, and will no doubt be happier than half the romantic marriages of the loves at first sight which so much interest our novel reading friends. He has purchased a fine house and is fixing up quite a nabob establishment- She sent out cake & wine to the widows & Orphans, everybody likes the bride and thinks she is justly rewarded for her charitable labours- and when they return from Niagara, will be greeted with joy by everybody- William Meredith & his wife are also very handsomely fixed- there is but one more to be married in the family- and then I hope long engagements will be discarded from fashion in Phila- It is so long since I have known James Hale, that I hardly know him at all- but I am glad to hear you speak so well of him, He is the only one of my old friend's sons deserving of her talents- and the one perhaps from whom least was expected- there were 2 or 3 considered geniuses- who are little better than adventurers- James went to the west- Married & has turned out a judge & an Author- Give my love to My dear Brother, and embrace your darling boys for me- God bless you my own dear Sister, you do not know what comfort the sight of your hand writing in Jos letter, gave to the heart of your R GRATZ

July 30th

* * *

TO THE SAME

Public services of Benjamin Gratz—political party passions in the United States—first orphan asylum in the country established at Charleston, South Carolina—other similar institutions—the Day of Atonement.

Is it possible My dear Sister, you had really no intention of coming to us when you raised that cruelly delightful hope? if you could see the blank faces occasioned by the perusal of your last letter- I am sure you would be sorry you had hit on that expedient to punish Jo for playing the same game- I had planned such a happy winter for us all- had arranged my house, which has been all nicely painted &

papered- fixed your chambers according to my dear Howards notion, and thought we should be so comfortable & agreeable all together, that I can hardly bear to relinquish the scheme- tho' one passage in your letter shews I had expected too much- and my heart tells me- without the complete family- without our dear Ben & all the boys- neither you, nor they nor I could realize the happiness in anticipation- I expected as Ben wrote to Mr Blair- that you would have preceded your Husband by a month or two- and that he would have joined us before the winter set in- but I will not tell you all my hopes- and all my disappointments because I would not have your brow clouded with one regret my love can spare you- only let me set you right in one particular that your *objection* to *bringing all* is inadmissible for I shall never be content to have one missing when you do come- I have good servants and can add to their number without any diffi- culty- am not afraid of a large family when they can be domesticated, and have already experienced how easily you can be satisfied with the homely accommodations we can bestow. So My dear Sister, pray think more of gratifying my affection for all your family- than any little inconvenience you may fancy in the arrangement of my household. We have been in such confusion for the last fortnight in repair- ing & cleaning- that I find it quite a pleasure to sit down and see all in order again, and shall feel quite at home when you & Ben's portraits are reclaimed from Mr Sully, who is varnishing them- he has sent his eldest son abroad as a por- trait painter, to spend this winter in Virginia- what would be his chance in the west? Kentucky has produced so many good artists in that department, that I suppose there is no room for strangers-

I hope our dear Ben has got through his unpleasant duties- public honors are rarely attained without pain & turmoil, he must have earned his popularity by services conferred- and consistent integrity- or he would not in the few years he has resided in your city have been so often appointed to offices of trust, and responsibility- I am sure he would act justly if his own brother was among the arraigned and I hope whatever may be the feelings of delinquents he will be justified in the end, and regarded in the community according to his merit- the frightful excess political excitement has taken in our country is to be deplored- I dread the coming week, when our general election is to take place- it is to be hoped the death of the young man who suffered last week will be a warning against deadly arms on that occasion- tho' the idea of a public funeral for the poor lad shews the degrading length party spirit will go- . . . .

If you have had measles in your Orphan Asylum- we have had small pox & varialoid- between 30 & 40 were sick at the same time- one died- Mrs Hall was so ill from anxiety & fatigue that we feared we should have lost her too- and now we have got an assistant matron, to relieve her from the excess of responsibility- she has used her strength for 20 years with unsparing faithfulness- and *we the board* are grateful and wish to make her as comfortable as we can- but cannot consent to her leaving us- tho her daughter has offered her a home- I hope you will be as prosperous- and as you may be considered the founder of your institution, I feel a deep interest in your success- Mrs Yeatman means to establish one in Tennessee when she returns home- and is going to get hints from ours- how abundantly the good seed spreads when successfully planted- Charleston S C had the first house erected for this purpose and some of the distinguished men of that state may be traced to that seminary of charity-

God Bless You My own dear Sister, I am obliged to leave

you for dinner is on the table- tomorrow is the day of Atonement and I shall have no opportunity of resuming my pentell My beloved brother & the children how ardently I love them- and how sadly I am disappointed that I may not hope soon to embrace them

All here send affectionate remembrances Elizabeth joins- and begs me to say, do Aunt Maria come- let me hear from you soon again My beloved Sister and believe me always your

devoted affectionate R G

Oct. 12th 1834

* * *

TO THE SAME

This letter describes at some length the visit of the famous Englishwoman Miss Harriet Martineau to the United States— the "satiric pen" of foreign visitors—Twelfth Night—April Fools day.

Decr 27th 1834
Saturday night

Yesterday My dear Sister I wrote a letter of introduction to you for Miss Martineau which you will probably not receive before June- but I am sure you will be pleased with her, She has been spending a month in this city, and made her home at Mr Furness;[1] now tho she has been entertained at "great mens tables"- gone the round of fashionable routs- received the suffrage of philosophers & poets- been admitted to all public institutions- from the academy of science to the grim penitentiary- I believe the most acceptable testimony I can offer of her worth, is the enthusiastic admiration of the

[1] See page 132, Note 2.

frank hearted Mrs F. You will find her perfectly well bred & unaffected- her conversation full of interesting anecdotes of men & manners- quite unassuming & willing to talk of her own works with candour and in all respects such a woman as one rarely meets, and cannot fail to admire- I believe you have read her tales- I know I have told you how much they pleased me- and therefore you may imagine how much gratified I was to find their author so accessible and warm hearted- if she turns upon us the point of a "satiric pen"[1] when she leaves the country I shall never again trust to my judgment in descrying the reality of candour from its courtly counterfeit- I was not able to entertain her, because Becky Cohen has been in a state of living death ever since her arrival and I could not tell from day to day whether I could keep an engagement but she was plentifully feasted here- and in giving her a passport to your acquaintance I have done more for her gratification, and our credit- than if I had given her ten parties.

And so your clothes were making a winter voyage while you were in need of their services- I was greatly annoyed at not meeting with an obliging stage traveller to Pittsburg to give them a more rapid conveyance from Phila to the Ohio- but even that would not have expedited their peregrinations as they were destined to taste the waters of the Mississippi- I hope if they like Elijahs mantle could not part the waters- they retain no parts of them on their surface, lest in these degenerate days such spots might not be thought an improvement to their beauty- I have just heard that Mr Crutchfield- so long detained here by sickness and by whom

---

[1] Reference is made here undoubtedly to Mrs. Frances Trollope, the mother of Anthony Trollope, the novelist. After her visit to, and three years residence in, the United States she had criticized the Americans bitterly and unsparingly in her book "Domestic Manners of the Americans". (1832).

I hoped to have sent your dress has gone home- but Hyman has promised to seek out some other traveller- in case of failure- I believe I must apply to your old friend R. W. Johnson for a frank- as I am determined if possible to have them sent in time for your occasions- a Bachelor's Ball is announced here for *Twelfth Night* - to which all the Belles are looking with eager anticipation- and would you believe it- we are so ignorant as not to know to what Twelfth Night owes its origin- pray My dear Sister enlighten us on the subject- some have conjectured that it owed its notoriety to the change of style, when Christmas was so far back on the calendar- but some learned authorities tell us that the Romans had a custom of choosing a king & Queen on twelfth night which they derived from the Greeks. I once heard a long discussion on the antiquity of "April fools" and here is another familiar custom equally obscure- however on such innocent points it is better even the learned should dispute- than on as trifling & unimportant differences of opinion on graver subjects which have kept the world in long continued ferment- and "broken the bonds of brotherhood asunder" in the great family of mankind- I was talking to a beautiful young enthusiast last evening belonging to the Orthodox church- who would not go to see Miss Martineau at Mr Furness' house- nor be induced on any consideration to enter the Unitarian church- tho' I verily believe the Apostle Paul could never have been more eloquent or more pious than the good preacher of that temple- they admit that his discourses are excellent moral lessons- but not religious- is not this a distinction in which religion is sacrificed to prejudice?

The sublime, beneficent-holy Spirit, to which all forms are but the outward costumes in which different nations chuse to dress it- is still the same and all who lift their souls on high in Adoration- may walk the earth in charity with one another but this is a strange turn to give "my April fool"- forgive me dearest Maria, as I am not expected to agree with the disputants I hear all sorts of opinions discussed- why did you not send me your Orphan Society report- it would have come just in time for my occasion- pray my dear Secretary let it come when you next write, it should be printed in your newspapers. You need not place your name to it, but the public like to know what is done with their money, and each subscriber likes to feel that they have contributed to the benefits you tell them have been received from their bounty- but I never see the Lexington papers unless My dear Brother directs them to us. . . . . I am charmed with your family sketches & adventures. Canewood has a thousand agreeable associations in my mind- there is no spot in Kentucky I should better like to visit- your boys will think their cousin Horace a dull city youth- totally ignorant of sports by field or flood- and will have to teach him all their country sports- but they will find him as boyish as themselves- and disposed to love them dearly. Sarah & Lizzie are inseparable- and are always happy together, Elizabeth[1] has had resolution to stay here during the vacation, her father thinking she had better not risk a winter journey- she is a sweet girl- very like her mother, and as happy & gay as at 16 she should be- I have just left them all at the next house discussing Bulwers last novel "the last days of Pompeii". Sally & the Dr dined with me today- I told her of your proposition for young settlers in the West and find it much to her taste- . . . . Jac saw Dr Coit[2] while in Phila and he said many fair things of you- he

[1] Elizabeth Blair daughter of Mr. and Mrs. Francis Preston Blair, and niece of Mrs. Benjamin Gratz. She attended school near Philadelphia and was an intimate friend of Rebecca Moses, a niece whom Rebecca Gratz reared.

[2] The Reverend Dr. Thomas M. Coit, President of Transylvania University at Lexington (1835-1837). Benjamin Gratz was a trustee of that institution.

was delighted to meet with such brilliant talents- so highly cultivated- and your husband too, had his share of commendation which I would fain tell you if I had room- Mr Biddle thinks him a very clever fellow- he received much kindness from him in Boston, and Dr Coit staid at his house here for some days- to use his lawyer phrases- he does not consider him equal to Horace Binney or John Sergeant- but likes him, and therefore gave him an introduction to his friend- he told Jac that if his wife consent, he would accept the offer of President to your college- I hope if he does they will be more to your taste than the Woods. I have only room to send the love of all here in a heap- and to beg you will tell your dear husband & children how devotedly I am their & your affectionate

Sister RG

* * *

TO THE SAME

This undated letter is postmarked Phila Jan 12. The writer mentions the graduation of Gratz Moses, a nephew, as taking place in the spring. As this young man graduated from the medical college in 1835, this fixes the year in which the letter was written.

"The Life of Hannah More" - a beautiful philosophy of life - the poet Cowper - the Reverend John Newton - the Orphan Society - "Hamlet, a Prelude" by Dr. James Rush - a students strike.

My Dear Sister

I have just thrown down "the life of Mrs Hannah More"[1] for the pleasure of holding a little converse with you, I am

---

[1] Hannah More (1783-1833) a well known English poet, religious writer and philanthropist.

charmed with this book- it contains such a large range of delightful letters from distinguished men & women- who write with the same freedom and ease which makes up the soul & spirit of genuine correspondence- one sympathizes with the writers who express such thoughts, as similar circumstances would bring up in our own minds & hearts, and tho they are better expressed than we might find words to put them in- yet they put us in good humour with ourselves, because we appreciate the beauty of their simplicity- there is one writer however, I am disappointed in- the friend of Cowper- the Revd John Newton[1]- he is so austere- self condemning and evangelical- that I cannot bestow on him one feeling of love my Cowper had prepared for him- and I think Mrs Hannah seems to stiffen and grow demure when she addresses him- some of her religious meditations seem to be the offspring of his letters- while Dr Proteus brightens her piety with a plea of heaven itself- I love a joyful gratitude acknowledging the gracious gifts bestowed by providence- and these men rich in holy gifts and set up as teachers to the community why "lead them up a thorny steep"- when the "primrose path" blooms so beautifully to the very garden of paradise. I doubt the philosophy of preparing for disappointments- for when we have experienced much happiness the arrival of crosses teaches us how to bear them- sunshine & storm are alike necessary to the salubrity of the natural atmosphere- and so must sorrow & joy temper our moral institutions for the growth of those virtues which make us capable of conceiving the end for which we are designed- I have read very few of Hannah More's works but mean to get some of them immediately- I have received your Orphan

[1] The Reverend John Newton (1725–1807), curate of Olney, the parish in which Cowper the poet lived. The poet and the clergyman were intimate friends and collaborated in the production of a volume entitled "Olney Hymns" (1770).

reports and congratulate you on the interest your community evince in your success- you will now go on prosperously and I hope at the end of 20 years you may be able to look back with as much satisfaction on your labours as we do here- but our good Mrs Hale is becoming very infirm- she is wearing out in our service- we have got an assistant matron- but she is no more to be compared to the principal- than I to Hecuba- your report is beautiful- if you have taken anything from mine, you have worked up the old materials so as to make them much better than when they were new- and in such a manner that no one would know them again- I am glad our meeting was over when your paper arrived or I should have been envious of the whole affair being so much more noticed in Lexington, than here- the Rev Mr James made us a preaching of considerable length- but his style is bad and his reading worse- however thank God a few of our pious friends attended- and ninety five poor little children were present- who sang a hymn written for the occasion in the Asylum by a young woman the teacher in our girls school - . . . . Hyman yesterday received a letter from Pittsburg mentioning that your box had been detained there some days on account of there being a scarcity of freight- but that it was sent forward on the 12th Decr so that I hope you have had your cloaks during the very cold weather last week- your dress &c is waiting for a western traveler and I hope soon to speed it on its journey- but should you want a hint of the present costume before the arrival of your box you must hear some of our ladies have been to Constantinople, and their heads are turned "a la Turke"- turbans are preferred to Caps and composed of any article- from velvet to golden gauze- our brother Jo has furnished some of his beautiful handkerchiefs which you know how to use. . . . .
Both our rivers are fast bound- and given over to skaters

and waggons, and I am told the gayest part of the city by sunlight- and moon light is on the Delaware. Elizabeth is in high health & spirits- she had a long letter from her father last week- with fair accounts of all the family- and she is full of anticipations for the summer when Montgomery & she will have both finished their educations-

Gratz Moses hopes too to graduate an M. d. in the spring- and to begin on the labours of his profession- if he can obtain a place in the Alms house, which is removed to the new building W. of Schuylkill, he will deem himself fortunate to reside there for one Year- and then will be cast on the world for a location- perhaps in the far west- unless your own medical school sends out its own pupils over the whole land[1]- Dr Hays has now a very good prospect of advancement as Dewees is retiring from practice- and he has been attending Ds patients during his illness & absence, but the old Dr has a son in Europe whom he hopes will succeed him, and therefore hangs on until he arrives- unfortunately however the talents of his son, cannot sustain him in his profession, and there are few who would be willing to receive him as a substitute, either for his father or Dr Hays-

Have you seen a book entitled "Hamlet a Prelude" by Dr James Rush? no one can understand it here- it has a double purpose- being a medical satire & drama- The students in our college have entered into a rebellion against Professor Coxe, and declined attending his lectures- they addressed a petition to the Faculty- who appointed a committee, and they have reported that the Institution is injured by Professor Coxes incapacity to fill his chair- in consequence of which he must either resign- or be requested to vacate- it is

[1] Dr. Gratz Moses settled in St. Louis where he became an eminent physician. He was professor of obstetrics at St. Louis Medical College (1851–1854). He was president of the St. Louis Obstetrical Society, and was health officer of St. Louis for some years.

thought Dr Jackson will be appointed in his place- all this may be interesting to our dear Ben- and has been so much so here, where Gratz is concerned that I could not help telling you- . . . . old John has brought in his tray and castors- it is Sunday and the privilege of an early dinner cannot be denied him- so dearest I must say adieu and May God Bless you every day prays your own attached sister RG

John begs Mrs Gratz will excuse him - he would wait any time to pleasure her- he begs Mr & Mrs G will be pleased to accept his remembrance-

* * *

TO THE SAME

Apparel sent to Lexington - marriage of Henry Hart - the warlike spirit of Andrew Jackson - a gay season - Hannah More's Life.

Tuesday night Jany 20th 1835

Last Friday My dear Maria your box was dispatched by the mail stage to Pittsburgh- to the care of Mr Hutchinson, with orders- that if the navigation was not open- to forward it on by the mail stage- so that I hope you will have your dress before the arrival of this letter- I should be very glad indeed to hear that your Bonnet & Cloaks were in use long since- they were sent in the Steam boat Lady Marshall, to January & Huston Maysville with other packages for Crutchfield & Tilford and sailed from Pittsburg on the 12th Decr- if you have not received them- Brother had better write to the persons above mentioned at Maysville about them- I expect My dear Sister when you open our present importation you will be reminded of the Irish servant, who being sent for a physician, called also at the undertakers as one would naturally require the other- having purchased you a gown & Turban I thought you would require a cape to suit a walking dress- and one to make it complete for an evening and so I exceeded your order by these articles- The Blonde looked so pretty with its coloured bows that I would not have them exchanged- knowing you could substitute the little scarf belonging to your dress while you wear black and I hope most sincerely you may enjoy health & happiness and wear them with a light heart- we heard a few days ago that Henry Hart was to be married immediately- I congratulate you on his success- for I know you have a mothers interest in his welfare and that his Lady-love is one you approve of- I suppose he will exchange his naval honors for the garb of a gentle cit- or country squire- unless the warlike spirit of our chief should be caught by the congress- and bring about something for our navy to do- if the season were more favorable I should recommend his making a visit with his bride to his friends here- . . . .

Jo has recovered, and begins to look better- he is recreating himself with a few friends at the whist table- he & Jac abandon tea parties altogether- Hyman sometimes goes- I more rarely still- for the last fortnight the city has been regaled by a succession of fetes- but as Sarah does not go out this winter I am not called on to bear a part, and only appear occasionally- if Julia Hoffman, who I expect in a fortnight is disposed to share in such scenes I suppose we shall be drawn into them- the Theatre they say has been very attractive but my time for such amusements has gone by- I have not been to see a play since Fanny Kemble retired-

I am reading Hannah More's life- and I hope it has reached you by this time- it is full of interesting letters, and incidents- she filled a high station in the literary circle of her day- and was honored for her talents- her piety and her benevolent activity in improving the moral & religious character of her neighbourhood- .... I heard last evening that our friends in Washington are well- I gave an introductory letter to a gentleman, who came back delighted with the attentive kindness of Mr & Mrs Blair- he thanked me for the most useful document he carried- he wants an office, and Mr B-s influence will do it for him

Elizabeth was quite a belle on Saturday Evening at a Ball- she is so full of brightness & vivacity that it is impossible not to be attracted- the party was at Pembertons and fixed on Saturday as the only evening she has permission to go out- Adieu May God bless you both with every blessing each could ask for the other- ever

My dear Maria, your own attached
Sister R Gratz

* * *

TO BENJAMIN GRATZ

Rebecca Gratz visited Lexington in the year 1835. This accounts for the long gap in the correspondence.
Mrs. Benjamin Gratz in Washington - home a dull place without wife and children - the Lexington boys at school in the East- differences in brothers - averting war with France.

January 11th 1836

We have just heard My dear Brother of your safe arrival home, and rejoice most sincerely that you escaped the many accidents a winter journey is liable to- home I am sure must be a dull place to you When Maria & your boys are absent- but then you have such numerous concerns to arrange, that you will not take time to be lonesome and as soon as you are disengaged from them, you will I trust find the Ohio safe &

free from ice- and wend your way back to us- Your boys are perfectly well, and satisfied, they were prevented going to Washington for the holidays by bad roads- but will probably go on with Henry Etting the last of the Month, they go regularly to school and their being here has been & is a great happiness to me- I never before had an opportunity of knowing their characters so well- Bernard has much good sense- and delights me- by the manliness & integrity of his conduct, he has a noble heart too- and safe qualities that promise well for his future well being & well doing- he shews more fondness for books than Howard- and thus makes up for a slower perception- they have both taken a fancy for the game of Chess, and pass their evenings in that amusement. Howards eagerness & impetuosity makes the loss of a game quite a trial- but he has a genius for it- and Jac takes an interest in teaching him- . . . . I fear the recent wet weather will disappoint Maria of her intended visit to Richmond by making the roads too bad to travel for pleasure- when we last heard they were busy preparing for a Ball- the girls have a gay time and I have no doubt Maria enjoys the novel scene as much as any of them- Mr Bartons[1] arrival will give some excitement too of a political nature- which will reach the drawing room- every arrival from France or England opens fresh views for speculation- the fall of nations seems to split on such a delicate point- that we shall either go to war- or be saved from it- by a qualifying If, as the money is all ready- waiting for the Message- I hope fresh ingenuity will be able to pick out of it a soothing paragraph, to supply them with an apology to do what they desire- and we too- it seems so silly & wicked too to throw away good money- after bad- and waste the lives of thousands for a point of etiquette

If you see Mrs Clay- pray present My sincere & affection-

[1]Thomas P. Barton of Kentucky, ambassador to France in 1835.

ate sympathy to her- I grieve for her loss[1]- and truly deplore that one so lovely and possessing so many sources of happiness should be so soon called from her earthy duties but God is wise & most merciful- and has surely judged right- I hope her husband will be comforted by the interesting children who are solely dependent upon him- Lexington has lost two valuable women, since we left, and they will be greatly missed in its society- pray My dear Brother, make affectionate remembrance acceptable to your Sisters Mrs Bledsoe & Boswell- is it true that the latter has lost her son in law Shelby[2]? to dear Sara & Jane, and all your family who were so kind to me last summer, and made me love them- tell them gratefully I remember them- they will try to cheer you during your . . . .[3]
not stay longer than your business requires- for I am sure neither you or Maria will be quite happy until you meet- and after all there are few things in life worth making a sacrifice of such comforts as you possess in the society of your family- Your sons send their love to you- they have gone to bed, tired with a battle of snow-balls- in which their school & another engaged this afternoon- but it is growing late and their seniors are dropping off too to seek repose- Sara Hays- the Capt.[4] and our next door neighbours have been passing the evening here- and our own Sara[5] salutes you with a loving Kiss- our Sisters are well- and we all talk of you with such a grateful happiness- that you are so good- so fenced around with blessings- and use them for purposes so acceptable to providence- the good of others- that to invoke a con-

[1]Mrs. Ann Erwin, the daughter of Mr. and Mrs. Henry Clay, had died in New Orleans.
[2]The first husband of the second Mrs. Benjamin Gratz, who was a niece of the first wife.   [3]Paper torn.
[4]Doubtless Captain Alfred Mordecai who married the Sara Hays mentioned here, a niece of Rebecca Gratz, June 1, 1836.
[5]Sara Moses who was living with her aunt Rebecca Gratz.

tinuance of His favors and pray that God may ever bless you is all, affection can ask- and this is reverently petitioned for by your devoted Sister R G.

* * *

TO MARIA GIST GRATZ

Hyman Gratz' Annuity Office - the United States Bank Bill - difficulties with France adjusted - Bulwer's Rienzi - novel reading.

Feb 17th 1836

Oh thanks to you My own dear Sister, for your two delightful letters last received- I came home from Sister Hays last night and found one had been waiting for me, in the faces of your honorable boys, who well knew under the sealed cover something was hidden that interested them- and yet they did not shorten My visit- or hint their impatience. I was glad you approved of my not sending your sons last week- the weather and the roads are such formidable objections to travel, that I have not the heart to expose them to the trial altho they would most willingly set out and they watch the skies most diligently wishing the snow, rain and the ice- running waters- but the Delaware 16 inches thick affords a solid passage to sleighs and wood carts- and amusement to multitudes of skaters while it denies to you the pleasure of embracing your boys. and our Brother Jo the opportunity he desires of visiting you at the great city.[1]

. . . .

I thank you, My Sister, and our kind friend Mr Blair for

[1] Mrs. Benjamin Gratz with her two younger children was visiting her sister Mrs. Francis Preston Blair in Washington. The two older boys were placed at a boarding school in Philadelphia.

your reception of Edwards[1] message, and as soon as he comes home will inform him of your offer- if I had reflected before I wrote, instead of telling you what I was bidden I might have been sure that I was troubling you unadvisedly- for in truth I had too little understanding of the business to make it clear to you- However he will be grateful to know he has such powerful friends at court and may push his fortune, at a more fitting opportunity

You ask about our Brothers- Hyman is at Harrisburg- trying to get some legislative act in favor of his Annuity office- by the bye I have just heard that the U. S. bank bill has passed complete, governers signature & all- whether for good or evil, time & circumstances must develope- it has been the subject of grand excitement & speculation here, & I suppose in most of the commercial cities- but you have heard all of the unpopular side and one cannot help wishing all the great departments of our government could be carried on amicably and united, as the proudest title of our country claims- I am delighted that our differences with France are adjusted without mediation, tho' I have not your objections, to the good terms of old England, and give her credit for many national virtues- I like better, that the Presidents message should have satisfied Louis Philippe- and if his first message was acceptable what will be the effect of his third? I am quite impatient to hear the compliments of the french chamber- (I beg your pardon for this digression, you will laugh at my politics) Jo said when he went out after breakfast that he thought he would write to you- if he does not I will remind him of your Portuguese proverb- he is right well and looks handsome in his black stock now that I have got accustomed to it- Jac has returned from his journey thank

[1] Edward Johnston Etting, a nephew, was in the navy.

God in better spirits- he is reading Rienzi[1] with as much perseverence as a school girl- you will think it a singular cause of pleasure in a grave character like me- that with spectacles on my brother should be reading a novel- but I do so dread habitual depression that I consider the time redeemed that is given even to light amusement, if it is drawn from moody idleness- Jac has sold some land, he thinks not well- but it has given him something to do- the cold journey gave him something to suffer- and mixing with the hurly burly at Harrisburg gave him something to think of - and as James Paulding says in his Backwoodsman
> "God helps the man who helps himself
> When help himself he can"

To His help too I attribute all the good change I see in our brothers spirits- well now, Jo has just come in- and maugre the . . . .[2] has not fulfiled his morning intention- for he bids me "tell Maria if she wants to move any where to let him know and he will come down to attend her"- that is as soon as these winter storms will let him- Howard has gone through the deep snow to get a pair of shoes- after working out in the yard to make paths & build forts- for this being ash Wednesday there is no school- and Bernard has been writing to his Father & you two long letters- . . . . embrace My little darlings for me- I long to see them again My best love to my dear Becky & Lizzie- your sister & Mr B. and believe me My sweet Sister most devotedly

your RG--

---

[1] Rienzi, *The Last of the Tribunes*, by Bulwer.   [2] Paper torn.

TO THE SAME

Since Rebecca Gratz states in this letter whose year is omitted from the date that six months had elapsed since the appearance of Washington Irving's "Astoria" and since that work appeared in 1836 the date of this letter is undoubtedly Jany 7th 1837. The Miriam whose marriage is recorded in this letter was Miriam Moses one of the nieces whom Miss Gratz reared after the death of their mother in 1823. Miriam Moses' marriage to Solomon Cohen of Georgetown, S. C. took place November 30, 1836. This also fixes the year of this letter.
Trade Unions - the suffering poor.

Saturday night Jany 7th

I can wait no longer My Dear Maria, for the first word to come from you, for I begin to feel uneasy at the long suspension of intercourse between us- let me see, I think the last letter informed you of a day fixed for Miriam's marriage- and she has been gone a whole month before your answer has arrived, perhaps you have had a letter from her at Georgetown telling you how happy she is, that she has been received with the greatness kindness by all Mr Cohens family, that she likes them all very much, and notwithstanding the new & strange circumstances by which she is surrounded, she is as absolutely contented as ever woman was- such is the tenor of her letters home and the minute accounts of her reception and the society around her, completely satisfies her friends here that she is indeed happy. Well then let me further assure you, that greatly as we all miss Miriam, we do not fail to rejoice, that she is thus- I believe all are reconciled to the change- such is the facility with which inevitable changes are submitted to in all human affairs- . . . .

We last week got through our Anniversary labours, and I am sorry to say Sister Secretary that we made a very beggarly account of an empty treasury- I do not know what is to become of the poor, unless they see the folly of these "trade unions" which seem to forget the wholesome old adage- "half a loaf is better than no bread" and hold out for high wages or no work- in your plentiful country they might go out and plant corn, and hemp, and produce enough to feed & cover themselves & families- but here they must either crowd our poor houses or beg- since they are bound in honor not to work, ... Have you read Washington Irvings "Astoria?" it is so old that I ought to be ashamed to mention it as new to me- but in fact I am six months behind in literary lore- having been so occupied with domestic affairs as to have had little leisure for reading- but now the excitement is all over, I shall resume old habits- and endeavour to refresh my mind with more wholesome food- but it will be long ere the loss of My dear Miriams society can be made up to me- you have only sons, so will gain another child when they marry but to part with a daughter is quite another thing- one whose mind has been trained under your own eye, in whom every year has developed some excellent quality- and every days intercourse has endeared to your heart- My dear Maria this parting has been a severe sorrow to me, and yet I rejoice in her happiness- and feel confidence in the high character of integrity & worth to whom she has allied herself- even Georgetown represented by her letters is a paradise to her- so entirely is the home of her beloved, the scene of her choice- I have so many questions to ask that I do not know where to begin- My dear Ben, & the boys each I would hear something about, and to each I beg you will give my affectionate love, I asked Mr Johnson about you all- but he had been seeing so many sights since he left

Kentucky that he seemed to have forgotten when he saw you- he was at all the parties and was greatly charmed- I only saw him at home, he dined with us on Christmas- but the girls met him at Ladies parties- he has gone to N York- every body charges me to give their love to you, and implore you to write- we are famished for one of your letters. Consider that it is six weeks since you have written. . . . . Our beloved Ben's happiness is a source of continual gratitude to you- and to God for having blessed Ye both with so many blessings- May they continue to encrease "even as your lives do now" prays, My dear Maria Your ever attached

RG.

* * *

TO THE SAME

Life's ephemeral blessings - the unexpected always happens - Julia Wright - a South Carolina winter - dangers besetting "men children".

January 15th 1837

I am greatly concerned My dear Sister to hear of our beautiful Carys misfortune. I was afraid you had some cause for your long silence but did not think of such a sad one- poor little fellow how soon his holiday pleasures were converted into pain & sorrow- but I hope he is restored to sight before this, and that all danger to his eyes & comeliness has passed away- We are constantly reminded My dear Sister by how frail a tenure we hold the blessings of this life and how every day we endanger their loss by our own acts and in pursuit of our own amusements- a dear little boy lost his life in our streets about a fortnight ago who had just left home with his brother, drawing their sled on the ice his foot slipped and he fell just under the wheel of a wood cart which passed directly over his neck- his brother ran home with the news- and his poor Mother came to the spot, to be carried home frantic with the body of her bleeding child- she is a delicate little woman, "whom the winds of heaven were not permitted to visit too rudely," and might be expected to fall a victim to this calamity- were it not that her beloved widowed Mother is very ill, and holds out a motive for exertion- thus the apprehension of a coming evil enables her to bear that which is inevitable. May God enable her to wrestle with & over come her grief for she has several children still dependent on her care-

We are all very much interested for Julia Wright who you may remember came to see Sara in Lexington, and was a schoolfellow of hers- her mother brought her back in the fall to finish her education with Mrs Sigorgnes- and returned to New Orleans, where both she & her husband died, within a few weeks of each other. Julia was sadly distressed to hear of her Fathers death, and the still severer loss has not been communicated- indeed until yesterday Mrs S received no direct intelligence of Mrs Ws departure altho other letters were in town stating the event- . . . .

Our letters from Miriam are most satisfactory - she writes every week and finds a Carolina winter much to her taste, her last was from a Plantation on the Santee, the residence of her Brother-in-law about 12 miles from Georgetown where the winter foliage of live oak & evergreens strike her as not more beautiful than singular- the presence of flowers in the open air, and all the luxuries of a southern climate have great charms for her- and her heart is attuned to harmonize with everything in her new home for she is still desperately in love, and her husband being the great man of the village, he & everybody around her, pay her homage (she says for his sake) but I have from others, that Miriam for her own sake is valued- and both you & I know her well enough to believe it- both her letters & Rosa's crave for information about dear Aunt Maria & Uncle Ben - . . . .

I am quite in love with My dear Bernards affectionate care of his little brother, he has the most patient self sacrificing disposition I ever saw in a boy so young, girls more frequently exhibit these endearing qualifications- but this shall be recorded among Bernards virtues- our dear Howard & Hyman have feeling hearts too and I hope will learn, in the pity they feel for Cary to be careful of getting into the like danger, that they may spare their mother from such distressing alarms- the parents of men-children must arm themselves with fortitude- so many dangers beset their youth, first in their sports- and then in the active pursuits of life they have so many "hair breadth scapes by field & flood" that were not the watchful eye of providence fixed on their path, and his protecting arm outstretched to guard them- there would be no comfort in sending them forth to win their way through life. May God bless your Boys, My love, and guide them safely, and virtuously and bravely, and May they feel & acknowledge their dependence on Him and reward their beloved Parents for all they receive at their hands- all here unite in tenderest love, with your attached sister

R Gratz

TO THE SAME

Mothers and daughters - the Reverend Mr. Dewey - the Reverend William H. Furness and his views - "Differing religions of men should not alienate people from one another" - "with opinion I will not war, while I see good men forming each creed that leads to the same end, the worship of God" - death of Judge Ogden Hoffman - the inauguration of President Van Buren - the Aurora Borealis.

Feb 19th 1837

I can hardly tell you My dear Sister how happy I was to receive your letter on Friday, ... every topick in your letter is full of interest to me. Mrs Boswell[1] took strong hold on my affections, she was confiding & kind, & I so pitied a widowed Mother, whose children were estranged from her- and whose labour & most harrassed thought were to be urged against those, who ought to have cherished her with devoted love. I am glad Mrs Shelby[2] has returned to comfort her- does it not seem that the hand of providence had interposed in her behalf in giving back to her the daughter she most loves, and removing one who might have worked both their ruin. I hope Laura will learn to honor and respect her parent too now that she has been living among strangers and feels how different that relationship is to all others in the world. Since I last wrote I have been to a party where I met Mr Furness, and at his church where I heard an excellent sermon from Mr Dewey- Mr Furness told me he & I ought to be inimical to each other- according to the usual system of

---

[1] Mrs. Joseph Boswell, a sister of Mrs. Benjamin Gratz.
[2] Mrs. O. Shelby, daughter of Mrs. Boswell, became the second wife of Benjamin Gratz. The first wife died November 4, 1841, and Benjamin Gratz married a second time July 6, 1843.

mankind- because in religion we were not *very* different, and yet not alike - I told him that I claimed the privilege of not being inimical to any mans religion- yet being firmly attached to my own- and so I hope My dear Maria are You, and being so, why should you suppose the fear of death might make you falter- since the God you serve, is the same who created you- appointed your duties- has given you a clear perception of his holiness- his mercy and his providential care, and guarding you through the paths of life, will not desert you in the "valley of the shadow of death"- and as his attributes cannot change in whatever state mysterious nature may place the creature man, whatever region the immortal spirit may inhabit- the same God whose breath made man a living soul- inhabits eternity to which that soul is destined. I cannot comprehend why the worship of God should be so fertile of ill will on earth, but I do not doubt some good end is to be answered and so I submit as far as regards my self and believe obedience is better than sacrifice, therefore am in principle as well as practice a conformist to the law- Now if even *this might not be necessary-* it cannot be wrong- while no moral or religious (spiritual) obligation is infringed - opinion makes the difference and with opinion I will not war, while I see good men forming each creed that leads to the same end- the worship of God.

You have heard that My dear Julia Hoffman has lost her Father,[1] he was an excellent man, and a firm friend of mine- I expect Julia to come to me, as soon as she can arrange her affairs- she will break up housekeeping for the present- and after a while live with her brother Charles, or George as circumstances may direct. We hear from Miriam constantly

[1] Judge J. Ogden Hoffman of New York who married as his second wife Maria Fenno, an intimate friend of Rebecca Gratz. This friendship was extended to his children by his first wife, Matilda and Julia Hoffman and their brothers.

and she urges us to tell her about her dear Uncle Ben & Aunt Maria, little Carys accident grieves her most, for she has not yet heard that he is well- Miriam & Henry Etting went this morning to Washington, the latter promised to take Miriam on his next visit, and she is gone to witness the inauguration- it is hard that Lizzie should have two visitors when she does not go out, (on account of her grandfathers death) but I suppose Miss Pemberton & Miriam will be satisfied with the public shows without parties. I am sorry that the answer to the business part of your letter will reach you so late- I waited for a private conveyance to send your bills, but will here give you the amount which will answer just as well- having got money from Jo to pay them all-

For Carolines cloak	$17.37-
Pictures & frames	98
Pintard 2 bonnets	37 50
cleaning feathers	6
Cary & Hart & Grigg	6
	164 87
deduct for Sara B	3 50
	161 37 ....

Miss Fraser says she has written to you, to patronise her magazine and I hope you will be able to serve her among your literati- she has very good talents, and it is a praise- worthy undertaking as they are much reduced, and her whole time is devoted to her sick sister, in whose chamber she has written a good deal, which she hopes may be useful and profitable- do you think I forget you while gazing on the splendid Aurora borealis which I find visited your hemi- sphere as well as ours? is it not delightful that these heavenly appearances may be gazed on at the same moment by friends so far from each other, that distance & mountains cannot intervene to shut out the glorious view- thus love, when all earth fades from our mortal eyes, shall we not together view the heavens and adore Him who liveth for ever - Jac is at Harrisburg, we heard yesterday that he was well- perhaps he has written to Ben, but he is so lazy in that way that there is no depending on him- our other Brothers are well and so is the whole concern- Sisters have each but a single daughter at home- they are cheerful tho' & well- . . . . God Bless you my dear Sister & Brother, pray do not be so long again without writing to me. . . . . Adieu Beloved Maria & Ben, ever your devoted   RG

* * *

TO THE SAME

The business panic of 1837 - reflections on changed relations of children to parents when they pass from childhood to youth and manhood - luxurious living during the Feast of Passover - the state's duty to children of criminal parents - the reorganization of Transylvania University - Dr. Caldwell - President Coit - "Grace is a passport to favor and by no means to be neglected."

April 30th 1837

I follow your good rule My dear Sister, on this occasion the rather because I am sure you will be anxious to hear that our brother Jo is no worse- and I do wish it were in my power to tell you that he is better- some days we are so flattered and next he retrogrades again- but his patience is not exhausted and as he does not appear to suffer- I still hope repose and slender diet will at length prevail- he is cheerful withal, when he has company to laugh or talk with him - and is wonderfully composed about money matters- which seem to agitate all the mercantile world. I hope with you (I believe) he is safe with regard to his own situation - tho' do not doubt he will be a poorer man. From all the workings of the complicated machine- which involves the whole business community- I am glad our other brothers are out of trade, for they have less forethought & discretion than Jo, and could not have prepared for the storm- Hyman left us on Friday for his southern tour, I hope he may find it possible to come home through Kentucky- tho he would be but a short time with you it would be a comfort to have had even a day in your house- and then perhaps you would take the opportunity of paying the visit you told Miriam of and which she is anticipating with so much pleasure- and Horace[1] too has gone from me!- this is a trial I will not attempt to speak of- your own heart can tell you- it was not merely parting with him, for I looked forward with pleasure to the hope of his entering on a respectable profession, with a reasonable prospect of success- but then our relations seem changed- the tender cord of childhood is stretched & strengthened- when we meet again, he will feel like a man who has laboured for himself- and with all the confidence & exultation I may feel in his advancement- still the change is painful- will you ever have such foolish yearnings? perhaps not, for you have many sons and have thought more & arranged your plans with better help- but after all we must leave the event to God! and there is comfort in that thought, and so My dear Sister- in his hands I entrust my beloved Horace, and feel that his own Mother could do no better- your letter was full of interesting matter, and but that you told me your own health was not good, I should be satisfied

[1] Horace Moses born in 1820 to whom Rebecca Gratz had been as a mother since the death of her sister Rachel Gratz Moses in 1823.

with all the other results of affairs in which your previous communication had awakened my interest. I hope you are careful of your self and treat your *head* as if it was a part of your body worthy of physical attention- the fact is that when one is cautioned to take care of their heads- that again is considered only in relation to its intellectual conventions its sentiments & feelings & aspirations- and the flesh part of it is considered not, is forgotten altogether- until painful experience tells that it has a local habitation as liable to disease as any other part of our frame- now dear Sister the sensibility of your head must not be neglected, and as it requires some attention from your other members, pray try to remember that it requires a quiet neighbourhood and do nothing to disturb it. You have told me from your scripture that "nothing that goeth into the mouth defileth" (spiritually) but you know that it may harm physically, and therefore abstain from hurtful food- I am prepared to preach experimentally, as I have just been released from a bed of suffering, from the effects of living too luxuriously during the feast of passover- I acquiesce entirely in your opinions of the Turners- they are equally criminal, but I think rather worse of the Man- for he adds meanness & treachery to his guilt- pray what will become of the children? must they be reared into another generation of vipers by such parents? it is a pity the state could not provide in such cases for its future citizens- I am glad Transylvania will be re-organized, and I hope on solid principles. I wish you had a Professorship for our nephew Gratz[1]- he is a young aspirant, working hard for reputation- I never had respect for Dr Caldwell, and only wondered how under the weight of his sins he would sustain himself in your society- pray how comes on President Coit & his pretty daughters? is your classical de-

[1] Dr. Gratz Moses, supra, page 153, Note 1.

partment the same as when we were in Lexington? I am much pleased at the figures our boys make in the ball room- grace is a passport to favor, and by no means to be neglected- Horace will never do to send to France, for he could not lead a lady out to dance, or support her thro the notes of a valse . . . . Mr Marx[1] has lost a deal of money $75000- but he is not ruined- Saml has gone to new Orleans to see if any thing can be recovered- and perhaps to avert further losses- the old gentleman is much depressed by the failures of so many of his friends- but I hope the domestic comfort of that amiable family will not be interfered with- . . . . God bless you my dear Sister & Brother, believe in the sincerest affection of your R G

* * *

TO THE SAME

The school of experience - Mr. Murat (Prince Joachim Murat) at Bordentown, New Jersey - the Gratz Alabama lands - the weaknesses to which aging flesh is heir - Carlyle's "Sartor Resartus."

May 28 1837

Your two letters my dear Maria reached me safely last week . . . .

Our brother Hyman came home very unexpectedly on Tuesday last- and I was unreasonable enough to be sorry that he had not taken time either to see Miriam at the south or pay you a visit- and yet as things have turned out I am very glad he is at home, for he has had a slight paralysis of his face, which being with his own physician is more satisfy-

[1] See page 94, Note 1.

ing than if he had been abroad- we perceived it on Friday- since which he has been bled & cupped, and I hope in a few days will be well again- he told the Dr he must go out tomorrow, and received for answer that he might be well content if he was permitted to do so in a week- God knows we are poor, frail creatures, and keeps us from the knowledge of our weakness, that we may be enabled to bear it! Hyman looked to be in perfect health on Wednesday- his complexion brightened by travel, and as the girls thought as handsome as ever and I saw nothing of his disease, until Friday afternoon after he was bled, we dined together, and he sat immediately opposite to me- as it is confined to a single Nerve, I fervently pray he may soon be restored. He found the country every where suffering actually or in anticipation of hard times, and could do nothing with his Alabama Lands but look at them- Jo is better, and down stairs but by no means well yet, that is, he is obliged to be so prudent to keep well that there are many lapses in his recovery, which a woman might avoid by the sedentary habit of her life, without very great sacrifice- as the weather grows warmer I hope he will get strong again- but we must not forget that in the autumn of life, the changing year does not renew our youth, and that disease is the natural warning of the wear & tear of our frames, preparing us for other changes to which they tend. In this great struggle for the riches of this world, which the political & commercial community are so much engaged in- I cannot but pause, and consider what a waste of happiness has been made- with health and competence, in this beautiful country- how much real enjoyment might be realized, if men would be content without riches- the ideal good- the idolatry of modern worshipers- I wonder if there will ever come a time when it will be the fashion to care little about money, and only value as riches the faculty of being happy? would you not like to visit the earth at such a period? does not the bible promise such a time when knowledge (of God) is spread over it, as the waters cover the sea? . . . .

The account we have of Washington is that your sister & Lizzy are well- Mr B. making his garden (who would believe such domestic taste occupied the private hours of the angry Globe)?- Caroline has returned to her fathers house, I hope Montgomery may be successful, and all the boys turn out as well as they promise- Frank is a sweet fellow and appears very amiable. . . . . Jac is at Harrisburg or Bellefonte- he did intend to go to Virginia[1] and pay you a visit- but says he cannot be so long absent now in these hard times- but if people do not fail they are comparatively well off- and so My dear Sister let us be thankful that your husband & his brothers are out of business- and that our dear Jo is a prudent man- or let us rather thank God for all his mercies and pray that we may be enabled to submit to his will in all things- Mr Moses & Becky have gone to Bordentown with Mr Murat[2] to spend the day- and Sara has gone to hear Mr Furness preach- but they both- and all the rest of the family desire affectionate remembrances to you and my dear Ben, and I send mine most warmly to my dear Boys too- . . . .

I was concerned to hear of the death of Miss Crittenden- I did not know her, but any misfortune to that family would call for my sympathy - pray present them my regards - did you ever receive "Sartor Resartus?" and how do you like it - when you go to Canewood again tell Cary to take care of my

[1] During her Eastern trip Mrs. Benjamin Gratz had sojourned for a time at Richmond, Va., to visit her niece by marriage, Mrs. Harriet Marx Etting.
[2] Joachim Murat, the son of the King of Naples, emigrated to the United States after the fall of the kingdom. He married a Miss Fraser of Baltimore who conducted a private school for young ladies at Bordentown, New Jersey.

tree- and tell all the boys to think sometimes of me- God Bless you my dear Sister & Brother- I offer my best wishes for your health and happiness, and am always with sincere affection your attached

Sister R G<small>RATZ</small>

* * *

TO THE SAME

A trip through New York State - the beauties of the natural scenery - James Fenimore Cooper's country - Natty's mountain cave - Cooper's quarrels with his neighbors - James Paulding - Washington Irving - "men are the worst patients."

Aug 27th 1837

Your letter My Dear Sister was forwarded to me to Cooperstown, where it was really a treasure- we were so far away from Kentucky that the sight of your handwriting seemed an assurance that a sisters love can find us through all space, and the chain did not drag at each remove but seemed to lengthen and bear me lightly through bright scenes each day- with the thought how much you would have enjoyed them with us. Sara wrote to you the very day I received your letter- and I suppose she gave you a sketch of our travel- at Fishkill- where the good old Judge was so pressing for you to visit his hospitable Mansion- and his mantle has fallen on his successors for they are all kind & friendly as he would have been- and such a noble Estate ought to be in liberal hands, for there is nothing wanting to make it the seat of elegant and tasteful enjoyment. Our dear Julia is treated like a daughter of the family and she has passed the summer with her friends pouring balm into their wounds and sharing their sorrow for the early fate of the daughter they have lost- then, to Albany & Utica & the Falls of Trenton!! oh how I wished you had been there to gaze & wonder & admire- but where could you go that your heart would not glow with admiration? I am sure not through the north or West of our highly cultivated country- nor through the mountains & glens, the rocky shores of Canada creek- nor the cascades of the Mohawk- in fact we have been making a tour of pictures- we staid several days at Cooperstown, and made acquaintance with a number of agreeable people, it rained so constantly that we did not mount to Natty's[1] mountain cave- but we sketched the hills wandered along the Lake, and saw the old Vale- but the magician[2] who drew such graphic sketches, was not visible Wand in hand - he had got into *a snarl* as the newspaper says, and kept out of sight, in fact I was sadly disappointed at not meeting him where I could hear him talk, he has offended his neighbours & they have banished his books & would not care if he were to visit the Mohecans himself - In New York James Paulding found us out, and seemed as glad to see me as he was twenty years ago- we talked a whole day together and renewed so many agreeable passages in our lives, that I would willingly go to N Y. annually for such another conference - Washington Irving came in too- and they were as brilliant as in the days of their youth - . . . .

Our brother Jo recovered his health at Saratoga, and looks so well that he has been complimented all round on his improvement- we returned on Friday- and the girls will follow next week- we found Jac languid & thin, he has been indisposed & depressed for several days- Dr Hays has him in hand, & I hope will soon effect a cure, I have just put on a blister at the back of his neck, to relieve a tightness across

[1] Natty Bumpo in Cooper's "Leatherstocking."
[2] James Fenimore Cooper.

his eyes- men are the worst patients, I would rather take the pain, than see them bear it- but we have no right to chuse even our trials, but much cause to be grateful for the blessings that are mingled with them in our cup of life- Rosa & Sara are both with their Mother, the former has entirely recovered and looks very charmingly- Sara[1] is a devoted Mother, and rarely has her little Laura out of her arms, it is a sweet little babe- she is going to take it to Richmond, to receive a grand fathers blessing- the family are all called together to see perhaps for the last time the venerable old man[2]- his health has been declining ever since you met him here- .... You have been spending August at Canewood- gathering an abundant harvest - was there ever such a luxuriant summer? the fields teeming with rich grain, and the trees laden with fruit- abundant showers keep the foliage green & the field verdant & gay with flowers- it really maketh ones heart glad to view the bounty of providence, what a happy lot is his who passes his life in such scenes, and can raise his thankful voice in adoration to the God who gives them- beautiful Canewood, my thoughts often carry me there, to a morning scene from my chamber window, the sun shining on that sweet lawn & the birds chirping- & the boys merry voices echoing thru the forest- shall I ever see it in reality again? God knows- but assuredly I hope so- give my best love to My dear Ben, and to all My sweet boys- .... Adieu My dear Maria, May you always be happy- having your husband & children, approving & beloved around you. ....

[1] Sara Hays Mordecai.
[2] Jacob Mordecai, the father of Captain Alfred Mordecai.

TO THE SAME

This letter reveals the fact that although Benjamin Gratz had married out of the faith he observed the Jewish festivals as is indicated by the reference to the observance of the Feast of Tabernacles in his home - the patriarchal home of Joseph Simon of Lancaster, Pa., the grandfather of Rebecca Gratz - a storm at sea - "pious zealots" - the Reverend Joseph Wolfe, the notorious Jewish convert to Christianity - Isaac Leeser's faux pas - Bulwer's Athens - Carlyle's Sartor.

Novr 5th 1837

You may be sure My dear Maria, necessity alone prevented my answering your interesting letter as soon as it was received particularly as you had experienced uneasiness at my long silence- but I have been sick & spiritless and therefore such a bad companion that I thought it more kindness to keep quiet and leave our brothers correspondence to suffice, for Jo told me several times that he had written- I am glad you were kind enough to find an excuse for me and kept the Tabernacle celebration, in scenes so naturally appropriate to the season- for My own part I was only once under the shelter of its roof- and partook no further of the feast spread before me- than a little bread & salt tho' I enjoyed the sight of goodly fruit & wine distributed in plenty and listened to a hymn of thanksgiving that we were permitted to meet at the sanctification of this festival & view the emblems of former rejoicing- the palm & branches of goodly trees- mentioned in scripture as taken by the youths & damsels- as they went out after the ingathering of the blessings of the year, to dwell in booths and rejoice before the Lord- has always had a great charm in my imagination-

I like the idea of cheerful gratitude and combining religious worship with heartfelt thankfulness in scenes where they had just reaped the benefits of their labor- and praying that God would enable them to use his gifts for their good and the benefit of the poor- this is making religion one of our daily duties- a habit of our lives- and the commemoration annually of some National event in our history, which at this period of the world is called "supersticious" observances has to me such a different bearing that I can hardly understand how a Jew can consider them oppressive or consent to forego them- Ben has told you of our Grandfathers[1] patriarchal habit of living- of his hospitalities to his brethren and his amiable disposition- he has told you too, how liberally and justly he dealt with all mankind- and how he was beloved by his neighbours & the poor who were within reach of his bounty- I remember & feel a yearning to view the old Lancaster homestead- and felt offended that it should have fallen into strange hands as long as one of his children survived who might have been sheltered by its roof- but dissensions crept in- and when the good old man was gathered to his fathers- there was no son to reign in his stead- the last day I spent in Lancaster I visited his tomb- the fence was broken, cows were grazing among the high grass & weeds that covered it- and I came away sorrowful[2] . . . .

I was much interested in your account of Bishop Smiths trial and your benevolent heroism in sustaining him in the

[1] Joseph Simon the pioneer Jewish settler of Lancaster, Pa.
[2] The graves of Joseph and Rosa Bunn Simon are now in good repair. The epitaphs on the tombstones are quite legible. On Joseph Simon's tombstone the epitaph is both in Hebrew and English. The latter is as follows:

> And Joseph gave up the Ghost
> and Died in a good Old Age
> an Old Man and full of Years
> and was gathered to his People.

hour when all else deserted him, I hope it will make him a better man- I have not much respect for pious Zealots- there is so much pride & uncharitableness mixed with their self righteousness that it seldom comes to good- we have a new made Christian Saint here, going the rounds of all the churches, who has recently been ordained a Minister of the Gospel & who, if I am not mistaken will disappoint his flock- the Revd Joseph Wolfe, the famous converted Jew- I read a book he published some years ago, his journal in Palestine which is as little to the purpose of religion as are the discourses I have heard he preaches- but the novelty of a Jew preaching the Gospel is irresistible and the churches are crowded- Leeser went to hear him, and was simple enough to write him a note in hebrew, pointing out some misquotations he made from a learned German author- which he turned to good account, by reading from his pulpit as from a Rabbi, wishing him to retract- . . . .

I am sorry to tell you that Mr Furness has been long suffering with sore throat, so as to prevent his preaching, and make him look very badly, but Dr Hays thinks he is getting well, and does not call it by the hard name -

Ask My dear brothers to accept my love, and believe My

> Joseph Simon Departed this Life the 12th day of
> the Month Shebat
> in the Year Corresponding
> with the 24th day of January 1804
> aged 92 Years in a good Old Age
> And Joseph walked with God
> and he was not for God took him -

> H S R I H

> The epitaph on the wife's tombstone reads
> The Body of Mrs. Rosa Simon
> Who departed this life
> the   day of May
> 69 Years

own dear Sister in the ardent affection, which ever prays for your happiness, and so May God Bless you- RG-
Tell Jac the Susquehanna has been seen on her passage. and is believed to have pursued her voyage unmolested by pirates.

* * *

TO THE SAME

Orphan Asylum affairs - the beautiful Kentucky country - a mild winter - charming home scene - Kentucky friends - the Reverend William H. Furness.

Decr 31 1837

I thank you most heartily My Dear Sister for your two last letters, and thus acknowledge my delinquency- but you know this is my busy season- and if you knew how much our labours are increased since we have lost Mrs Hale at the Asylum, you would not wonder that we are busy- so much doing & undoing- and finding things done wrong, that there is quite a bustle when we are to come before the public and shew what we have been about- I have been working in the dark too for more than a month- for in that time the children have had the measles, and not having had it in my childhood I have been made by the solicitude of my friends to avoid its contact out of my own house, and so I think it my duty to be more attentive since the doors are open to me again- but this is a long apology instead of telling you that our brother Jac got home on the 26th inst much better than when he left us, and though still thin, and taking great care of his diet I feel quite satisfied that his journey into your lovely country and loving society has done well for him- I am sorry he had so little of our dear Ben's society- had he known what a mild month was to conclude the year he might have sunned himself on the western side of the mountains, and still have found the rivers flowing uninterrupted by ice- I was a little surprised and sorry too at the accounts you give of yourself, you should certainly have taken better care of your family during the absence of your husband- .... Sally Hays returned home a week after Ben left us- she regretted much that she did not see him- but he would have carried you a sorry account of her appearance, for she was sick on her voyage and is thinner & paler than when she went away much to her mortification, having in all her letters boasted of her improvement in the climate & society of her native home- and who would not feel well & happy in such a return- she found no change but agreeable ones during her absence- her dear Parents & family circle, all greeting her with such fondness- her youthful companions & friends all flocking around her- and the servants who had watched her looks and 'tended her as much from love as from duty, still answering her calls and serving her son with the pride and pleasure their faithful attachment to her induced- it is quite charming to listen to her details-

Her eyes sparkle, and she is as voluble as if she were unwilling we should lose a single scene or trait of the picture she has so much enjoyed- particularly as she winds up by saying- well, we cannot have everything in this world- and I am very happy here- and could be anywhere with My husband- and so Miriam says even in Georgetown and I have no doubt Becky[1] will say in New York, when the time comes for her to make the trial- .... Tell My dear Ben I received a visit for him a few days ago from Mr Short, who was very much annoyed on finding himself too late in returning

[1] Rebecca Gratz Moses married Jonathan Nathan of New York, June 17, 1840.

his courtesy, until I assured him, that I would transfer it to him by letter, he then said something civil of the opportunity it gave him of paying his respects &c- and I introduced his agreeable relations in Kentucky upon the tapis, we talked of them for some time, until I made him feel proud of their talents & consequence, and I hope he will put a codicile to his will in favor of your young friend Mary- now if there should happen to be a beauty among the younger girls it might go as far towards making her fortune, as Marys good sense & orthography which he commends in her letters. . . . .

Gratz Moses[1] will go next week to the South for his bride he appears very happy in the anticipation- and I pray he may realize all his wishes for domestic life- I have seen too little of the lady to judge of his prospects in that respect, the character she bears in her own town is excellent- and she appears gentle & intelligent- if their years were reversed it would be a better match, but he is desperately in love- I shall deliver your kind message when he comes to town and know it will gratify him- . . . . remember me to the dear friends who remember me- Jac has quite flattered me by telling how I was enquired for- . . . .

God Bless you My dear Sister. I cannot express all the obligations I feel to you- for the sweet visit of our dear Ben- but estimate your love, by the sacrifice you made in willingly parting with him- it made us so happy- and now he is restored to you, I can speak of it, without making you sad- embrace him & the dear boys for me, and believe me always most devotedly your affectionate

R GRATZ

[1] Dr. Simon Gratz Moses married Mary P. Asche, January 24, 1838, at Wilmington, N. C.

(con'd)

Our friend Mr Furness is in very bad health- but I hope not desperate- the book you mention I have not read- he asked me if I would provided he sent it to me- and when I reminded him of his promise- recommended Sartor Resartus as much better- do you think so?

* * *

TO THE SAME

First mention of the Hebrew Sunday School which Rebecca Gratz founded in 1838, the first of its kind in the United States. This school is still in existence and has grown to very large proportions.

Character more important than mental attainments.

April 24th 1838.

I have this Moment My Dear Sister dispatched a letter of introduction to you by Oscar Dewees- but when you will receive it- matters not- it seemed too tantalizing to be writing to you with such uncertainty and then to say nothing that was likely to be at all interesting, when I might tell you how many family concerns were on my mind and in my heart- the first then is to tell you that except the ticking of the clock I have been two days without an audible companion for my morning hours- yesterday Julia & Horace left us at an early hour - the first to pay a few attentions to her brother George before his departure- and Horace to hurry forward that he may spend one day at Niagara before George joins him at Buffalo- I conclude that Jo has told you how Horace unexpectedly obtained the situation he applied for on the Erie railroad, and that George Hoffman by the same good luck is also appointed, two vacancys having occurred in the places they applied for- then Mr Moses had fixed on the same day to move and Sara went to help them, and Jac is absent- but it is no real hardship to be alone- particularly when one has so much to think of- to pray for- and to be thankful- Some one has written "our very wishes give us not our wish"- I think he should have made some qualification of the sentence to make it true- our accomplished wishes do not leave us free from care- and if he means that happiness is not the result, it may be true, for nothing worth wishing for can be enjoyed without the price of anxiety and care- as you will experience when one of your boys leave your parental roof to seek their fortunes and make their own destiny in the world- it is true we have many hopes and consolations when they exhibit character on which we can rely- and I really depend on firmness of principle and love of truth in the youngling we have just parted with, he has discretion too and an enduring spirit, that may be better in the end than shining parts, and he went away pleased with the profession he has chosen, and full of high hopes- as young and ardent minds ever do- May He who led his ancestors through the wilderness where there was no path be his guide also, mid all the perils of life, and make him worthy of *His* care- . . .

I met Mr Furness a few days ago and he told me he was going to recommence his official duties- I preached prudence to him for a little longer until the weather was warm and settled but fear he will not wait- and if it were not for my Sunday school I should like exceedingly to witness his return to his congregation- he promised me a new book written by a friend of his- and I told him what you wrote about his own- it has gone through another edition and he says is improved-
. . . . I hope Jac will make you a visit, and induce you all to accompany him home, it would be delightful to pass the

summer in your society some where when the city is too hot- we can go to the seashore, or some other place that you prefer- and then you might find some School if you want one for your boys-

Embrace My dear Nephews for me - God Bless them and their dear little brothers and may they all unite in weaving blessings for their beloved parents for whom My prayers, daily ask abundant good - ever your R G

* * *

TO THE SAME

The coronation of Queen Victoria - "The Great Western" - Sir Walter Scott - An accomplished American woman - contrasts in sisters - Harriet Livermore.

May 25th 1838.

A rainy morning, has given me, My dearest Maria- what I prize more than sunshine- an opportunity of writing to you- for I had made an engagement at the Orphan Asylum which the weather would not let me keep- and I mean to spend it much more to my taste, in prattle with you- you are careful not *to say* anything that may encourage the hope of seeing you but on comparing a passage in your last letter to me with another in Jo's, my imagination & my wishes have been travelling fast to meet you- and arranged all things with perfect convenience, and to my entire satisfaction- so that I shall not be surprised when you announce your whole plan, ... I hope My Sister your health is improved and that you will only have pleasure to seek in your summer tour- what think you of a steam voyage across the Atlantic to witness the coronation of the Queen Victoria? "The great

Western" is to return for such an accomodation and no doubt some of her Majesty's loyal subjects will take advantage of it- I have just seen an old friend from Albany who has returned from a seven years residence abroad, in which time she visited all the principal places of resort- passed several summers in Switzerland & winters in Italy & France- was a month at Naples while Sir Walter Scott resided there, and through the kindness of a Scotch friend enjoyed frequent opportunities of being in his society- she told him, that in sickness and in sorrow his books had solaced her pain & grief- and that she owed him the homage of her gratitude- he accepted this compliment with sensibility, and gave her permission to come when ever it suited her to his apartments- if he was not disposed to see her- she must stay with his daughters- and it is told (tho not by her) that Sir Walter said Miss Bridges was the most agreeable woman he had ever known- the friend who introduced her, told him she resembled his Jennie Dean, and thus obtained her an interview, which led to such enviable results- well now I must tell you now she has returned home- she has even more simplicity of manners than when I knew her 14 years ago- for time has mellowed her vivacity into an even flow of cheerfulness- her enthusiasm has not lessened but is spent on objects of high natural beauty- or on exquisite works of art- and she has so much good taste that she neither obtrudes her knowledge & experience in conversation, nor declines to satisfy curiosity but is so natural and unaffected that you feel perfectly easy and at home with her- her Sister the companion of her travels on the contrary looks so full of superiority of what she has seen, that you do not feel inclined to ask her any questions- I wish you could have seen our friend Miss Peters' enjoyment of Anna Bs society- she took her for an entire Blue- and thought to make the most of her- but for all that Miss P is an excellent woman- and so if you please- I will differ from you in opinion, that it is a pity we could not speak just what we think- if we were to say all- how constantly we should bring out little defects- which only shade great virtues but do not hide them- and thus offend against the golden rule- that binds society together- two other personages have come across the waters- that interest me greatly- Mrs Hardman Philips- who may say with Naomi "the Lord hath dealt bitterly with me I went out full- and have returned empty"- she has been the mother of five- and has come back childless--poor lady, I have not yet seen her- for her grief was so much renewed by coming among Sophy's friends that the Dr forbid her seeing them until she has recovered her composure- and Harriet Livermore, who executed her pilgrimage to Jerusalem- and talks in scripture phrase of all she has seen & suffered-

But I forget My dear Maria that you care more to hear about people you know- and the friends you love- Mrs Louisa Myers has written me too, a very feeling letter, God Knows what is wisest & best- and doeth according to his will- "but the human understanding comprehendeth it not-" of Mrs Marxs death, we must "hold our peace"- she was an excellent woman I believe, and of such there is safety even in death- the unexpected mercy of Mr Marxs recovery, his family now entertain better hopes- and both these dispensations, must touch the hearts of his children, and reconcile them to the will of the ruler- . . . .

How sorry I am that you have lost Mrs Short's society- and that your two agreeable male friends have quarreled- what can resist ambition & self interest in Man's nature- the bonds of brotherhood are broken, and every rational consideration- and substantial source of happiness sacrificed to station- I am afraid your Transylvania will suffer, by these frequent breaches, and, I really shall regret anything that injures beautiful Lexington- .... I am glad to hear My dear little Hyman has begun a correspondence with his Uncle it must be refreshing to Mr B[1]- to exercise his affections on family objects and indulge himself on subjects instructive & genuine- for what so heartless as politics- and from all I have seen of him in private life- I should think, the Globe must be a more hateful burden than ever Atlas bore, we were very desirous of having a visit from Elizabeth, and Sara wrote for her to come with Mr Hays & Ellen- but her parents would not part with her- she had been sick- Mrs Paulding told me she was charmed with Your Sister- they passed a fortnight in Washington last month-

Our last letter from Jac was dated Clarksburg- and he did not say how much longer he would be there- but he wrote in good spirits- he seems to be up & doing among the lands of our Fathers estate and I hope will not be labouring in vain- present my ardent affection to My dear Ben, and your boys, and believe me My dear Sister with unvarying love your
R G-

[1] Francis Preston Blair.

TO THE SAME

The year of this letter is omitted from the date but it is fixed by the mention of the birth of Gratz Moses' first child. This child was born November 24, 1838, at Bordentown, New Jersey.
Sunday School class - Mrs. Hemans' "Hebrew Mother" - exposition of Genesis by the Reverend William H. Furness - T. I. Wharton's addresses- the anti-foreigner riots of 1838.

Philadelphia Decr 16th

I have been counting the days for a whole week My Dear Maria, in hopes each would have brought me a letter from you, and tho perhaps one is on its passage I shall not wait its arrival, because my busy time is approaching and I may not find leisure to write again, until I hail you on the New Year- I have been up to Bordentown to see Gratz little son, he came to town and seemed so proud & happy in the character of Parent that I had not the heart to disappoint his wish to introduce him to my love - and as all the children of my sister have a peculiar claim upon me, it would have been churlish to refuse- his wife is really a fine woman, so rational, and mild, and kind hearted, that this would alone entitle her to the regard of his family- but she adds the charm of a well cultivated intellect- and strong principle of rectitude- which must claim their respect also- . . . . I am yet uncertain whether Julia will make me her annual visit or not, so when you think of her on a morning in the little breakfast room- say what would I not give for some of the interesting conferences we held together- out of which we both I trust gleaned some useful knowledge- it is true we each have the means of improving ourselves from the same book in our separate homes- but I believe we gain more by comparing opinions than by solitary study- and so My dear Sister, if you tell me what portion of scripture you are engaged on I will read it, and our meditations may again be communicated- in My Sunday School I have taken the life of Samuel to read & comment on- and find it deeply interesting- Hannahs earnest desire & prayer for a child- and her self sacrifice in devoting him- is almost as touching in the language of Scripture- as Mrs Hemans has made it in her beautiful poem "The Hebrew Mother"- . . . . our favorite orator Mr Furness gave a most beautiful lecture the other evening on Genesis- and verily- I thought he illustrated his subject most aptly- the hall was crowded, and the most deep & fixed attention prevailed, I wished you could have heard him, for I never heard him more eloquent in the pulpit, and he managed a popular lecture so as to abate nothing from the reverence & dignity of his clerical character- on tuesday next our dear Bens friend T. I. Wharton is to enlighten us- I omitted going last week because the orator had been making some violent insurgent speeches at public meetings on the disorganized state of our political situation, and the outrage was felt by all the Whig party or in other words those who respect the laws- I do not know when Harrisburg will be left to civil government- the military are still there to keep the peace- but I am not going to trouble you with subjects you can learn better from the newspapers- if you wish to learn them at all- . . . .

Our family affairs continue much as you left them - I look at the dry branches of the willows and remember how constantly you admired their graceful foliage but spring will renew their beauty- and I hope My dear Maria we shall look at them together and again praise them- and the hand that so bounteously clothes them & all nature with richness and beauty- we have had very little cold weather yet, none that impedes our usual exercise in the city, tho' enough to stop steam boat travelling in our rivers, which the girls think hard of as they could go up to Bordentown unattended in that way, and are obliged to get an escort by the railroad. . . . . present my love to them- Hyman saw Mr Clay when he was in town- but gleaned nothing from him about our Kentucky friends, except that he had seen Ben the day before he left home- God Bless you My dear Sister. May the approaching New Year find you in health & happiness which I pray may encrease "even as your lives pass"- believe me ever affectionately

Your RG

* * *

TO THE SAME

Sins of omission - New Year's Day reflections - a day of reckoning.

Jany 9th 1839

A thousand thanks Sweet Sister, for the happiness your two last letters have bestowed - I did not mean to have been your debtor on the New Year - but old Time on his silent march overtook me before my duties were fulfill'd and will, I fear, have many registers against me- when my great account is called for- of omissions- not only through ignorance but delays- it is well to have a point in every year to sum up our accounts as well for our moral improvement as for the affairs of business with our fellow beings- and truly I have had a charge this morning that will carry me back through many years of my life, to examine my conscience- for actions and motives of action- for feelings indulged, without the sanction of judgment- and to trace consequences through a long train of causes, up to the present unsatisfactory result- . . . .

There is a part of your letter My Dear Sister, that gives me much concern, you speak of your health as seriously affected- but as your dear husband is watchful- and Dudley your leech, I hope soon to have better accounts- Your New Years gift I treasure, in "My heart of hearts"- and give due credence to your husbands feelings, nor indeed is my confidence one jot the less- nor has my love ever known abatement- it is agreeable sometimes, and why not on the New Year- to examine our hearts and renew compacts when we can, of affection and truth as we do leases- strengthening the old ones by free and willing offerings- and sometimes raising our grateful estimation- by the memory of our full loves and hopes of future improvements- every parent realises such feelings- and in the various relations I have been placed in, both private and public, I have experienced it too- . . . . Sara's[1] letters always speak of Lizzie,[2] and your Sister- the last was written on the 1*st*-all the pageantry of the *coast* was displayed on that day- and your niece bore the palm of admiration among the fair and young- . . . . Jo has kept his health and spirits amazingly for the winter- except in the beginning he has not complained of cold- and is so much interested in the Gas works, that he goes up to the N. Liberties once or twice a week in any weather- he and all the rest of the family reciprocate your good wishes and pray for the restoration of your health- and the completion of your happiness- half of your boys are no longer children- and the others are fast outgrowing the title- I keep their gauge by some of their old companions, and since Horace has put

---

[1] Sara Hays Mordecai, who was living in Washington.
[2] Elizabeth Blair.

on a long coat- fancy him and Bernard a couple of young gentlemen- say the kindest words of affection to all your sons for me, and tell them they can never outgrow my love- . . . . and I repeat again and again my warmest assurance of being your and my dear Brothers most fond and devoted

RG-

* * *

TO THE SAME

Accidents by rail and steamer - legislative enactments necessary - Stevens' "Palestine" - Combe and Spurzheim on phrenology.

Phil - Feb 8th 1839

Thanks my Dearest Maria for your consideration in saving us the alarm of seeing our dear Brothers accident first in the Newspaper, I pray God he is recovering from the effects of it before this- we shall never be secure from the dangers and carelessness in steam travelling until the Engineers of Railroads and steam boats are made responsible for all accidents that occur- and I think this would be a fit occasion for an appeal to the legislature of your state to begin the work of reform- Will you not have the kindness to write again, or induce our dear Ben to do so (if he is able) in order to allay anxiety as to the extent of injury he has sustained- you behaved like a heroine as you always do on great occasions- when you have time to summon firmness- and now your other agreeable powers will be employed to make confinement sit easy on the invalid. . . . .

You ask me My dear Sister, what books we are reading besides the bible?- Why we have accompanied you thru Palestine with John Stevens and had all our veneration excited in the wonderful news of the excavated city- and our patriotism warmed amidst the desolation of Jerusalem!!- and are now deeply interested with George Combe and Spurzheim on the science of phrenology- Combe has just finished a course of the most interesting lectures I ever listened to- and many a time have I wished for you, to exercise your mind in this study of nature through a medium, which if not true (which I believe it is) is so ingenious and plausible, in the lessons of Combe, that it opens a channel of thoughts leading to high and holy contemplations- If you have not read a small work of his on the Constitution of Man[1] I can recommend it, as highly interesting and useful- what you would particularly like in his lectures, is his application of phrenology to the improvement of education and he addresses it to women and mothers particularly with good effect and gives examples from numerous anecdotes that have fallen under his own observation- in the experience of 20 years devoted to practical science- he is quite different in practice and precept to Dr Caldwell- . . . . Bless you My dear Brother and Sister. May you and yours be ever in his holy keeping prays yr sister RG

* * *

TO THE SAME

Special Providence - Interpretation of Exodus XXXIV - Prescott's "Ferdinand and Isabella."

April 25th 1839

Day after day has passed My dear Maria, in the hope that I should have a letter from you, until I can no longer resist

[1] First published in 1828.

the desire to write and quicken your memory of the long standing debts you owe me - this is either the third or fourth letter since I have been blest with the sight of your handwriting, and I find your husbands correspondence with his Brothers too circumscribed to satisfy me- or compensate for the treasures of your pen- so long withheld- To be sure you are not accountable for this charge- as no one is obliged to pay for a commodity they have neither asked for or ordered and which by the bye may cost more in the perusal than it is worth- and so I beg you will inform me, if the same notion has occurred to you- but I shall in the meantime remembering all your former kindness- and the interest you took in all our affairs go on to sketch another home scene for your magic lanthorn, for in our house hold we have almost as many changes as would suit that instrument- Jac & Horace are both gone again for the summer, at least the latter, who will hardly come again until "November's surly blasts make field & forest bare"- and one hardly likes to think of such a season, and the luxurious blossoms promise such an abundance of summer fruit- but thus our lives are made up- the future continually intrudes on the present and we dare not assure ourselves that the hopes we are so fond of framing will ever be realized- yet God is so bountiful to us that we have as much cause to be grateful for what He denies as for what is granted- knowing that wisdom & mercy are the attributes of his power & inconsiderable as we are, individually or collectively among the works of his creation, he considers us worthy of his care- it is perhaps easier to conceive that God regulates a Universe, than that every minute being from the least atom that has life & motion is especially his and shares his superintending providence- yet this is His greatness- When Moses asked to be shown the divine Glory- and was told- "I will cause my goodness to pass before thee"-

he must have felt that the whole book of nature was open before him- and every sight & sound & smell proclaimed the glory of God- how delightful it is at this season to hear the birds attuning their little harmonious voices- even in their cages- telling us as Cowper said of his captive "the oppressor keeps his body bound- but knows not what a range his spirit takes"- does not the caged songster teach us a striking lesson? but I proposed a family picture, and have carried you into the air in a bird cage- and Gratz's wife- in whom you took so much interest- came to town yesterday with her lovely boy five months old- to visit his grandfather, who never saw him before- and has so enchanted his young aunts- that I do not expect to have another reading day for a week, tho' we are in the midst of Prescott's interesting "Life of Ferdinand & Isabella"- and have for sometime had quite an attentive audience for 2 hours every morning Julia & Sally included- .... I sent you some caps by Mrs Hunter, which I hope will suit you- they are the latest fashion and much used here- remember me affectionately to My dear Brother & nephews- .... what are your plans for the summer? How I should like to meet you at Canewood for a few weeks or at the Sea Shore- or any other place but most especially in my own chamber where we have so often conferred together- God Bless you dear Sister pray let me soon hear from you and believe me always

Your affectionate R GRATZ

TO THE SAME

Family letters - the Orphan Society - a "stupid immoral novel" by Lady Bulwer - contrast between Bulwer and Scott - criticism of Prescott's "Ferdinand and Isabella" - Isabella's character - "the Secret Societies of the Middle Ages" - "man's inhumanity to man."

May 27th 1839

If I tell you now My Dear Sister, how delighted I was to receive your letter- you may remind me that it was a fortnight old before I made the acknowledgment but, truly it has been in my heart acknowledged daily, and always most gratefully- and I have been twenty times on the point of telling you so before- but I am not going to enumerate the causes of delay, for I have been sick & dizzyheaded in the last ten days- and had to part with Julia on Saturday, so I am sure of your sympathy, and having gained that point, may proceed in the hope of interesting you further- some one says that family letters, should be a kind of domestic newspaper- this is a good idea provided one was furnished with incident & anecdote worthy of record- but the even tenor of dull city life afford few circumstances of the kind, and I should be sorry to impose the idle rumours which would liken a letter to a newspaper, on you, when perhaps common honesty might oblige me to contradict them in my next sheet- I was pleased to see our friends Mr & Mrs Macadistor yesterday, and to hear the good accounts they bring from Kentucky of all your dear family. Eliza tells me you are again Secretary of the Society and I am glad of it, for your boys are no longer so young as to require all your attention, and I know by experience how richly one is repaid for all the trouble & thought that is spent on that institution, and you have even more to attach you to it than I have- for you are the Founder as well as the principal Manager- and there are many here who could fill my place, without my being missed if I withdraw- .... I have been reading a most stupid immoral novel,[1] by Lady Bulwer, for no other reason than because it is said to be the picture of their own life, and I have always thought so badly of her husbands character that my curiosity was awakened to know how they would make it out themselves- I must say I feel less respect for her Ladyship since she has spoken of herself- but I hope it will have the good effect of putting down the fashion of admiring the poison distilled from the profligate pen of her husband, since his character is to be fully exposed- we may indeed turn with delight to the pages of Sir W Scott, and find in his life & letters such nature & purity as gives a brighter glow to his genius & his virtues- have you read Prescott's "Ferdinand & Isabella"? if not, I think it will interest & entertain you- I must confess I turn with disgust from the intolerance & superstition of the age- and can scarcely agree with the historian in his praise of Isabella's benevolence & piety when the stake and the gibbet were continually reeking with the blood of Jews & heretics- it is a bad argument for one in so responsible a situation as the Queen that she was under the dominion of her priests- however great allowance must be made for the spirit of the age she lived in, and she was the admiration and wonder of her day- I have been reading an account of "the Secret Societies of the Middle Ages"- and there too we have nothing but fanaticism & persecution- In-

[1] The novel was entitled "Chevaley or the Manor Honour." The marriage of the famous novelist, Edward Bulwer Lytton, was most unhappy. The couple were divorced. In 1839 Lady Bulwer published this novel in which she caricatured her husband in most scathing terms. Her attacks on Bulwer continued to the time of his death.

stitutions founded under the auspices of religion- made first the tools and then the victims of fiery zeal & superstition- what a revolting picture does every history of human society present- we must turn to individual exceptions if we would be reconciled to our own species- and fortunately in every age such may be found to plead for Mercy on their erring fellows- . . . . Miriam writes, how happy it would make her to meet you & her Uncle Ben at her own home again- this world would be too happy if all we love might be collected in one charmed circle, and enjoy the delight of that communion of perfect love & confidence- which is sometimes & at distant periods permitted to occur- Say a thousand kind things for me to My beloved brother, and the dear boys- and then My dear Sister pardon all my stupidity, and love me with as true an affection as I offer to your acceptance- ever

Your attached R GRATZ-

* * *

TO THE SAME

Mrs. Murat's school at Bordentown - a Napoleonic episode- Dr. Gratz Moses - Henry Clay at Saratoga Springs.

Sept 22nd 1839

My Dear Sister

Immediately on the receipt of your letter I wrote to Mrs Murat, and have just received her answer saying that she has three vacancies, and will be most happy to have your little friend under her charge- I perfectly concur with you in opinion that this is the most eligible situation for Mary Boswell[1]- indeed I think it the most desirable family a girl

[1] A niece of Mrs. Benjamin Gratz and the ward of her husband.

can be placed in who is separated from her own home for while their education is properly attended to, their affections are cultivated by those little attentions and sympathies so indispensable in female intercourse- Mrs Murat & her sisters take such an interest in their pupils happiness that they seem like members of one family- and if you inform them what particular branches what accomplishments &c you wish Mary to cultivate they will no doubt be influenced in the direction of her studies accordingly- Mr M[1] is at present in Europe, the death of his mother made it necessary for him to go, she has left to his son Joachim, all the property she could dispose of in her own right- but this good fortune to her child makes no difference in Carolines[2] plans- it must be years before any arrangements can take place on his behalf- and she is determined to achieve her independence, and support her family by the means, she has found so satisfactory & successful, and for which she is most respected

You were right My sister in assuring Mary that she may depend on my affectionate interest, to do all that she may require of a friend here, and to introduce her to the kindest attentions of her instructress- and any hints you may send from her medical adviser will be acceptable- Gratz Moses is

[1] Napoleon Lucien Charles Murat, second son of Joachim Murat, the king of Naples, and Caroline, the sister of Napoleon Bonaparte. After his father's expulsion from Naples and subsequent death, the family suffered many vicissitudes. The two sons came to the United States, the younger arriving in this country in 1825. He married Georgiana Fraser of Baltimore; upon the loss of her fortune Mrs. Murat and her sisters opened a boarding school at Bordentown, New Jersey. Mrs. Murat and Rebecca Gratz became close friends. After the revolution of 1848 Murat returned to Europe and was reinstated in his rights when Napoleon III after the coup d'etat of 1851 became emperor. His son Joachim referred to in this letter was born in the United States in 1834 and later on played a conspicuous role in France as Prince Joachim Murat.

[2] Miss Gratz here undoubtedly confuses the names of Murat's wife and mother; she should have written Georgiana.

about leaving Bordentown to seek his fortunes in your Western World, his wife & child are at present in Phila- I think his predilections are in favor of St Louis- but he cannot decide until he makes a survey- he is adrift- "the World before him where to choose & Providence his guide". We shall be sorry to part, but he has a most excellent discreet wife and a lovely boy- which will make any home happy to him where he can secure the means of living comfortably & I believe he is fully capable of making a reputation in his profession- . . . .

Our journey to the Springs has greatly improved my health, tho' at first I was not sensible of the benefit I derived from the water- for I caught a cold that spoilt all my good looks- however I now feel well again- we were too late to see Mr Clay, or to be witness to the excitement occasioned by the presence of the great men of the nation assembled there- but this suited me much better than bustle and noise- but I think your patriotism would have been gratified by the honors paid your distinguished Countryman- give my most affectionate love to My dear Brother, and tell him, to make his wishes known about his interesting ward and rely on my doing all in my power to satisfy him, & contribute to her comfort- . . . . I began this letter crooked[1] & cannot go straight so you must accept it as it stands as I have no time to write another before the Tabernacle commences- and I want you to be in possession of this by the earliest conveyance- . . . . God Bless you My dear Sister and grant to you & My dear Ben, every thing your hearts desire, for your children- and for the continuance of your mutual happiness- ever believe in the love of your devoted Sister

R G

[1] Reference is made to the crooked lines of the letter which were running obliquely and not straight.

TO THE SAME

Orphan Society affairs - Mrs. Hemans' biography by her sister Mrs. Hughes.

Jan'y 15 1840

It is very long My dear Sister since we have held any intercourse with each other- but if my memory is correct you are in my debt a letter, however, if you will permit me to believe that I can entertain you for half an hour, I will occupy the time, between the girls going to bed, and Jo's coming home, to tell you how much I miss your letters in this long suspension- Mary Boswell talked so much of you & the boys & my dear Brother that I could almost fancy myself in the loved circle around your domestic fire side- she spent a fortnight with us at Christmas time, and won her way to our hearts, she wrote to Sara how happy she was on her return to Bordentown to find her first letters from home- her health good, and she enjoyed excellent spirits- several of her school friends were in town with her- since her departure I have been busily employed with Orphan affairs- you did not send me your report to help me out and we had no sooner carried them through the Annual than one of the Teachers resigned- and now we are put to fresh trouble but this is a trifle as times go- all who meddle with public concerns must expect changes, and when the men have so much harder trials it is not worth while to speak of ours- . . . .

Mrs Biddle has just sent us a book, which she highly recommends "Womans Mission"- have you seen it? have you read Mrs Hemans memoirs by her sister, Mrs Hughes?[1]

[1] The Memoir of Mrs. Hemans by her sister Mrs. Hughes appeared in the edition of Mrs. Hemans' Collected Works published in 1839.

it is a delightful book and represents the poetess as lovely & pure of heart as her sublimest effusions would indicate- is it not strange that with such a character & beauty- she should have been a deserted wife? her sister too must be a lovely woman, fit to be the biographer of Mrs Hemans- Sara had a letter from Lizzie yesterday your sister is well, but she says her Father is not- I suppose the excitement of politics must be a wasting disease at this season of the year in Washington-

Pray let me hear from you soon My dear Maria, I long for one of your family sketches, my nephews are all growing to be such important personages, that the picture in my minds eye they left is only a miniature of their present size, and you only can portray them as they advance in form & character. I hope you will bring them to see us next summer, our dear Ben almost promises us a visit- Jo is much better in health- he has been celebrating John Vaughans birthday- I believe his 87th and the good old citizen is as joyous on these occasions, as if they were novelties- a club has been formed, bearing his name, who meet on his birthday to drink his health in the oldest & best wine they can procure- he does not look as if he could witness many more revels of the kind- our sisters send you their love, Richea came from Baltimore looking quite well- and Fanny has been able to walk abroad quite like other people- but we are all growing old, and bear the marks of it right visibly- but dear sister the love that time ripens and makes perfect glows in our hearts for you & yours, may God ever bless you prays your affectionate

RG

TO THE SAME

The year of this letter is omitted from the date. This letter and the following one dated Feb. 23 must have been written in the same year since both mention the novel Mariamne which Rebecca Gratz had been reading. The year of this letter is fixed by the mention of Mary Boswell's attendance at the Murat private school in Bordentown. In the letter dated Sept. 22, 1839 Miss Gratz wrote to her sister-in-law that she had arranged for the acceptance of Miss Boswell as a pupil in the school. Mary Boswell came from her Lexington home shortly thereafter. The date of this letter is therefore 1840.

Your letter arrived My Dear Sister on a day when, wonderful to tell I was dining with Sister Hays and Ellen, it rained so fast that I could not get home & Mr Etting came in and told me there was a letter from Lexington, which I had been so *long desiring-* yet could not for some hours obtain! well but it was most welcome, and delighting, for it brought you all before me, in the dear home scene I love to bring before my minds eye- and allowing for the growth of your sons is as familiar as if I had been there yesterday- "rising early- attending to your children" and seeing to the affairs of your household- this is what an intelligent female writer, calls bringing great principles into common use, and is among the happy influences of "woman's mission"- and thus My dear Sister I delight to think of your employment, ... Jo's health too has much improved, and if he has not written to our dear Ben before this, you may assure him, that it must be from some other cause, he sometimes gets lazy with his pen, and puts off writing as alas, many of us do with no better excuse, until we are ashamed of ourselves, and even lose the skill to do it well, when at last our consciences demand it of us- Jac[1] was home for two days last week, and then returned to the turbulent scene of his legislative duties.

I am deeply interested in a novel, of rather a singular character, called Mariamne, the last of the Asmonean Princesses- it is a tale of Palestine, and written in the oriental style, but you know the history of Herods wife is tragical enough to make the truth more romantic than any fiction, and ones feelings have no relief in this sad tale but to know that the sufferers are gone to their rest, having lived and borne oppressions & sorrows, greater than are now inflicted in civilized warfare, except we turn to our own borders, and blush for the native sovereigns of our soil- now hunted by enlightened freemen, with a spirit more savage, than that practiced by their own hostile tribes-

I am glad to hear that Mary Boswell is so well satisfied with her school, she writes to Sara sometimes and in her last letter says she studies more than she ever did before, and loves her teacher very much, they are every day expecting Mr Murat's return- his mothers estate, will give them something handsome- but he is embarrassed, and will have debts to pay out of it- his son's fortune will however be large, by the time he gets possession- Gratz will probably be home in March or April, and long before that time we shall have to part with his amiable wife and son- we have all become much attached to them, and hope he may succeed in his profession, whatever location he may choose for his future residence-

Among the daily occurring changes of fortune in this working day world, I have just heard of the family of Wm Cox (Mrs Mather's brother), they were educated in Europe, and are fine accomplished girls- who are coming to town, to

---

[1] Jacob Gratz was a member of the State Senate of Pennsylvania at this time.

endeavour to get situations as teachers of Music- Mr Cox has been residing at Wilkesbarre, and there unfortunately embarked his property in some manufacturing establishment that has failed- he too I understand means to take a similar situation- it strikes me that if they were to go together to some new or thriving place they would haply succeed much better and live much happier than they could in this community where all their companions and connections, without being able to serve them, are richer and more fashionable than they- Mrs M. has offered them a home, and she will do all a kind hearted relation can do- but that will not maintain their whole family- . . . . I am delighted now & then to have the Lexington girls here, & get them talking about home, they tell so many amusing anecdotes of home, and the people of your town, that methinks it is like revisiting the streets of your city, reading familiar names- or knocking at the doors of old acquaintances- . . . . I have many agreeable recollections of My old friend Mrs Vertner, and hope to sometimes live in her memory- tell her how sadly poor Gertrude Merediths life is passing away- her Father infirm & depressed both in spirits & fortune- and her sister, the youngest of her dear Mothers daughters- consuming with a silent sorrow- but indeed Miriam, has redeemed her character, by the most praiseworthy devotion to her family and the quiet duties of domestic life- she told me in a note I received from her some time ago- that she was happier in the midst of her sorrows, than when she smiled in ignorance of better things- I hope her unworthy husband will never return to claim her- or again agitate her life with the allurement of his fickle love-

Jo has just come in and says he thinks every day of writing and knows he ought to have done so before- he sends his love to you & dear Ben- who may soon expect to hear from him- I am just interrupted by a visit from Louisa & Elizabeth Gratz[1]- God Bless you My dearest Maria believe me always with true affection Your Sister

RG-

Feb 10th

* * *

TO THE SAME

The year of this letter is omitted from the date. As stated in the introductory note to the last letter this epistle must have been written in the same year since both mention the novel Mariamne. Another indication that this letter was written in 1840 appears from the mention of the second examination of the Hebrew Sunday school. This refers doubtless to the annual examination. Since this school was founded in 1838 this second examination took place in 1840.

The distractions of city life - the purpose of the Sunday School - Mendelssohn's Jerusalem - the Ten Lost Tribes of Israel - the Cabala - the enemies of the Jews - the uniqueness of the Bible.

Feb 23rd

I like your proposition vastly My dear Sister, that we write to each other, at least once a fortnight whether we have news or not- foreign or domestic, for if there be lack of interest in daily occurrences- there is no lack of love to sweeten discourse, upon any subject that arises in our minds and an exchange of thought is even more profitable, than recounting events in every day life- for after all Solomon has declared "there is nothing new under the sun," and therefore we may rest satisfied that searching for news is but labour lost. I acknowledge tho', it is pleasant to note the experience of our friends in verifying this truth, and when you tell me

[1]Daughters of Simon Gratz, the oldest brother of Rebecca Gratz.

that my nephews improve in any sort of knowledge it does not abate my satisfaction, to remember, that the King of Israel was more learned so many years ago, but I sometimes feel humbled at my own ignorance when children ask me questions on serious things - that have not been familiar to my own reflections. Living in large cities we waste so much time in trifling pursuits- walking about the street- and exchanging uninteresting visits, that we are apt to consider a rainy day or a slight indisposition as so much time wasted, being then necessarily kept quietly at home, so you see I may quote your adage with equal propriety here, and feel it more poignantly, because so many years of life are spent, and yet the evil is not put away- we are now preparing for a second examination of our Sunday School and I am gratified at the evident improvement of a large class of children in religious knowledge, more particularly as I find it influencing their conduct, and manners, and gaining consideration in the minds of their parents- it will be a consolation for much lost time- if this late attempt to improve the degenerate portion of a once great people shall lead to some good- and induce wiser and better Jews to take the work in hand. I have just received a manuscript translation of a work of Mendlesohn on Jerusalem,[1] from which I expect great pleasure & labour too- for it is difficult to read & more difficult to understand, perhaps I might be better able to answer your questions, when I have perused it. You give me credit for more *lore* than I can boast, but with regard to the tribes of Israel, I do believe there are descendents of Judah, of Davids

[1] This famous book of the philosopher Moses Mendelssohn is not a treatise on the Holy City but is in its first part a dissertation on the relation of church and state. The argument is for the separation of church and state and for freedom of belief. The second portion of the book deals directly with Judaism. Here Mendelssohn sets forth that Judaism has no dogmas but is ceremonial legislation. This thesis of the philosopher has been the fruitful source of much controversy.

line in existence- the Jews of Spain claim that descent- and tho' they have no doubt been mixed with other tribes- who emigrated with them, they probably have preserved their geneology entire, the priests & Levites are known distinctly, and most families have some traditional knowledge of their ancestry- the "Cabala" is a mystical work[1] little understood and I never heard it considered a divine Revelation- I believe it is written in Chaldean- the religion of the bible- or the law of Moses, is alike for people & priest, was publicly delivered and teaches them to "love the Lord thy God with all thy heart & with all thy soul & with all thy might"- in public & in private- the bible and all Jewish books I have ever seen teach the same- you must not go to the enemies of that religion for information of their tenets and any writer who contradicts the books of the pentateuch cannot rightly interpret the Jewish religion- the wise men among the ancients had a fixed rule to enterpret the scriptures, and did not accept any opinion that disagreed with, or contradicted the text, much learning has been spent- and numerous volumes written to illustrate the word of God, but tho no other book was left in the world to speak of the wonders of his doings the Bible alone contains all the Jews require to keep their religion by- yet the sacred vol. and all other history tells how shamefully they have at different periods forsaken the law- and fallen into idolatry & unbelief- sinned, been punished- repented & sinned again- I wish you could get "Mariamne" an historical novel, that I have just read it is so deeply interesting and so well written- but you know all about her character & sufferings, and it is heart sickening to know that the author must follow her to the end through

[1] The Cabala is not a book as stated here but is the term used to designate the esoteric or mystical lore of the Jews. There is a large cabalistical literature; the chief cabalistical book is The Zohar which dates from the beginning of the fourteenth century.

sorrow & oppression, and end her life on the scaffold- . . . .
Our Sisters are well and desire you will accept their best
love- every now & then Mr Etting has feeble attacks, that
warn us of his advanced age- he has just passed over one-
and is well again- Jo received a letter from Dear Ben yester-
day- which we are delighted to get, for there had been such a
lazy spell passing between them that I felt quite impatient
to see the writing of his hand again- My best love to my dear
Brother- . . . . God Bless you my dear Sister believe me
with true affection always yours RG

* * *

TO THE SAME

*This letter which is undated is postmarked Phila May 3 but
the year is not given. The date is fixed however by the reference
to the coming marriage of Rebecca Moses which event took
place June 17, 1840 when this favorite niece of Rebecca Gratz
married Jonathan Nathan of New York.*
  *Death of Miss Harriet Fraser, sister of Mrs. Joachim Murat
- letter from Maria Edgeworth.*

I take shame to Myself My dear Sister, that our correspondence should have slackened any after the little vigor-
ous exchange of letters that passed between us some weeks
back, because I am sure neither of us consider private con-
veyances any necessary spur to the occasion and I should
have apprised you, that a package of books to your address
for the Orphan Asylum was dispatched by Mr Griggs on the
14th April to be packed with Collins & Timberlakes goods- I
have sent you such books as have been approved of in our
Asylum School, to the amount of $23.34. of which $10 is
charged to your account. $5 given by each of our brothers
Hyman & Jo- and the rest from Griggs- when times are better

and your stock is out, I shall be glad to serve you more liberally- The boxes containing your other articles have I hope arrived before this, and I beg you will let me know if they suit your taste, and fit you and whether I have exceeded your wishes in adding anything to the expressed order- not with an expectation of offering any remedy for the present occasion- but as a future guide, when it may please you, to have things sent from here- you know it always gratifies me to procure things for you, and fancy how they look upon you, but my grave taste may not be in accordance with the fashions at Lexington, and so I would be advised how to please you better- I got $100 from Jo, which has paid for everything.

Mary Boswell has been with us about three weeks and will return to Bordentown on Monday next- it is honorable to the feelings of the girls, that they relinquished a whole week of their vacation, because they could not bear to leave the family during Harriet Frasers extreme illness, but I did not like that their young hearts should be unnecessarily afflicted like that and sent Horace up for Mary, Sarah Ashe and some others who were to spend the month of April in town- Becky Moses went to her friends in time to see the last offices of affection close on poor Harriet, who died on Saturday last- she has long been a most deplorable sufferer to spinal disease, but such a sublime example of patience, piety & disinterestedness that no one could witness her trials without being benefited- and filled with admiration & sympathy. Mary speaks with much affection of Mrs Murat and the family generally, and is a great favorite with them all- I think they will now have no alloy to their cheerfulness and comfort, and trust when her dear Guardian[1] sees her he will be satisfied with the progress of her education-

[1] Benjamin Gratz was the guardian of Mary Boswell, a niece of his wife.

I hope My dear Maria, you will accompany him in his promised visit, particularly as he has some thoughts of fixing on a Northern College for your son- I shall be rejoiced to see your dear boys once more, but they have grown into men since we parted. Horace has changed too but has not gained a great deal in height- the depressed state of public enterprise in Penna has affected his prospects in his profession- there are no improvements going on here, and he is out of employment, but I hope will get something to do in the state of N. Y. where they seem to manage things better, & George Hoffman may be able to procure work for them both . . . .

Becky is preparing for a new scene of life, which will deprive us of her society before the end of summer- I expect she will be married in June, but it has been so long talked of, that I scarcely realize how soon it will be true- Jac paid us a visit of ten days and then was obliged to go to Centre county- on tuesday his duties again call him to Harrisburg, where if we may judge by the passed[1] he may be kept half the summer- I have received another letter from Miss Edgeworth, with the present of a book written by her Father "An Essay on professional education"- she expresses herself well on the character of Washington which she says is the purest recorded in history- Miss E. is the last of those illustrious women, who were so conspicuous for their genius, and its useful employment during the last half century- Hannah More- and many others- and it is her highest praise that she has done so much to raise the character of her poor country men- I have an intelligent such woman living with me, who lived in the neighborhood of Edgeworth Town- and she says. Miss E lives on the easiest terms of hospitality, and good will with her neighbours and amidst the blessings of the poor- pray My dear Sister let me hear from you soon- it is almost

[1] Slip of pen for "past."

a month since the date of your last letter- Miriam continues her weekly accounts, she is better situated in Savannah than in her former residence- she has more society and a larger field of usefulness- she is very busy just now, helping to get up a fair for the orphans, so you see there is a sort of sympathy in all our occupations, ...

Present me most affectionately to My dear brother and nephews. . . . . Good Night Sister, the watchman is calling the midnight hour- May The Guardian of Israel watch over you- and grant you peaceful slumbers prays your affectionate & faithful

R Gratz

* * *

TO THE SAME

Canewood's beauties - the Book of Jashar - citizens' meeting to protest against Damascus blood accusation.

Aug 27th 1840

I received your letter from Canewood My dear sister and was right glad to be carried back in idea to that delightful home scene of your family and the beautiful country I so much admired and enjoyed in the agreeable visit we made there together- I have a thousand times reflected on the bright moon light evenings we passed so quietly wandering about the lawn, or sitting in the shade of majestic trees conversing of one interesting matter or other, till the forest seemed peopled with their original inhabitants which the footprints of man rarely intruded.

I should like to have made one of your summer party- to have seen your namesake nieces, and heard your observations on the book of Jashar[1], that extravagant chronicle of bible characters- there is a portion of it very agreeable to me- but so many improbable histories and some impossible exploits entirely destroy its credibility, and one cannot but wonder that the author or his translator, could expect it would ever pass for the veritable book of Jashar referred to in the Scriptures. An intelligent hebrew Scholar, raised my expectations so high, in favor of it before it appeared that I confess I was sadly disappointed, when I found it impossible, as I proceeded in the work, to class it with anything better than an old romance- It was very affecting to hear Abraham & Isaac conversing on the sacrifice, as they journeyed to Mount Moriah, and to find that Jacob shared the fortitude and faith that supported them - but the introduction of Satan, and his malignant effect on the life of Jacob is shocking - particularly as the next event recorded in Scripture history is the death of Sarah- it is true she had reached a good old age and in the course of nature, might be called on to resign her life, and happily too, for as a wife & mother she was blessed, and triumphant, but we would rather think she had gone down peacefully to "the place appointed for all living," than to be killed by sudden joy- and the fallen angel the agent. Those who would take the bible history as the foundation of these works should be careful never to violate the spirit and influence of the Sacred book, nor assign motives for events not borne out by its authority- The beautiful history of Joseph too is spoiled in this book- and Moses suffers so many

[1] The Book of Jashar mentioned twice in the Bible, Joshua x, 13 and I Samuel i, 18 was a book of heroic songs. It was lost and nothing was known of it except these two references. An anonymous book of the same name, being a midrashic elaboration of the earlier Bible stories was composed about the twelfth century. The first edition of this Hebrew compilation appeared in Venice in 1625. An English translation appeared in New York in 1840. It is to this translation that Miss Gratz here refers.

adventures, that we scarcely recognize him as the plain man "meek" & "slow of speech" as he records himself to be- but enough of this, we are threading another passage in Jewish story as heart thrilling as any recorded since their dispersion - I mean the massacres at Damascus[1] and the still enduring sufferings of the poor tortured prisoners, who are accused of unnatural & unlawful crimes of which it is impossible they can be guilty- in Europe & America great exertions are making for their relief- there is a meeting to be held this Evening here, and I believe all the community feel an interest in it- Hyman received a very gratifying letter from Dr Duchesnel offering to cooperate with the Israelites in any measures devised, and saying had a general meeting of citizens been called, our Christian friends would have freely attended- but what can be done, unless the Governments of Civilized Nations combine to save them - the Jews have no representative powers, and can only act in their individual capacities, the support of the countries of which they are citizens- and the application of their wealth to purchase their brothers lives is all that they can do- and perhaps this is as far as human aid can go. God in his Mercy, may touch the hearts of their oppressors, or break their bonds when all visible means fail.

Jac left us on Tuesday for the West. I was sorry his presence at Bellefonte was required, or I should have liked him to have been here tonight. . . . . you ask about Mr

---

[1] The notorious Damascus case of blood accusation against the Jews stirred the Jewries of Europe and the United States to the depths in 1840. A monk Father Thomas had disappeared. The cry was raised by enemies of the Jews that they had killed him to use his blood at the Passover feast; European governments became involved. President Martin Van Buren, through his Secretary of State John Forsythe, urged the United States Minister at Constantinople to use his good offices in behalf of the persecuted Jews. See Proceedings of The American Jewish Historical Society, viii, pp. 143-144.

Moses will- I hear he has left each of his daughters (six in number) $15000 and divided the rest of his property between his sons but have not heard what amount- the house will be sold and his daughter Mrs M. go to live in Norfolk with her sons. Miss M. has been invited by her nieces to live with them, but I do not know which she will choose, she is independent, worth $20000 I hear- . . . . I will get Lady Ms "Women & their Mothers"- and will then answer your question- our brothers and sisters send you their love, and so do all our nieces- We have not heard of the Blairs since they went to the Springs but I hope Lizzie is better, or they would certainly have written to Sara as L and she keep up an active correspondence

I hope our dear Ben will be able to make us a visit this fall- if Jac goes to Wheeling as he expected, they ought to meet and come home together

I have some doubts whether you will be able to read this letter, for all the materials are bad, and badly used, but may try to decypher enough to convince you of my real affection dearest Maria for you and all your dear family- Cary's birthday does not pass us by unheeded - Horace claimed our good wishes on the same date- he is away and comfortably employed- . . . . God Bless you all with your hearts desire & make you happy prays yours true friend and sister R G

TO THE SAME

Howard Gratz at school in the East - a trip to Cuba - a granddaughter of Thomas Jefferson - American protest against the Damascus case.

Oct. 27th 1840

I have great happiness My dearest Maria in telling you of the safe arrival of our dear Ben & Howard which I should have done before had I not thought that you were already informed of it- it would not be easy to describe the pleasure we experience in having all our brothers together once more- if you and the other dear boys were with us we should have nothing to wish for- Howard has so grown that I can scarcely identify him with the little fellow we so much loved five years ago- but he has improved quite as much as he has grown- Reuben says he is just the thing he ought to be- so frank and gay and natural in his expression and has such an open expression of countenance that he wins our hearts and confidence at the same time- they found Mary Boswell in town and he has a whole set of school girls to beau- he drove Mary and Sarah Ashe out to the Girard College this morning and is already familiar with the city localities- I can appreciate the sacrifice at which you parted from him but hope the advantage he will derive from it will reconcile & reward you- if he is placed anywhere in our vicinity I shall be careful of his comfort and at any rate his Uncles will see to it that he is well attended to- we are daily expecting Lizzie Blair & her Father who has determined to accompany her to Havannah I hope her state of health is not so desperate as you apprehend, tho' her physician & parents think it proper that she should avoid our winter climate- our dear Ben has written to Mr B- to urge her mother to accompany her as it seems such a sad thing to place an invalid among strangers in a strange country- where she would if sick pine for the tender care of her affectionate Mother and they would be equally unhappy in the separation. Mr. Blair will make the voyage with her, and then return, she is to stay with Mrs Meckelhaar[1] formerly Miss Randolph, the granddaughter of Mr Jefferson who resides there- the vessel in which they propose sailing leaves N York about the fifth of next month- and tho several days have been appointed for her coming on here, to consult Dr Jackson, she lingers back to the last that she may be as long with her mother as possible, I hope Ben's letter will induce Mrs B to come with her at least to the port of embarkation-

Becky has been to pay us a three days visit, she looked so happy and satisfied with her residence in N York that we cease to regret her absence, she just missed her uncles, Jac came home the day after she left, and a few days after Ben & Howard- I am sorry she did not postpone it until now- and have the pleasure we are enjoying- for which My dear Sister, we are so much endebted to you- . . . . Ben has gone to spend this evening with our Sister Hays & Sarah, Howard & Jo have taken Mary to the Theatre to see or rather hear Mrs Wood and Hyman to the meeting of Israelites- to hear news of our Damascus brethren which has recently been received from England- Sara is not allowed to breathe the night air in consequence of a disease in her throat and therefore could not make one of the party to the theatre. . . . .

Howard says he will write to you as soon as he gets to school- he is quite well and so is your husband- God bless you

[1] Mrs. Septimus Randolph Meckelhaar, the last surviving granddaughter of Thomas Jefferson, died in Washington Sept. 16, 1887. See *Domestic Life of Thomas Jefferson*, by his great-granddaughter, Sara N. Randolph, New York, 1871.

My dear Maria, we think of you and talk of you every day- May you enjoy health & happiness from the conviction that you have bestowed it on your affectionate Sister

R G

* * *

TO THE SAME

The presidential election in 1840 - William Henry Harrison - Henry Clay's assistance - Cuba as a resort for tubercular affliction - "a Benjamin's portion."

Decr 6 1840

I thank you a thousand times My dear Sister for your last animated delightful letter- the account of our dear Bens safe arrival was most gratefully received- I never enjoyed the full & complete happiness of his visit until he had returned in safety to his beloved family for then I felt that we had indeed received a blessing free from all penalty & drawback- but you had some trial besides being without his presence for a month- you were sick and would have been consoled by his society and yet Dear Maria your generous nature resolved to utter no complaint on that account, for the spirit of cheerfulness was diffused over your letter, and you mention your sickness as a mere circumstance- I am glad Ben returned home in time to receive & welcome Genl Harrison- he had quite a triumphant entrance into your city- the banner state has a right to exult and the visit to Lexington was a befitting compliment to its distinguished Citizen- Mr Clay certainly deserves all acknowledgement from the President elect and if he is consulted in all the duties of the station we shall feel confidence in the wisdom of the new administration- you must have felt your heart warm toward the friend of your parents, and given him your full suffrage- we were quite agitated for the fate of Penna during the election struggle, but now think it was a most honorable triumph considering that the opposite party counted on at least 20000 majority- I trust the whole country will have cause to rejoice in the change

I am very sorry for the fate of your bonnet, it was Paris make, and finished in such good taste, with such pretty materials that I thought it preferable to any M^e could make, shall I get enough velvet of the same pattern to make another crown, and send it by Major Tilford? you are so ingenious I am sure you could fix it without detriment to the bonnet, and if you write immediately it will be in time for this opportunity- I have just written to Howard- since his first communication to Sara we have not heard from him, but I suppose he finds it easier to write home, and perhaps does not find time for more, we shall expect him in a few weeks- but I am afraid he will find this severe snow storm makes the country look very dreary- however, there will be nothing to win him from his books. . . . .

We are anxiously expecting to hear of our dear Lizzies arrival at Havannah and trust her state of health will be improved- I feel encouraged not only by Dr Jackson's opinion, and the accounts of success in so many cases that have come under our knowledge- Julia tells me her niece Mrs King is entirely recovered, she went away last fall, we feared in a worse condition than Lizzie, and is now able to spend the winter in N. York- besides strong symptoms of family complaint, she was labouring under great depression of spirits from the loss of her brother- but the change of climate, exercise on horse back in Cuba, and amusement from foreign customs combined to effect her cure- may it be so with our interesting invalid- pray My dear Sister, give my best love to dear Ben, and my nephews, ... and accept a Benjamins portion for yourself- from all our house as well as from your own true and loving sister

R Gratz

* * *

TO THE SAME

Sisterly sympathy and affection- indignation at custom of placing children in House of Refuge among convicts.

We were happy My Dear Maria in not hearing of our dear Bens illness- until we heard of his recovery- some Gentleman told Jo that he was indisposed, which he did not repeat at home, but the joy of receiving a letter was great indeed, when he recognized Ben's writing- and then for the first time told how anxious he had been- but I am disposed to find fault with you My sister, for not getting one of the boys to write, while you were too much engaged, because I do not wish to be saved the pain- or lose the privilege of sharing the trials under which you and My dear Brother suffer, but I thank God for his recovery and most heartily congratulate you thereon- .... I had a letter from Mary Boswell on Tuesday- they are preparing for a weeks visit to the sea shore. Mrs. M[1] is to have a house to her own family and will remove all the school into sea air for a little while which is particularly agreeable to Mary- she has two or three new pupils, young ladies from Carolina who I hope will make up Marys losses-

Howard was with us a few days this month- and looks very well, both health & spirits excellent but I know Jac has told you all about him, for he was so gratified with Mr

[1] Murat.

Ws report that he could not rest until he had shared his pleasure with his parents-

I have at length My dear Sister, sent you a summer dress- the various delays in attending to your request- first by my being out of town, and then not finding a conveyance, that the shops were emptied of early importations and the muslin I have sent was really the best choice I could make for the season, I hope it will suit your taste and in a few weeks- that is, the early autumn importations may enable me to find something pretty by way of decoration- I hope to hear from you very soon, and that you will confirm Ben's account of himself and add his entire & perfect restoration- please offer him my most affectionate love- . . . .

I have just been called away on a business that interests me very much- application was made for the admission of a boy into the Orphan Asylum, by a person who had received him from his dying mother- had indentured him to be adopted as his own son, to change his name, educate & give him a trade- at this period the child was three years old- he is now five- and they brought him to me with such evil reports of his character that I thought it necessary to get the consent of the Board- this was obtained but thinking the man who had taken him with such promises ought to pay some consideration, he was told so- and while I supposed he was making preparations to relinquish the child- found he had (perhaps to save the fee) placed him in the house of Refuge- a child 5 yrs old to be brought up among convicts!!. this appears so shocking that we intend to get him out and take him to the Asylum- It is impossible that such an infant can deserve to be punished to such a degree, and if not, what must he become living among old offenders?- you shall know the result if we succeed, and make him a good boy- if not it will be time enough to place him in the prison after the experiment has been tried- I pray Dear Sister let me hear from you soon- give My love to the boys- will you not send Bernard to see us this fall, if you do not mean to come yourself? but if ali can come- it would delight the heart of your affectionate

RG.

* * *

TO THE SAME

Serious illness - "heartless community of a boarding school."

July 27th 1841

You are restored, My beloved Sister, and with heartfelt gratitude I return thanks to God for the blessing- our dear Bens letter gave us all so much happiness, that I could do nothing but spread the glad tidings at home & abroad- the post carried letters to New York, and to our dear Howard, who I was afraid might possibly not have received his Fathers letter, and I am pleasing myself with the anticipation of his next communication which I know will be joyous- I did not let Mary know how very sick you were lest it would either keep her from going to the shore, or destroy the benefit she expected- but told her the hopes (which are now realized) that she would get better news by the time she returned- you must give my Dear Brother a thousand thanks for his comforting letter, I wrote to him so recently that I will spare him this time, and trust your recovery will be so rapid, that he will not be long employed in nursing . . . .

Miss Craig dined with me yesterday- the poor child is by no means satisfied at Sigorgnes, indeed she does not mean to continue at school, and is very sorry she did not go to Bordentown- she goes tomorrow to the country with Mr Rockhill- from the many little annoyances she related, I do not wonder that she longs to go home- some timid sensitive characters are never understood in the heartless community of a great boarding school, and totally unfit to make their way through them- a determined independent girl- with less talent, would hardly be subject to them or would soon get rid of them- I think it probable Ben's letter will determine Mary to postpone her visit until she finishes her education, as she told Jo nothing would induce her to go, without the certainty of getting back in a short time- she did not say anything about it when at home-

I must not fatigue you My Dear Sister with a long letter, but I could not resist the desire of embracing you, and conveying the united love and congratulations of our Sisters & Brothers to you and our dear Ben- all the clouds of anxiety are breaking away which have encompassed our family- the numerous invalids are convalescent- Sally Hays writes from Burlington that she is better- Horatio's child is also getting well- and we hope Isaac Moses[1] will improve- his father heard once from him after he arrived at the springs-

God bless you dearest, let us hear soon of your progress to perfect health and be assured of the ardent affection of your attached Sister

R GRATZ

[1] The oldest son of Solomon and Rachel Gratz Moses.

TO THE SAME

Visit to Saratoga Springs - the "balsamic waters" - Catherine Sedgwick - Lucretia and Margaret Davidson, youthful poets - Washington Irving's memoir of Margaret- Miss Sedgwick's edition of Lucretia'a poems - the mother who like Rachel "weeps for her children and they are not" - the curiosity of the crowd - the marriage mart - a society scandal.

Saratoga Springs

Aug. 10th 1841

The day before I left home My Dear Sister I received your letter, and with heart felt gratitude returned thanks for the blessing of your recovery. . . . . as soon as dear Ben's hopeful letter arrived, Jo offered to accompany me to N. York- and once disengaged from business he determined that we should spend a week here, and drink these balsamic waters- and so I most unexpectedly find myself in this scene of gaiety, folly & fashion- where old & young pursue the giddy round, "converting pleasure into toil, and fancying toil a pleasure"- we are in a house containing five hundred persons from various places- out of which *you* would extract abundance of amusement and instruction, while I can only pick up a few crumbs that are dropped in my lap- for you know I never possessed the facility of catering for myself- or bringing in a quota to the common stock- however I will freely share what has been afforded me, and first introduce you to a very interesting personage with whom I have become acquainted- the Wife of My old friend Robert Sedgwick. She is here in attendance on her invalid husband and inhabits a more retired position, to which I often resort- they lately visited Europe with their distinguished Sister- the object of this voyage was Robert's health but it resulted in many agreeable circumstances tho' the immediate object was only partially attained- he is still a sufferer- Catherine was here when we first arrived, arranging papers with the Mother of those astonishing young poetesses - Lucretia and Margaret Davidson[1]- we went yesterday to see their portraits, Mrs S-s name being mentioned produced us further favors- their mother sent us several volumes of M's poems and romances- many not published- and numerous specimens of drawings- (self-taught) of these girls. The eldest died at the age of 17- the second at 16- a brother equally talented- is now consuming away in the same fatal disease at 22- Washington Irving has recently written a Memoir of Margaret and selected part of her productions- and Miss Sedgwick is preparing a similar Vol from her old edition with additions of Lucretia's writings- it is but justice to mention that these excellent persons, have given their labours to the parents who are in straightened circumstances- I hope some good ladies here who have wealth and influence will patronize this unfortunate family, and make the sad Mothers heart rejoice again- who now like Rachel "weeps for her children because they are not"- the throng are easily led to something new, Mrs Meredith having mentioned our visit many are curious & others perhaps from higher motives desire to see Mrs Davidson-

I wrote to Howard the night before I left home having

[1]Lucretia Maria Davidson (1808-1825) and her sister Margaret Miller Davidson (1823-1838) were two youthful poetical prodigies who attracted great attention in the literary world at this time. They were the daughters of Dr. Oliver and Margaret Miller Davidson. Lucretia's poems were published in 1829 four years after her death in a volume entitled "Amir Khan and other Poems." Margaret's poems were introduced to the literary public by Washington Irving. The poems of the two sisters were published together in 1850.

that day received a very agreeable letter from him, if we had intended to make this journey, I think it probable Jo would have brought Mary Boswell, but she was at the sea shore- and I am glad it was so, for I think this is the worst place a young girl can enter- altho Many Mothers came expressly to *bring out* their daughters (to bring them out indeed to the gaze- the familiar gaze of adventurers - who learn the possessions & expectations of every fair aspirant- and taint their purity by presumptuous association)- the Ladies waltz here too- beautiful girls just from the schools, waltz with mustacheoed foreigners - perhaps with impostors - for who can know what company they keep in public houses - dressed as all dress here, in the most expensive manner -

There was a great outrage committed the other day in NY. which has occasioned much excitement- the son of bishop O- who some years ago was convicted of *forgery*, and other dishonestys ran off with a Miss *Bibbee* aged 16- or rather induced her to make a clandestine marriage, which was consumated in his fathers house, in the presence of several of the family *at 3 oclock in the morning*, at which hour she left her home & returned to it undiscovered, two or three days after she was missing- and then her parents learned the fact, which well goes nigh to destroy them- and the Bishop lies under the censure of sanctioning & concealing this outrage- several relations of *the bride* are here- her Aunt related these circumstances to me, and bitterly grieves for the misery & disgrace she has involved on herself- I believe Ben knew her family- they are of the aristocracy of N. Y- but besides all this private evil- what can be said of the state of society- if the head of a church is allowed to commit such outrage on the peace of a community he is bound to guard- & admonish and lead in the path of duty- moral as well as spiritual- had justice been administered, this culprit would

Philadelphia March 15th
1852

Our Brother Is this day My Dearest Ben handed me your letter to read, and the munificent present of $150 as a Purim gift. I know not how to express my thankfulness, not alone for the money, but the loving consideration which induced you to remember me, at the "season of gifts." I will endeavour to use it well for your sake, and of part of it, make some poor heart glad, and bless you for it. Surely no women have ever been more blest in Brothers than we have — Ye have not only carefully labored to produce means out of the tangled & perplexed affairs of our Father's estate for our benefit, but supported us during a life long period with generous & delicate liberality.

I ponder on these things with heart felt

* * *

It seems hard to be so long unseen as the time shortens when we may meet in this world — but May God bless you — ever & for ever — prays your affectionate & devoted sister
R Gratz

FACSIMILE OF LETTER FROM REBECCA GRATZ TO HER BROTHER BENJAMIN
(Reduced)

have been suffering the penalty of his crime- but his sentence was put aside in consideration of his fathers sanctity- and now they both deserve reprobation- . . . .

Dear Maria, how my heart sickened at the description of your illness- and the sufferings both you and my dear Ben endured- it is penetrated with gratitude to the Great & Good God who has restored you both to us, and to your loving family- I shall never forget Howard's touching expressions on his father's letter which he sent for my perusal- may your fondest hopes be realized in your children-

Jo thinks he has already benefitted by the waters- and I believe I shall too- tho I do not *feel* it yet, in a few days we shall to go N. York where I shall pay my visit to Becky. I have secured a room in her neighborhood, so that I shall be always in her room when she can have me. . . . . what a precious world this would be if we could see those we love whenever they or we needed each other- but God has made it otherwise for our good- God in His wisdom can not err, may you be ever blessed- dear Maria, adieu, your

R G.

* * *

TO BENJAMIN GRATZ

Death of Mrs. Benjamin Gratz - separation in time of trouble - tender sympathy.

Novr 12th 1841.

O My Dearest Brother, how does my heart weep for you, and with you for the bereavement it has pleased God to visit upon you- The unexpected calamity came upon us, with a suddenness that encreased our grief- for we knew nothing of our Beloved Maria's illness until she was past recovery. May

He who is most Merciful, support you under this greatest affliction of your life, and visit you with consolations which can alone come from *him*- the blessings that surround you, in the dear Children she has left, will bring comfort to your heart, and the love she has bequeathed you in them, will still speak of the happiness, begun here to be made more perfect in that state where no separation can rend it from you- would that I could know how you and the dear Boys are and strive to minister to your comforts- I am grateful that Gratz Moses was near, with his affectionate attentions, in the hour of trial, and that he had the privilege of seeing one we all loved so much . . . .

I wrote to Howard as soon as I heard of his Mother's illness and told him to come home- he suffered so much among strangers, when he was sick last summer that I was unwilling to have him exposed to the same feelings again, and I think it quite probable he will arrive today- poor fellow, Sara received a letter from him last evening- he was well & happy-

When you can make the exertion, my dear Brother, please write to him, or get one of his brothers to do so. I wish too it will not be many days before we again hear, if Gratz has left you we shall be grateful to some other friend to let us know how you all are. The distance seems interminable now when one's whole heart and spirit longs to be near. I cannot now speak of my sorrow, tho you know I have a true & loving sisters share, and few have been so blest in sisters as I have or mourned with keener grief their loss, but you my beloved brother, fill my heart with sympathy, even in proportion to the estimate I had of your married happiness and the worth of your now sainted Maria. May God bless you & your children is the constant & ardent prayer of your affectionate sister

R Gratz

TO THE SAME

This letter is dated Friday 19, 1841, the month being omitted but the letter is postmarked Phila. Nov. 19.
Grief assuaged by responsibilities - the hereafter.

A thousand thanks, My Beloved brother for your kind letter, it relieved our anxiety for your & our dear boys health- and our feelings went forth to meet yours in the truest sympathy- indeed we all so loved your best beloved- and so fairly estimated her high and noble qualities, that your grief became our own- in the loss you deplore

Howard and Mary Boswell are here, and we have been a mourning family each pouring out the recollected instances of affection, benevolence or wisdom with which every heart is stored, and all ending in lamentations for you the greatest sufferer and for your Sons who share your bereavement- But God does not afflict without leaving us consolation in the duties & responsibilities we are called on to fulfill and yours My dear Brothers, are of a nature, to continue the tie of love, which can never divide you from the Memory of our dear Maria, her children are your care and the objects of your fondest love, and their progress in life, their characters, and filial love will fill your heart with what would have filled hers, had she been permitted to continue with and share your labours of love to them-

I thank you My dear Ben, for giving me an account of her last days- I longed to know every particular and wrote to Sara Bodley for information which I feared would be too painful to relate- I thank God that she breathed out her pure spirit calmly - and that her bodily sufferings were mitigated- in a little while we shall be reunited, and this life will not be too long to remember and cherish the love of those who made our happiness here, and will ever brighten the joys of the hereafter-

Our Brother Jo is at Bellefonte, from whence you will no doubt hear from him. Howard is quite well & hopes by this days mail to receive your letter, which will be brought from New Haven- he appears to like his situation there, and I hope will derive all the advantages you anticipate from residence there, yet I cannot conquer many woman's fears for the dangers & difficulties that encounter a youth, among so many, and various characters, and often influence their own- Howard is a great favorite I hear, and possesses qualities to retain favor- he will probably return in a few days, and so will Mary- her vacation is over but she has staid home, because her feelings were too much exercised to apply her mind to study . . . .

May God bless & comfort you My dearest brother, prays most fervently Your devoted

Sister R Gratz

Friday 19th 1841

* * *

TO ANN BOSWELL GRATZ

Benjamin Gratz married as his second wife Mrs. Ann Maria Shelby nee Boswell, a niece of his first wife, July 6, 1843.

The serenity of the faith in God - the ills to which flesh is heir might be worse - belief in overwatching Providence - death of Mrs. Montgomery Blair - Prescott's Mexico.

January 29 1844

The New Year came in very sorely to me, My Dear Sister Ann, tho I have great cause to be grateful, that the result of my accident has been so harmless- I had been reading in my chamber and just after the midnight hour struck- laid down my book, intending to go to bed, when I tripped over a rocking chair on which Sara was sitting, and fell- my face was struck with great force against a wardrobe- and bruised so badly that I have been up to this time greatly disfigured- and suffering much pain from the slightest touch- the muscles of my neck were also sprained- and for some hours exquisitely painful but it has all passed away except the sense of divine goodness- in preserving me from greater ill, from an accident which appeared so dangerous- "It is not in man that walketh to direct his steps"- is constantly verified by our experience, literally as well as morally- and perhaps never more impressively than when the ordinary circumstances of security are interrupted by unforseen accidents- I hope I shall not appear presumptuous to you (as I know I should to many people) by believing that a kind providence is employed "in all the good & ill that chequers life"- and when we feel it extended for our benefit- may be humbly grateful- not in vain of the special care- a human parent has a special care of each of their offspring- then surely our heavenly Father, may, nay does extend his Mercy over all he has created- and without his care, we cannot walk safely across our chamber- under it, may tempt the tempestuous ocean and tread the dreary forest- . . . .

I am much obliged to you, Dear Ann, for the picture of home you have sketched, there is nothing I more desire than the domestic happiness of My Dear Brother's family- his children are all dear to me, and in winning their affection, you increase my gratitude- . . . . I am glad to hear such favorable accounts of Howard. I hope he will do justice to himself, if he studies, he will no doubt succeed, for he has talents that have not been sufficiently exercised and improved- poor Montgomery Blair has met with a sad affliction in the sudden death of his wife- we had letters from Dr Moses mentioning it- she had not been in good health for some time- Mary Moses has also been ill, but was recovering when the Dr. wrote- it appears that the autumn & winter have been sickly extensively in our cities, but I hope since the cold weather has commenced, it may have a salutary effect - the last four days have been so cold as to fill our rivers with ice and completely stop the navigation for a time- . . . .

I have got the poems you recommended by the sisters Wall and think there is a great deal of poetic beauty in them- but as you observe a vein of melancholy & romance of feeling pervades the vol. - knowing the young authors, and the peculiar circumstances of their early life- the pieces to me have the charm of genuine feeling- tho' as a critic, should say there was not sufficient variety- Have not yet read Prescott's Mexico- but from the pleasure his former work gave me- expect to be highly delighted with it- the subject is so rich & new- our Whig politicians are in good spirits- the presentation of Mr Clay's picture, has drawn many together to make speeches- they have a long time to keep up enthusiasm, but I hope this time they may succeed-

You must present my affectionate love to my brother and the boys- Bernard has almost outgrown that title but not my tenderness for him- remember me also to Gratz Brown,[1] he was a fine boy when I saw him and promised great intelligence- you have quite a family of students- our brothers & sisters desire to be kindly remembered- you need never apologize for writing long letters to me, as I feel flattered by

[1] Son of Judge & Mrs. Mason Brown, a cousin of the first Mrs. Benjamin Gratz; he was named Benjamin Gratz Brown in honor of Benjamin Gratz; he was the candidate for the vice-presidency of the United States on the Democratic ticket in 1872; the ticket was Greeley and Brown.

the kindness that dictates them and entertained by the agreeable matter they contain- and am sorry to return you such a dull sheet in exchange- .... believe me with sincere wishes for your happiness, My Dear Sister Ann, affectionately yrs

RG

* * *

TO THE SAME

The younger members of the family in St. Louis - proposed visit to Lexington and Mammoth Cave - the presidential campaign of 1844, Henry Clay versus Polk.

Philadelphia March 24th 1844

I was just going to inflict a letter on My Brother Ben, when yours came Dear Sister Ann to save him that unmerited punishment- I began to feel anxious for some information about you all- and am sorry to hear that you have been indisposed. I hope that you are entirely recovered and that all are enjoying health again.

Hyman's still suffering with his arm gives me some uneasiness, is it not a very unusual affection? can it be the consequence of his attack of fever? or is it entirely a local disease? dear fellow! it is very hard to be so disabled- would not change of air be useful to him as the season advances, I wish my brother would send him & Cary to pay us a visit- it is so long since we have met, that I fear I shall be entirely forgotten by the young folks-

It was very kind in you to tell me so particularly about all your household- at the very time my heart yearned for such information; I began to feel I was losing interest in My dear Brother's regards, as he never addresses a line to me on any occasion, tho he knows how jealous I am lest long separation should rob me of any portion of his affection- but this idea is not harboured for a moment, he does not love to write, and rather chooses that you should save him the labor and a much more fastidious person, might thank him for such a substitute, My Dear Ann, and so do I- I had a letter from Howard[1] last week, and tho he gives a very good account of himself, he says nothing about his studies, so Frank's[2] information is the more gratifying. Frank seems fond of Dr Moses[3] family, he speaks of the children, in a manner that proves he takes an interest in them, which is a good thing in a young man- it would be difficult to live with Mary without loving her, she has so many fine qualities blended in her character, she is agreeable, and amiable, and sensible and good- free from all selfishness, upright in judgment, and "walking humbly with God"- I am sure you would be pleased with her & I think a longer acquaintance would confirm your good opinion of Gratz- their removal was a great deprivation to us all- I too regret he could not have settled in Lexington, for then I might hope to see them again- tho' now it seems improbable that I ever shall- .... this month has been very trying, it has advanced in disagreeableness up to this day- having commenced with bright warm weather putting forward the foliage & green grass- and then bringing rain & storm & ice, when we were looking for spring- but soon we shall be rid of her- and trust her capricious sister & successor will put a smiling face on- that we may celebrate the passover in bright weather

I am glad to hear My Dear Bernard is becoming fond of

[1] Henry Howard Gratz, son of Benjamin Gratz, was living in St. Louis at this time.
[2] Francis Preston Blair Jr., a cousin of Howard Gratz.
[3] Dr. Simon Gratz Moses, nephew of Rebecca Gratz, who had settled in St. Louis.

books- every gentlemanly accomplishment will encrease his resources- and he has such excellent qualities & principles that I rejoice in every acquisition that will make him happier, the only fault I find with him is that he will not write to me, give my love to, and tell him so, love too to my sweet Cary- he was the beauty and the cadet of the family when I saw him, and he is still in my mind's eye the loveliest of children- pray beg him to send me a specimen of his improvement in writing. I am afraid you will hardly be able to decypher this- I am greatly fatigued by a long walk after sunday school but could not bear to omit the opportunity of thanking you for your welcome letter. You say Dr Bush has been attending you, what has become of Dr Dudley? have you & my brother changed your family physician? good Mrs Thrashley will I hope not put herself to any inconvenience in preparing for our journey to the Mammoth Cave, as no time has been fixed, and in the circumstances of this life, there are so many chances against the fulfilment of more probable events, that this also may fail- my last letter from Mary Boswell mentions that she has been indisposed. I hope they will not fix themselves at housekeeping until she has again visited the sea shore which proved so beneficial to her last summer.

When may we hope to see you this side the mountains? I should have urged a visit this spring but rumours have reached me which made me fear a refusal- present me most affectionately to My dear Brother and nephews- and Mary Boswell and accept the love of our sisters & brothers, who are much gratified by your kind remembrance- the dreadful catastrophe of the Princeton, appalled us for a time- and is still a subject of deep feeling- Capt Stockton is suffering great anguish of mind and mortification at the result of his high plans & expectations, but perhaps, at no time should the explosion have taken place when fewer lives would have been lost- a few days previous several hundred persons Ladies & Gentlemen were surrounding the fatal gun- when it was fired with even a heavier charge than that which exploded, it has put an end to the gaiety of the season at Washington- Next year I hope we shall see better scenes at the Capitol- Will you not meet us there to see Mr Clay[1] inaugurated? we talk of such things with high hopes here, tho' a whole year off- and we "know not what a day may bring forth"- good night, believe me very affectionately your sister

R Gratz

* * *

TO BENJAMIN GRATZ

There is a long gap in the correspondence between Rebecca Gratz and her brother; this is the first letter addressed to him since the death of his first wife in 1841. It is possible that there were letters written in the interval, but they do not seem to have been preserved. The latter portion of the letter is addressed to Mrs. Gratz.

May 13th 1844

I was rejoiced My dear Brother to receive a letter from you again, and to hear such good tidings of your family- nothing could have been more agreeable to me than to accept your invitation and return with our dear Bernard, but Miriam Cohen is in New York on her way to pay us a visit, and we expect will spend the month of June here, if she is not induced to remain longer. Bernard left us this morning

[1] This wish was not fulfilled, since Henry Clay was defeated for the Presidency by James K. Polk.

to pass two or three days in New York with his Cousins, for Sara left home the morning after he arrived here, and extorted a promise from him to do so if he determined to journey westward before she got back- indeed it was hard for her to obtain her own consent to leave him; her arrangements were made & her sisters expecting her before Bernard arrived.

I regret that you did not send Cary with his brother- you know the change of air is always recommended in the whooping cough, thank God, he is getting well without it, I am told it often happens that this disease is taken a second time- tho numbered among the infantile evils which are to plague us no more, Sally Cohen has had it violently this winter, in her old age- our Brother Etting is very frail indeed, yesterday he had an attack from which he apprehended he would not recover- but in a short time it passed off leaving him as well as usual- but admonishing as by how slight a thread his valued life is held- in a few weeks he will enter his eighty second year, so we have only to be grateful, and regard his lengthened days as a special favor. . . . .

I have restricted myself to one page, My Dear Sister Ann, that I may not exceed wholesome bounds for weak eyes, while I tell you how happy I am to hear that you and my little niece are well, and doing well I am told the little lady[1] is a beauty- and what mother does not desire this blessed distinction for a daughter- I have heard many speak of the perils of beauty, who spoke very wisely, but I doubted the sincerity of their hearts, if they would not still say that they would encounter the peril to possess the gift- indeed an expression of goodness is so necessary to beauty, that I believe it is independent of features in a great degree, and therefore

---

[1] Miriam, born April 13, 1844, named for Miriam Simon Gratz, the mother of Benjamin Gratz.

an amiable & good mother, may always beautify her daughters by bringing them up well, giving them examples of good temper, and the graces of a gentle speech (this is very old maidish) I did not mean to write anything on this page but good wishes- and I beg you will accept an abundance for both mother & child- and if after all the babe does not turn out a beauty- (babys change so) I will try when that is ascertained to say as much in favor of plain faces, as will satisfy any mother or rational being- that God has abundance of good gifts beside beauty to bestow, and a grateful heart cherisheth them, and is blessed- I hope soon to hear that you are abroad again, this fine spring weather will soon restore your strength, and then you will describe your daughter to me- believe me very affectionately your

R G

* * *

TO ANN BOSWELL GRATZ

Rebecca Gratz had paid a visit to Lexington in the summer of 1844; she speaks of this visit in this letter written on her homeward journey. The year of the letter is omitted from the date but the recipient noted it on the back of the letter.

Wheeling Saturday night Oct 26th

My Dear Ann

Your affectionate concern, when you parted with us after the fright, was so impressed on your countenance, that I have thought of it a thousand times since and regretted that my pleasant visit terminated with such a scene. I wrote from Maysville to tell you that all had gone on well, the first day of our journey- we had a pleasant party- but indeed I had left too much behind- to enjoy even Mrs MacAllister's agreeable conversation and could not rally myself to reward her efforts- on the same night we got on board a very good boat, and arrived here about 10 o'clock last night- I cannot say we found any persons among the passengers to interrupt our meditations, so we took to our books- or talked over our Lexington friends. The weather was delightful, and the river in fine order. "The Cutter" was the first large boat that came up, so we gained in every way by not leaving you earlier and I assure you My dear Ann, my heart is full of grateful recollections of every days kindness experienced from you and each of My dear Brother's family- I love the dear boys for many traits of character that I had not before an opportunity of knowing & look forward for nothing but encrease of happiness for you all- We leave Wheeling tomorrow morning, expecting to get to Cumberland in time for the Cars on Monday morning & to reach Washington the same evening- . . . .

This place exhibits a scene of active business- boats constantly arriving & departing- loading & unloading- soldiers parading- political songs & huzzas- with all the usual tumult of an excited population- Horace & I walked about the town & hills this morning- & have had ample amusement since looking on "The busy world" We met a party of Philadelphians going to N. C. last eve'g from whom we heard of our friends- . . . .

I have scribbled on in defiance of bad pen & ink- without regard to your convenience in deciphering- if you can only make out my love and thanks My dear Ann, for all your kindness there is little else to be gathered- you will hear from me soon after our arrival in Phila

God Bless you- believe me very sincerely your affectionate sister

R G

TO THE SAME

Winter scenes- "mutual forbearance a necessary household commodity" - Irish agitators - Daniel O'Connell - election excitement - anniversary of Orphan society - Henry Clay's defeat for the presidency in 1844.

Decr 28th Saturday night 1844

I thank you My Dear Ann for your kind letter, I was beginning to be desirous of hearing something from Lexington for I assure you the interest my visit renewed in my dear Brothers family makes me desirous to be familiarly acquainted with all the sayings & doings of the house, I go over again and again the scenes of the last summer and would keep up the train of events as they pass- you tell me both your children were sick, I am sorry Miss Miriam has found out that troublesome infant malady the croup to plague with but if taken very early in its first stage, it is easily conquered. Mary's letter to Sara received today, says you are all well again, it would be matter of much surprise if I could say the same through all the branches of this large family, where colds are rife- running from one member to another- but in the general acceptation of the term All's well- may be understood that there is no particular illness- and with this allowance I can thus report altho Brother Hyman has been three days in the house with a moderate attack of lameness (very like the gout) tho he does not call it so, and sister Hays was not able to go with Ellen to dine at Mr Ettings- because of a cold- Horatio's nursery too is full of hoarse children in consequence of the beautiful warm bright days preceding Christmas- and that day too was more like Oct or April than the 25th Decr- but winter has come at last - we had a snow storm yesterday and the streets are covered beautifully with a white carpet which in the moon light looks cold enough for the lovers of winter- but, would you believe it, ten days ago Sara gathered a bunch of Roses from a garden, in which there were many bushes in full bloom- I hope your climate has been as mild, and then you could wait patiently for the arrival of your winter clothes which I hope have arrived before this. I was very unfortunate in boxes sent by sea to Miriam, the ship was lost and her pickles & preserves I fear sent to the fishes in the deep- but there is no danger of that kind to disappoint you- . . . .

I am very glad to see that our dear Mary and her mother are getting on so happily in their own house, with every thing so comfortable about them, it must certainly be their own faults if it were otherwise- there is no condition in life which does not require the exercise of our virtues to make us happy- mutual forbearance is a necessary household commodity between companions as well as in every other domestic relation- it must exist between mistress & servants, or we should never be fixed, particularly where the latter are free to change whenever an offense is given and our hibernian community- released from the oppression of their own country, seem to think all the rest of the world made for them- Mr Moriarty the Catholick priest who has gone to Ireland- has been making speeches- and giving a theme to O Connel,[1] which will make him more obnoxious than ever, and I fear do mischief here, by encreasing prejudice but you must not think us still under the dominion of a mob- we have been as quiet as old Philadelphians ever since the election was decided.

My wishes have come to pass with regard to my friend

[1] Doubtless **Daniel O'Connell**, the great Irish orator.

Becky Fisher, I heard the other day that letters had been received by the President of the Missionary Society, from Africa saying that if Mr Hazelhurst returned, it would be only to walk into his grave- and advising them not to send him out again- under such circumstances, it is not probable that they will go to that station at any rate, and tho I believe Becky's missionary enthusiasm unabated, she cannot wish to pursue it at such hazards- we are just on the point of the Anniversary of our Orphan Society- & the children have the whooping cough- so we shall not be able to make them sing- nor allow them to interrupt Dr Bethune, who is to be the orator- I suppose your meeting is over- & I hope your difficulties too- while ours are just commencing- . . . .

I have nothing to tell our dear Ben, of any of his old friends- it is so long since he has been here, that I should not know where to begin. I hope Mr Clay's defeat will not prevent your coming in the spring- we have enough to regret about it without that additional-

Give my best love to my brother and the dear Boys O how sadly I feel for poor Hyman- the long long suffering of that arm- and yet no positive amendment!- kiss your sweet babe for me- and believe me My dear Ann, with great sincerity your affectionate sister

R Gratz

1838   1913

THE HEBREW SUNDAY SCHOOL SOCIETY
OF PHILADELPHIA

SEVENTY-FIFTH ANNIVERSARY CELEBRATION
MARCH 2, 1913, 8.15 P. M.

HORTICULTURAL HALL, BROAD AND LOCUST STS.

REBECCA GRATZ
BORN IN PHILADELPHIA 1781; DIED 1869

"A Woman that feareth the Lord she shall be praised"

TO THE SAME

The ills that childish flesh is heir to - mothers' tasks - the soul of good in things evil - musical events - Henry Clay's admirers - roses in winter.

Philadelphia Jan 28th 1845

My Dear Ann

As soon as I received your letter announcing the arrival of the long expected Box, I commenced a reply which has unaccountably disappeared from my portfolio- and it is now almost too late to express my pleasure, at the satisfaction given to the respective parties concerned- for the gloss of admiration has worn off, and I have only to hope that their usefulness will at least equal their beauty. I begin to feel the ill consequence of not having written before, for I am anxious about your sweet little Miriam and wish to hear that she has recovered from the discomfort you mentioned, tho' do not consider it of any serious import as long as her health is not affected by it- indeed it sometimes happens when these affections are thrown on the surface the constitution is less injured- I expect when Miriam's diet is changed by weaning that she will grow robust, and then the irruption will disappear. You need not fear to particularize all her little ways when you write to me, I love to hear of her improvements for I take great interest in young human beings- & try to find out what the future woman is to be- by the early development of character & disposition- My sympathy goes out to poor mothers too- they have so much to do & to observe- so many physical & moral ailments to nurse into health & good- and with all their care, are so often interrupted by seasons of trial-

I was surprised a few days ago by a visit from Mrs Menefee, who I had understood had gone home, a full month ago with her Brother- she told me her sister's indisposition prevented their travelling - that she is now better. Mrs M. looks very pretty, she came with Mrs Lathrope, and I *have heard* that the Widower, who has just moved into his handsome new house is very much charmed, so perhaps, one of those masked incidents, which looks like evil, and turn to good in the events of human life may be in progress here. If Miss Jewett regains her health and her beautiful sister is induced to change her state, we may congratulate ourselves on such an acquisition to our gay circle- but this is taking a great liberty, when I confess that I am so little abroad, that until called to receive her visit, I did not know the ladies were in the city. In fact I have never lived more recluse than this winter, a few of my kind friends & neighbors make up the whole of my society. Julia Hoffman & Sara are always cheerful companions at home- family calls keep me in exercise, and what other social duties give interest to my life seem as years roll on, to fill up my time more consistently with my taste than the present fashionable manner of disposing of it- I am quite sorry that circumstances prevented Mary's spending the winter with us, there would have been such good opportunity of improvement in her favorite accomplishment, music for we have had a succession of great geniuses, giving concerts & lessons- and I should have so liked her to spend domestic evenings with Sara & Mrs Butler who are both good musicians- however, there is much more beauty in performing our duty than in any other accomplishment and I should not love her as well if I did not think her happier in that right sphere than she could any where else, where that was sacrificed- Becky Fisher, you know is married, and gone to the south with her husband, for the double purpose of improving his health, and collecting funds for his mission, we are in hopes that he will find some station in the West or South, that will keep him from going to sacrifice himself & wife in Africa- I saw her mother yesterday and thought the lines of care had deepened on her brow, and her flesh had wasted in the struggle of parting with her darling daughter, and then Dear Ann, I doubted whether Rebecca's first duty was not to her doting Mother.

I am glad to hear Mr Clay receives so many manifestations of affection, he will be further gratified by the notice taken of the result of the election in foreign prints and I hope yet more- by the efforts of his Phila friends to give substantial proofs of their regard- . . . .

To My Dear Ben present my most affectionate love, I long to see one of his precious letters- it is some time since Jo has received one- and mine, he seems to have quite forgotten- did you ever know such a set of bad correspondents, as the men of our family are? except Howard, it is hard to get a letter out of them, and even from him I have not heard for more than a month- kiss my sweet Miriam for me, and pray let me hear soon from you, remember me to all my Lexington friends, how is Becky Bruce? I could ask a great many more questions if I had room- but they should be about your own household- I saw Mrs Strothers and her pretty daughter and animated son, when they were in the city, her old friend & schoolfellow Ellen was here to greet her- Good night My dear Ann, believe me very truly & affectionately your sister

R G

TO THE SAME

This letter is not dated but the recipient wrote on the back "answered Aug. 5 1845."
  Lady Willoughby's Diary - descending the vale of years - tender memories of the parental home.

My Dear Ann

They have published Lady Willoughbys[1] Diary, and as you were so well pleased with the extracts you read, I send you the Vol quite sure your admiration will not diminish as you proceed, I am only sorry that it was not written by the veritable Lady whose name it bears- living in the troublous times of Charles Ist and experiencing the identical scenes so beautifully described- bearing with so truly a feminine grace the trials, and feeling with such chastened sensibility the duties of her station- in every character of woman's mission- . . . .

I will not say I envy My brother the pleasure of his visit- but I shall accompany him in idea, and rejoice in the gratification he & Dear Ben will experience in meeting after so long a separation - we cannot often hope to be together with such distant homes- as we are all descending into the vale of years- but the memories of a long series of uninterrupted affection lights up the past, and keeps the mind & heart fresh in all the feelings of former attachment. We were brought up in a happy home of family love- the domestic scene is still dear to us all- No one who has ever enjoyed it can forget the

---

[1] Willoughby Elizabeth, Baroness W of Penham. So much of the diary of Lady Willoughby as relates to her domestic history and to the eventful period of Charles the First (Some further portions of the Diary of Lady Willoughby) 2 vol. London. Chiswick printed 1844–48 (A fictitious diary. By H. M. Rathbone). British Museum Catalogue.

treasure of parental love- it influences every after scene of life- and mixes in our devotion to the great Author of our being- Our Father in heaven! excuse me Dear Ann for writing in such a vein- and believe me affectionately yrs RG

* * *

TO THE SAME

This is the first letter in this correspondence which has not the address on the back of the letter sheet itself; it was evidently sent in an envelope. This explains the remark about cheap postage at the close of the letter.
   Contrasts in New York - mob excitement - abolitionists in Kentucky - visit to Saratoga Springs - bazaar for the Academy of Fine Arts.

Phil. Aug 31st 1845

I was much rejoiced, My dear Ann on my return home last Sunday to hear the happy news of the birth of your son,[1] and of your safety- most sincerely do I congratulate you and my dear Brother on this event and embrace the little treasure of a nephew with many blessings- what does sweet Miriam say? she will not feel jealous of the young stranger, for her own loveliness will secure favor, who ever may appear to share her triumph- I suppose you have by this time decided on his name, he is just one day older than Becky's son Jonathan, I was with her when he was named, and left her quite well, considering her babe was only nine days old- she made such a strange miscalculation that two whole months of expectation hung heavily upon her previous to his birth, but her health did not suffer, & she looks so bright and

[1] This child died in infancy.

happy with her three baby boys, that I look on her with wonder and admiration- her husband's limited means does not cast a shadow over her brow, tho it induces her to make every prudential arrangement in her household and exercise her own activity in the care of her children, she has the rare & noble trait of character, which dares to meet the evil with the feeling & deportment of a gentlewoman, she is cheerful, and thro devoted affection to her husband & children happy- the weather was so warm, and our brother Jo had preceded us home, which obliged us to hurry on, so that we could not stay in N Y any longer- but I left Becky with great regret- N Y is what I suppose London must be- there is so much splendor & so much misery- such magnificance in some parts & such filth & noise & discomfort in others that a stranger who has the luck to be lodged in one part of it, can form no idea of what is suffered by another in the opposite direction- for my part I never wish to be there in hot weather unless my home is in a friends house- we were at the Mansion House, over a mile from Beckys dwelling, and of course must drive to her house, and this deprived me of the opportunity of looking into their pretty shops, the usual attraction of the street- in Broadway-

Why Dr Ann, what a desperate set of people you have become,[1] but you have improved on Phila- you do quietly what they would do in a tumultuous mob- I hope neither city will have any more such work on hand- it is a pity & a shame that in this beautiful country men cannot respect the rights of each other- is Mr Clay insane that he should have attempted such a plan in Lexington? He might surely have known trouble would ensue- I grieve for the poor blacks

[1] Doubtless reference is made here to the mob that stormed the newspaper office of Cassius M. Clay the leading abolitionist in Kentucky, on August 18, 1845. See *Life of Cassius Marcellus Clay* (Cincinnati, 1886), Vol. I 107, III.

whose condition will be worsted- and their chains be riveted, whereas, if let alone for a few years they would be likely to wear out in Kentucky- how do they behave under this excitement? They must have a horror of any Abolitionist coming into the state, the best of them do not consider them as friends- and the bad are only more set on mischief by the encouragement of their interference- how painful all this must be to the Warfields- will it not raise up new troubles in your social circles? . . . .

Our brother Jo was delighted with his visit to Kentucky- I knew he would be, we found him at Saratoga looking much better for his summer trip, in health & spirits. My visit to Saratoga was very pleasant & useful. I did not deem it so necessary as my friends did, but was certainly benefited by it- Sara too was greatly served by the waters- she got poisoned several weeks before, I believe by going through a graveyard in which many rank weeds were growing- her face & neck were swollen & sore, bathing & drinking however has restored her, and she looks quite like herself again- . . . . I am busy in making preparations for the Bazaar for the Acadmey of fine Arts- Hyman & Horace are so much interested that I could not decline tho' the whole business is so new to me that I fear my table will be the most indifferent among the Lady patronesses- we have sent circular beggars far & wide, but such applications are so numerous that I fear our share will be small, tho' being for such an object no sect will have an object in declining, and in the autumn so many strangers are in town that if we have pretty things there will no doubt be buyers.

Isaac Moses joined us at the Springs, he is certainly wonderfully changed since I last saw him, his health is perfectly restored he has turned into industrious habits, been successful, and resolved to sustain his character which in a strange community a stranger, he had to build up for himself- and I am happy to say he seems to be well received & respected among his fellow citizens whom he has met in his journey- he is in N. Y. at present, both he & I see a strong resemblance in little Gratz Nathan,[1] and your Miriam- Gratz was two years old in May, very lovely & beautiful, as your sweet daughter was when I saw her- they are cousins you know- you must present my best love to my dear Brother, thank him for his letter which I perused & will answer some of these days- cheap postage, my dear Ann will sometimes cost you some patience, as I scribble on quite indifferent how much paper I cover, as you will not have to pay more coin for it- but even a letter has its limits and you will be thankful that mine draws to an end- remember me to your friend & neighbour Mrs Reynolds & her sisters- Mrs Vertner Miss Sydney & my other friends particularly Mrs E Warfield and believe me your affectionate sister

R G

* * *

TO THE SAME

The naming of children - custom among Jews not to name child after living parent - night thoughts - "Lord, deliver us from candid friends."

Monday Novr 24th 1845

My Dear Ann

Had the inclosed arrived one day sooner it would have sent our Beloved Ben on his way rejoicing but he left us yesterday afternoon with a little shade of disappointment

[1] Son of Jonathan and Rebecca Moses Nathan.

and anxiety, for the want of your accustomed letter, and tho' he may perhaps be with you when this arrives (as he seemed but half disposed to stop at Washington) I make it the occasion of another letter to you- besides which, I want to unsay a piece of impertinence in my note of yesterday, where I used the disputed name for your little boy- tho' I assure you it was by no means My intention to decide so important a question- and you know from the previous expression of my opinion that (dearly as I love My brother)- it would not be my choice. I know not what induced Ben to ask me if I had written to any one, upon the subject of his child's name. I told him as nearly as I could recollect, what I had said to you, and thought by his reply, that I had been mistaken on the ground of his objections- and foolishly supposed there were no others. At dinner (after my note was sealed & delivered) I introduced the subject and found both his father & Uncle Jo opposed to it- but it did not occur to me, that *my* expressions were of any consequence and my note was unrecalled- Young says "a deathbed is a detector of the heart" but I may go further and say a nightly pillow is a reflector of each days deeds - and mine often echoes back inconsiderate words and acts that I would recall or wish undone and I accused myself last night of helping to increase a desire in you, which would not be gratified- I believe I have two prejudices on this subject- the first growing out of circumstances in our sisters families- who both gave the same name to two children, and the precious little inheritors were both unfortunate- The second that it is not customary among pious Jews to name a child after a living parent- it does not occur in the Scriptures from whence we take our customs as well as laws- but it is very common in modern times, and I have no *reasons* against it- only a prejudice.

quere- might not the boys be jealous of a name sanctified in their memories by one passed into the skies?[1]

Now dearest Ann, after saying so much in confidence to you, let me assure you, that what ever may be the name of your darling, I shall love him most dearly- that your happiness & that of all My brothers family is so very near to my heart. I think of you very often- with the same feelings expressed to you last summer- that time alone is wanting to bring all things to their right places- "be not weary in well doing" is an excellent motto for by patience all good works are completed- it is said- discretion is the one thing needful- how much more elevated is the virtue in domestic life. Unfortunately female moralists sometimes laud candour as the favorite test of friendship- and care not how deeply they lacerate the feelings- and poison the peace of families- by telling all the harsh & unkind things said of them- from such friendship "God Lord deliver us" - we are quick enough to discern malice & ill will- quick enough to catch the pernicious infection- that turns the milk of human friendship into bitterness, our friends then, should . . . .[2] on the ground, or give to the winds every word that is calculated to do mischief- and leave us in peace to enjoy what God has given to us, to work out our own happiness. I hope our dear Ben has had a pleasant visit- it was too short, and has passed away too quickly- I wish you and your dear Children had been with him to have staid a month longer, in which time we might have shewn something of our cities gaiety & a great deal of its comfort & the love we bear you- I missed My dear Brother sadly last evening- . . . . for most of our evenings were spent together. Give My love to the dear

[1]The oldest son of Benjamin Gratz, who had been named after his father, died in 1830.   [2]Paper torn.

boys & Mary & kiss your children for me- deliver the inclosed to My brother with My love, and believe me dear Ann

       faithfully yours RG.

* * *

TO THE SAME

The Blair family - misunderstandings - Henry Etting's appointment to the Navy Yard at Brooklyn.

       Decr 8th 1845.

 I was going to write to My Dear Ben to thank him for his kind & most welcome letter from Maysville, when yours My dear Ann arrived, and knowing he gladly receives offerings of love and gratitude from your hands, I will make you my messenger, to tell him how joyfully I received his greeting that far on his journey & how you completed my pleasure by talking of his safe arrival at home.

 It is delightful to hear that his visit made him happy, for it assuredly spread much gladness among his family & friends- he was sad at parting with Cary[1]- no wonder, for he was never separated from him before, and the dear boy has so many lovely & loving qualities that his Father will daily miss- but they will return to him with two fold value, in the sense of duty which urged the sacrifice- and in the improvement he will derive from his studies-

 You are amiable My dear Ann, beyond measure in yielding to others, what alone concerned yourself. I am ashamed of the agency I had in the business and would by no means interfere with your taste or wishes on the important subject-

---

[1] Youngest son of Benjamin Gratz by his first marriage; the boy was placed in school in the East.

call your boy by any name you fancy. I shall love him dearly as I do his brothers- and the little darling Miriam- that sweet name, harmonizes with all my feelings- it was honored, in the person of My mother, who was universally beloved in her generation- and bore herself meekly through all the changes & trials of her life- yours is the fourth grand daughter that has borne it, and I could not wish them a better inheritance than that a portion of her spirit may descend upon them-

From the disposition in which Dear Ben left us I did not much expect that he would stop at Washington, tho' I urged him to do so, in order to remove the feeling of enstrangement I perceived in him- I received a note from Lizzie[1] expressive of disappointment, but saying that he had promised to see them during the coming year, which I hope will be fulfilled, for then *we* may hope to see *you* also- If you & he have no objection we will send the boys to spend half their Christmas holidays with their Aunt Blair, Lizzie says her Mothers heart is bent upon having them- . . . .

James[2] is to be married next month, Lizzie has taken a small house in the city- as exercise is essential to her health, she is forbidden to ride, & in the country cannot walk at this season- Montgomery[3] is also at Washington, and I suppose he will carry a wife back with him- what has become of Frank?[4] he may say with Beatrice "all are going to the world but me"- has he return'd from the Rocky Mountains? where is his lady love- poor child if she waits until his fortune is made at the Bar, I fear she will not marry in her *teens*, but Frank has fine talents & good nature- love may give him industry-

[1]Elizabeth Blair Lee, niece of the first Mrs. Benjamin Gratz.
[2]James Blair.
[3]Montgomery Blair.
[4]Francis Preston Blair. These three were brothers of Elizabeth Blair Lee.

Jo is much pleased with your approval of the Carriage, he prides himself on his taste in those matters and little doubts it in his wines- but cannot flatter himself that you will enjoy the latter luxury, tho' you may the first- I had a letter from Sara to day from Savannah, she had a very sick passage of 8 days - but having found her sister[1] well, seems to have forgotten her sea sickness, after promising never to take passage that way when she can journey by land- I expect Julia Hoffman tonight- and of all the nights in the year, this is the most inclement for a journey- it has been snowing & raining & freezing all day- so much for having an engaged brother for an escort- he has been detained from his fair one, by business that even a storm is no consideration- Miss W drove down at the risk of her neck to let me know I might expect Julia to night- . . . .

Our Sisters & brother send their affectionate greetings to you & our brother Ben- and the dear boys- Mr Etting continues comfortably well- and the rest of the family as usual- Henry Etting has been appointed to the Navy Yard at N.Y.- which will take him from home, but is a very good station- I hope your little darlings have recovered, and that your rest is restored- it is a bad thing for a nurse to lose rest, you do not tell me whether you are strong & have flesh enough or whether you give all your substance to your boy- you must remember that a good mother should look ahead, and try to preserve her constitution for future usefulness. . . . .

A thousand thanks My beloved Brother for your kind letter from Maysville, it made my heart glad to trace your considerate love in greeting us on your journey, we were so sorry to part with you- so anxious when gone that you should speed on your way home- May God Bless you- ever
yrs R G

[1] Miriam Moses Cohen.

TO THE SAME

The South in Winter - "hired help" - the magnetic telegraph - new railroad in the iron region of Pennsylvania - evils of the sedentary life - compensations - the Marshall - Clay duel.

Feb 13th 1846

I am extremely sorry my dear Ann to hear that you have been so much indisposed, as our recent letters from Lexington mention- Mrs Strother told our sister yesterday that you would probably spend the month of March at the South, this has made me fear that you have not improved since our dear Ben's last letter as he says nothing of such an intention- but I should be glad to have this communication confirmed by yourself- it would be a much more agreeable remedy then the drugs of your physician and no doubt more efficacious- you could take Mary along as a nurse & companion- and escape the rude winds of the coming season most pleasantly - Sara[1] writes that spring has already opened and the sweet violets in bloom in her sister's garden- indeed she included one that perfumed her letter. Miriam would be delighted if you would make her a visit, and then in four days you might come on to Phila and complete the good work by a sojourn among your husband's family- we should be so happy to welcome you here- you must not consider this my first letter of inquiry, for I have one before me which was commenced ten days ago when interruptions prevented my finishing it- and somehow or other- (as you know sometimes happens in housekeepers arrangements) it was neglected and now rises up against me. I could give you a long string of

---

[1] Sara Moses who was visiting her sister Miriam (Mrs. Solomon Cohen) at Savannah, Georgia.

cogent reasons or apologies from the kitchen- if you knew anything about "*hired help*"- but "where ignorance is bliss 'tis folly to be wise"- I will tell you tho' what I know will be interesting from the kindness of your feelings towards your relations- our dear Sara Mordecai has lost her youngest child Emma after only the illness of a few days- her fatigue & distress produced illness and she is still confined- but I hope the worst is over- our venerable brother Etting is quite ill- he has rarely left his room during the winter tho' a part of every day saw his friends and enjoyed cheerful conversation in which he freely partook- he is now in bed and when I left him last even'g appeared to be suffering intensely the effect of a severe cold on his nearly exhausted frame- it set in with a chill succeeded by fever- and seems to have assumed the character of intermittent- Henry, who is his very attentive care taker when at home- is now resident at the Navy Yard at Brooklin- but his wife and the rest of the family are around him and the magnetic telegraph could recall the absentee in an hour, should he be required-

Our boys have not once written since they returned to school. I wrote to Cary and enclosed him invitations to his cousins wedding and party- as they promised to write if anything was wanted to contribute to their comfort, I interpret their silence favorably for boys find no pleasure in letter writing unless some particular object requires it

I shall lose the society of my friend Julia Hoffman earlier this spring than I expected- her brother is married and about to settle at "Wiconisco" as engineer of the Lykens Valley railroad- and she will accompany her new sister to their new home, some time next month- the bride & groom are going to make a preparative visit immediately and they carry my Horace with them, he has taken employment again as an Engineer, with the hope of obtaining a situation more to his fancy in the erection of a furnace - the road is to lead into an Iron region which is the object of this present engagement - Horace feels the necessity of advancing himself in life- while waiting for opportunities of business- he has employed his time in cultivating his mind- but the evil of too sedentary a life is that it has made him unsocial & independent of intercourse with general society. When this wears off however, I hope something will appear of advantage to his future happiness. When thrown among men, he will be estimated according to his worth, and if it is his fate to struggle on, labouring in solitude he will still have resources to draw from that will lighten labour by the reflection & recollection of all he has heard of and read of who have trodden the same path. "there is a divinity that shapes our ends, rough hew them as we may"-

Give my love to Mary and tell her I shall write to her soon- I am rejoiced that she designs us a visit in the spring- I see by the papers that young Shelby is supposed to have been deranged when he committed that dreadful outrage- insanity is often made a plea for guilt- some penalty should fall on the relatives or guardians of the insane who are left to prey upon society in an irresponsuble condition- Tom Marshall too seems to have fallen into an excess and again redeemed himself- I should be sorry to entrust any one I loved to his keeping- who finds it so difficult to keep himself- Is there any truth in his having fought a duel with C. M. Clay[1] in which both were wounded? so say the newspapers.

How are your darling Miriam, and your dear boy, I should love dearly to embrace them both, you must describe Mason[2] to me, and tell me how you call him, if he is fair- or

[1] For account of duel between Cassius M. Clay and Thomas F. Marshall, see *Life of Cassius Marcellus Clay* (Cincinnati, 1886), Vol. I, 140.
[2] The boy was named Mason Brown Gratz after Judge Mason Brown, an intimate friend of Benjamin Gratz.

whether you will call him Brown- give my best love to my dear brother, to Bernard & Hyman and accept for yourself the sincere affection of your sister

R G

* * *

TO THE SAME

The year omitted from the date of this letter is fixed by the mention of the infant son of Benjamin Gratz by his second marriage; since this child was born August 15, 1845 and died June 24, 1846 the year of the letter must be 1846.
Hudson's Shakespearean readings - homeopathy and other medical isms.

Philadelphia March 24th

I was delighted My Dear Ann to receive your letter giving a favorable account of hour health & hope your recovery will be rapid as the spring opens upon you, and you are induced to go out and meet the glad offerings she spreads over the face of nature- already the first buds are coming out on our trees- the willows in their fresh green and the various coloured crocus ask a welcome, most willingly accorded- your heart will rejoice too in the presence of your Son,[1] and I think you will find him greatly improved in health as well as in his studies- the Boys have only been here a few days & I should be glad to keep them a week longer if I did not find they were yearning to be at home. I shall give this to Jo with a charge that he does not deliver it until two days after his arrival. that you may enjoy his company first without the

[1] Joseph Shelby, son of Mrs. Gratz by a former marriage, who was at school in the East. He gained renown in the Civil War when he fought for the Confederacy. As General Joseph O. Shelby he was one of the well-known leaders in the Southern army.

intrusion of even a letter- Jo seems to have the spirit of mirth inborn in him, for he is as merry as a bird, or rather as a boy let loose from School, which he illustrated in a way to justify the adage- I saw your friend Mrs S a few days ago- we went together to hear Mr Hudson[1] lecture on Shakespeare- the character of Hamlet was his subject- and he viewed the play in some new lights, he is a very eloquent and original person, and has been quite popular here, an eastern man, who had his fortune to make & began with mechanicks- going thro' many active *notions* as other Yankees do working with mental as well as bodily activity until he found his vocation was to impart as well as imbibe- and I believe it is now his plan to study for the church- but I should think the stage would suit him better than the pulpit- there are such transitions in his style manner and voice- he does not observe any rules of oratory - digresses and speaks aside - or rather apart from his subject, if any sudden idea crosses his mind- with an accompanying expression of countenance sometimes of deep passion & sometimes of mirth- which he transfuses to his audience- but with all he is awkward and plain looking- yet I should like you to hear him, for I am sure you would enjoy the time spent in listening- our young gentlemen much prefered the circus or theatre or some other more youthful entertainment & so can give you no account of him- I was in company last evening with two Kentucky ladies from Hopkinsville; Mrs or Miss . . . . . & Miss Cross but did not find that they were familiar with any of my friends- The elder lady was intelligent, & the younger modest but I doubt if they were much entertained- it was at

---

[1] Henry Norman Hudson (1814–1886), famous Shakespeare student; author of *Lectures on Shakespeare*, 2 vols., Boston, 1848; *School Shakespeare*, Chicago, 1870; *Shakespeare, His Life Art and Characters*, Chicago, 1872. He issued an edition of Shakespeare's works, with life and notes, in eleven volumes, Boston, 1851–56.

a Bridal family party- and if they were tired I could sympathize with them-

I am glad My dear Mary is coming so soon, and under the escort of Hyman this is really joyful for it speaks well for the condition of his arm- change of climate may finish the good work by its effects on his constitution. My dear Brother will be shorn of all his sons save the baby but I trust happily- his purchase for Bernard must give great satisfaction, and I hope prove the commencement of a prosperous & useful life- in a little while he will be looking for a wife- & how I hope he will be directed in that important search, that his heart & his eyes may be fixed on such an one, as will be a help meet, and a guide & a guard & a companion hereafter- he is so good that his wife should make his home a little Paradise even if she had to make butter, as well as "dress his garden"

You describe two lovely children, I pray all your hopes may be realized in them- and that you may be spared to fulfil all the duties of a mother- I did not know that you had been so seriously indisposed- the care you have taken of yourself & the regular simple diet may eradicate the dyspepsia which has so long troubled you- I conclude you have not been nursing Mason- which office never suited you- tho' your babes are not the sufferers- . . . .

I suppose Mrs . . . . has not yet returned to Lexington her Sister Mrs . . . . considers herself in bad health & has put herself under the care of a homepathic. I think much mischief arises from the idea that their small doses can do no harm- when if they have any effect at all, it must be because they are much stronger but every age has its mania- ours has many. Mesmerism & homepathe- & Hydropathe, and many other hard to be believed systems which must grow into certainties or be swept away among the cobwebs of idle theories-

Brackenborough in Vermont is the Theatre of the Water system- Julia had a letter the other day from one of the patients a delicate lady who had gone to try its efficacy- what would you think of rising from a bath, wrapping wet sheets around you, and walking many hours, with a tin cup at your girdle that you might stop and drink cold water at every spring or pump you passed- spend the day in bathing drinking walking always in wet or bathing- it appears to me little less than madness- yet such is a system gaining converts- . . . .

Wishing you every happiness & health to enjoy it believe me to be my dear Sister most affectionately

Yours R Gratz

* * *

TO THE SAME

Resignation - Mrs. Grant of Laggan - unusual letters.

Phila July 10th 1846

My Dear Ann

Our boys have been home and have spent a few rainy days very pleasantly here- pleasantly to me, particularly because I could see no vestiges of discontent lurking in the minds of either of them and they returned most willingly to school- our brother Jo expresses such entire satisfaction in the judicious & proper management of Mr Bolmar- his vigilant attention to each individual pupil and his discernment of proper character in his young charges that I was rejoiced to find the boys growing more reconciled to his government and acquiring more confidence in him-

Their young Cousins Mary & Sara being home made their

holiday pleasant but poor Jo had just heard of the death of his little brother[1] and his sensibility & affection for you were awakened- he looked very bad until he had written and poured out his sympathy- I hope you have been enabled to comfort him by a letter ere this and that in endeavouring to do so you have drawn arguments from your own chastened heart that will return into it a full measure of consolation. It is so obviously our duty to receive the will of God with humble & grateful hearts whether he bestows or withdraws the blessings we treasure in this life- that it requires only a little time to collect our strength to bear such trials as are apportioned to us. I hope both you and my dear brother realize this feeling and are resigned. Your little darling daughter must plead for your smiles and her caresses will be sweetly soothing to you-

I am just now reading the memoirs and letters of Mrs Grant of Laggan[2] by her son (the sole survivor of twelve children) most of whom lived to grow up to maturity- & she survived them all- perhaps you have met with the "letters from the Mountains" which were published about 40 years ago and have an extensive reputation in this country- she was in America in her youth- and these letters were genuine written to her friends & published when she became a widow- as a source of pecuniary assistance- I wish you could meet with her letters they would interest- console- amuse, and strengthen you for they are the production of an enlightened & chastened mind- and written in a style that

[1] Mason Brown Gratz, the infant son of Benjamin Gratz, died June 24, 1846.
[2] Mrs. Anna McVicar Grant "Letters from the Mountains being the real correspondence of a lady between the years 1773-1807". London 1807. The book was republished in New York 1903 under the title "Memoirs of an American lady, with sketches of manners and scenes as they existed previous to the Revolution," by Mrs. Anna Grant, with unpublished letters and a memoir of Mrs. Grant by James Grant Wilson.

makes you love and enter into communion with the writer- she corresponded with some of my personal friends. I have read some of her letters in manuscript and feel as if I had known her- she died at the advanced age of 84 yrs-

Our Mary is improving her musical talents by very regular practice and taking singing lessons- thus far the weather has been favorable- whether wet or dry it was not too warm for exercise, but the last two days have given us midsummer heat and I fear she will find the city oppressive- her health is excellent - she perseveres in a strict diet, but has taken no medicine- walks every day and makes herself very agreeable

Our brother Jac is still in Virginia - I am sorry for his detention for it is more difficult to put up with privations in a dirty tavern at this season when ones comfort depends so mainly on cleanliness & wholesome food

I hope you are all enjoying health and pure air, the country is delightful & beautiful but you cannot feel the change as desirable as we do- having that beautiful green field[1] before you and extensive gardens behind- This morning's paper mentions Frank Blair's safety at Taos which must be quite a relief to his Lady Love- we have all been uneasy about him - his family quite distressed at the danger which seemed to encompass him-

Remember me most fondly to my brother and the boys and kiss sweet Miriam for me- believe me dear Ann most truly and affectionately

Your Sister
R Gratz

Remember me to your good old Dinah

[1] Known now as Gratz Park named in honor of Benjamin Gratz.

TO THE SAME

Year of this letter is omitted from the date but the recipient wrote on the back "answered Nov 2d 1846"
    A mother in Israel - family gathering on the Sabbath - Jewish holidays.

Philadelphia Oct 18th

I do not know My Dear Ann if you have ever experienced a period of total inability to apply yourself to an occupation- if you have not- then I must fail to make you understand why your last interesting letter has been so long unanswered, and I fear you have attributed my silence to a wrong cause- I do indeed lament that your heart lingers so painfully over the memory of a lost blessing- because that is a grief irreconcilable- and perhaps would we comprehend aright might be numbered among the trials a righteous judge designs to make us more sensible of *his* infinite mercy- and prepare our hearts better to serve him. You say right- our Sister Hays does sympathize with you, and was alone deterred from writing- lest she should not succeed in addressing you at the time or in the manner to make a letter acceptable- she has been often called upon to resign those she dearly, tenderly loved- in infancy- in youth and at maturity she has wept over her offspring- the first blights of many sweet maternal hopes- but when to these were added the recollection of years in which those hopes seemed realized and the cares of maternal watchfulness were exchanged for the pleasures of companionship the trial was ten fold more severe- I wish you could see what a benignant expression rests on her countenance, over which so many sorrows have passed- all her surviving children were gathered under her roof last week- Sara[1] & Ellen[2] had their children with them, and the whole family party was complete- now she is again alone- they could not prevail on her to leave home this winter, but has promised her daughters to visit each of them in the spring. . . . .

We had a visit from Genl Tronwyle and were greatly entertained with his enthusiastic account of his foreign tour- he has brought back many flattering testimonials of his reception and the estimation he was held in, for his zeal in the good cause, among these a beautiful likeness of Father Mathew[3]- the danger he was exposed to in "the Great Western" & his escape from shipwreck, form a very interesting portion of his details- many events may be crowded in a short space of time- and how large a portion of our lives pass away when "we take no note of time- but by its loss"

Our Brother Etting, tell Ben is doing very well- and is delighted to see his boys, I found him yesterday talking very animatedly to Hyman- Sisters both send you their love- we meet as often together as we can always on the Sabbath at our eldest sisters house- she never goes abroad, but is so hospitable and cheerful, that we assemble, in pretty large companies there- three generations together- and Reuben looks like a patriarch, at the head of his tribe- the Tabernacle is just over, and the New Year has thus far been prosperous and gratefully welcomed-

Kiss your darling little Miriam for me, and give her my blessing of the season - may she live to be a blessing to her parents - tell dearest Ben I send him my best & most affec-

---

[1] Mrs. Alfred Mordecai.
[2] Mrs. Samuel Etting.
[3] Theobald Mathew, known as Father Mathew (1790–1856) famous Irish advocate of temperance, notably among sailors. Was in the United States 1849–51, and spoke in many places in advocacy of his pet cause. Numerous societies were named for him in the United States.

tionate love - his dear boys make me go over his young days again - our brothers send their love to you both - & I beg My dear Ann that you will believe me sincerely your affectionate Sister - R G

* * *

TO THE SAME

Family sorrows- mother and daughters - the Mexican War, "this wicked war" - benefit of a good education.

April 24th 1847

My Dear Ann,

I do not like to return evil for good or sadness for joy and the bright aspect of your last letter has been for several days pleading for a reply which my sombre feelings could scarcely do in a befitting manner. I know that even the pleasure of your son's company has not kept you from sympathizing in the melancholy event that has greatly affected us- poor Isaac Moses'[1] untimely death and the melancholy circumstances attending it which debars us from the consolation of knowing anything about him- it seems that he walked out and was heard of no more until his remains were found some miles from the city- several days after he left Mrs Ogden wrote that he was missing but it does not appear that any one sought for him, and it was not until after almost a fortnight had elapsed that his body was accidentally discovered sitting with his head resting against a tree- God only knows whether a sudden summons or protracted sufferings closed his mortal career, and this sad uncertainty adds to his fathers grief- Mr Moses' health has not been well for some

[1] Oldest son of Solomon and Rachel Gratz Moses.

time and this blow- together with Horace's departure for Mexico are severe trials at his age-

Lizzie returned home yesterday and our Sister Hays accompanied her as far as Baltimore where she means to stop with her daughter Ellen for about a week, then will proceed to Sara at the Arsenal where Ellen will join and accompany her to Rosa's near Richmond- you do not know what an event, this journey of our sisters appears to her and her girls- they have so desired to have her visit them, and have written so constantly about it, that when she made up her mind to go, they fancied they had gained a conquest- and I have heroism enough to rejoice on their account, tho' I shall miss her greatly. Poor Mrs Montgomery Blair has had a hard struggle for life- no one thought she could have survived- her babe was born dead- and she was so low- that all her physicians despaired of raising her. Lizzie was kept in great anxiety- but happily she is getting well- it was fortunate her husband arrived before her illness- so she had all she loved around her and her mind being easy the reaction was unalloyed- last week I had quite an alarm by hearing that a person was killed at Frankfort bearing your family name, and knowing you had brothers in the neighborhood feared the sorrow might touch you My dear Ann- but as we have heard nothing from any of the family- I trust those dear to you have been spared from so great an affliction- poor dear Mr Clay & Mrs McKee- how my sympathy has gone with them under their irrevocable loss- this wicked war- I cannot think even the glory of our successful battles can pay for such lives- our city was illuminated for the victories gained but many of our friends would not join in such mocks of festivities- until all are safe- let us show our light hearts by brilliant illuminations then they say- when Peace is declared and the wailings of sorrow no longer heard-

When are we to expect the young students back? I am glad you found them so much improved and I am glad they are wise enough to return for the benefit of a good education is too great to be neglected, and they are just at the period to appreciate and to receive it. . . . .

Sara Moses is much distressed at the death of her brother and Mary does all she can to comfort her- they have been such close companions, that they will find it hard to separate- they study Italian- walk- talk- play the piano & sleep together- Mary has greatly improved you will find, in health & accomplishments & in self regulation, which of course follows in all mental cultivation- she is at present making preparations to assist at a musical entertainment at Mrs Peters, the british consuls lady- a party long talked of & postponed during lent- there seldom occurs a better opportunity for improvement in singing than she has enjoyed the last winter- a party having great talent & skill meet once a week statedly to practice- and have performed at Mrs Peters concerts every fortnight- besides various other intermediates, so that you will find Mary quite accomplished in Italian singing as well as in her own sweet English ballads which I confess are much more delightful to me - give my best love to My Dear Brother and all my nephews- . . . . Adieu My dear Ann Believe me always with much sincerity your very affectionate Sister

R G

A letter from Ben confirms my fears respecting your brother - most sincerely do I sympathize with you & pray that God may comfort you, My poor Sister

R G

TO THE SAME

Gratz Brown - the beatitude of heaven - mother love - early marriages.

Philadelphia May 27th 1847

My dear Ann

The boys left us on Monday morning after spending a week with us which I assure you we enjoyed very much, as they were in good spirits and went back to West Chester with willing minds. I sincerely hope they will have a happy and profitable session I think Jo much grown & improved. Gratz Brown met them here, his example is a bright one for imitation, he will graduate this summer with great credit, he only misses *the honor* by a single vote, the other candidate having been longer in college, it was pleasant for the boys to meet and encouraging to those in the middle of their course to find their friend & companion so near the goal-

I have grieved for you & with you My dear Sister in your recent calamity- it was a sad bereavement indeed for you- and the friends who loved him, but for him perhaps a happy release from hopeless sorrow. There appears no condition in human life more afflictive and destructive to happiness & morals than such an ill-advised marriage, as your unfortunate young brothers- and the consolation you have to lean on is that he died innocent- the victim and not the partner of crime - I have thought a great deal of the devoted affection his mother bore him- how fondly she anticipated the days on which by appointment they met in the country- when he was somewhere at school- May not this love begun here between such relations be continued- and form some portion of the beatitude of heaven? there can be no love more pure more perfect or more enduring than a mothers- what a blissful refuge to the stricken spirit- after the disappointments of such a life to be comforted- "as a mother comforteth"!- we are not permitted, My dear Ann to choose our affliction- if we learn to bear those that have been appointed to us by our Creator- and submit ourselves to *his* will we shall be visited by his mercy, and our offering be accepted. The mystery that hangs over poor Isaac's fate, adds a severe pang to his mourning family but there is consolation in the sympathy & respect of his fellow citizens- his life was solitary and wanting in many comforts to a man of his disposition- Alas! who can estimate the loss of a mother to a young family- the training eye of maternal watchfulness not only forms & regulates the character of her offspring but clears their path from unseen & unsuspected dangers- Isaac lost his at a critical period of his life- and had none when his experience taught him to retrace his steps, but thank God he did retrace them- and had it pleased *Him* to have prolonged his life- he might have been happy in the domestic scene- . . . .

I am glad to hear that Miss Anderson[1] has recovered, will you describe her to me, I do not mean her appearance, but feel interested to know what kind of person Howard has chosen to be the partner of his life- he has never mentioned to me his engagement, or his views- early engagements are good things if their fulfilment is not too long postponed. They incite a man to form habits of industry- with a reward in prospect men set to work with spirit- and the desire to keep the love & respect of their Beloved- is an all powerful motive for deserving it-

Everybody tells me of the loveliness of your sweet Miriam,

---

[1] Henry Howard, the third son of Benjamin Gratz, married Minerva Anderson at Lexington, October 5, 1847.

until I ache to see her. The boys talked of her continually & comparing her with children here- she seemed to them a queen of fairies- give my best love to my dear Brother and a kiss to her- also much love to the boys- . . . . Adieu My dear Ann, I wait impatiently for your promised letter and am affectionately yr

R G

* * *

TO THE SAME

Rebecca Gratz Bruce a namesake - the love of flowers - poetry in education - further deprecation of the Mexican War - shame to the United States.

Phila. July 22nd 1847

My dear Ann

Becky Bruce will tell you how entirely the arrangements of her party defeated your kind intentions in my favor- Yesterday afternoon she brought me your letter, informing me that they had been four days in town and would leave early this morning, that her friends were waiting her return, to take her to the Chinese Museum and then to the Opera, so that every moment of her stay in Philadelphia was appropriated.

She still looks delicate but gave a very good account of her health & the enjoyment of their tour- I should have wished to have paid some attention to the dear child, whose Mother I hold in great respect and to whom we are under many obligations for services & kindness, & for the personal compliment she has paid me in giving her daughter my name- but on this occasion I have been disappointed.

Your letter dear Ann was full of interest- I take great

pleasure in the description of your beautiful garden- which you know we talked about when I was with you, and you were only cultivating it in idea- the employment of your successful efforts must be very gratifying to you - but I could not have imagined that your sweet little Miriam would so early imbibe a taste for flowers, and store their names in her memory - I delight in her facility and in your judicious management in bringing the beauties of nature under her notice- the pure & innocent & refined all love flowers, they seem a creation of pure benevolence with which God has ornamented the earth, to make it more lovely- and to gladden the heart of those who dwell on it- I have a friend, who has been long in affliction- she calls flowers her good angels- for they have power to soothe her in sorrow and give a sensation of gratitude while she inhales their perfume and looks on the perfection of their beauty- Miriam loves poetry too, the darling! when she fully comprehends the philosophy of that exquisite poem, she will wonder at her infant minds being attracted by its deep & solemn truths its verses portray- you must give her memory rhymes for her present exercises- and simple hymns which her mind can apply- I know you will not burthen her memory- or task her for the gratification of others, because your good sense will prefer to see her natural development than force out the germ of intellect before its proper time . . . .

Miriam Cohen is on her passage from Savannah- we have heard of Horaces arrival at Pensacola, I cannot tell you how glad I am he has left Mexico- I feel so much more sorrow & disgust, than heroism in this war, that I could not bear to think of his being in any way connected with it. When we were obliged to fight for our liberty- and rights- there was motive & glory in the strife- but to invade a country and slaughter its inhabitants- to fight for boundary- or political supremacy- is altogether against my principles & feelings and I shall be most happy when it is over- tho many bleeding hearts will be left over losses of their dearest & most beloved victims- The Washington will come directly to the U. S.- . . . . present My dearest love to My beloved Ben & his boys- . . . . accept our sisters' love with mine & believe me every- most affectionately Your R G

* * *

TO BENJAMIN GRATZ

Birth of Benjamin Gratz's second daughter Anna - betrothal of Sara Moses to Henry Joseph of Montreal, Canada.

Your letter My dearest Ben gave me very sincere pleasure not only because it confirmed the good account we had received of your dear Ann & her babe,[1] but because every expression of your affection is most grateful to me- I never doubt its existence and feel that I shall always return it, since it has endured thro' many trials & long separation- but in this human state, whatever be our convictions the occasional reassurance of fervent recollections and loving thoughts, makes our hearts glad and gives a new & quick pulsation of joy- and such do your letters produce- your dear little girls have a living interest in my heart and I pray for them, that they may be as happy in each other as I have been in mine- Miriam must be a sweet prattler and by all accounts very beautiful.

I hope by this time Ann has perfectly recovered and enabled to join in the festivities of the season, tell her I wish her a happy New Year and many succeeding ones- It has

[1] Now (1929) the only surviving child of Benjamin Gratz, Mrs. Thomas Hart Clay.

been a period of peculiar interest & trial to me, for My dear Sara- the child of my tenderest affection has just engaged herself and I shall lose her society- the gentleman Mr Joseph of Canada, is I believe better known (personally) to Mary Boswell than myself- for the intimacy was commenced when they were at Cape May last summer- as far as I understand he is a young man of irreproachable character- a merchant in good business and respectable connections- he has been long attached to her- ever since she & Lizzie Blair were in Montreal- but no intimacy grew out of it until recently- Tho I can make no reasonable objection if her happiness is concerned, it is a very severe trial to me- no one can look into the uncertain future- and the child you have reared and cherished and treasured so dearly can hardly be transferred to other protectors without reluctance & misgivings- Sara is one of the most lovely & gifted characters I know so it would be difficult to find a person we think should be good enough to match her to- . . . .

Sara desires me to send her best love to you - she intended writing to you herself and telling you her own story, but feels a difficulty in putting her intentions into execution- her old fancy of visiting Canewood on such an occasion must be relinquished for a nothern summer- . . . .

Thank God all our family circle are well- and I ought to be happy & grateful- but My dear Ben when your darling daughter is going to be married you will be able to understand a feeling not easily defined- but certainly too full of anxious care to be called happiness- believe me with sincerest affection My dear Brother devotedly Yours

R Gratz

Jan'y 2nd 1848

TO ANN BOSWELL GRATZ

The loss of friends - impending loneliness - life on a southern plantation.

Philadelphia Feb 6th 1848

I ought much sooner My dear Ann, to have replied to your most gratifying letter but I hope you will be kind enough to excuse me and believe that the little stranger you introduce with your own name was taken directly to my heart- and that I shall not only love her for your sake but bear in mind the tender motive which associates her with the friend you loved- and lamented- Mrs R was indeed a loss to you- we rarely can replace such a companion- but in the innocent caresses of her sweet namesake you can dwell on her virtues and bring up memories that are dear long after the habit of daily intercourse has ceased to be missed- poor old Mr Hunt must finish his days in solitary mourning for his loving daughter & kind nurse- for none can be to him what she was- the loosing of such ties break up our hold on life- and are perhaps the best preparation we can receive for our own departure- did she leave a child younger than little Kate whom I used to see & admire three years ago

You must miss Mary & Mrs Thrashley very much from your fireside- but you cannot be lonely- your own little darlings and Howard's clever wife will fill the gap if *you* ever feel the want of society- for the first time I begin to realize such a state- When Sara leaves me on whom I have so long leaned- who has been reared by my side slept in my room, and been in the place of a daughter to me from her infancy up to the present time it seems as if I should be quite lost without her- and this anticipation haunts me painfully already- of an evening when she is at her piano every brilliant note reminds me that I am not long to be so charmed- our tete a tete sewing parties, the books we read together- all our social habits speak of the time when I shall no longer have her- but when I look into her face or hear her speak of the bright days of happiness dawning on her young hopes- every selfish regret is hushed and I sympathize in her feelings of confidence and love- we have had no accounts of Mary from N Orleans yet, the papers say they arrived on the 19th I hope her health will be improved and that she will have much pleasure in her visit- but I hope she will not be fixed there for life- she is not calculated for a planters wife nor do I think a southern residence would either improve her happiness or character. Mary is very lovely but requires more active duties than she would have, surrounded by dependents & slaves- you may laugh at this notion of a mistress's duties- but my dear Ann I only mean, that few not brought up among them & taught to feel the responsibility of that station can accomodate themselves to fulfil them- and then comes inertness- and little comfort- . . . .

I often think of my Lexington friends and try to place myself in your pleasant circle but find the deepest interest around your nursery fire with my dear brother looking proudly on and trying to hide how much he feels with womanlike tenderness- . . . .

Yesterday we had more snow than has fallen this season- and today there is nothing seen of it on the streets- The whole winter has been mild and bright & beautiful weather- & the walking perfectly good- The wise folk who do not accept any present enjoyment without predicting that it is to be paid for with interest expect a hard Feb. & late spring- . . . .

What does Howard mean to do? practice Law, or try a quicker road to fortune? may success follow his footsteps & prudent industry direct them-

Adieu dear Ann, write to me as soon as you conveniently can- and believe me always very truly your affectionate sister

R Gratz

* * *

TO BENJAMIN GRATZ

A new invention, the daguerrotype - the Malbone miniatures of Rebecca Gratz and her sister Rachel Gratz Moses - the European revolutions of the year 1848.

Philadelphia April 22nd 1848

My Dear Brother

I have just heard of an opportunity to Lexington which enables me to send a daguerreotype likeness taken from a miniature of our Sister Rachel which I think you will be glad to have, this ingenious invention, has been a great source of pleasure to many in preserving the likeness of distant friends- and as Sara Moses is so soon to leave home she has been taking advantage of it and among others obtained one of her Mother. I have often regretted that I did not take my miniature to Kentucky to shew to Ann, particularly as her darling Miriam is said to look like her- and even a mother's eye would not object to the resemblance to one who was so beautiful as was our sister- May she be as lovely in character also! Mary has a thousand little anecdotes to relate about her- very interesting and very clever- indeed she brings you all so often before us by her graphic description of the family circle that we feel drawn nearer to you- and almost impatient to see as well as hear of you

Our sisters health is improving since I wrote last. They are suffering with severe attacks of cold which confined them to their beds- and as strength does not return as rapidly to the aged as at an earlier period of life, continued longer invalids- our brothers are all well- they make a great pet of Mary, and she appears very cheerful & contented- a great many of her old friends have greeted her warmly- and she has already joined a musical club of Doregos pupils among whom she is spending this evening. Mr Joseph arrived yesterday- their wedding will be private, and they leave immediately- every arrival brings fresh & stirring news from Europe- whatever good may come in future from these revolutions- there seems to be a fearful period of suffering & bloodshed to be gone through first- enough to make any woman's heart quail-

Give my love to dear Ann, and all my dear nephews & nieces- .... our brothers, Sara & Mary desire their affectionate remembrance- and believe me my dearest Ben, with devoted affection unalterably

Your Sister
R Gratz

* * *

TO ANN BOSWELL GRATZ

Death of Reuben Etting- the country and the people in Canada- Henry Clay's loss of the presidential nomination to General Taylor - a duelist in the United States Senate, "a duelist is a murderer."

Philadelphia June 25th 1848

All the time I was sick My dear Ann I thought of your charming letter and felt that you did not know how much pleasure it had given me and how grateful I was for it- then came dear Ben's letter, and this was so rare a blessing that I could not resist writing to him immediately, notwithstanding my indebtedness to you, and since my recovery all the strength I have has been used in daily visits to our bereaved sister- we do not think the death of our dear venerable brother an evil, for he prayed for it as a blessing- his spirit was weary of imprisonment in its worn out tenement, and he longed to be at rest- but his place is vacant and the faithful loving companion of more than half a century is so missed by our sister that she sits as one amazed how she can live without him- . . . .

Our letters from Sara shew that "she has her content so absolute," it would be unkind to regret her change- her husbands family are very agreeable to her, his Mother affectionate & cordial in her reception, & his sisters pleasant companions - she likes driving about the country, and visiting all places which exhibit to her the customs & manners of the old Canadians, the french population particularly amuse her, with their primitive costume, and proud defiance of their present rulers. She has been invited to hospitalities which being in mourning she could not partake of- but from sociable visiting seems to have formed a pleasing impression of society in Montreal- being a Military Station they have fine bands of music, of which you know she is very fond. They have not yet gone to house-keeping, but have private apartments in a hotel, ... private entrance & table- when she becomes better acquainted with the country & people she will begin to feel a desire for a more permanent home establishment . . . .

Dr Moses has brought home his family from Texas and is again established in his profession, he thinks without having lost anything by his absence, his old patients were quite glad to have him back again, ... how do Mr Clays friends take the result of the Convention, and how does the sage himself bear it? I am mortified for him, that he did not, in the full strength of his triumphant personal popularity, while the whole country were turning out to do him honor decline being a candidate for public office. Then had his political friends persevered & given him their nomination, his feelings would have been spared from mortification & perhaps his chance been even better than it stood when the convention met. The Whigs would no doubt have prefered *Mr Clay* tho' they thought that *Gen* Taylor would be more likely to succeed, and they could not risk another administration- Military titles seem the only qualification looked for in President making- I do not like your losing Mr Crittenden[1] out of the senate- and sending a duelist in his place- There seems something very inconsistent in putting a law breaker, in the place of a law maker- and disguise it, as they will by any code of nominal honor- the duelist is a Murderer, and God has denounced that crime as unpardonable- "ye shall not take the price of blood"- The end of my paper warns me to have done- . . . . Farewell My dear Sister Ann, remember you have three sisters here who claim all the privileges of that title to love and embrace you and believe me faithfully

your affectionate R G

[1] When John J. Crittenden was elected governor of Kentucky in 1848 he resigned from the United States Senate and was succeeded by Thomas Metcalfe who filled the unexpired term till March 3, 1849. Crittenden was reelected senator in 1855 and served until 1861.

TO THE SAME

Saratoga gaiety - Sabbath observance - Grace Aguilar's "Home Influence" - departure of Mrs. Murat for France.

Sept 15th 1848

My Dear Ann

I have been in so unsettled a state since my return home, with the comings and goings of our family & friends that I have not yet found leisure to give you an account of our summer doings as I fully intended- knowing you and My dear Brother take a lively interest in our concerns- Sara & Mr Joseph were with us but a short time, but we enjoyed every moment that was given- they did not arrive at Saratoga early enough to partake of its gaiety- the Fancy Ball of which Mary has sent you an account was over- tho had they been there they would not have attended it being given on Friday Evening- the illuminated garden was very beautiful and seemed to realize those memorable descriptions familiar to readers of fairy tales - & the salon must have appeared equally illusive as it was thronged with representatives of every nation, and every period since men & women learned to trick themselves out in fine dresses- our Mary was tastefully arrayed in the rich dress she had last winter when she left me to join the group- we were all benefited by our visit to Saratoga- delighted with our journey thro' New England- and grateful to find ourselves at home again- without any mishap on the way and meeting our dear friends here in their usual health. . . . .

Our brother Jac has not yet reached home his business in Virginia detains him much longer than he expected- I am very glad he went to Lexington first, the pleasure he there enjoyed has nerved him against his present privations for he can live over the thoughts of your feasts both mental & physical- and endure the contrast with more patience, ...

I see they have just published a new novel "Home Influence" by Grace Aguilar, which was lent to me by an english lady some time ago. I wish you would read it, and give me your opinion of its merits, because I see many excellences in it, and found it deeply interesting- I know nothing so touching as the distresses and difficulties of childhood, and am glad to see them treated with consideration and sympathy by matured intellects- I doubt whether at any period of life more intense misery could be experienced by those involved in unintentional wrong than poor little Ellen suffered- it is to be lamented the gifted author did not live[1] to complete her design of continuing the subject through another work- but enough has been done to admonish parents & children that "Truth in word thought & action is the only safe guide of life"

I have just had the pain of parting with our friend Mrs Murat[2] & her children, who embark for France in a few days to join her husband, and in the unsettled state of that country, there seems no security that the favored of the day may not be proscribed by the next in power . . . .

Embrace your darlings for me, I wish I could do so myself for I want them to know me- on our journey I had the happiness of seeing My friend Mrs Butler[3]- whose persecuting husband has forced her to this country by suing for a divorce on the plea of her having deserted him, tho' it is well

---

[1] Grace Aguilar died September 16, 1847.
[2] Prince Joachim Murat played a great role in the Second Empire under Napoleon III, the nephew of his mother.
[3] Fanny Kemble.

known he drove her out from her privileges of Mother & wife- long before she attempted to earn a maintenance for herself in a profession she loathes- to My beloved brother give my tenderest love, and always believe me My dear Ann, your affectionate Sister

R Gratz

* * *

TO THE SAME

Mrs. Butler's (Fanny Kemble) domestic troubles - Grace Aguilar's power of portrayal - Henry Clay in private life - fashionable society - ease of travel compared with hardships of former days.

Philadelphia Decr 11th 1848

I did not wait for your letter My Dear Ann tho' I was very glad to receive it, but felt that our correspondence was becoming very languid, and intended writing to you for some time before its arrival- our best intentions however are often thwarted, and that was my case in the present instance- a very old friend of My youth- with whom in sisterly affection the best years of my life were passed was suddenly removed, and her death, brought up so many dear recollections, and the distress of her sisters interested me so much, that I devoted my time to them in their grief- then came My friend Mrs Butler, and her affairs engrossed my time and interest so that I should have tired you with the subject, particularly as all the newspapers were full of it- she came here accompanied by her excellent friends Mr & Mrs Charles Sedgwick- and received flattering attentions from all her personal friends here which tho she was in no condition to accept were agreeable evidences of their sympathy- you have no doubt seen the pleadings- the judgment of the court is not yet known- and she has returned to the privacy of her village home- our dear Lizzie Lee[1] went home last week, very much benefitted by her visit, her husband joined her here, so that she enjoyed his society and was quite contented, you know what very agreeable conversational talents she possesses-Mary was delighted with her companionship and our house was again brightened by their young light hearted merriment. I am glad to have Sara's friends feel at home in it, tho' every day they missed & wished for her presence . . . . I am glad you like "Home Influence"- I wish the gifted author had lived to complete her design of carrying her character thro' life, with such a beginning we might have expected her own portrait in one of them, and a charming group of practically good people more natural & easy than Hannah More's and quite as good as the Hanleys. Miss A was herself an example for good daughters . . . . We were very sorry to hear how very sick Mr Clay has been, I hope he is out of danger now, and will soon regain strength & spirits- there are other fields of honor & usefulness open to him free from the cares of state, which he may embrace and make the latter days of his life even more famous than its prime- & he has too great a mind to allow of entire inaction & repose- What are you doing this winter? your babies are big enough to allow you time to devote to business & pleasure- and your husband having finished his domestic fixings ought to accompany his wife into polite circles- we hear of the great wedding in Louisville, were you not invited? pray if you were, give us a description of the marvellous doings - those Wards are the Thorns of the west and should have their fame spread for their magnificent aspirings- Mary has been

[1] Elizabeth Blair, so frequently mentioned in these letters, had married Lieutenant Lee of the United States Navy.

invited to a grand Fancy Ball in N. York to be given by Mrs John Stevens, on the opening of her new house or palace in College Square, Ben knew her in days of yore (Maria Livingston) she took a great fancy to Mary (as most people do) last summer at Saratoga and sent us all tickets to her fete- whether Mary will go or not, I cannot tell- she went a few weeks ago (When her Uncle Jo had some business there) to an Opera- since the Railroad affords such easy travelling- an 100 miles to a frolic is no such great affair- five hours will suffice- when we had to travel in stages, it took some time to make up ones mind for the journey- and two days were necessary to complete it- I was born too soon My dear Ann, to be fashionable- was always slow and now tho' indifferent to fatigue- have no desire to leave home, except for an object of greater importance- Sister Hays has just stopped in & finding me writing to you desired I would give her best love to you and our dear Ben, put mine along with it Sister, and tell him it comes warm from the heart, we treasure him among our choicest- . . . . My love to each of My beloved nephews & nieces and regards to all friends- believe me ever your R G

* * *

TO THE SAME

Flowers "good angels" - Mrs. Butler's (Fanny Kemble) divorce - the California gold mania - Italian Opera - the drama's decline - Shakespeare out of fashion.

Phila Jany 29 1849

You have been kinder to me My Dear Ann than I deserved, and my heart is very grateful to you, your long charming letter remained unanswered and yet you remembered to send good wishes to me in the season of festivity at the New Year- most warmly do I reciprocate those loving remembrances- and if it had not been a period of extra occupation for me you should have heard from me before. It so happened that many postponed duties crowded upon me- some out door claims which the loss of friends occasioned- and domestic interruptions which every housekeeper is liable to- made me at last imagine that I might as well yield up my volition altogether- but before the first month of the new year has gone, I hope to wipe off my old debts and feel myself free to enjoy morally & physically the social blessings I possess-

It is delightful to have such good accounts of you all- as your letters and our dear Ben's furnish us with, your precious little daughters must be perfect loves- tell dear Miriam her violets retained their sweetness & beauty when they arrived in cousin Mary's letter, and that her uncles & aunts all smelt & admired them. I am glad she loves flowers and hope they will always be "good angels" to her, which nature always supplys to those who entertain them. I have a friend who has been unfortunate in many circumstances of her life who says flowers are her "good angels"- They have such power to give her pleasure- she can always cast aside her sorrows to look at, arrange and admire flowers. I have wondered sometimes at their power to attract notice when her cares are most oppressive- The Ward wedding has been much discussed this side the mountain, and I was glad to have an authentic account of it- Mrs Lawrence has a great many eccentricities, among her better qualities, and has the talent of doing a good many queer things. I hope the marriage so distinguished in its celebration may turn out more rational than one could expect by the spirit with which it was got up- if money were as adhesive as it is proverbially the contrary, they might always buy notice, but unless they can be contented sometimes to live in retirement the world may go hard with them- I am glad to find you & My dear Ben, are interested in poor Fanny Butler's history- the Judges have not given Mr Butler a divorce, as was anticipated by those who knew the laws- and I see by the papers that she is making another effort to maintain herself by reading Shakespeare to the Bostonians- I expected she would be obliged to work or apply to the court to allow her some means until something was decided upon- and expected from her independent spirit that the former would be her choice- It is a pity a compromise could not be effected by which he could be released from marriage bonds and she, given the custody of the children- for both and all their sakes this would be their happiest arrangement, if he wishes to marry, as is suspected & reported- the little girls had better surely be taken care of by their own mother - and they would be a sad care & charge on any other woman- indeed I do not think the most unexceptional man in the country, would be a good match with the encumbrance of such children- who have had no domestic control for three or four years and are now approaching womanhood- do not mistake me, in supposing that such a state of things does exist- Mr B will not be likely to confer such a happiness on his wife as to give his daughters to her- if he intends to marry he would be more likely to follow Sir E L. Bulwer's example- I have just had news that our niece Becky Nathan has another son, making her number four- The boys can tell you what a bright warm hearted little person she is- and how she lives in a little plain domicile, as happy & contented with her state, as if she were surrounded with luxury- it seems her pride to be surrounded by her children, and overcome difficulties which other persons would think desperate- her

Father went to New York with Edmund,[1] who sails on the Falcon for California- he has the gold mania, and means to adventure there- James Blair sails in the same steamer- he has leave of absence for a year, and has embarked in a business which promises to be profitable. I told him his wife was very badly treated, by his voluntary absence when his profession obliged him to be away- Sailors are never at home on shore- except Lizzie's husband who seems happiest in taking care of her- Mary is well and has just made an engagement to sing at a small party on Monday next, she has improved very much, but gives most of her time to Italian singing which I sometimes rebel against, and obtain some of her beautiful ballads- but I find myself growing fonder of Italian music- its richness & passion seem most adapted to her powers and is certainly much grander- even tho you do not understand the poetry- Italian Operas have completely taken place of Theatricals- and of course the drama is no longer what it ought to be- or what it was in my day when Shakespeare was in fashion .... everybody here sends much love to you and Ben to whom please make my best love acceptable- believe me, My dear Ann, very truly and lovingly, your Sister, kiss my sweet Miriam & Ann for me, ever your R G

[1] Edmund Moses son of Solomon and Rachel Gratz Moses and nephew of Rebecca Gratz.

TO THE SAME

Year of letter omitted from date but in all likelihood it was written in 1849 as indicated by the mention of the arrival in Philadelphia of Sara Gratz Joseph with her husband and child from Montreal. This child was born January 28, 1849. Railway travel - Mrs. Kemble's Shakespearean readings.

Do you not consider it kind of Me My Dear Ann, to absolve you of nearly half the blame of our sluggish correspondence? *It is not quite* a month since the receipt of your last letter- but I must not take too much credit for following your example as my time has been more than usually occupied- first by a visit from our dear Mary, who spent 10 days with us, and was here when Sara her husband & child arrived- .... My dear Sara left us this morning. Mr Joseph could only spare a fortnight to us- they have a very sweet intelligent little girl, to whom they are both very much devoted- I was disappointed My Dear Ann, that your last letter did not contain a plan of your summer journeyings- When you would start what route you would take, and when we might expect to welcome you at No 2- pray do not keep me long in suspense, or disappoint us of the happiness of a visit from you & our dear Brother and the sweet little girls- .... The long session this year, will give you an opportunity of seeing congress assembled, when you visit Washington if you come in over the Mountains- do you love travelling? if you do I can anticipate for you a great deal of pleasure- to me it is a great enjoyment- tho' I must confess the convenience of Steam & railways is purchased at the price of much enjoyment to lovers of the picturesque. In my young days when fatigue was unfelt, I should have been

sorry for the change- time is now a consideration with one-
. . . . Jac is still an invalid- our other brothers are well- I wish you could enjoy Mrs Kemble's Shakespeare readings with us- it is not possible to give you an idea of her power- the Bard himself never heard his plays so truly personated- she seems to understand every character in the whole play and give appropriate tones to every speaker, exhibit every passion- varying her voice & manner to the very cadence of the scene she reads of- in another week she will have finished- & I never expect to witness Shakespeare representations more!

Give My love to My dearest Ben- Kiss your little darlings for me- . . . . believe me ever affectionately

Your Sister RG

April 22nd

* * *

TO MR. AND MRS. BENJAMIN GRATZ

Year of letter omitted from date but it is fixed by the mention of the seventy - eighth birthday of Mrs. Reuben Etting, the oldest sister. She was born June 18, 1771; the date of the letter therefore is 1849.
Death of Elijah Gratz Etting - the Clay-Turner duel - the horror of duelling.

Philadelphia June 18th

I am indebted to both My Dear Brother & Sister for the kindest and most welcome letters and hope they will permit me to address them together as they are constantly associated in My mind & heart, and as both have so affectionately expressed their sympathy to our bereaved sister. Anns letter to her penetrated her heart with gratitude- and she shed many tears over Dear Ben's sweet words of consolation- I am glad to tell you that she is recovering from the shock of Gratzs sudden death, tho she mourns his loss with all a mother's clinging to her first born- the amiable domestic character & habits of Gratz[1] makes her daily & hourly miss him, he was ever attentive to her smallest wishes and always present to perform them- but she is reconciled- he was taken away without much suffering and there was nothing in his illness to leave a painful recollection of him. . . . . I was extremely shocked this morning to see by the paper that Cassius Clay was killed, in a duel in which both parties lost their lives- was his antagonist the son of the ill fated Mrs Turner who was murdered when I was in Lexington? For I pity the unfortunate Mrs Clay- and all the family of these victims- Misguided men! if they had no scruples of conscience at sacrificing their lives, the gift of God! might not human affections have saved them from involving their unhappy wives in such desolation & ruin! no laws can be too rigid against this barbarous custom- honor, false honor against every principle of right- either religious or moral- There is a young man, a cousin of Horace Moses's just about returning home, branded by a similar act- having killed a man in a duel- he is about 24 yrs old- a light hearted amiable lad, who a few months ago, was hailed as the benefactor of a community in Texas, having gone to a village where the Cholera raged & the inhabitants were panic struck, deserting the sick & flying from danger- with his characteristic courage & good nature, he went among the sick & dying, administering remedies and attending to the wants of the suffering- he was lauded for his benevolence, & followed by the gratitude of the populace- a change has come over the fair page of his

[1] Elijah Gratz Etting, the oldest son of Reuben and Frances Gratz Etting, born July 14, 1795 died May 25, 1849.

history and the curse of Cain incurred- to wipe off a stain
from his insulted honor- My dear Brother will think this a
womanish view of the matter but Ann will sympathize with
me- commerce with the world does not oblige us to mingle
wrong & right together- and do a wicked thing to prove that
we are brave- Lizzie writes that Frank Blair is about returning to St Louis but that both he & Montgomery are to bring
their familes to Silver Spring[1] to be in the summer- . . . .
This is our Sister Ettings birth-day. She has reached her
78th year & is blest with an unbroken constitution, and
possesses a temper & qualities that make age lovely &
venerable- She bids me present her love, and affectionate
thanks to dear Ann for her kind letter and a blessing to her
dear Ben & his boys- . . . .

God Bless you both- believe ever in the true affection of
your devoted Sister RG-

* * *

TO ANN BOSWELL GRATZ

*Marriage of Mary Boswell to Elisha Riggs of Washington -
panorama journeys - the Gratz family in St. Louis.*

Phila Novr 18 1849

It is indeed a long time My dear Ann since we have held
converse together, and so many interesting occurrences have
& are to take place in which we have mutual feelings that I
sometimes wonder I did not break silence long ago- My
heart is so full of our dear Mary's destiny that had we been
together it would have formed the subject of unremitting
discourse but it is just the thing one writes least about tho'

---

[1] The magnificent country home of Francis Preston Blair, the father
of Lizzie Lee and Frank and Montgomery Blair, near Washington.

it fills up our thoughts- In another week I shall lose her society, she is to be married at St Thomas church on Monday morning at 11 o'clock and will go immediately to New York with Mr Riggs' parents,[1] who come on to the wedding, after a visit of a week or two they return here, and will proceed to Washington to their own house, which I hear is a very good one- handsomely fitted out with all things befitting the condition of her new alliance. I like Mr Riggs very much, he is intelligent, sprightly and very devoted, his manners are plain and his taste domestic- I do hope that our child will be very happy, she is now nervously alive to everything, and were it not for the business of making preparations for the occasion- would probably be sick- Lizzie Lee came on Thursday and they have just gone to church together - Mr Clay has been to see Mary and is to be present at the wedding- perhaps will give the bride away (if there is any objection to my performing that office) which she says is her first choice- I have executed your commission by purchasing a very beautiful point lace cape & cuffs which cost $78- she is highly delighted with this present, being of a character, that never grows old and out of fashion- Mary will be married in her travelling dress, an embroidered cashmere- The wedding costume is a white brocaded silk & your point Lace- but she can not wear it on the occasion as they leave at 12 o'clock, and the risk to her health would be too great at this season to go so attired to church in the morning- I wish you and my dear Brother were here, the wedding will be private only a few invited guests and the family- Mr Riggs brings one or two friends with him.

I hope your little Anna has quite recovered and that all

[1] Elisha Riggs was a member of the great banking firm of Corcoran & Riggs. He was one of the most prominent citizens of Washington. His partner was the donor of the famous Corcoran Art Gallery in Washington.

your dear household are well- we had a very pleasant visit from Miriam in October, she has two very lovely & good children and seems to be very happy- Mr Cohen is a very devoted husband, & seems to admire her as much as he ever did. They talk of a western tour next year- and we amused ourselves by appointing a meeting in Lexington after you have made a visit to our middle states. It is so much the fashion to form Panorama journeys & voyages that we mean to make ourselves moving machines and take the picture of our world- which means the residences of all our loved ones- I want to see your children greatly- and Howards little girl- whom her Uncle Hyman praises most lovingly- . . . .

You must have had some difficulty in consenting to Jo Shelby's departure for St Louis, he is so amiable affectionate & clever that his society to you was of great consequence but it was entirely right- he has gone to such a thriving place- and where he has so many friends! . . . . you must give my love to Jo when you write to him, and tell him to go un- ceremoniously to Gratz Moses's, and make himself at home in his family- when they know each other it will be mutually agreeable and there are so many of our connections there that they may have quite a family gathering- Mary is writing at the same table with me- and desires me to give her love to you and her Uncle Ben, to thank you both for her beautiful present- she will very soon do so for herself- and tell her Guardian how much better he calculated her expense than she did herself and how much she thanks him for his foresight- Now Dear Ann, in your kindest manner, give affectionate love for me to my dear Brother, and your darlings and accept the greetings of our brothers- My love also to our dear Nephews all- and ever believe me most sincerely your affectionate sister R G

TO THE SAME

Decr 20 1849

Yes My dear Ann I can duly appreciate your heroism in consenting to the departure of your husband for he has just bidden us adieu- after the short sweet visit for which we are indebted to your acquiescence- he has left one bright hope to cheer us- the promise of bringing you & the children to see us next summer- his appearance among us, was as unexpected as it was joyful and tho' it has past, his visit was a blessing & a delight- even Sara & Miriam who did not profit by it, seemed to have felt glad that his countenance had brightened the home they both love- I had a letter from Miriam this morning too late as was the inclosed to benefit him- willing I would have sent yours after him but knew it would not reach him at any stopping place, and so consign it to your care for him on his return- his stay in Balt. will not exceed many hours and as it is probable he will pass Ellen & Josephine on the road, there will be none to feel great disappointment there- tho' I know Ellen will grieve when she arrives this day to find that he has gone- I wish too that he could have seen Mary in her own house, she writes very happily and I sincerely hope you will find all your wishes realized on that score. There came by todays mail invitations to an entertainment at Silver Spring on the 24th given to the bride- our dear Ben will tell you all about his kinsfolk here and how very much they desire to see you face to face- and as you have never been on this side of the mountains I promise myself a great deal of pleasure from going about with you- you must see the Ocean and the falls of Niagara & the beautiful lakes and the Canadas and the springs and all the natural & artificial curiosities that abound in the regions of the north & east- which I think may keep us busy during the summer besides making a long & sociable acquaintance with your relations who are all disposed to love you-

Our dear Ben has been well all the time he was here- a great many of his friends sought him, and would gladly have kept him longer if the season had permitted a safe delay- but we were not willing he should suffer on a winters journey from severe weather- it rains today but is not cold and will not affect either the mountains or the river- so hope he will be with or very near you when this arrives. . . . .

I pray that you may have a happy meeting with your beloved, and spend in all domestic joy- My thoughts go with him on his journey & hail him with dear love at the home of his heart- believe me my dear sister affectionately yours

R Gratz

* * *

The Rev. J. M. Raphall's lectures on the "Poetry of the Hebrews."

Philadelphia Jany 23rd 1850

I received your letter My Dearest Ben with grateful pleasure- I can well imagine the joy occasioned by your safe return and could see the bright faces associated to welcome you- your visit was a delightful one to us all. and we hope it will please God to let us meet again in the spring with the additional happiness of having Ann & the children of the party . . . .

I am sorry you did not see Mary in her new house, that you might further satisfy her friends of her new position- both her own letters and Mr Riggs' speak as if they were happy and satisfied with each other & all the world- . . . .

We have been enjoying a very superior intellectual treat in the lectures of Dr Raphall[1] "On the Poetry of the Hebrews" The first night Julia's & my report induced Jo to go to the next and he became so interested that he has not missed one since, & is quite enthusiastic on the subject. He is on his way to the South, as far as New Orleans, should he pass thro' Lexington on his return, I hope you will see him, he has two sons with him- they remain in Balt. a fortnight, where he is to lecture- these beautiful delineations of Bible poetry tho' more particularly interesting to the Hebrews- attract the attention of our Christian clergy, who not only visit his lecture room but have sought his acquaintance-

Our sister suffers less with her eye than when you were here, but is still inflamed- and there is little other change in the family- a letter from Henry now & then delights his mother and gives an impulse to Isabellas monotonous life- sister Hays is well has been to a party to meet Dr Raphall & attends his lectures- . . . . Sara writes constantly- and would remind you of her mother when she speaks of her child - she always sends her love to you - and so does Miriam. Jac is quite well, tho' we see little of him in the parlour- he loves the indulgence of his easy chair and carries his books & papers into his chamber to enjoy them- Jo does not complain of the weather- nor Hyman of anything- the club room loses none of its attractions, tho' I am sometimes a little jealous about the reputation of my table which suffers by comparison with Auguste's luxuries- but *they- we* all agree about the happiness of seeing you enjoy the home feeling & home faces of the old household and the love which brought you to

[1] The Rev. Dr. M. J. Raphall was one of the most prominent rabbis in the United States in his day. He came from England in 1849 and served as rabbi of the B'nai Jeshurun congregation of New York City from that year till 1866.

it- . . . . God Bless you My dearest Ben, believe me ever fondly & gratefully your affectionate sister

R G

* * *

TO THE SAME

Philadelphia Novr 12th 1850

I was truly delighted My dearest Ben to receive your letter, giving so agreeable an account of all your dear family and bringing you all before me, just as I wish to see you, each pursuing your habitual occupations, and enjoying the blessings of providence in this delightful season- it is pleasant to look back on the past summer when you were with us- you are indeed unchanged My dear Ben in the fresh & glowing attachments of your youth- and it is a happiness to feel that they are met with corresponding love- it is not often that so large a family grow old with so few losses- and in all respects having so much cause to render thanksgiving to Almighty God for manifest blessings- I hope we are properly grateful- . . . .

My friend Julia will not be in town till December, I shall be glad to have her- but I have learned to live alone, or rather to do without a female inmate- I have been fortunate in so long possessing the companionship of loving & affectionate children- many mothers might have envied me- and still I occasionally enjoy their society- Julia will I hope always spend the winter with me, but as long as her brother stays in the mountains she will continue with him- his wife is very fond of her-

I heard yesterday that the husband of one of Ann Nicholas' daughters (Dr Maloney) was going to congress from

Illinois- if his wife accompanies him, it may lead to a renewed intercourse in her fathers family, as since the death of the parents Saml Nicholas seems to be interested in the children- our sisters & their families are very well, and send affectionate remembrances- they all talk with so much pleasure of Ann, the dear little girls & yourself that it was really worth all the trouble you took in bringing them here- to have left such a lively interest in the home circle of your own family- I do not know which of the little ladies we all love best, indeed their beautiful conduct, good manners and endearing qualities are a never failing source of conversation- & their little cousins talk as much of them as if their opinions as well as their love was a matter of consequence-
. . . . Tell Ann I wish she could have heard Dr Raphall's lectures on the post biblical history of the Jews- they are so very interesting, so eloquent & so instructive. They are attended by a very intelligent class of the community- the last one will perhaps bring a larger audience, as people will want to hear what he has to say of the present race. One would scarcely expect to find a family so hard & cold hearted, as the Wickliffs in a country where nature is supposed to prevail over fashion and the distinctions of rank- and where humanity is so generally extended to foreigners & strangers- poor Mrs W if she loved her husband must surely feel the want of sympathy in his family- I hope the good people of Lexington are more kind to her, than her kinsfolk- the old Duke must beware of the example of King Lear, and not give his daughter all, while he is liable to the elements-

Give my love to Ann and tell her she is a letter in my debt, and that she need not fear to fill a page or two with the prattle of my pets. The old Earl of Baleares wrote that people were very apt to leave their Portraits to their descendents shewing their features & statures- but he thought it more satisfactory to leave the picture of the mind, and in the habit of putting down every days thoughts & incidents, there were few lives so barren but would afford something to add to the stock of human knowledge and to be useful to their posterity- we are much obliged to him & his children for a most agreeable book (The lives of the Lindsays) for following out this plan- now your children will be so grown before I see them again that I should like to keep up my acquaintance with them uninterruptedly- Miriam will soon become a fine study- & sweet little Anna with her bright & ardent mind must not be lost sight of- I love them both dearly- give My dear love to all your sons- My beloved Brother and believe me fondly your affectionate sister

R Gratz

* * *

TO ANN BOSWELL GRATZ

Cholera in 1850 - Hyman Gratz at Hollidaysburg - Sabbath observance - Jenny Lind in Philadelphia - Henry Clay's barbecue - the Southern malcontents - the abolitionists - Miriam and Anna Gratz - the training of young children - Sabbath greeting of peace.

Friday Oct. 18 1850

We were desperately tired My dear Ann, of waiting for the first news of your arrival at home, for the Telegraphic message never arrived, and your & dear Bens letters of the 7th Instant brought the first intelligence but as you told us at Wheeling of the state of the river, we fancied you were wending your way prosperously- never dreaming that your feelings would be shocked by such a disaster as losing a fellow passenger by Cholera! but it is not given us to foresee where our danger lies nor to measure the goodness which shields us from it- we are getting on very quietly here all our Summer visitors are gone - but beautiful bright summer weather continues to cheer & smile on us - the autumnal mornings & evenings are scattering the leaves about our doors and remind me that nature is changing the visible world - and preparing for winter - this is the first day of rain for a long time- yesterday Hyman joined a party on the new route to Hollidaysburg - but I expect he will leave it & return home as he would not like to spend the Sabbath (a rainy day) by himself in Harrisburg his original plan- I think a little recreation will be useful to him- as he was prevented making his northern tour- Jac continues a rover- he has been away for a week past-

Jenny Lind is here- gave her first concert last evening- and is to repeat it to night & to morrow night but I do not think I shall hear her- It is one of those extravagances which moderate people & old ones too may not indulge in- the lowest price of a ticket is $5 and if it were $500 many might fill her room at that price - what think you of Roots notoriety for giving $625 for the first one sold at auction, but the sun shines to make his fortune - and he can afford it - I suppose you have been to Mr Clay's Barbacue and join the multitude who delight to do him honor We were all sorry when he was disappointed of the Presidency - little imagining that he was designed for a higher destiny. I am a little frightened about the Southern Malcontents - they are so hot headed & so wrong headed that they do not seem to see what dangers they would bring about their own ear- Now they throw themselves into the power of their greatest enemies (The Abolitionists & their slaves) . . . .

My heart clings to our little pets I should like to see them every day & watch the development of their characters, so lovely & yet so different sweet sensible Miriam, playful, artless Anna- . . . . I think My dear Ann we agree exactly about early teaching- it should be made pleasant & easy- but not neglected- a little time every day devoted to learning something will amount to a good deal- besides forming a valuable habit- if we urge a child to learn much, and praise her for it, she becomes vain & superficial- but to require what is learned to be understood- and not give her complicated ideas to study which she can not comprehend is much the best plan-

I was amused one evening by hearing a lady repeat what her little son had said to her one day- when I found it was words put into his mouth by a teacher of which the boy understood little, and certainly did not originate a single idea- There is one thing you have very judiciously avoided- you never talk nonsense to your children- they have nothing to unlearn- childish thoughts are not foolish- little stories they invent- and little plays they amuse themselves with- are beautiful they are true to nature- and affect me sensibly- sweet little Anna's examination of Minna Haights dress at Saratoga would have rebuked her Mothers fashionable dressing- more than any criticism- . . . .

Adieu it is near the hour of Sabbath- peace be with you all my dearly beloved- R G

* * *

TO THE SAME

Removal of Howard Gratz to Missouri - Marx Etting appointed midshipman at Naval Academy at Annapolis - the United States Navy - sale of Canewood - movements of the Blair family.

March 10th 1851

I am rich indeed this week My Dear Ann for I have letters

to answer from both you and My Dear Ben, and I most joyfully come to pay my dues, as *ye* are *one*. I shall not write two letters this time, but I beg you will not think me such an unprincipled debtor as to deny the fact, and it would not avail me much, with a person of such a correct memory, as your ladyships- henceforward when a great chasm occurs in our correspondence I shall take it for granted that I am the defaulter, so if you would not subject yourself to the imposition of two letters for one, you must be reasonably punctual- both your & my dear Brother's letter are full of interest to me, I first congratulate Howard & Minerva on the birth of their son- and then lament that they are going so far from home, I do not think well of going to "a new country & commencing a new business," his Father's counsel should be Howards guiding star- he has had little experience in the ways of the world- was not brought up to commerce and knows nothing of the people among whom he is going to live- I hope Mr Anderson is capable and willing to be his friend & adviser, and pray from my heart that they may be successful & happy. . . . .

Marx Etting[1] has obtained his suit and will date in May a Midshipman- his great joy on the occasion will satisfy his Mother tho' she is loath to part with her darling- in the Autumn he is to go to Annapolis where the naval school is situated, two years is allowed for his education, & then to sea- he will be seventeen by that time, the latest period for admission, there is great advantage in the new arrangement, of preparing them thus for the service- formerly a boy had no chance of studying, and when put into the Navy at an early age- must forego many advantages which they now possess- . . . .

[1] Frank Marx Etting, eldest son of Benjamin and Frances Marx Etting.

TO ANN BOSWELL GRATZ

My winter has been so quietly spent, that I scarcely know what is doing in the world around me- the only evenings I have spent abroad have been at musical entertainments- or family meetings but with Julia for a companion I am never lonely. Horace brings us books- foreign news &c to amuse our evening fireside- and we take daily exercise abroad- our sisters & brothers are well- a pretty regular correspondence gives us the domestic annals of our various nieces abroad, which I assure you are very interesting to Mothers & Aunts. Henry Etting writes long letters from Naples, he expects to be home next summer - I have not seen Mr Bell - Hyman called but he was not within- I sent your shawl & books to be packed with Mr Cochrans goods and put two little volumes in for my children. Maymorn for my dear flower loving Miriam, and Mama's birthday for my pet Anne, she having Mama's name will like that title- I was sorry the bundle was sent before I found some little books that would have suited her better- give a great deal of love to both for me, and a heap of kisses- and so dear old Canewood is to pass out of the family- I have no doubt it was a costly possession for some time- and since the old Beverly family are disposed of would go to ruin, if left uninhabited. I often think of the three happy weeks we once spent there, when the walls were hung with beautiful family pictures, representing the Belles of another generation and the old library held odd vols of a choice collection, which spoke eloquently of other days, when the lovely dames there represented were in the pride of youth. . . . .

Our Sisters & Brothers send affectionate greeting- I believe they all write to you, at least they talk of doing so, in order that they may receive your letters in return, Sally Hays covets the same indulgence- Julia sends her love- Believe Dear Ann in that of your affectionate Sister   R G

TO THE SAME

Bernard Gratz' visit to Philadelphia - children and fine clothes - Henry Clay's domestic misfortunes - Benjamin Gratz becomes a private gentleman - children's pleasures.

Phila June 10th/ 51

My Dear Ann,

It seems like a pleasant dream that our dear Bernard has paid us a visit- so unexpected, and of so short duration, but he told us so much of our western friends and their concerns that I enjoy its effects even now- when he is far away- I received a letter from Mary full of regret that he did not go to Washington, and Mr Riggs, who has just returned from New York says he enquired at several hotels in hopes of overtaking the party- but they had gone- of the party I saw too little to speak- Many superior claims on their time- bad weather and their own preoccupation deprived me of the pleasure, but as Bernard was the one that I care to have, I do not feel inclined to find fault with anything- I am exceedingly gratified My Dear Ann that I was so fortunate as to please you in my purchase and that the Box arrived safely- if your climate resembles ours this summer, you have as yet had little use for thin clothes but I should dearly like to see my little darlings tricked out in their new suits. There is a consciousness in the air of those little folk when they think themselves fine that is very amusing to behold- I have known persons, who considered dress of the utmost importance, and insisted that people felt better & acted better when they were well dressed than in their every day habits- I wonder what effect the new Costume so much spoken of in the newspapers, will have on the female world, who adopt it- . . . . how glad I am to hear of Lucretia Ervin's[1] marriage- I loved her Mother, and rejoice there is a prospect of the poor girls doing credit to her memory. What are public honors to the head of Mr Clay when domestic griefs crowd around his hearthstone- his children & his childrens children filling every private avenue with sorrow- shame & adversity- I know no spectacle more sad than to see such a man- honor'd- beloved, and labouring for the good of all- & above all for his country- with such a desolate home for his affections- but God has given him the comfort of seeing his granddaughter rescued from danger, and I hope her brothers too may become prosperous & happy-

I congratulate you and My dear Ben, on his becoming a private Gentleman, and hope he will use his freedom freely in our favor, and come more frequently to see us- you are right to let my own little Anna learn to dance with her sister- let them learn all pretty & agreeable accomplishments- "where virtue is, these are most virtuous" says Shakespeare, and why should not we put all innocent appliances in our childrens power to enjoy- pleasure is but short lived, and we must not let the proper season pass- you can mix graver studies for use, but there is still time for dancing & mirth. Bless the darling children, embrace them for me, and tell them Aunt Becky would be charmed to see them dance, and gather all kind of pretty & sweet flowers in the garden of youth- . . . . excuse this rambling letter, my dear Ann, and believe me your affectionate

R G

[1]Granddaughter of Henry Clay.

TO THE SAME

Anxiety - Dr. Gratz Moses - the cholera - Miss Cooper's "Rural Hours" - Fenimore Cooper's novels - Lieutenant Lee, commander of the Dolphin.

Philadelphia July 15 1851

Why Ann, Sister Ann what have you all been doing that not a word has reached us from your midst? we have waited in daily hope & expectation of a letter, until impatience has changed into anxiety- our dear Brother is not usually so forgetful nor you so unmindful of your epistolary debts! . . . .

We have had a delightful season thus far- a few warm days- was sure to be succeeded by a pleasant change- and thus midsummer has arrived with abundant good & beautiful vegetation, and general healthfulness for the season, we talk of our last summers enjoyment in your society- and the loveliness of your little girls- fancying their growth & improvement by those of similar age around us- and giving you full credit for the portion of time bestowed on their education- we have heard that Mary Moses returned home much improved in her health but do not get frequent accounts from them- I suppose the Drs[1] time at this season is fully occupied, they seem doomed to have the Cholera brought to them every year, tho' I suppose it has lost its terrors as an epidemic- for what evil do we not get familiarized to when it so often reappears?

I am reading a book which I think will please you (if you have not already read it) Miss Cooper's "Rural hours", it is such a graphic picture of country life with all the sources of interest and admiration open to an intelligent and refined

---

[1] Dr. Gratz Moses, a nephew, practicing medicine in St. Louis.

person, amid scenes of Nature- animate & inanimate. I am told it has been beautifully illustrated- but the copy I have is only illuminated by the pen- I would rather read it than one of her Father's novels- I see by the papers that Mr C is recovering from the illness announced as dangerous- . . . . Lizzie passed thro' with her husband on Friday last, Mr Lee commands the Dolphin on a voyage for which it is preparing in New York, and will probably sail about the 1st of August- please give our dear love to our Brother & all the dear ones around you, and have the goodness my Dear Ann, to write at your earliest leisure to your affectionate Sister

R Gratz

* * *

TO THE SAME

The year of this letter is omitted from the date but on the back of the letter occur the words "answered Oct 9 1851".
Visit to Montreal - comparison with American cities - the fine approach to the Canadian metropolis - the Friars.

Montreal
Sep- 3rd

My Dear Ann

You will be surprised to receive a letter from me, dated from Her Majesty's dominions, I have been here almost a fortnight, having accompanied My dear Sara home, & cannot but regret that you did not come to Canada last year, to see what a different sort of city this is from our U. S. places- you would be struck with the narrow streets imperfect pavements, and low houses in many streets, when you suddenly come upon magnificent Churches- fine gardens, convents- and rich possessions belonging to the priests- hear as much french as english spoken by the inhabitants, and at every turn find you are in a foreign country- tho' but a days journey from Saratoga- The approach to Montreal is beautiful- the City lies on the bosom of the noble River St Lawrence and stretches more than a mile along the shore, where a fine quay fronted by large buildings present themselves, the domed market place and numerous steeples of the churches have a very imposing appearance and the beautiful mountains in their verdant covering bound the whole view, the day we arrived the heavens were dressed in fantastic white clouds which reflected in the water and crowning the mountain tops added greatly to the prospect, and gave a fine first impression- Sara is very pleasantly situated in a retired part of the city, has good neighbours on the street, and a large garden opposite belonging to the Friars, where fruit & vegetables are abundant and the black robed inhabitants, are daily seen from my chamber window- book in hand strolling for hours together- as no woman kind is admitted into their dwelling I cannot vouch for the good order of their household but the garden appears well-cared for-

I have been invited to visit Quebec & Three-rivers by members of this family, but at present am suffering from a cold which has given me pains in my limbs- they tell me here, from imprudence in leaving off a flannel garment on a hot day, which I thought myself *very prudent* to put on, for two or three cold ones which preceeded it. This climate differs very much from ours, even in Summer. I received your letter only a few days before I left home, and was then very uncertain about coming away- Jo was at Saratoga, Jac. left on the morning we did. Hyman had the gout, so that if I had been well myself, I should have remained but they urged my coming so earnestly that I yielded and am so much improved in health that I hope to return somewhat stronger in the course of a fortnight. I beg you will give my best love to my

dear brother, the sweet little girls and their brothers. When
I heard from home, Hyman was well- neither of our other
brothers had returned- Adieu my dear Ann believe me ever
affectionately your

R Gratz

* * *

TO THE SAME

*Purchases for the Lexington Family - the World's Fair at
Crystal Palace, London, England - Kossuth, the Hungarian
patriot, in the United States - illness of Henry Clay - Francis
Preston Blair's anxiety for his son Montgomery ill at St.
Louis - Henry Etting's return from Europe.*

Philad Decr 8th 1851

I am highly grateful My dear Ann at my success in pleasing you by the purchases I made for you, it is very agreeable to select for a friend so easily suited. I thank you for the compliment to my taste, and hope you will not think you pay too dear for it from the following account. Bonnet, box & packing $22.31- cloak & dress (Levys) $55.75, childrens bonnets $12, mantua making $9.50- I should indeed like to see My dear little girls & their Mother too, in their winter bravery. I have never seen such magnificent stuffs of all descriptions as have been imported this season - the worlds fair collected such a variety of beautiful manufactures which have been distributed in our markets among other countries, that one may wonder at the perfection reached in delicate & rich fabricks- but the world's Fair is over- and the great Magyar has filled up the place it occupied in mens minds- Kossuth has been pouring out streams of eloquence to astonish & delight the people of England- but I do not think he has been so happy here- he has a little overstepped the modesty of his position, in the expectations formed of the views of our government towards him, he wants liberty & a home- but not a foreign home- and I think the temper of his New York oratory will, or ought to make him less popular with the American people than he has been- . . . .

Mary wrote last week that she was shocked to see the change in Mr Clay- and the papers since, announce that he has been ill- what a pity that his wife is not with him! in such a comfortless place as a Washington Hotel, the attendance of a tender nurse would be so important to the invalid. Lizzie wrote me that her Father had been to see him- she said he had left home so hastily in consequence of Montgomerys reported illness that he had made no preparation for a longer stay, and was obliged to hurry on, business requiring his presence- the account he brought of all our kinsfolks in St Louis was very agreeable . . . . Henry Etting's business has detained him at New York, which is very tantalizing after so long an absence, particularly as he has not been well- but in a few days more I hope he will be released. . . . . give My best love to My dear Brother, and our lovely little girls- there is no danger but they will learn fast enough dear little Anna will amuse her fancy by agreeable suppositions- while Miriam will seize on more tangible things- they are both wise enough for their years- and happy which is the great end of life- May God assist them to choose what is to make them permanently so- . . . . believe me ever your affectionate.

Sister R Gratz

TO BENJAMIN GRATZ

A Purim gift - appreciation of brother's affection - Kossuth's ill return for American hospitality - the grief of separation.

Philadelphia March 15th 1852

Our Brother Jo this day My Dearest Ben handed me your letter to read, and the munificent present of $100 as a purim[1] gift- I do not know how to express my thankfulness, not *alone* for the money, but the loving consideration which induced you to remember me, at the "season of gifts"- I will endeavor to use it well for your sake- and of part of it, make some poor heart glad, and bless you for it, surely no women have ever been more blest in Brothers than we have- ye have not only carefully labored to produce means out of the tangled & perplexed affairs of our Fathers estate for our benefit- but supported us during a life long period with generous & delicate liberality.

I ponder on these things with heartfelt gratitude, and see in them the working of an over-ruling providence, who hath implanted the desire to do good with the power, and made it more blessed to give- than to receive- yet this day your gracious gift has been most gratefully received- . . . .

You speak My sentiments about Kossuth- he has been completely humbugging the people throughout the country- he can no longer mistake the government, and therefore offends against the hospitality he has received by urging his views. . . . .

Jac has been quite indisposed today with Chills & a severe

[1] See page 17, Note 1.

cold- his spirits have been better, at least he has been less nervous for a few weeks past but he looks badly. I feel much less anxious about him since he has gone out, and sees more persons willingly- give my love to dear Ann, I will write to her very soon, but shall not be able to tell her half as much news as her friend can, as I have neither been out or received company all winter.

Julia & I often talk about her, I am sure they would be good companions- both being intelligent & cultivated ladies, she begs to be remembered to you most kindly and thro' you to Ann. God Bless you My dear Brother, I yearn to see you again it seems hard to be so long separated as the time shortens when we may meet in this world- but May God bless you- ever & forever- prays your affectionate
& devoted Sister
R Gratz

* * *

TO ANN BOSWELL GRATZ

Henry Etting's return from a trip around the world - gifts - Smyrna melons - Kentucky's fertile soil - nature's bounty - trip on the St. Lawrence river - Henry Clay's failing strength - Mrs. Clay's invalidism - Mrs. Rush's ball and receptions - spring fashions - "Episodes of Insect Life".

Phila May 7th 1852

Pardon me My Dear Ann, for so carelessly executing my commission as not to inform you *directly* that your comb was a present from Henry Etting- in order that I may not be guilty of a similar omission please note the inclosed seed of fine Smyrna nutmeg melons to the same source. Henry has brought out various things picked up in his travels, and says these are from the finest fruit of the kind he has ever eaten, he has distributed them among his friends in hopes they may somewhere find a climate that will suit them- and as you have a soil so productive in good things I hope your vines may produce them in perfection- and now let me thank my darling Miriam for her flower seed, which I carefully gathered out of my lap, as they fell from your letter- and only have been waiting for the weather to be suitable for planting them- her early love of flowers is inherited and I rejoice that she possesses such a source of happiness- Nature is always true and they who fix their affections on her productions will never be disappointed tho' sometimes their hopes may be deferred for a season- I have a friend who calls Flowers her good angels- for they have charm to soothe her saddest thoughts

Sara[1] paid us a little visit, she only spent the holidays[2] in Phila- her husband would gladly have left her one month here, and return for her in May, but she considered his convenience and went home through a most stormy season, when the ice king was just breaking up his power over the St Lawrence, and they had to go part of the way in a canoe- & part on sleds which was both dangerous and disagreeable- her little girls are much grown. . . . .

The late accounts of Mr Clay are sadly discouraging- Lizzie Lee writes me that Mary Riggs is constant in her attentions, being twice every day with him- Mr Crittenden & Pendall are also careful of his comforts- alas! what is the greatness of this world to a man in his dying hours- what the voice of Fame, compared to the soft soothing of domestic love? that such a man as Henry Clay should die, among strangers to his blood- is indeed a sad reflection!

I have thought often of his sweet daughter Ann, and the

[1] A niece, Mrs. Henry Joseph of Montreal.
[2] Passover.

devoted love she bore him but they will soon meet in happier scenes- I pity poor Mrs Clay that she could not have been with her husband on this trying occasion- I remember on one occasion hearing her express such a noble confidence in him, that I felt she knew & was proud of his character, one can scarcely estimate the sacrifice of feeling she must have made during this long & trying winter, herself an invalid so far away but who can control their destiny? . . . .

Tell our friends the McAllisters they went away too soon to see Sara, and go to Mrs Rushs Ball- which is unparalleled in the annals of American entertainments- its report has almost made me regret that I did not go- or that my chance of seeing the splendid establishment is so far postponed- Mrs Rs receptions are on Saturday mornings- so until she closes these I shall not even attempt to leave a card, when she is at leisure to receive a sociable visit, I will call- . . . .

Today, a bright warm sun has brought out blossoms on every seasonable thing- and filled our streets with well dressed women- coats & muffs are cast away for more becoming light garments, painted butterflies have not more various colours- speaking of butterflies reminds me of a beautiful book we have been reading "Episodes of Insect Life"- I think it would please you- there is such a fanciful tracing of analogy in the works of nature- between the smallest things that live & move up to the greatest. . . . .

Give my best love to My dear Brother, and my much loved little girls- I should love to have a long talk with them- when they can write down what they would tell me I shall be sure to send an answer- kiss them for me- accept the love of our brothers & Horace- and believe me, My dear Ann, affectionately yr sister

R G

TO CARY GRATZ

Phila Aug. 8th 1852

Thank you, a thousand times I thank you, My Dearest Cary[1] for the pleasure your letter gave me- It was very kind in you to relieve my anxiety about your safety on your journey- in these times of excitement about frightful steam heat accidents and the dangers all travellers are exposed to from the reckless and wicked indifference to human suffering practiced on all our waters by Captains & other officers of steam boats- I hope the penalties, imposed on those who sacrificed so many valuable lives on the Henry Clay will be followed up in every similar case. Two years ago when we were at Saratoga Mrs . . . . came to see us and brought us a book she had edited- the Correspondence of her Mother[2] & Uncle John Q Adams - written in France & England, when their Father was our Minister abroad- the good lady was full of literary zeal & pride for them and some vanity of her own poetical pretensions- but she was a valuable woman, a good mother, and kind neighbour- she was one of the victims- having embarked with a party of six, only three of whom were saved- her son-in-law & a lovely young woman perished with her.

I conclude Hyman did not overtake you on your rapid journey but hope he reached home well- I feel so grateful to both of you, for the affectionate kindness that brought both of you, and evinced itself during your most gratifying visit- Sara too blesses you for the pleasure you gave her- she is now

---

[1] A nephew, the youngest son of Benjamin Gratz.
[2] Mrs. William Stephen Smith, the only daughter of John Adams, and sister of John Quincy Adams. She had married William Stephen Smith who was Washington's aide-de-camp 1781-1783.

with her husband & children at Cape May- she first took them to a Mountain House in the neighborhood of Montreal but the child grew worse & they had to return home- the Dr recommended sea-air and so they are at the Cape, where they met Mary Riggs & her children- so I expect to see them both, when the season is over-

I am charmed with your account of your little sisters, they are rare children indeed- lovely in contrast- the precious intelligence & dignity of Miriam will be a guide to her more vivacious sister- Anna's quick sensibility which glows in her animated countenance, and is so lovely in early development may require as she advances some regulation, which Miriams example will afford her- If these two sweet children will grow up to love each other as I trust they will you will see, My dear Cary, how beautifully they will harmonize, and how happy they will be in each others friendship- the love of sisters & brothers such as I have sometimes seen- and have experienced- is among the best gifts of nature and I thank God for the blessing of a Mother in whom all such affections centred- . . . .

If you will write me occasionally, My dear Cary, and let me know how you & your brothers prosper in what is most interesting to your individual concerns, I will endeavour to find some entertainment for you in return- if you can be amused by scenes which are passing in our busy, fashion seeking community- I sometimes wish Dickens or Punch might pick up matter for a few pages here- I hear your Uncle Jo is enjoying Saratoga- we are all well & dull enough at No 2- . . . . tell my sister Ann I shall write to her very soon- and My dear Cary believe me always your most affectionate & loving Aunt

R Gratz

TO ANN BOSWELL GRATZ

Joseph Gratz and Washington Irving at Saratoga - "The Days of Bruce" - nature and the romance of history - the city's summer desolation - Captain Alfred Mordecai.

As you have had recent information from our boys, My dear Ann, you will excuse me for leaving your letter so long unanswered, particularly when I tell you that our Sister Etting has been ill, and if I had written sooner, it would have been to create anxiety, instead of giving you the comfort to say she has recovered, and was sitting up in her easy chair yesterday, surrounded by so many of her affectionate relatives that I thought it best to steal away with Rose Mordecai and leave the rest to entertain her- strength is now alone wanting to make her well again, which in a few days I hope will return- our brother Jo writes- with animation of his pleasures & improved health at Saratoga- where among his usual friends he found Washington Irving, as bright, kind & agreeable as ever, and very little changed in good looks- I am sure this meeting with his old friend must have been delightful to him- renewing the associations of youthful days to one whose spirit retains its elasticity so unimpaired as our brother must give rare enjoyment and from what I hear Washington is as little changed in feeling as Jo himself- I am glad to tell you that our Brother Jac has greatly improved, he has had no return of indisposition, which makes me feel greater confidence in his recovery- . . . . do you ever read novels? if you do, I have a great mind to recommend "the Days of Bruce"[1]- I have wept over it so plenteously, that

[1] An historical Scottish novel by Grace Aguilar published in 1852.

according to young peoples opinion, it must be good - and it is thus far a criterion - scenes from nature, affect our feelings most, and the romance of history - even when the characters are fictitious - take strong hold of us, as they bring back our recollections of true characters & events - the Bruce is dear to us in history & in song - and is a very fit hero for romance -

You acquitted yourself admirably in the reception scene you describe- Govr Fish reported himself highly gratified by your hospitality, and if he did not demonstrate as much to the elder as the young Anna, it was only the sense of propriety that prevented- sweet little Anna deserves to be a pet because she is generous as well as lovely, and will not envy the superiority of her gifted sister- and the sweetest hope I entertain for them, is that they grow up loving each other, and admiring the qualifications each is most remarkable for- you have the happy privilege of training them- two nicer subjects could not well be committed to your care. I dearly love them both, embrace them for me- give my best love to My dear brother and all my nephews- . . . . our town is much deserted- and very disagreeable- the dwelling houses in our neighbourhood with closed shutters- either for absentees or mourning- and the hammers & trowels constantly sounding on our ears from building not *improvements* . . . . I am just called- Alfred Mordecai came to dine with me- Adieu My Dear Ann, believe me always your

Affectionate Sister
R Gratz

Augt. 13th 1852

TO BENJAMIN GRATZ

Death of oldest sister, Mrs. Reuben Etting.

I should have replied to your, and Ann's affectionate Letters My dearest Ben, ere this- but alas I had nothing to say but a repetition of sad & sorrowful feelings- or the detail of our poor nieces' sufferings- Isabella[1] has been very ill since her poor mothers death- no doubt distress accelerated her disease which at all times for years has been so very severe- I am with them daily and the presence of their most affectionate Aunt Sally Etting is duly appreciated- and gives them much consolation- yet the loss of such a parent is not likely to be borne without much mental suffering- they are doing as well as possible- and try to submit to the Divine Will- aiding each other and deeply sympathizing with each other in their individual bereavement- for more than a year Miriam has devoted herself to home duties and strict attendance on her mother while poor Isabella when free from her afflictive spells of coughing was ever by her side- so they have prepared themselves, with consolation from a sense of having performed their duties- and a consciousness that they were acceptable to the beloved departed- Henry was much benefitted by his journey to the Virginia Springs tho' he was much shaken, on returning home to find his mother in the agonies of death- or rather sinking calmly into the sleep- which terminates our existence here- she recognized him- but could not speak- and expired with her hand clasped in his- poor fellow! his heart is sadly disappointed- the hope of seeing her enjoy the fruit of his labor has ended- but the

[1] Isabella Etting, daughter of Mrs. Reuben Etting.

charge of his sisters will still interest him- and the privilege of having passed some months with her after his long absence- when she had reached a great age- will be a future source of grateful memory- . . . .

God bless you My beloved Brother- May we embrace you in health & comfort- and may you & yours long enjoy happiness together is the fervent prayer of your affectionate sister

R Gratz

Phil Oct 15th 1852

* * *

TO ANN BOSWELL GRATZ

Unanswered correspondence - letters of Lady Montagu and Madame de Sevigne.

Philadelphia Jan 16th 1853

I am quite amazed My dear Ann on receiving your last letter to find how delinquent a correspondent I have been- during the visit of My Dear Brother, I did not write because you heard more agreeably from him everything I could tell you- and when I took up yours of the 22nd Novr I felt reproved that it was found among my unanswered letters- that was the last I received. What could have become of the *Three, you* so undervalue I cannot tell but had they reached me I should certainly have thanked you for them- Lady Montagu nor Mme Sevigne could not interest me as your letters do, for they could not tell me of the things I love to hear- or the persons whose doings and sayings are dear to me-

And with all your humility my good Sister, there are few persons so gifted in the art of making agreeable letters as yourself- What return can I make you for the interesting details of your dear childrens progress in the good gifts God has graced them with? the picture of My beloved brothers happy home is most grateful to me, and I thank you my dear Ann for so training your daughters as to ensure encreasing comforts for his encreasing years- . . . . give our best love to dear Ben & your darling little girls- and believe me ever affectionately yours- pardon my delinquencies which can never grow out of intentional neglect believe me- ever truly your sister- R G

* * *

TO THE SAME

The railroads - Benjamin Gratz in Washington - Baroness d'Oberkirch's Memoirs - Marie Antoinette and the French Revolution.

Novr 23rd 1853

I was going to write to my dear Brother when your kind letter arrived this evening My dear Ann, and am most happy to greet you together- a Telegraph informed us of his safe arrival- and then I gratefully enjoyed the happiness he bestowed by his visit- and returned thanks that he had been guarded through the perils of his journey. It is wonderful indeed in how short a space of time the distance is traversed, and when it is safely made without accident we can fully appreciate the advantages we possess in these times of Railroads and steam- I was glad to hear dear little Anna had quite recovered- for I think the mention of her illness marred the latter days of her Father's sojourn here- his presence had a great influence on our brother Jac, I think he is more careful of himself & he has not had any unfortunate turn since-tho' he looks wan & feeble- Sister's health is better, the cheerful companionship of Laura[1] has its salutary effect on her spirits- . . . .

I am very glad my dear Ben was satisfied with his intercourse with all our Washington friends I have always thought they knew how to appreciate him- Mary at least has never varied in her affectionate estimation of his truly parental interest in her, or in a grateful return of attachment-

I am reading a pleasant memoir of a German Baroness D'Oberkirch[2] who flourished at the french court, in the early part of Marie Antoinettes time- it is full of graphic sketches & anecdotes of the characters of that day- names with which we are familiar- and who are so life like & present- that one might imagine they are still flourishing on the stage of existence tho they are given to us by the authors grandson- It was a corrupt period of history of a corrupt nation- and many unhappy ladies nearest the throne were victims to the licentiousness & inconstancy of their husbands- a prelude to the horrible tragedy which succeeded- . . . .

My best love to My dear Brother & his sons- and believe me My dear Ann affectionately your sister

R GRATZ

---

[1] Laura Mordecai, granddaughter of Mrs. Hays.
[2] "Memoires de la Baronne d'Oberkirch publies par le Comte de Montbrison son petit fils." 2 vols. Paris 1853.

TO THE SAME

New Year reflections - the disaster to the steamship San Francisco.

Phila Jan'y 8th 1854

A Happy New Year to you My Dear Ann, and to my beloved Brother- and the dear little girls- and to all we love. My heart is full of good wishes for you- and of the hopes that cause of your silence is rather the festivities of the season, than any less agreeable interference. I am right happy to tell you we are all comfortable, in our domestic circle, and right grateful to Almighty goodness for granting so many blessings in the evening of our days, every new era of time calls on us to reflect on the past and make due acknowledgements for the mercies granted- . . . .

Tell Hyman we are grieved & shocked at the fate of an old favorite of his, Valeria Merchant- who, with all her family are passengers on the ill fated steamer San Francisco - on her passage to California- as it is feared she perished in the late storms at sea- the steamer was seen in such peril- that scarcely a hope remains of her escape- and 800 troops & passengers the officers wives & families who accompanied them it is feared are lost- our newspapers are filled with disasters by fire & flood- which emphatically show us the terror of all earthly possessions and make us rejoice in trembling while we thank God for our preservation from suffering- . . . .

Write soon My dear Ann and believe me ever sincerely your affectionate

R G

TO THE SAME

Nature's bountiful provision - Pentecost, the feast of flowers - Rebecca Gratz' godson - Anna Cora Mowatt.

Philadelphia May 5th 1854

My Dear Ann

It is a long long time since we have conversed together, and though I know our brothers have kept you informed of our condition and the sweet assurance of remembrance is conveyed to me, yet my fancy is busy picturing you and the dear children in various ways, & I feel the want of more certain information- Maria Abercrombie too has mentioned you in her letters to a mutual friend- but (am I unreasonable) all this is not so satisfactory as if you told me yourself how you & your darlings are employed, and when you are to set out on your western tour; Mr Barry came for his grand daughter Julia Buchanan, and started yesterday on their home journey, Gratz Moses' little children have also come in, and are at Washington with their Uncle Wm Ashe's family- our brother Jo left home this morning for Centre County & Julia departed last Monday- in all this moving scene, with bright skies overhead and the earth covered with beautiful flowers who can but feel the bountiful provision made by God & nature for our happiness- or withhold an offering of gratitude for the blessings of the year.

I received a letter from Miriam saying she contemplates making us a visit in August when she means to proceed to Montreal, and carry her children to make acquaintance with their cousins. The sisters[1] have not met for several years, and

---
[1] Miriam Moses Cohen and Sara Moses Jeseph.

I am glad they will have Gratzs children also to join their family group- . . . .

We today commenced the disagreeable process of painting & housecleaning, so you may imagine me as busy as a bee- tho' I shall do no more work than a drone- I suppose My dear Miriam is enjoying her flower garden, I wish I could send her a very beautiful bouquet brought to me by my godson[1] for the Pentecost- which is the season of Flowers- embrace her & my sweet Anna for their loving aunt- . . . .

I hear of our dear Becky that she is going to her friend Anna Cora Mowatts[2] wedding which is quite an excitement to her, did you read her autobiography? she is quite a character and loves notoriety even in the solemnity of her bridal hour, her taste is decidedly Theatrical, but she has many noble traits of character & strong affections- fare well my dear Ann ever affectionately your sister

R G

[1] Charles J. Cohen whose mother Mrs. Henry Cohen was one of the most intimate friends of Rebecca Gratz. Mr. Cohen, whom the editor met a number of times several years ago, had distinct childhood recollections of Miss Gratz. He showed the editor of this correspondence his copy of the small book "Recollections of Rebecca Gratz by one of her nieces" which was presented by the author, Mrs. Alfred Mordecai, to "the godson" of Miss Gratz, namely, Charles J. Cohen. See also *An Old Philadelphia Cemetery, the Resting Place of Rebecca Gratz*, by Mary M. Cohen, page 77 (Philadelphia, 1920). Miss Mary M. Cohen, well known as a student of Browning, and Miss Katherine Cohen, the sculptor, were sisters of Mr. Charles J. Cohen.

[2] A well-known actress and authoress (1819–1870); she was the daughter of Samuel Gouverneur, a New York merchant. She married first James Mowatt of New York, an attorney, and secondly, William F. Ritchie of Richmond, the marriage here referred to.

TO THE SAME

Home education - alternation of play and study hours - Joseph Shelby - the cholera - Sara Mordecai - Chestnut St. fire - newspaper account of disasters.

Philadelphia July 6th 1854

Do not suppose, My dear Ann, that I would acquiesce in the decision your generosity & modesty set forth- your letters have a two fold interest in them, first they bring me intelligence of those I dearly love- and secondly they are so well expressed & intellectual that as a matter of taste they would be valuable- your last gave me a lovely picture of domestic life- your plan of home education is wise and I trust your children will look back on their early days with the poets view of happy childhood- free from those drawbacks schooldays so often register- the delight of garden play hours is only an exchange of useful lessons- they grow familiar with nature, animate & inanimate and cannot fail to see a God employed in all the various productions that meet their eyes and as their minds mature will learn to adore their Creator with grateful love, through all the blessings scattered so lavishly upon them. I was glad to hear Jo Shelby paid you a visit, which took off the edge of your disappointment, in being obliged to postpone your western tour- The Autumn is a pleasurable season for travel and I hope the Summer will pass away without any great anxiety about Cholera, there seems to be a wide spreading report of its existence in various directions but less panic than its visitation formerly created- I am sorry Maria Abercrombie does not find Lexington agree with her, she promised herself so much pleasure from her visit- she is a person likely to become a slave to habits and I suppose misses the routine which makes up the business of her life- living at a boarding house with no strong interests, a restless seeking abroad among her friends for something to occupy her mind gratifies her self love- with the idea that she is doing good to others- Mrs Dr Page is a friend to whom she has devoted herself since the death of her excellent Parents who were Marias best friends- she told me, she did not know how she would bear a long separation from her- & indeed the deep affliction of Mrs Page interests all who know her- give my love to Maria & Mrs Vertner. I am endebted to both for their good opinion-

How fine you will be when all your beautiful improvements are completed. I can sympathize in the turmoil of its process- we were nearly four weeks out of order- with painting- whitewashing papering &c, which in our small house fully inhabited, was no trifling job, but now we are to rights again and look clean- Sara Mordecai[1] & three of her children are here, she was sick of chills at the Arsenal, & they are now trying to get country accommodations in the summer- rather a difficult matter so late in the season, as she does not want to go to expensive watering places - her Mother is quite well. sends her love to you & thanks for the promised letter, . . . last night there was a most extensive fire in Chestnut St, as the newspapers will tell you, for all kind of disasters teem in their pages- embrace your darling girls for me and give my tenderest love to my dearest Ben, I can only admire your judicious plan with your children & rejoice in your good fortune in obtaining good instructors & companions for them- Adieu believe me ever dear Ann your affectionate sister

R G

[1] A niece, wife of Major Alfred Mordecai.

TO THE SAME

Words of consolation - Isabella Etting's death - Major Alfred Mordecai at Constantinople.

January 8th 1856

My Dear Ann

We have this day received intelligence of your Dear Ella's death, and most sincerely do I sympathize in your distress- so recently have I been called on to witness the close of a dear sufferer's life- that my heart would suggest to you consolations derived from the very love you bore her living- in the thought that *she* is at rest no longer subject to pain & change- you had the happiness of seeing her so recently- exchanging the tender offices of sisterly affections- doing all that was permitted you, to alleviate her condition- and receiving treasures of tender recollections, to soften the grief of separation- The many Blessings that surround you, My Dear Ann, will speak to your grateful heart- & you will not murmur that it has pleased God, to remove one who has long been prepared by bodily infirmities to leave a suffering world.

You would pity our poor desolate niece Miriam Etting in her bereavement- for she has no one to supply the place of the sister she has lost- the great object of her life was to visit Isabella's sick room- she has gone back to her lodgings- & I trust will learn to bear her trial patiently- she has heard from Henry, who is well, and expects to be on the station at Cuba where his letters will reach him- sister Hays is well, much comforted by the presence of Sara Mordecai's society-the Major was still at Constantinople on the 5th of Decr[1]- our brothers are all well- the Music books for dear Anna were sent last week by Mr Andre in a package direct to Paris with an understanding that they were to be forwarded to Lexington immediately - . . . .

Give my best love to my Dear Ben, and to the darling little Girls - we have not heard recently from St Louis. I suppose Mary is at school and too busy to write, the Dr is a bad correspondent even to his Father- Horace talks of going on his journey next week- but if this extremely cold weather continues will find the North too severe- our streets are filled with deep snow banks- and sleighing the business of the season-

Farewell my dear Ann May God bless you, and give you comfort is the sincere wish of your affectionate sister

R G

* * *

TO BENJAMIN GRATZ

Appreciation of a brother's generosity - the greater equanimity of women than men - marriage of Sarah Butler, daughter of Fanny Kemble.

Phila March 25th 1856

My Dear Ben

Our sister joins me in grateful acknowledgment for your generous present which our brother Jo communicated to us from your letter received yesterday. I have no words to express to you My dear brother, the feeling your ever generous consideration imparts- happy for us, we have never known a

[1]Major Mordecai, chief of ordnance of the United States Navy, had been sent to the seat of the Crimean War to study the naval situation in that war.

want which our brothers have not been prompt to supply- indeed I do not believe the possession of fortune could compensate for such manifestations of your love- our brother Jo is suffering with a cold- he has not enjoyed this very severe winter, he could not take his usual exercise- nor the generous wine so agreeable to his taste- but I hope spring will come at last and bring its usual blessings- the old women of the family bear these changes of weather with more fortitude, perhaps because they have no right to complain of any infirmities that are incident to years- and are of more equable temperament. Hyman has been well, since the slight attack of gout and has recovered his good looks- he never complains of anything- but is affected by the want of hearing, which deprives him of joining in conversation- Jac's lameness continues to give him trouble- they all send love in which Horace & Julia unite- . . . . Tell Dear Ann I have thought a great deal of her- and of the new trial- tho' one that brought comfort with it- the arrival of her sister's remains to her last resting place- the scriptural expression of being "gathered to their Fathers", seems such a natural desire, we feel a holy wish to have it fulfiled for those we love.

I have just had a visit from my young friends the Butlers- Sarah came to tell me of her engagement to Mr Sandford of N. Y.- he has written for the consent of her mother- Mr Butler has sanctioned their wishes- and I hope Mother & daughter may again enjoy the happiness of being together- give my best love to Ann and the dear children- did Hyman go to the South? remember me affectionately to him & Bernard and believe me, ever my dearest Ben, with devoted affection your attached sister

R G

TO ANN BOSWELL GRATZ

The coming of spring - Death an angel not the "king of terrors" - life a preparation - letters from Paris.

        Phila April 2nd 1856

Your reproaches were just, My Dear Ann, and yet I never meant to neglect you- I do not know how it happened, but I became in debt to all my correspondents, and I have chosen you as to be first paid this morning- this sweet mild day gives us the promise of Spring- and altho a month has been recorded in the Calendar- Nature only now begins to give us a taste of her balmy season- I know you have been sorely tried, in your late domestic loss! let the dear ones blooming around you exercise their happy influence on you, and resign contentedly, that which it has pleased God mercifully to have taken away- we have good reason My dear Ann, to be grateful for some bereavements however they may afflict our hearts. Who should desire the life of a long suffering friend, when only pain has long been their portion- pain, which has prepared them to meet death, as an Angel. The Scriptures tell us of "the angel of Death". We call him "the King of Terrors"- he is only so to the wicked in their own case- and to us when he appears wrestling with those we love- In the last year, we have suffered much, and many times from these visitations- we must view them as blessings- warning us how to live- that we may be ready to die also- We have just had a sad visit from Josephine Etting[1]

[1] Daughter of Solomon and Richea Gratz Etting of Baltimore; her mother was a cousin of Rebecca Gratz, being the daughter of Barnard Gratz; a brother Samuel had married Ellen Hays, a niece of Rebecca Gratz. This is the Ellen mentioned here; she died November 23, 1855.

she staid a fortnight, & her Father came to take her home- They are the saddest mourners I have ever met with- their minds & hearts undisciplined to bear grief as it should be borne, in fact our dear Ellen had been the great support of their lives- and until they lost her, they were not sensible how entirely they depended on her- poor Josephine, at five & twenty is a child in self government, and now has a hard lesson to learn but she has very good sense and I trust her future life will be governed by it-

Horace had a very agreeable letter from Lizzie Lee a few days ago, giving good accounts of Silver Spring & its inmates, she says her Father is deep in Politicks- she promises me a visit in due season. Mary Riggs has entirely recovered, and is amusing herself with gay hospitalities- she writes me that her husband did not expect to be three months abroad- that they had been putting their place on Georgetown heights in order, so that she might remove her children there as soon as the season requires a change which will be a more comfortable arrangement than journeying with them to the Springs .... I have been perusing some very amusing letters of the Murat family & the french court, from Miss Fraser- .... give my best love to My most dear brother, Ben- and to your darling children- believe me Dear Ann very affectionately your Sister R G

Solomon Etting was the first Jew to hold public office in the city of Baltimore. He was a member of the City Council in 1825 and later served as President of that body.

TO BENJAMIN GRATZ

Ogden Hoffman's death - Major Mordecai's arrival from Europe - Hyman Gratz and the Academy of Fine Arts - Annual exhibition - Mr. Leeser's loss by fire.

Philadelphia May 1st 1856

My Dear Ben

I sent by the express to day a box to your address containing a Jar of *Potted Shad-* which I hope will not be shaken into an entire mess - the cold waters this spring have been very unfavorable to river fish - the Shad is particularly late and small- I was afraid to wait until they got larger, lest it might be too warm to send them- at any rate you will see that we remembered your taste when the season arrived, that might gratify it- Indeed My dear Brother, there is no season that does not bring you to our thoughts by some pleasant & affectionate memorial, no time that you are not in our hearts and cherished in fondest love.

We have just received telegraphic intelligence of the sudden death of Ogden Hoffman, Julia leaves in the morning- he died to day- we suppose his illness must have been very short, as there was but a few hours between the first intimation of it- and the announcement of his death- unfortunately George is absent, but this accompanies Julia in the morning-

Major Mordecai arrived in the Peoria on Tuesday, he looks very well and seems to have enjoyed his whole tour greatly - tomorrow he proceeds to Washington, where the officers meet, after greeting their families- Laura will go with her Father and proceed to Richmond with him- his family continue here, until his return, to make arrangements for their future residence, Tell My dear Ann I received her letter yesterday, for which I truly thank her- a rainy day prevented my attending to her commissions, but shall try to execute them without delay-

Our brother Jo, desires me to tell you he will write to you very soon, *as soon* as he feels right again- he is almost well, but is still dependent on Sunshine & warm weather for his comfort- he has resumed his visits every evening to the Club house, which is a strong evidence of returning health. Hyman is busy all the day- the Academy of Fine Arts[1] is in the first week of the Annual Exhibition, and I assure you he looks very venerable among the directors. Jo is better, he has been able to walk out again since the weather has been pleasant- our city was last night again the scene of a most destructive fire- wherein much property was lost- it was among stores- in a well built part of Market Street- and extended most fearfully- in the previous fire poor Mr Leeser lost several thousand dollars in books. . . . .

God Bless you, My dear Brother, believe me always with devoted affection

Your attached
Sister RG.

* * *

TO THE SAME

Jacob and Hyman Gratz die within a month of one another - Rebecca consoles her brother Benjamin.

Our Brother Jo requested me to write to you My Dearest Ben, what can I say to comfort you? Alas we are deeply

---

[1] Hyman Gratz was one of the founders of the Philadelphia Academy of Fine Arts; he served successively as Director, Treasurer and President of this institution.

afflicted, God has smitten us with a great sorrow- two of our Beloved Brothers are taken away by *His* will, and we can only bow submissively under the stroke of His Almighty power- We dare not rebel for we have been much blessed in having been possessed of such good and beloved relations- everybody sympathizes in our grief & testify to the worth of the departed. May He strengthen us to bear his visitation and not sin. Our dear brothers[1] have escaped from pain & suffering & infirmities in this life, and gone to rest from their labors- "May *he* in whose hands are the souls of the living and the dead" comfort you My dear Ben-

Jo & Sister & Horace are well and we all send tenderest love to you & yours- do not be anxious about us, for we bear up for each others sake, and are doing as well as you could expect or desire

God bless you prays your affectionate sister

R GRATZ

Sunday Feby 1st 1857

* * *

TO ANN BOSWELL GRATZ

Visit to Joseph Shelby - benefits of travel for young people - Saratoga.

Phila July 6th 1857

I congratulate you My dear Ann on having accomplished your wish of visiting your son in his own home and having returned to your own, so happily and comfortably with the Dear girls- they have no doubt picked up much in store for after enjoyment- the great & wonderful & beautiful in nature- the incidents of travel- the variety of people- manners & customs of the places they have visited all so new and

[1] Jacob Gratz died December 24, 1856, and Hyman Gratz, January 27, 1857.

full of interest- It is a privilege to travel with young people- they renew our early impressions, and give us back the pleasure long past but never to be forgotten- . . . . Our summer thus far has been very cool, and wet, on the 3rd & 4th we had fire in the dining room- our brother Jo is very susceptible to sudden changes, and not being as strong as he used to be, requires an equal temperature- . . . . I do not know what my destination may be, it seems settled by the family that *I must* accompany Jo to Saratoga- which is very repugnant to my feelings- the only suggestion that throws interest into the scheme, was from My dear Ben that he would meet us there, and as he *almost* promised, when he came again you & the girls would accompany him, I have dwelt on the idea with affectionate gratitude for his considerate goodness. My leaving home of course depends on our Sister's health. This year she is alas! the *only* consideration- My kind friend Julia Hoffman is still with me, and will continue as long as the weather permits. A summer in town is very trying to her, and she wishes to spend some time with her brothers family- to go with me would be a sacrifice, as she dislikes Saratoga- . . . . .

Give My dear love to My brother, and your children, and to my nephews, ... Adieu My Dear Ann, believe me
affectionately Yours RG

* * *

TO THE SAME

The financial panic of 1857 - the soul of good in things evil - affection for brothers and sisters - the Jewish Foster Home.

Phila Decr 3rd 1857

You must not suppose My Dear Ann, that I have been indifferent about the contents of your last letter- because it has remained unanswered- nothing that gives trouble to My own dear Brothers can possibly be so to me- but I am so ignorant of business matters, so perplexed by the fluctuations of money concerns- that I knew not what to say about them. I hope Dear Ben's sleep is now undisturbed and his mind easy about his sons- the *panic seems* to have passed away, and though many rich men in our community have been shorn of their wealth, and hundreds of poor men & women thrown out of employ- we cannot but hope the better times will come "with healing on its wings" to point out remedies to all that suffer- to the young it will give experience- to the old consolation- do not suppose My dear Ann "I reason for others, & only feel for ourselves"- living as I have always done, on the affection & protection of loving brothers & Sisters I have no individual joys or sorrows. When all are well & cheerful with them I am happy & grateful- when they are taken away or afflicted, My heart bleeds, but I "know that My Redeemer liveth" and strive to submit to *his* decrees.

What a sad letter I am writing and here is my brother Jo, sitting beside me, reading the newspaper and Sister Hays, thank God, quite well in her own comfortable parlor, perhaps at this moment listening to her little maid, reading the scriptures- Rosa Mordecai has been home for a month, and is not expected to return till after the New Year, & Julia Hoffman is in Baltimore for a fortnight so we two old women are thrown on our own resources- My Sister's want of sight makes her very dependent, but she has an intelligent cheerful girl, who is attentive and acceptable to her with whose services Sister is content- we spend a part of every day together- The hard times have put our ladies on the alert to support our "Foster Home" they are now preparing "a Fair" to take place on the 15th ins. I feel doubtful of its success but give my mite in furnishing- which many busy hands are employed for- . . . .

Give My dear love to My brother, and the rest of his family- in which Sister unites, and also in affectionate good wishes, for health and happiness to you My dear Ann

R Gratz

* * *

TO BENJAMIN GRATZ

Death of sister Richea Gratz Hays - a beautiful character - the Gratz family burial reservation in the Spruce St. cemetery.

Sunday Decr 12 1858

Horace has written to you so frequently My Dear Brother that I hope you have not suffered any uneasiness at my long silence. You are always so indulgent to me- in what I do & in what I leave undone- that I have fearlessly avoided writing until I could acquire fortitude to speak of our recent affliction with composure. Dear Sister! the close of her life beautifully illustrated the purity of its course- it was so peaceful! Death had no terrors for her- It was an Angel received her parting breath, and left its impress on her countenance- until we lost sight of it forever!

I have heard from Sara Mordecai since her return home- we are all thankful that our Sisters wish to be buried next to her husband was gratified- upon examination of the ground it was found that a space had been left according to her desire- and also other vacancies in our family reservation are there.[1]

Farewell My Dear, Dear Brother May God bless you and make your life happy is ever the prayer of your affectionate

R Gratz

[1] Mary M. Cohen, *An Old Philadelphia Cemetery*, etc., page 81.

TO THE SAME

Year of letter omitted from date but supplied by recipient in note on back, viz., 19 April 1859
The Passover - the changes wrought by the passing years - memories.

Phila April 17*th*

I cannot express to you My Dearest Ben, My thankfulness for your last letter, and the hope you have given me of seeing you before the 26*th* - I have forborne to write lest my great desire to have you come- might be urged too strongly- but as you say to Horace that if possible you will be here, I am content to abide by your convenience- sorry that you should have other cause for anxiety, I would by no means have you make a sacrifice of your interest or comfort. My health is very good for one of my age, and I am blest with affectionate companions- Horace and Julia are very very kind, Sara Joseph means to pay me a visit. I have written to her not to come until after the sale when My mind will be in a freer state to receive her- and the solemnities of the Passover ended- the festival formerly so joyful- is changed by the memories that crowd on me of the departed, and I am selfish enough to prefer passing them in quietness- . . . .

God Bless you my dear Brother believe me devotedly your affectionate

R Gratz

TO ANN BOSWELL GRATZ

Year of this letter omitted from date, but the recipient wrote 1859 on the back of the letter.

I cannot tell you my Dear Ann what inexpressible joy and consolation I derived from our Beloved Ben's visit short as it was, and unexpected, it gave a new turn to my feelings- which began to warn me how uncertain our meeting in this world was becoming-

Horace tried to repress my hopes of seeing him this summer, when his sons misfortunes were known, as their business might trouble him, and his indisposition detain him at home- under these depressing considerations I was endeavoring to school my wishes- when *he* appeared- God bless him for all his kindness to me now & always- I thank you tenderly My dear Ann for your letter announcing his safe arrival at home- it was a pleasure to see him even for so short a time- as he designed to be at St Louis today- I hope when he returns, he may be at rest to enjoy the domestic happiness you and the dear girls provide for him- I am glad you think he improved during the trip, it generally benefits a convalescent to change the air, and Ben is such a good traveller, that the Railroad does not fatigue him. We expect Julia Hoffman this evening- unless the rain prevents- I was very sorry she was not here to see my brother, he seemed so to bewail my loneliness, but it does not grieve me. I am perhaps more solitary when surrounded by living people who interrupt the quietness of my home habits- Dear Ann, you will say this is wrong and I hope a more healthful state of feeling will be accorded to me if I live- for I accustom myself to talk of those who are gone and on whom my thoughts will dwell- give my dear love to your girls and believe me My dear Ann your very thankful and affectionate Sister

R Gratz

Monday June 20th

* * *

TO BENJAMIN GRATZ

Business reverses- Gratz and Horace Moses - differences in brothers - early marriages.

Philadelphia July 17th 1859

I thank you My Dearest Ben for your affectionate & interesting letter- I rejoice that your health is restored, and that your visit to St Louis afforded you so much satisfaction, in the first place that Dear Cary sustains his reverse of condition in so manly and correct a manner- we may apply to Business what correctly applies to every other condition of human affairs "It is not in man to command success- he may do more, he may deserve it"- and with the consolation of unimpeached integrity, I trust your sons, My beloved Brother, will rise out of their present troubles- wiser and better able to combat with the trials and affairs of life- That you met with estranged connections, who sought for reconciliation, was gratifying to your benevolence- it is thus we wish to live with all our fellow creatures- I thought Henry Hart was always a favorite in your family- indeed I do not know any of the Gists through all its branches who are or who were not endebted to your kindness.

Bessie Moses[1] returned home about ten days ago- Howard stopped with us one day on his return home and offered to take her to St Louis, but she was then waiting for a party

[1] Daughter of Dr. Gratz Moses and grand niece of Rebecca Gratz.

her Father had written to her about. I am glad the Dr gives such a good account of his condition- but suspect he is rather short in ready money if one may judge by his letters to Horace, or the state of Bessies purse. The brothers differ in one respect - Horace never runs in debt and would rather wait for a thing until he could pay for it than take it in anticipation- hence his admonitory letter to Gratz- but tho' thus differing in opinion & practice they are very loving brothers- I trust the Drs children will continue to give him happiness- they love him very much, Bessie I believe (tho' she did not tell me) is engaged to the brother of Mr Carr who married Mrs Moses daughter- he is a youth of about 22 she 18- the western girls, hardly leave school- before they are candidates for matrimony, and if a boy has a fortune they are likely to succeed- I should be sorry to have my pet Mary do so, for I think she has talents if properly cultivated to make her a fine woman and I am sure she has qualities to make her a good one- but alas! want of right training spoils many fair specimens of God's work- Gratz Cohen[1] arrived on Tuesday last- and tomorrow his parents go to the White Sulphur Springs Va- I had no doubt Frank Etting[2] would glory in Kentucky- he came home last night- I have not yet seen him-

We have had some very hot weather but only at intervals- then refreshing rain cooled it off and prepared us to bear a repetition- but this is favorable summer weather and our household are blest with health- . . . . Take my precious brother my hearts devoted love, to you & yours with kisses to the dear girls- ever your affectionate R G

[1] Son of Solomon and Miriam Moses Cohen.
[2] Son of Benjamin and Harriet Marx Etting.

TO ANN BOSWELL GRATZ

The artist Rothermel - Frank Blair's political prospects - John Brown's raid at Harper's Ferry.

Philadelphia Decr 12 1859

My Dear Ann

We have breakfasted two days on your excellent Butter and sent a part of it to Sally Hays- it was preferred to our Phila make- in our household it was likened to the Irish butter so highly prized for exportation- and verily you have provided so liberally that it might serve for a winters supply- I send you our sincere thanks not only for what you sent but for what you intended to send and most of all for the affectionate remembrance of our recent intercourse, while we live I hope it will always be thus with my beloved brothers family. I am glad to hear of your dear children's progress in all useful knowledge, and graceful accomplishments- the interest their parents take in their studies quickens their desire to learn, and God has been bountiful to them in many good gifts which they must cultivate for their own happiness and *His* glory- I am sorry our friends the Vertners have so little happiness in their old age from the beautiful Rosa they so loved & cherished- there has been too much attention paid to external charms, too little direction to the right cultivation of her mental powers- her talents and beauty, should have made her a lovely and estimable woman, a crown to her husband- to whom her children should rise and call her blessed! instead of which alas! she seems to be hastening to become a victim to vanity and misdirected talents- I am very glad My dear Ben is pleased with the picture- Rothermel[1] has risen to great fame as an artist, one of his pictures "The Giants Staircase" sold last week at auction for $980. The day we received Ben's letter we went to Miss Williamsons who promised to send your dress by the next dispatch, I hope you have received it . . . . I have had letters from all our nieces - they & their families are well - Miriam & Sara both send loving messages to their Uncle & you- *he* has always been their *beau ideal* & Miriam was thrown into ecstasies by the arrival of his photograph. . . . . I have heard nothing from the Blairs this winter- Lizzies promised letter has not yet arrived- Henry Etting said she looks very well- I suppose Frank will be very busy in the political arena- that miserable Harpers Ferry affair will be made use of to keep up excitement. I hope when the executions are over, peace will be restored- farewell my dear Ann- love to all your house from all of ours- ever your loving and obliged sister

R G

* * *

TO BENJAMIN GRATZ

Cary Gratz - Laura Mordecai - Washington Irving's death.

Phila Decr 21st 1859

The year is drawing near its close, My Dearest Ben- and I know your engagements usually multiply at this season- My thoughts live very much with you, at all seasons, and when I can picture you at home with a serene brow in the midst of your darlings I feel grateful and happy- a rumour reached me a few days ago that Cary was engaged- if it be true, I hope it gives you pleasure for I know you deeply

[1] Peter F. Rothermel, a well known American painter.

consider what is for your childrens good and have no selfish views or prejudices to oppose to their wishes- and this dear boy has been so loving and beloved, that to see him happy would be a crowning joy to your age- Laura Mordecai has been with us for a few days. she is a very charming woman, well educated, intelligent & amiable her manners so correct & cheerful that she stands apart from the general desire for Belleism of our city girls . . . .

I suppose you brush up your own scholarship in behalf of her (Miriam's) Latin exercises, but, my dear brother, nature has bestowed an early ripening to her intellect and with you & her Mother's home training she will not require a school to keep her from being a woman too soon- a happy girlhood is the lovelist period of life- and its memory cherished with fondness in after years.

Our friend Washington Irving has descended to the Tomb full of honors & glory! alas how few of his early friends are left to give a heart offering to the general mourning- his nieces & nephews were around him and his only surviving brother- much his senior . . . .

Give my dear love, accompanied by that of Julia, Laura, Horace & Josephine to our dear Ann & the girls. Sweet Annas bright smile dances before me now and believe me my precious beloved brother ever your affectionate

R Gratz

TO THE SAME

The Democratic convention at Baltimore - business recovery - real estate "improvements" - sale of home.

Philadelphia June 24th 1860

I hope My Dearest Ben my silence has not given you any anxiety about us, we have been quite well- and perhaps my greedy wish that you would join our larger family circle than we could expect might again be collected here, influenced me to put off from day to day writing to you- tho' you were ever in my thoughts and while the nieces were here often the subject of our loving discourse- Miriam & Mr Cohen came to spend a day with us last week- the latter attended the Democratic convention at Baltimore, and stole away to give me the pleasure of a little visit- Dear Miriam looks in full health, and is the picture of contentment- no one can be happier in the domestic sense or more grateful to the Almighty giver of all good than she is- and truly Mr Cohen repays her tenderness and our great regard-

You may be assured my beloved brother, of my entire sympathy in all your cares & anxieties about the condition of your sons- Cary is young and will soon recover energy enough to begin anew business and the experience of his present difficulties will teach him caution in his future efforts. Howard & Hyman have such strong inducements for exertion, that they cannot fail to exercise their talents industriously for the support of their families- . . . .

We are at present a good deal annoyed by the noise of our neighbors improvements. He is converting the house next door into a store, which will place a wall close to our steps-

and as all the houses west of us in the row are empty and liable to the like change, we have put a bill of sale on our door- as we should certainly be driven out if Mr Cochran shall either sell or build on the other side- . . . .

My heart is joyful when I think of your darling girls and trust they are preparing to make the evening of your life bright and happy and repay their dear mother for all the care and devotion she is bestowing on their young days- present me fondly to them all and to your dear sons. I hope good Bernard is prospering to his hearts content- . . . .

In the assurance My beloved Ben that you will come when you can conveniently I rest satisfied for I would not have you here at a sacrifice to your home engagements- always loving you & trusting in your love, absent as well as when together I remain fondly & devotedly your affectionate sister

R Gratz

* * *

TO ANN BOSWELL GRATZ

Agitated public opinion in 1860 - Kentucky and the Union- letter of the Secretary of the Treasury, Howell Cobb, to Georgia.

Phila Decr 13th 1860

My Dear Ann

Our dear Ben's letter to Horace yesterday relieved me from great anxiety both on account of the health of your family- and on Cary's absence on such an occasion, but as he writes in good spirits about these most interesting subjects I feel too grateful to complain of the postponement of My dear Brother's visit- indeed in the present agitated state of the public mind- I suppose every good citizen feels it his duty to be at the post where his influence is strongest. I hope

Kentucky is free from secession principles or dangers- and that our beloved Union may survive the dangers that threaten- our household enjoy health, our visitors made the autumn pass agreeably- Julia was abroad about 7 or 8 weeks during which time Laura Mordecai Josephine Etting & Lizzie Lee were here but not all at the same time- Julia returned before Lizzie left- I have rarely seen a more lovely child than Blair Lee- he is larger than children generally are at five years old & he is not yet 2- and has great beauty & smartness- Howard[1] saw them here but his visits were so short- and their politics so antagonistic that I do not think he delighted in her society but I did in his account of his amiable wife and children- . . . . There is to be a mass meeting to-day in which the Bishop takes a part, as well as the Mayor- our city is decidedly Unionist- I should think Ex Secretary Cobb[2] has over shot his mark in the letter to Georgia- what wise or honorable man can be influenced by one who has held office up to this time in a government he so denounced at the moment he can inflame the passions of men for its destruction . . . .

Give to my beloved Brother a heart full of tender love- and to your dear girls a Benjamin's portion- I long to get a letter from you speaking fully of them, and your domestic history- there is too much of sameness in mine to afford much on record- my only visits are to the family- or the Institutions I have adopted as part of my avocations

God bless you all- let us pray that He may help us & our country out of all danger- & believe me Dear Ann

Affectionately yours R G

[1] Howard Gratz was a southern sympathizer.
[2] Howell Cobb of Georgia had been the secretary of the treasury in Buchanan's cabinet from March 1857 - December 1860. He was a leader in the secession movement, acting as president of the convention of the seceded states which drafted a constitution for the Confederacy.

TO BENJAMIN GRATZ

Secession - conciliation proposed by Senator Crittenden of Kentucky.

Phila Janr'y 21st 1861

I am greatly concerned My Dear Brother that you have suffered any anxiety on my account, my indisposition was not at any time alarming, and I am now well again, and took quite a long walk this morning. Glad as I should be to see you, I do not wish to have you leave home, in the present state of affairs when every man should be at the place, where his influence for the good may be needed. I pray fervently that Kentucky will be firm in the Union- the seceders are bringing ruin on their own heads as well as the deepest distress on the whole country- would that the spirit of conciliation proposed by Mr Crittenden could obtain a triumph, I believe most of the southern states would gladly reconsider their hasty movements, and leave S Carolina to her evil counsels. . . . .

The weather here is quite mild again, we had only a few days of severe cold then came rain & snow the last two days clear and mild- as I can now take exercise abroad shall soon be as strong as a person of my age can expect to be, and I assure you My Dear Brother I surely feel most gratified for the blessing of health so bountifully bestowed on me through a long life-

May God Bless you My Beloved Ben, give love to Ann & the girls for me-

ever your devoted Sister
R G

TO THE SAME

March 21st 1861

I thank you My beloved Brother for the dear letter informing of your safe arrival at home- how welcome you must have been to poor Ann, who had to bear her sad trial alone- and yet I was glad you did not arrive while your house was the house of mourning- it would have been such a shock.

Death has had many missions of late among those we loved or were familiar with, but "Gods will be done" in giving and in taking away- offer my tender sympathy to Ann- she has great consolation in having ministered to the departed through many infirmities- I have not been abroad since you left but my cold is fast disappearing and if the weather were settled think I might very safely take out door exercise. Julia is also free from rhumatism and down stairs greatly to Horace's comfort- whose bachelor's life was very lonely after you left- Henry Etting is still absent so we know nothing of the doings at Washington, in which our friends are interested- . . . .

May God Bless you My Dear Ben, most fervently prays your affectionate sister

R Gratz

* * *

TO THE SAME

Death of Julia Hoffman.

I thank you My beloved Brother for your kind and sympathizing letter received this day. It was indeed a severe and unexpected bereavement that took my much loved friend and companion from me- In all her illness Julia never considered her life in danger nor did the Dr or ourselves fear such a fatal result of her painful disease- but it was God's will, to take her from "the evil to come" and she resigned her spirit with the most tranquil submission into His hands- but oh My dear Brother the loss of her society is to me, a trial only to be borne by the conviction that her whole life was a preparation for a happy futurity, and her death the death of the righteous- her love and care of me could only be appreciated by those who witnessed it, and was continued to the last hour, but I will not pain you by dwelling on my grief. I thank you my Dear Ben for the sympathy you express- and the true character you have drawn of *our* friend- . . . .

My dear Brother, at my advanced age it is not to be expected that I should possess as much vigor as in times gone by. But I am quite as strong as when you last saw me and still hope that I may have the happiness of embracing you again, when the war & rumors of war will leave you free to meet us again- God bless you my precious Brother, and grant health and happiness to you all

Your affectionate
R Gratz

May 8th 1861

* * *

TO THE SAME

Henry Etting goes to sea- the able men of the family in the Philadelphia "home guard" - Cary Gratz in the western army.

It was a great happiness to hear from you My Dear Brother- at a time when we know how troubled you are about the state of our country- and the uncertainties that perplex and agitate your community- it is bad enough here- where every days account is of war & outrages incident to war- but the minds of the people are made up, and their energies seem all directed to one point- while you have to struggle and keep watch over the disaffected- May God watch over the Union- and help those who labor for its pre- servation- Lizzie Lee & her boy left us this morning she left her husband at Brooklyn on the point of sailing a week ago, but he has been detained longer than he expected and she went home to day, taking Miss Jesup with her, her sister Mrs James Blair has her family at Bethlehem for the season, or until Washington is more quiet & safe- Henry Etting goes to sea also, in the Colorado, fitting at Boston- all the other able men of the family are drilling in the "home guard" and Cary away in the western army keeps our interest alive in all quarters- . . . . I thank you my dear Ben for wishing to pay us a visit- but indeed I would not have you undergo the perils & anxiety of a journey or have you absent from your family on any account. Thank God, my health is good and my strength rapidly improving- I walked a few squares yesterday without fatigue- and when the weather is fair hope to resume my habit of daily exercise- Major Mordecai's family are at present at Dr Hays'- not yet determined whether to take lodgings in the country for the summer, or a small house in town & get settled at once- it is a hard con- dition they are reduced to, but they all bear it wonderfully well, considering the change from the luxurious home, at Wahcoleet- . . . .

Give my love to dear Ann & the girls- . . . . I am grate- ful that we are not cut off from the comfort of hearing from you- our relations here are as usual & always desire to be remembered to you

God Bless you My Dear brother, ever with devoted affection

                                your own R Gratz

June 7th 1861

* * *

TO ANN BOSWELL GRATZ

The South against the North - members of the same family in fratricidal conflict - Missouri's position in the Civil War - Jo Shelby.

It is very long My Dear Ann, since we have written to each other, and I do not think it fair that the non intercourse law should exist between us- I do not like to torment my Dear Brother with frequent letters which may trouble him to answer, and yet do so long to hear from or about him in these long separations while so many painful scenes are passing between us, that I am sure you will indulge me with one of your pleasant kind letters every now & then even if you find you get only a stupid reply- . . . .

We are very desirous of hearing about our dear Cary- Frank Blair did not come to make his report and as Mrs Biddle is in the country I do not expect to see Appo before she goes to Washington- I have written to Lizzie to make enquiries of Frank for me-

Today I had the rare treat of a letter from Miriam Cohen[1] through a private opportunity to N. Y. which was forwarded to me- her family are well, and in her own sweet way she uttered kind thoughts that made my heart glad- 'tis sad times when the natural flow of familiar intercourse is to be either stolen or only accidentally enjoyed- she tells me there

---

[1] A niece who lived in Georgia.

is not a young man *at home* in all their large connection- of course they have all gone to fight against us! What have we to expect from Congress? . . . .

This is the hottest day of our season- thermometer 86- none of our family talk of leaving the city this year for pleasure- I hope none will be called on for service in the field- what is the position of Jo Shelby[1] in this terrible struggle? Missouri seems to be most turbulent- we feel much worried about Gratz Moses- the young Dr[2] is still with Sara in Canada-

Fare well My dear Ann, give my dearest love to my brother and accept a most affectionate portion from your attached

R Gratz

July 8th 1861

* * *

TO THE SAME

Year omitted from date of this letter but it is fixed by the death of the youngest son of Benjamin Gratz, Cary, who was killed in the battle of Wilson's Creek, Missouri, August 10, 1861.
  The hope of reunion in another world - the horrors of civil war.

Aug. 23rd

Thanks, what grateful thanks My dear Sister, do I owe you, for your most kind letters, over which I have wept again, and again- and prayed for my beloved Brother- whose grief I share, but cannot measure even by that which fills my heart- all human sympathy are but drops of comfort, in his

[1] Son of Mrs. Benjamin Gratz by a former marriage. He enlisted in the Confederate army and rose to distinction as General J. O. Shelby.
[2] A son of Dr. Gratz Moses of St. Louis, nephew of Rebecca Gratz.

great sorrow, but God in *his* mercy will open a fountain of consolation to his mourning spirit- the beloved son, whom "He gave; and hath taken away" will rise in an angels form, to whisper peace- memorials of all his virtues & loveliness- his pure and innocent life, and brave qualities, the noble heart as tender, and full of filial love- all perfected and immortal- will in future be to him- his very son- his beloved Cary.

You Dear Ann, and the treasures that are surrounding him, will win him from the indulgence of feelings which have so overwhelm'd him- and I trust restore his peace- experience has taught me, that it is thus God deals with us, we live on, cherishing those that are taken from us, as tho they were only removed from sight- with the hope of reunion in another world. . . . .

I hope My Sister, you can excuse my impatient pleadings- I had sent my letters before yours arrived- forgetting that though further away, we got information nearly as soon as you did.

Your second letter, which I have also received, gives me great comfort, as it tells me Ben is more composed- I trust the efforts of his friends will be successful in obtaining the dear remains- Frank Blair is now on the spot to aid them- I pray most fervently that Kentucky will not be involved in this dreadful strife- we live here in constant agitation- every days account of wrongs & outrages perpetrated by kindred on each other- of familiar friends becoming bitter foes, is too appalling to be realized, in our late happy country - even members of the same family warring with each other. Lizzie Lee & her son are at Bethlehem- all the females of the family excepting your Aunt Blair, are driven from their home- she will not leave her husband- tho' both are surrounded by troops and are uncertain of an hours safety-

Give dear love for me to My Brother, and all the children. I am glad Bernard is with you- his presence must be a comfort to his father- remember me most kindly to Judge Brown- and believe me always My dear Ann your grateful and affectionate

Sister RG

* * *

TO THE SAME

Remains of Cary Gratz - civil war - Kentucky and the Union - the hope of future reunion with the dead - the Day of Atonement.

Phila Sept 12th 1861

I have long thought of you My Dear Ann, and sympathized in the anxiety, which I knew must silently be preying on your peace of mind- on account of your Son Jo Shelby whose name I have seen mentioned in the Southern Army, so fatal to our Beloved Cary- I heard previously to your letter, of the hopes entertained that we should probably recover his dear remains- and trust his good brother Bernard may have the consolation of bringing to his bereaved Father the privilege of depositing them in holy ground.

Dear dear Ann, what changes have taken place in our once happy country. One can hardly realize they are *at home* - in the U. S. of America- and are at war with each other- I have been reading some loving letters from some so near to me in blood & affections whose arms are perhaps now raised against the hearts at which they have fed- and the bosoms of those, who have cherished them- this I cannot but lament as among the horrors of war. The recent news from Kentucky is very cheering. God grant you may be successful- and retain your allegiance to the Union- such men as Holt & Anderson & Crittenden must encourage your patriots to fight in the good cause. I hope the Governer will be true to his promise-

Just received your letter of the 9*th* thanks Dearest Sister, for your consideration of me, in the agitation of such a moment- I pray with you, that our beloved Ben, may be comforted, and like David, resigned to the dispensation of the Almighty- hoping, tho his beloved son, can no more come to him- they shall be reunited in another world- How I wish by sharing I could lessen My poor brother's grief!-

I sympathize with you, too My dear Ann, in the anxiety which is so harassing by the uncertain accounts the papers bring of the contending Armies- we may pray for Jos personal safety- tho' we cannot for the success of his arms- Faith in Him, who in justice & in Mercy rules over the destiny of all, must give us patience! Tomorrow will be a holy day with us- Sabbath & day of Atonement, when memorials of the dead mingle with petitions for the living- and we endeavour to purify ourselves by devotion, confession & repentance - you will all be remembered by me, in the house of prayer-

My health has greatly improved within a few weeks. I feel stronger than during the hot weather, and live very quietly. Miriam Etting dined with me yesterday, and asked me to give love & sympathy to her Uncle & you- my tender greetings to all around you- and grateful affection to yourself My dear Ann

R GRATZ

13*th* Sept

TO THE SAME

Joy at Kentucky's loyalty to the Union- the Richmond hospitals - the Fremont - Blair controversy- "no faith in politicans" - difficulties of epistolary communication between North and South.

Philadelphia Oct 30th 1861

It is a long time dearest Ann, since I have written to you- yet I have a very interesting letter to answer- and a day seldom passes without my thinking of you and my beloved brother- so many sad & stirring things happen in this unhappy state of our history that ones Mind is continually harassed & perplexed to know what is to happen next. I am joyful about Kentucky, and hope her loyal sons will so far outnumber the rebels that they will be afraid to shew their faces, on the soil that was honor'd by their patriotic Sires.
. . . . Phila is much over cast about the recent disasters- in which many of our prominent citizens are involved- our friend Mrs Fisher sadly grieved about her grandson Capt Mackoe who is a prisoner & wounded (slightly they say) but from accounts of the Richmond hospitals, they are destitute of every comfort- we thought as you do, about Mr Blairs mistake in the Fremont affair but he justifies himself on the plea, that it was a public affair- the great mortification they suffer, is having assisted to place them in power to do so much mischief- it seems to me that our friends are deficient in knowledge of human character- like other sanguine people they act from feeling- and misjudge those they love, who they think are as guileless as themselves- they have now made enemies of the Fremonts and the struggle will be between the General, and Frank,- if the former succeeds in his

present command what will the government do? as I have no faith in politicians I am hopeless of seeing the right done unless Divine providence in pity to this noble country should put it in the heart of our rulers to take counsel by His holy law, and remember that we are one people and are shedding Brothers blood in this unholy war-

I had a letter from Miriam last week, the first since August- she says "My thoughts have been with you all continually & my tender sympathy (though unexpressed to him) is with My Dearly beloved & stricken Uncle, when you write to him do tell him all you know I feel for him, for no one so well as you know how fondly I cling to this darling Uncle"- poor Miriam! separated from all she loves except her own household, must have suffered greatly for want of information from home- her letter came open, under cover to the commanding officer at Norfolk 10 cts being inclosed, and postage p'd to Fortress Monroe whence by flag of truce - I tell you this, as it may facilitate your intercourse with your Jo, if he is in a southern camp - give my best love to My own Dear Brother and your dear girls- . . . . In happier times I hope we shall all meet again- tell My beloved brother how my heart yearns to embrace him

May God bless you all prays your affectionate

Sister
R Gratz

* * *

TO BENJAMIN GRATZ

This letter has on the back in the handwriting of the recipient the words "Becky Gratz May 1862".

Thank you my beloved Brother for the assurance that you were safely in the vicinity of your home, where I hope you found all the Dear ones well- and made happy by your return- I think over the precious hours we spent together, and pray we may meet again under happier times when peace & good will will reign throughout the land- give my best love to Dear Ann, and our sweet girls & also to my nephews- Becky and her little girl brought Gratz to us on Friday- they are all well- the Etting invalids are better- poor Edward seems to be fading away.

Horace sends you his love. God Bless you My darling Brother ever yours R GRATZ
Sunday morning May 17

* * *

TO THE SAME

Sick soldiers returning from the war - "this unholy strife".

Sunday June 6th 1862

Your letters My beloved Brother, are the day spring of My life and make me feel young again- through the warmth of the affection they express- . . . . we are very much here, as you left us, and our city is so quiet, that if we did not know what a dreadful struggle is going on- and witness the squalid appearance of sick soldiers returned from the war- and read the more appalling accounts of the battle fields and hospitals we might enjoy the beautiful season, flourishing around us- the Flowers seem to spring up every where- the bounties of Nature, seem to reproach the wickedness of man in this unholy strife- and Women too! more monstrous still, who step out of the sphere God designed them to fill in such times of trouble- I imitate you My dear Brother and never discuss the vexed question with our opponents in politics-
. . . .

We talk of you daily & nightly- we had a very interesting visit from our friend Fanny Kemble- who sails soon for England- God bless you dearest Ben.

Ever your devoted RG

* * *

TO THE SAME

Dismissal of McClellan - the destitute condition of soldiers in the Union army - Theodore Etting in naval academy - Charles Etting in Union army.

Phila Novr 14th 1862

Your letter my beloved brother was most gratefully received, Ann and the Dear Girls have been very kind in writing frequently to allay my anxiety during the fearful period of your tribulation- yours too came safely. Mrs Mayo came to see me a few days ago- and says Col Gracie was much pleased with his intercourse with you (notwithstanding your difference in politics) I am surprised Major M[1] has not answerd your letter- no mention was made on the subject, Horace seeing it advertized told him about it- & subsequently heard it had been removed, the Major's associates here are among the disaffected, (the Ingersols- Moncure Robinson, Wm B Reed &c) so I fear what ever sentiments he might have entertained in the beginning- they are now so far implicated on the wrong side that he will find it difficult to recede- poor Sara is victimized being the only loyal member of the household the subject therefore nearest all our hearts is never discussed in their household- . . . . unfor-

---

[1] Major Alfred Mordecai, after a most distinguished career resigned from the United States Navy in the early years of the Civil War.

tunately there are too many sympathizers in the wrong cause, in all our cities. . . . .

I am glad to hear Dear Bernard is at home. God grant there may be no need for military efforts- he is a brave soldier- but I am a very coward for those I love- you have done wisely in not increasing your home family- young children would interfere greatly with your comfort & habits- nor would Ann find it contribute to her happiness- I love my little visitors but the cares & anxiety attendant on their rearing are only suited to young folks. I know My dear Ben that you cannot leave home, nor dare I wish it - duty well performed is the only source of happiness which the world cannot take from us. My health is good- if I live to see better times, the joy of embracing you, will be greater from knowing that you can come without a sacrifice, in the mean time we will write to each other lovingly-

There is no appearance of light breaking upon the affairs of our country- the dismission of Genl McClennel[1] has greatly shaken my hopes, and seems to have appalled those who looked upon him with due confidence in his worth & patriotism- Lizzie writes me that her Father strove with all might, to avert the evil- in vain,- she also says every word about the destitution of the noble army is true- their Genl would not move until they were clad- they marched by here, barefooted & ragged- so that her Mother even on Sunday all day gave needles and thread to mend their rags- where can the fault be, that such things can exist, when such quantities of clothing & shoes are furnished? we hear the enemies soldiers are well clad- and our brave fellows are suffering- "There seems something is rotten in the state of Denmark." who can find it out?- I am glad your dear girls are so usefully employed, and trust your home will be cheerful & happy by

[1] McClellan.

their efforts & improvement- Edward Etting is rather better, his son Theodore, will soon leave for Newport, for the Naval Academy- they hear frequently from Charles, who writes very manly letters having chosen the Army as his profession, does not complain of the hardships of a soldiers life- Horace sends his best love to you, accept mine My beloved brother- & May God for ever bless you, R Gratz

* * *

TO ANN BOSWELL GRATZ

Phila Jany 27th 1863

My Dear Ann

I hope you have not suffered uneasiness from my unusual silence tho' I acknowledge it mortifies me to think I have been neglectful of your last kind letter- I believe I have been more busy- more lazy and a little annoyed by a cold which in this damp warm weather I have found it hard to get rid of- Horace has kept me prisoner at home, and so I have been looking over domestic omissions which having recently changed our man servant, have been staring me in the face- Well, we have changed for the better, got an industrious, colored man in place of an idle white one. My cold is better, and I only wait a change in the weather to be well again-

I hope My dear Brother returned from Frankfort in good health and accomplished his mission to his satisfaction, without too great a tax on his patience, and that Kentucky is quiet- The changes and chances and mischances that reach us from the Political world do not seem to advance our progress through this terrible war. I hear so rarely from Washington that I fear Lizzie has nothing pleasant or hopeful to communicate, and that she devotes herself to private friendship, in taking care of Sara's husband,[1] who is still at Silver Spring- I believe I wrote to you that his physician thinking a few months' absence from home would expedite his recovery- Sara went home from here, that he might be satisfied the children were well cared for in his absence.

Tell the dear loyal girls, their soldier cousin Charles, is recovering but not deemed well enough by his Drs to return to duty at the expiration of his furlough, this has been extended, and we hope both health & spirits will be recruited before he goes back. The family are all doing well- Theodore keeps a good standing at Newport, and their mother exerts wonderful energy in her new cares & responsibilities. . . . . At last I have received a very interesting letter from Mary Riggs full of love for all her friends here- and of Patriotism to her beloved country- she says Bozzie beg'd her to bring him home, that he might see Uncle Ben & Aunts Lizzie & Becky- Mary is proud of Kentucky her native state and seems to feel her separation more than ever. I think it not impossible her husband will be obliged to return on business- it must be difficult for Americans to live abroad unless they have funds invested there- Mr Riggs was just recovering from gout when she wrote- . . . .

God Bless you all according to his Holy will prays your affectionate

R G

[1] Henry Joseph of Montreal.

TO THE SAME

England's sympathy with the South - rebels in the north - Purim celebration.

Phila March 11th 1863

My Dear Ann

Your last letter was so full of interesting matter, and so graphic in describing the condition of Kentucky and its requirements that I could not resist sending it on a mission- where it might be useful to the country, so I enclosed it to Lizzie and requested her to show it to her Father, who might make good use of it- on returning it to me she says, "I read what you said to Father, and he read carefully Cousin Anns letter, which he will duly report to the President in person- I return the letter as you desired & her name will not be used"- Lizzie mentioned our Dear Ben's letter to her father- you are working together in this holy cause, which may God prosper! and bring back to us peace throughout our beloved country- the part which most interests me at present is where you dwell because the immediate aid has been wanting and so much might be secured by a few good officers- I feel as if our turn would come, from the fleets preparing in Europe, in our unprotected harbors- England with her minister at our court, is in feeling acts & words doing all she can to aid our rebels- and is watching an occasion to do openly what it is easy to see she desires- The Lord Mayors feast received Mason with honors- the illustrated News gives portraits of confederate Generals & Statesmen- & Punch is full of satires on the U. S. and strictures on their great men- white & black

But my Dear Ann it is a happiness to hear that you are all

well would I could relieve my beloved brother from some of
his anxieties & annoyance- . . . . tell Dear Ben, our Purim
evening was celebrated this year on the 4th- his loving
thoughts and good wishes were more precious than all else on
the occasion. I pray it may please God to permit us to meet
again in this world and the memory of the past be sanctified
to us by blessings still in store to crown his life in his own
happy household. Adieu My dear Ann, give my love to all
around you, and believe me affectionately your

R G

* * *

TO BENJAMIN GRATZ

Family dissensions resulting from the war - Canadian sympathy with the Southern cause - Kentucky loyalists - Philadelphia in war time.

April 15th 1863

I thank you My beloved brother for your most kind letter,
which relieved me from much anxiety- I never for a moment
doubted the good faith of your household- but was under the
impression that Mrs S. had come to reside with you and
feared you might experience difficulties & incur responsibilities which would interfere with the harmony so essential
to domestic comfort- I trust dear Ann will pardon me if I
give her a moments concern- my heart goes with her in the
peculiar interest she has in this connection where her private
feelings are so much in conflict with the condition we most
approve and desire to accomplish- My love for Miriam & her
children makes me realize all she suffers for those so near to
her- we heard that Miriam was in Virginia on account of the
illness of her son, whom they had taken home to Savannah-

but what their present condition may be is yet to be determined- one of Gratz's sons is in Canada with Sara, sent there to keep him out of the way of mischief, but he seems tainted with the politicks of his father- Sara & her husband are truly loyal, tho' it seems the community in which they live is full of southern sympathisers and no doubt ready to adopt any English measures- I am rejoiced that Kentucky is ably supported and I hope will be safe through all coming time- I marvel at the apathy of our community- with the knowledge of Fleets of iron clad steamers preparing abroad which might enter our rivers and lay our cities in ashes no movement of defense is made. Phila is as full of idle people, the streets & shops crowded & except in the exorbitant prices asked for commodities & freely given the presence of war is unheeded- except indeed in the active works of charity for the sick & wounded brought to our hospitals. My Dear brother, I am too old to do any good, but feel deep interest in all this & pray for better times . . . .

Give My love to your sons and their families- and believe me, ever dearest & beloved Ben your affectionate Sister

R Gratz

* * *

TO THE SAME

The hydra-headed rebellion - Morgan's capture - troubles in Kentucky - New Year's Day and the Day of Atonement.

Friday morn Sept 21st 1863

I have so entirely recovered from my indisposition, that I was sorry My Beloved Brother you had been made anxious about it- Dear Ann & Miriam told me about your journey and its results. I was glad Ann and Jo Shelby's wife were saved the painful necessity for a longer journey- these are times when every days events are eagerly enquired for, and we are grateful when sad events or threatened dangers are not recorded.

I have felt a great deal for you My Dear brother, who for so many months, have been anxiously watching, and striving to avert the dangers around- this dreadful rebellion seems hidra headed- I hoped when the traitor Morgan was defeated Kentucky would have rest and the law abiding community restored to order, and security- but it seems you are still surrounded by evil spirits, requiring the strong arm of authority- I am grieved that you were obliged to make sacrifices so near home, but if you get relieved from the pressure of care, it is by no means to be lamented. No property, no wealth can be enjoyed, while a deep seated obligation is left to prey on the mind- thank God you have domestic love & happiness around you, which I trust you may long revel in, and have health to enjoy- It will make us very happy My dear Ben to embrace you, and any of your beloved family who will accompany you- . . . .

Our wanderers are returning from their summer tour- The Holidays (New Year) on Monday week will find them all at home- this day is the anniversary of our Parents death- which never passes, without bringing fond & sad memories to me. May God accept My deep felt penitence, for all the sins of commission & omission of duties, of which My conscience accuses me. towards these best of parents- we have had letters from Miriam as late as 1st Aug. written in good spirits- Gratz was with her, she sends love messages to you & all her relations & friends - her children all at home - but not a word of fear or indeed of any thing but personal condition & feelings - Alfred[1] writes constantly to apprise his Mother

[1] Alfred Mordecai later General Alfred Mordecai in the Union army. He was a son of Major Alfred and Sara Hays Mordecai, the latter a niece of Rebecca Gratz.

of his health - expresses himself like a soldier - sans fear or reproach- poor Sara! she glories in his position, not withstanding a Mother's fears for his safety- Charles Etting is at present on duty here. where he will probably be detained for some weeks- Theodore at sea . . . .

God bless you. my own dear Brother, be cheerful & happy prays your devoted sister

R Gratz

* * *

TO THE SAME

Phila May 13 1866

This moment My beloved Ben, I have heard of your affliction- and my heart claims the privilege of sharing your affliction- of mourning with you the loss of your precious son- long separation from those we love is among the severest trials of this life- particularly when sorrows oppress those we dearly love. Oh My brother my heart mourns for you- even as if I were with you, to miss the daily intercourse of your son[1]- his warm affectionate heart was ever so full of love that he was endeared to all who came under its influence, and my memory of all the overflowing kindness of his life will keep his memory ever green in our hearts- alas, I feel so isolated from you and your beloved family- that I feel as if worlds already separate us yet my heart clings to you all with unwonted tenderness

My beloved Brother and Sister, accept my tenderest love and sympathy- give my devoted love & sympathy to all your dear children and believe me ever most affectionately your own Sister & friend

R Gratz

[1] Hyman Cecil Gratz, died May 3, 1866.

Editor's Note: No letters remain to be added. This epistolary output, extending over well-nigh sixty years, presents a vivid picture of the lovely personality who stands forth as one of the glories of American Jewish womanhood.

INDEX

A Winter in the West, 197
Abercrombie, Maria, 394, 396
Abraham, 281
Academy of Fine Arts, 315, 317, 403, 404
Adam, 168, 169
Adams, John Quincy, 76, 77n, 97[1], 385[2]
Aesop, 99, 100
Africa, 310, 313
Aguilar, Grace, 350, 351, 387[1]; death of, 351[1], 352
Albany, 3, 242, 253
Altoona, Pennsylvania, 1[1]
America, 58, 160, 186, 282, 331
American:—s, 82[1], 434; —cities, 377; —Jewess, 59[1]; —hospitality, 381; —people, 380
American Jewish Annals, 2[5]
American Jewish Historical Society, (AJHS), proceedings of, 73[4], 74[2], 75[1], 98[1], 152[1], 282[1]
Amir Khan and Other Poems, 293[1]
An Essay on Professional Education, 279
An Old Philadelphia Cemetery, the Resting Place of Rebecca Gratz, 395[1], 408
Anderson, Minerva, 339, 339[1]
Antoinette, Marie, 391, 392
Asche, Mary P., 249[1]
Ashe, Sarah, 278, 284
Ashe, Wm., 394
Astoria, 227, 228
Atkinson, General Henry, 183

Backswoodsman, The, 226
Baltimore, 10, 23, 43, 44, 96, 97, 107, 109, 110, *et passim*
B. and M. Gratz Papers, 19[1], 165[1]
Barbados, W. I., 75
Barmitzwah, 75[3]
Barron, Commodore James, 27[1]
Barrys, the, 134, 138, 167
Barton, Thomas P., 222
Bayard, Harriet, 53
Bayard, Mrs., 50.
Becky, 178, 196, 226, 285, 295, 315, 316 (*see also* Moses, Rebecca)
Becky, Aunt, 78, 85, 121, 375, 434 (*see also* Gratz, Rebecca)
Bedford, 10, 48
Bell, Aunt, 2, 21, 98, 162, 173 (*see also* Cohen, Mrs. Solomon M. [nee Simon])
Bellefonte, 240, 282, 298
Berkshires, the, 1[2]
Bethlehem, 422, 425
Bethune, Dr., 310
Bible, 274, 276, 281[1]
Biddle, John, 18
Biddle, Logan and J., 20
Binney, Horace, 215
Black Hawk, 166, 167, 183, 184
Bladensburg, Maryland, 27[1]
Blair, Elizabeth, 184, 186, 214, 342 (*see also* Lizzie)
Blair, family, 321, 371
Blair, Francis Preston, 43, 43[1], 44, 45, 163, 164, 255[1], 322, 322[1], 379

INDEX

Blair, Frank (Francis Preston, Jr.), 302[2], 332, 361, 413, 414, 423, 325, 428
Blair, James, 322
Blair, Montgomery, 43[1], 120[3], 150, 176, 178, 180, 182, 184, 299, 322, 361[1], 379, 380
Blair, Mr., 46, 48, 49, 56, 163, 193, 209, 224, 285 (*see* Blair, Francis Preston)
Blair, Mr. and Mrs., 221
Blair, Mrs. Francis Preston, 45, 46, 132, 164, 184[1], 214[1], 224[1]
Blair, Mrs. James, 422
Blair, Mrs. Montgomery, 298, 336
Bledsoe, Mrs. Jesse, 45[1], 188, 223
Bloomfield, camp, 2, 7, 8
B'nai Jeshurun, congregation, 366
Bodley, Mrs., 101
Bodley, Sara, 297
Bohlen, a German young man, 109, 110, 111
Bonaparte, Charlotte, 57
Bonaparte, Joseph, 57[1]
Bonaparte, Napoleon, 267[2]
Bonapartes, the, 57
Book of Jashar, the, 280, 281
Bordentown, New Jersey, 57[1], 238, 240, 256, *et passim*
Boston, 2, 2[5], 3, 9, 92, 133, 141, 148[1], 158, 215, 328[1], 422
Bostonians, 356
Boswell, Ann, 97
Boswell, Mary, 266, 267, 269, 271, 272, 278, 284, 288, 294, 297, 303, 343, 344, 361, 362, 363, 364, 365, 374 (*see also* Mary)
Boswell, Mrs., 113, 223, 232
Brackenborough, 330

Bristol, 204
British Court, scandal of, 40
British Museum, catalogue of, 314[1]
Brooklyn, 321, 325, 422
Brown, Gratz, 300, 338
Brown, James, 105, 107[1]
Brown, John, 413
Brown, Judge Mason, 326[2], 426
—and Mrs. Brown, 300[1]
Browning, poet, 395[1]
Bruce, Becky, 313, 340
Buchanan, cabinet of, 418[1]
Buchanan, Julia, 394
Buffalo, 250
Bulwer, Lady, 264, 265
Bulwer, 144, 146, 214, 224, 226[1], 244; Sir E. L., 356
Burlington, 178, 291
Bush, Dr., 303
Butler, Mrs., 312, 351, 352, 354, 356 (*see also* Kemble, Fanny)
Butler, Pierce, 132, 204, 205[1]
Butler, Sarah, 204, 399
Butlers, the, 205, 400
Byers, Vincent, 19[1]
Byron, Lord, 72, 130, 146, 147, 186[1]

Cabala, The, 274, 276
Cain, 361
Caldwell, Dr., 30, 33, 166, 235, 237, 261
Caldwell, Mrs., 34, 41
California, 354, 357, 393.
Canada, 126[4], 149, 242, 342, 343, 347, 364, 377, 424, 437
Canadian; —s, 348; —Metropolis, 377; —sympathy, 436

INDEX

Canewood, 13, 24, 25, 30, 179, 181, 184, 188, 214, 240, 243, 343, 371, 373
Canton, China, 207
Cape May, 343, 386
Carlyle, Thomas, 238, 244
Carolina, 141, 148, 152, 166, 288
Chaldean, 276
Champlaine, 178
Chapman, Dr. Nathaniel, 18, 93, 155, 159
Charles, the First, 314[1]
Charleston, 148, 152, 163, 208, 210
Charlotte, Queen, 40
Chevaley or the Manor Honour, 265[1]
Chicago, 328[1]
Child, Mrs., 140, 141
Christendom, 62
Cincinnati, 76[2], 98, 316[1]
Civil War, 327[1], 423, 426, 431
Clarksburg, 255
Clay, Cassius M., 316[1], 324, 326, 359, 360
Clay, Henry, 58, 59, 76, 93[2], 96, 97, 124, 125, 126[1], 129, 151, 152[1], 160, 163, 164, 183, 184, 258, 266, 268, 286, 300, 301, 304, 308, 310, 311, 313, 336, 347, 349, 352, 353, 362, 369, 370, 373, 375, 379, 380, 382, 383, 385
Clay, Mr. and Mrs. Henry, 223[1]
Clay, Mrs. Henry, 45[1], 123[2], 186, 187, 222, 360, 382, 384
Clay, Mrs. Thomas Hart, 126[3], 342[1]
Cobb, Howell, 417, 418
Cohen, Becky, 212
Cohen, Charles J., 395[1]
Cohen, Gratz, 412

Cohen, Mary M., 395[1], 408[1]
Cohen, Miriam, 227, 228, 230, 231, 304, 341, 363, 364, 394[1], 423
Cohen, Katherine, 395[1]
Cohen, Mrs. Henry, 395[1]
Cohen, Mrs. Solomon, (nee Simon), 2[2]
Cohen, Sally, 305
Cohen, Solomon, 227
Cohen, Solomon and Miriam Moses, 412[1]
Cohens, family, 108, 227
Coit, Reverend Dr. Thomas M., 214, 215, 235, 237
Colorado, 422
Combe, George, 260, 261
Combs, Col. Leslie, 133, 134
Confederacy, The, 327[1], 418[1]
Confederate, army, 424[1]
Connecticut, 148, 152, 178
Constantinople, 217, 282[1], 399
Continental Congress, 84[1]
Cooper, James Fenimore, 108, 241, 242[1], 376
Cooper, Miss, 375, 376
Cooper, Thomas Apthorp, 81, 82[1]
Cooperstown, 241, 242
Corcoran and Riggs, 362[1]
Corcoran Art Gallery, 362[1]
Corree, Abbe, 28
Correspondence between Solomon Etting and Henry Clay, 152[1]
Cowper, 131, 193, 216, 263
Cox, Mrs. John, 64
Cox, Wm., family of, 272
Coxe, Professor, 218
Craig, James, 137, 138
Craighan, Col., 196
Crawford, William Harris, 76[2]

INDEX

Crimean War, 399[1]
Crittenden, Senator, 339, 419, 427
Cuba, 284, 286, 287, 398
Cumberland, 307

Dale, Com., 80
Dallas, Alexander James, father of Capt. Dallas, 115[1]
Dallas, Capt. Alexander James, 115
Damascus, Blood accusation, 280, 282[1]; —brethren, 285; —case, 284; Massacres of, 282
David, the King, 150, 275, 427; harp of, 189
Davidson, Lucretia Maria, 292, 293
Davidson, Margaret Miller, 292, 293
Day of Atonement, The, 6, 73, 180, 181, 208, 211, 426, 427
Deaf and Dumb Institute, 32, 43, 44, 49
Dean, Jennie, 253
Decatur, Captain Stephen, 27
Decatur, Mrs., 27
Declaration of Independence, 84[1], 93[1]
Devon, 153
Dewees, Oscar, 218, 250
Dewey, Reverend Mr., 232
Dickens, 386
D'Oberkirch, Baroness, Memoirs of, 391, 392
Dolphin, The, 376, 377
Domestic Life of Thomas Jefferson, 285[1]
Domestic Manners of the Americans, 212[1]

Dorsey, Dr. Philip Swing, 14[3], 15
D'Orval, Mde., 101, 103, 188
Duchesnel, Dr., 282
Dudley, Dr. B. W., 93, 104, 259, 303

Eaton, Mrs., 132
Edgeworth, Maria, 277, 279
Elizabeth, Queen, 184; court of, 46
Elkin, Abraham, 86, 87
Ellen, (*see also* Hays, Ellen), 21, 23, 26, 50, 62, 78, *et passim*
England, 50, 204, 222, 225, 285, 366[1], 379[1], 385, 431, 435
English, actor, 82[1]; —ballads, 337; —captain, 3, 4; —reviewers, 11; —translation of the book of Jashar, 281[1]; —travellers, 186
Episode of Insect Life, 382, 384
Erwin, Ann, 133
Erwin, Lucretia, 375
Esther, Book of, 17[1], 381[1]
Etting, 305, 323, 325, 334, 387
Etting, Benjamin (Ben), 94, 116; —and Frances Marx, 372; —and Harriet Marx, 412
Etting, Charles, 431, 433, 434, 439
Etting, Edward, son of Reuben Etting, 35, 130, 225, 433
Etting, Elijah Gratz, 359, 360
Etting, Frances, 94[1]
Etting, Frank, 371, 372, 412
Etting, Gratz, 5[2], 12, 111, 129
Etting, Harriet, 94[1], 240[1]
Etting, Henry, 115, 158, 164, 222, 321, 323, 325, *et passim*
Etting, Horatio, 94[1]
Etting, Isabella, 108, 149, 389, 398

INDEX

Etting, Josephine, 401, 402, 415, 418
Etting, Miriam, 115[2], 266, 308, 389, 398, 427; —and Henry, 234 (*see* Miriam)
Etting, Mr., 271, 277, 308
Etting, Mrs. Reuben, 133, 135[1], 359, 361, 389
Etting, Mrs. Samuel, 334, 334[2]
Etting, Reuben, 85, 347; —and Frances Gratz, 360[1]
Etting, Reyne, aunt, 198
Etting, Sally, 389
Etting, Samuel, 96, 135
Etting, Solomon, 152[1], 402; —and Richea Gratz, 115[2], 401[1]
Etting, Theodore, 431, 433, 434, 439
Eugene Aram, 144, 146, 147
Eve, 42, 154, 168, 169
Exodus, Book of, 261

Fairfax, family, 201
Fauntleroy, Betsy, 201[2]
Federal Constitution, 93[1]
Fenno, Edward, 12, 38
Fenno, Maria, 233[1]
Fillmore, cabinet of, 185[1]
Fisher, Becky, 310, 313
Florida, ceded to United States by Spain, 41[1]
Forsaken, The, 142
Forsythe, John, Secretary of State, 282[1]
Fortunes of Nigel, 54, 56
Fourth Continental Dragoons, colonel of, 2[3]
France, 50, 55, 105, 107[1], 221, 222, 224, 225, 238, 253, 267[2], 350, 351, 385

Francis, Willing, 14
Frankfort, 107[1], 336, 433
Fraser, Miss (Harriet), 234, 240[2], 277, 278, 402
Fraser, Georgiana, 267[2], 267[3]
Fremont, controversy of, 428
Furness, H. H., 132[2]
Furness, Mr. (Reverend William H.), 131, 132, 161, 192, 211, 213, 232, 240, 247, 250, 251, 256, 257
Furness, Mrs., 141, 145, 146, 212

Gaskell, Mrs., 101
Genesis, Book of, 256, 257
George III, history of, 41
George IV, 40
George Washington the Image, and the Man, 201[2]
Georgetown, 227, 228, 230, 248, 402
Georgia, 109, 203, 417, 418
Giants Staircase, The, 414
Gibraltar, 50
Girard College, 284
Girard, Stephen, 57, 58, 133, 136, 196
Gist, Ann, 123[2]
Gist, Colonel Christopher, 197, 201
Gist, family, 201[2]
Gist, Maria, 10, 11, 13, *et passim*
Globe, organ of Jackson administration, 43[1]
Goodwin-Stoughton affair, the, 21
Gouverneur, Samuel, 395[2]
Gracie, Col., 431
Grant, Mrs., 330, 331
Gratz, 2, 8, 9, *et passim*

Gratz, Ann Maria Shelby (nee Boswell), 298, 299
Gratz, Anna, 342, 380, 386, 388
Gratz, Barnard, father of Mrs. Reuben Henry Etting, 115[2], 135[1], 401[1]
Gratz, Benjamin (Ben), 1, 2[1], 3, 4, *et passim*
Gratz, Bernard, son of Benjamin, 57, 82, 83, 85, 100, *et passim*
Gratz, Cary, son of Benjamin, 105[1], 121, 128, *et passim*
Gratz, Elizabeth, daughter of Simon Gratz, 274
Gratz, family, the, 72, 91, 141[1], 361, 408
Gratz, Howard, son of Benjamin Gratz, 68[1], 78, 79, *et passim*
Gratz, Hyman, brother of Rebecca, 2, 9, 10, 17, 22, *et passim*
Gratz, Hyman, son of Benjamin Gratz, 79, 85, 87, *et passim*
Gratz, Jacob (Jac), brother of Rebecca Gratz, 6[1], 7, 8, 13, 15, 29, 32, 37, 43, *et passim*
Gratz, Joseph (Jo), brother of Rebecca Gratz, 5, 6[2], 10, 12, 15, 17, 20, 21, 32, 37, *et passim*
Gratz, Mason Brown, 326, 329, 331[1]
Gratz, Michael, father of Rebecca Gratz, 3, 9[1]
Gratz, Mrs. Michael, 2[2], 139[1], 198[1]
Gratz, Minerva, 372
Gratz, Miriam, Mother of Rebecca Gratz, 3, 305[1]
Gratz, Miriam, daughter of Benjamin Gratz, 311, 313, 315, 318, 395, 438 (*see* Miriam)
Gratz, Rebecca, *passim* (*see also* Becky, Aunt)
Gratz, Simon, brother of Rebecca Gratz, 37, 40, 44, 56, 62, 73, 84, 86, 87, 274
Gratzs, the, 60
Greeley and Brown, ticket of, 300[1]
Guest, Jona, 19

Hagerstown, 77
Hale, James, 208
Hale, Mrs., 210, 217, 247
Halleck, 147
Hamlet, character of, 328
Hamlet a Prelude, 218
Hamilton, writer, 184, 186
Hannah More's Life, 219, 220
Hare, Dr. Robert, 14[2]
Harrisburg, 44, 47, 111, 225, 226, 235, 240, 257, 279, 370
Harrison, William Henry, President, 285
Hart, Col. Nathaniel G. S., 123[2]
Hart, Henry, son of Colonel Nathaniel G. S. Hart, 123, 150, 194, 200, 205, 219, 220, 411.
Hart, Jo., 180
Hart, Mrs. Nathaniel G. S., 45[1]
Hartford, 112
Havannah, 284, 287
Hays, Dr. Isaac, 7, 8, 14[1], 63, 80[1], 159, 193, 197, 205, 218, 242, 246, 422
Hays, Ellen, 12[2], 96, 97, 135[1], 401[1], 402 (*see* Ellen)
Hays, family, 2
Hays, Henry, 108
Hays, Maria, daughter of Samuel and Richea Gratz Hays, 85

Hays, Miss, 92
Hays, Moses Michael, 2[5]
Hays, Richea Gratz (sister), 85, 91, 101, 109, 143, *et passim*
Hays, Rosa, 50
Hays, Sally, 198, 203, 248, 291, 373, 413; —and the Dr., 214
Hays, Samuel, 2[5], 78, 85, 255
Hays, Sarah, daughter of Samuel and Richea Hays, 85, 126, 142[2], 144, 154, 223
Hays', the, 35, 196
Hazelhurst, Mr., 310
Hebrew Mother, 256, 257
Hebrew Sunday School, 250, 251, 252, 256, 257, 274, 275
Hetty, aunt, 40
History of Lexington, 27[1], 114[1]
Hoffman, Charles, 35, 77, 144, 186, 187, 197, 200
Hoffman, family, 120
Hoffman, George, 250, 279
Hoffman, Judge Ogden, 12[1], 59[1], 232, 233[1], 403
Hoffman, Julia, 77, 78, 121, 135, 136, 143, 147, 220, 233, 250, 256, 312, 323, 325, 420, 421 (*see* Julia)
Hoffman, Maria Fenno, 12[1]
Hoffman, Matilda, 59[1], 233[1]
Hoffman, Mrs. Ogden, 58, 59, 61
Hollidaysburg, 369, 370
Holyoke, Mount, 178
Home Influence, 350, 351, 353
Hopkinson, Judge, 126
Hopkinsville, 328
Horace (*see also* Moses, Horace), 51, 61, 67, 68, 71, *et passim*
Hudson, Henry Norman, 327
Hughes, Mrs., 112, 269

Illinois, 368; —and Wabash claim, 18, 19
Indiana, 18
Indian; —s, 41, 42, 112
Ingersols, the, 431
Irving, Washington, 59[1], 163, 166, 183, 185, 227, 228, 241, 242, 292, 293[1], 387, 414, 415; books of, 147
Isaiah, Book of, 133[1]
Israel, 74, 280, 333
Italian, manner, 337; —music, 357; —opera, 354, 357
Italy, 50, 253
Ivanhoe, 26, 29, 30, 32, 59[1]

Jackson, Andrew, 76[3], 77n, 96, 97[1], 107, 125, 125[2], 159, 166, 219; administration of, 43[1], 123[1], 131; cabinet of, 122, 124; organ of, 135[2]
Jackson, Dr., 219, 285, 287
Jacksonians, 76[3]
James, Rev. Mr., 217
Jefferson, Thomas, 84[1], 284, 285
Jeremiah, Lamentations of, 102, 103
Jerusalem, 102, 254, 261
Jerusalem, 274, 275
Jewish allegiance, 76[2]; —books, 276; —Community, pioneers of Cincinnati, 98[1]; —Encyclopedeia, 25; —festivals, 244; —fold, 76[2]; —Foster Home, the, 406, 407; —holidays, 333; —religion, 276; —rites, 76[2]
Jewish Pioneers of the Ohio Valley, 98[1]
Jews and Masonry, 2[5]
Job, Book of, 102, 103, 116

Johnson, R. W., 213
Johnston, Judge, 167
Johnston, Mrs., 164, 167
Jonas, Abraham, 98[1]
Jonas, Benjamin Franklin, 98[1]
Jonas, Joseph, 98[1]
Joseph, Henry, 126[4], 154, 342, 343, 347, 350, 358, 434[1]
Joseph, Sara, 350, 353, 358, 377, 378, 383, 383[1], 384, 385, 394[1], 409, 424, 431, 434, 437
Joshua, Book of, 281[1]
Judah, tribe of, 275
Judaism, 275
Julia (*see also* Hoffman, Julia), 24, 25, 97, 141, *et passim*

Kappell, Elizabeth, 207
Kean, Edmund, 43
Keating, Professor, 132
Keene, Miss, 58
Kelly, Miss, actress, 81
Kemble, Fanny, actress, 163, 166, 202, 204, 205[1], 220, 358, 359, 399, 431 (*see also* Mrs. Butler)
Kemper, Mrs., 12
Kenilworth, 45, 46, 184
Kennedy, John P., 185
Kentuckians, 12, 31
Kentucky, 9, 10, 11, *et passim*
Keys, Reverend Abraham Israel, 73, 74, 75
King Lear, 368
Kossuth, 379, 381
Kremer, Representative of Pennsylvania, 72, 76, 77*n*

Lafayette, 68
Laggan, 330, 331

Lake George, 178
Lancaster, Pa., 9[1], 56, 139[1], 198[1], 244, 245
Last Man, the, 192, 194
Last Days of Pompeii, the, 214
Latimer, John R., 207
Leatherstocking, 242[1]
Lebanon Springs, Mass., 1[2]
Lee, Ann, 50
Lee, Elizabeth Blair, (Lizzie), 259, 283, 284, 287, 322[1], 353, 361, 362, 402, 418, 422, 423, 425 (*see also* Lizzie)
Lee, General (lieutenant), 31, 353[1], 376
Leeser, Reverend Isaac, 108, 192, 193, 244, 246, 403, 404
Leicester, character of, 46
Leslie, Hope, 112
Levy, Moses, 82
Letitia, mother of the Bonapartes, 58[1]
Letters from the Mountains being the real correspondence of a lady between the years 1773–1807, 331, 331[2]
Lexington, 11, 13, 15, 18, 21, 24, 25, 34, 41, 42, 45, 47, 54, 64, 68, 91, 98, 102, 114, 121, 122, 124, 126[3], 127, 129, 133, 134[1], 139, 166, 169, 174, 175[1], 176, 182, 187, 194[1], 197, 200, 214, 214[2], 217, 219, 221, 223, 230, 238, 255, 271, 278, 286, 301, 302, 306, 307, 308, 313, 316, 324, 329, 339[1], 345, 346, 350, 360, 363, 366, 368[1], 379, 396, 399
Lexingtonians, 77
Liehman, Walter, 152[1]

Life of Ferdinand and Izabella, 261, 263, 264, 265
Life of Gouverneur Morris, 146, 147-8
Lind, Jenny, 369, 370
Livermore, Harriet, 252, 254
Livingston, Maria, 354
Lizzie, 214, 226, 234, 240, 270, 336, 357, 377, 380, 383, 414, 432, 433, 434, 435 (see also Blair, Elizabeth)
London, 40, 314[1], 331[2], 379
Louis Philippe, 225
Louisiana, 98[1], 105, 107[1]
Louisville, 353
Lykens, valley, 325
Lyle, Mary, 14
Lytton, Edward Bulwer, 265[1]

McAlisters, the, 384
McClellan, Gen., 431, 432
McKee, Mrs., 336
Macbeth, 82[1]
Mackoe, Capt., 428
Malbone Miniatures, the, 346
Maloney, Dr., 367
Mammoth Cave, 301, 303
Mariamne, 271, 274, 276
Marshall, Tom, 324, 326
Martineau, Harriet, 159, 211, 213
Marx family, 118
Marx, Joseph, 94, 238, 254
Marx, Richea Myers, 94, 254
Marx, Samuel, 123
Mary (*see also* Boswell, Mary), 60, 278, 285, 290, *et passim*
Maryland, 185[1]
Mather, Mrs., 272
Mathew, Father Theobald, 334

Maysville, 166, 219, 306, 321, 323
Meckelhaar, Mrs. Septimus Randolph, 285
Memoires de la Baronne d'Oberkirch, 392[2]
Memoirs of an American lady, with Sketches of manners and scenes as they existed previous to the Revolution, 331[2]
Men and Manners, 186
Mendelssohn, Moses, 274, 275
Merchant, Valeria, 393
Meredith, Gertrude, 273
Meredith, Mrs., 51, 81, 89, 293
Metcalfe, Thomas, 349[1]
Meredith, William, lawyer, 51, 208
Mexican War, 335, 340
Mexico, 298, 300, 336, 341
Michigan, 187
Mikveh Israel, congregation, 72, 73[2]
Middletown, 152
Middle West, 114[1]
Milton, 146, 147
Minis, Dinah Cohen, mother of Sally, 80[1]
Minis, Isaac, 80[1], 176[1]
Minis, Mrs., 203
Minis, Philips, 157, 158
Minis, Sally, 80, 157, 158, 177, 178, 181, 197, 205
Miriam, (*see* Gratz, Miriam *and also* Etting, Miriam), 107, 109, 118, 176, 178, 191, *et passim*
Missionary Society, 310
Mississippi, 212
Mississippi, river, 96
Missouri, 54, 371, 423, 424
Monroe, Fortress, 183, 429

INDEX

Montagu, Lady, 390
Montgomery, 193, 195, 202, 218, 240
Montreal, 126[4], 155, 342, 343, 348, 358, 377, 378, 383, 386, 394, 434[1]
Mordecai, Alfred, Captain, 85[2], 142[2], 223, 243[2], 387, 388, 395[1], 397, 398, 399, 403, 422, 431, 438
Mordecai, Emma, 325
Mordecai, Jacob, 140, 142, 243[2]
Mordecai, Laura, 232, 243, 392, 403, 414, 415, 418
Mordecai, Rose, 387
Mordecai, Sara, 243, 325, 334[1], 396, 397, 398, 408, 438[1], 439
More, Hannah, 215[1], 216, 279, 353; *Life of*, 215
Morgan, 438; capture of, 437
Moriah, Mount, 281
Moriarty, Father, 309
Morris, Gouverneur, 197, 201
Morrison, Col. James, 26, 27, 30, 31, 34, 40
Morrison College, 27[1], 193
Morton, Mrs., J. R., 125[3]
Moses, biblical, 262, 276, 281
Moses, Becky, 23, 25 (*see also* Becky and Moses, Rebecca Gratz), 74, 120, 278, 279
Moses, Bessie, 411, 412
Moses, Dr. Gratz, 237, 266, 267, 300, 348, 376[1], 376, 411[1], 412
Moses, Dr. Simon Gratz, 153, 249, 302
Moses, Edmund, 357
Moses, Gertrude, 61
Moses girls, 154

Moses, Gratz, 120, 215, 218, 256, 296, 363, 394, 424
Moses, Solomon and Rachel Gratz, 61[1]
Moses, Horace, 35[1], 106[1], 236, 360, 411, 412 (*see also* Horace)
Moses, Isaac, 110, 130, 291, 317, 335
Moses, Mary, 300, 376
Moses, Miriam, 16, 116[2], 324
Moses Myers the Jew, 151, 152[1]
Moses, Rachel Gratz, 35, 65[1], 236[1], 346
Moses, Rebecca Gratz, 214[1], 248[1], 277 (*see also* Becky and Moses, Becky)
Moses, Sara, 324, 337, 342, 343, 344, 346, 347, 348
Moses, Sarah, 106[1], 107, 126, 223
Moses, Solomon, 35[1]; —and Rachel Gratz, 23[1], 74[4], 110[1], 291[1], 357
Mother's Book, The, 140, 141
Mowatt, Anna Cora, 394, 395
Moylan, Stephen, Genl., 2[3]
Murat, Joachim, King of Naples, 125[2], 267[2]
Murat, Mr., 272
Murat, Mrs., 267[2], 277, 278, 288, 350, 351
Murat, Napoleon Lucien Charles, 267[2]
Murat, Prince Joachim, 238, 240, 351[2]
Murat, the younger Prince, 125
Myers, Adeline, 5, 137, 138, 141
Myers, Etting, 97
Myers, Moses, 5[1]
Myers, Mrs. Louisa, 254

INDEX

Naples, 253, 267², 373
Natches, 38
Natty Bumpo, 242¹
Napoleon, III, 267², 351²
Nathan, Becky, 356 (*see also* Becky, Moses, Becky, Moses, Rebecca Gratz)
Nathan, Jonathan, 248¹, 277; —and Rebecca Moses, 318¹
Nathan, Gratz, 318
New England, 132, 350
New Haven, 298
New Orleans, 12, 34, 37, 38, 93, 93², 96, 97, 101, 187, 223¹, 230, 238, 345, 366.
Newport, 433, 434
Newton, 130
Newton, Revd. John, 216
New York, 3, 9, 12¹, 22, 59, 60, 61, 73, 75¹, 98¹, 107, *et passim*
New York American, the newspaper, 144
Niagara, 2, 208, 250, 364
Niagaras, the, 20
Nicholas, Ann, 367
Nicholas, Saml., 367
Night Thoughts, 166
Norfolk, 5¹, 123, 138¹, 152, 283, 429

O'Connell, Daniel, 308, 309
Ogdens, family, 60
Oliver, Dr., 293¹
Olney Hymns, 216¹
Orphan Asylum Society, (of Philadelphia—of Lexington), 23, 24, 26, 49, 52, 53, 112, 176², 182, 190, 210, 214, 216–7, 247, 252, 264, 269, 277, 289, 308, 310

Ohio, 11, 187; —railroad, 114¹; —river, 47, 139, 212, 221

Page, Mrs. Dr., 397
Palestine, 246
Palestine, 260, 272
Paris, 98, 113, 287, 392², 399, 401
Passover, Feast of, 15, 17, 18, 21, 29, 97, 236, 282¹, 383², 409
Paulding, James, writer, 11, 14, 122, 124, 126², 147, 159, 226, 241, 242
Paulding, Mrs., 255
Paul, the Apostle, 213
Peixotto, Reverend Moses Levi Maduro, 73, 74, 75
Pennsylvania, 43, 62, 72, 76, 93, 160, 272, 279, 287, 324
Pensacola, 115, 341
Pentecost, 394, 395
Peters, Miss, 123, 135, 136, 151, 207, 253, 254
Peters, Mr., 13, 337
Philadelphia, 6, 15, 23¹, 33, 41, 43, 44, *et passim*
Philadelphian, 93, 307, 309
Phillips, Leah, 139
Phillips, Levi, 108, 139
Phillips, Mrs. Hardman, 254
Phrenology, 194, 195
Physick, Dr. Philip Syng, 63, 123
Pittsburgh, 10, 11, 13, 48, 91, 123, 129, 212, 217, 219
Poetry of the Hebrews, 365, 366
Polk, James, 301, 304¹
Pope, 146, 147
Portland, 114¹, 194¹
Portuguese, 225
Pratt, Mme., 113

Prescott, William H., 261, 263, 264, 265, 298, 300
Princeton, 303
Proteus, Dr., 216
Purim, Festival of, 15, 17, 17[1], 435, 436; —gift, 381

Quebec, 378

Ranck, historian, 27[1], 114[1]
Randolph, John, 205, 206
Randolph, Sara N., 285[1]
Raphall, Rev. Dr. J. M., 365, 366, 368
Rebecca, character of, in Ivanhoe, 32, 59[1]
Recollections of Rebecca Gratz by one of her nieces, 85[2], 395[1]
Reed, Wm. B., 431
Reich, 122, 124
Revolution, French, 391
Revolution, the, 2[3], 84[1]
Richea, sister of Rebecca Gratz, 2[5], 270
Richmond, 9, 92, 94, 118, 222, 240[1], 243, 336, 395[2], 403, 438
Rienzi, 224, 226
Riggs, Elisha, 361, 362, 365, 374, 434
Riggs, Mary, 383, 402, 434
Ritchie, William F., 395[2]
Rocky Mountains, 322
Robert De Paris, 124, 126
Rome, 58
Rosh Hashanah, 7, 8
Rothermel, artist, 413, 414
Rural Hours, 376
Rush, Dr. Benjamin, 93[1]
Rush, Dr. James, 218

Rutledge, Reverend Mr., 106, 141[1], 152

Sabbath, 73, 333, 334, 350, 369, 370, 427
Sacred Rolls, 73 (*see also* Scriptures)
San Francisco, 393
Sargeant, Mrs. John, 50
Saratoga Springs, 41, 186, 203, 242, 266, 317, 350, *et passim*
Savannah, 38, 80[1], 177[1], 280, 323, 324[1], 341, 436
Sartor Resartus, 238, 240, 244, 250
Schuyler, General, 1, 1[1]
Schuyler, Aunt & Uncle of the Gratz's, 3
Schuylkill, 318; canal of, 32
Scott, Charles, General, 13, 13[1]
Scott, Mrs., 13, 45, 170
Scott, Sir Walter, 30, 45, 47, 54, 59[1], 124, 126, 137, 139, 140, 252, 253, 264, 265
Scripture; —s, the, 59, 84, 164, 197, 199, 257, 281, 319, 401
Sedgwick, Catharine, 109, 111, 112, 292, 293
Sedgwick, Mr. and Mrs. Charles, 352
Sedgwick, Robert, 292, 293
Sergeant, Henry, 68
Sergeant, John, 215
Seixas, Benjamin Mendes, 74[2]
Seixas, David, 26, 28, 49, 51, 98
Seixas, Gershom Mendes, Reverend, 28[2], 74, 98[1]
Seixas, Jacob, 74
Seixas, Miriam, 74
Seixas, Zipporah Levy, 74[2]

INDEX 453

Sevigne, Madame de, 390
Shearith Israel Congregation, 73[4], 75[1]
Shakespeare, 34, 132[2], 149, 202, 203, 354, 356, 357, 359, 375
Shakespeare, His Life, Art and Character, 328[1]
Shelby, Joseph, (Jo), 327[1], 363, 396, 405, 423, 424, 426, 435
Shelby, Mrs. O., 232
Shelley, 186[1]
Shelley, Mrs. Mary Woolstonecraft, 192, 194
Sigorgnes, Mrs., 147, 182, 192, 230, 290
Silver Spring, 361, 364, 402, 434
Simon, Hetty, aunt, 42 (*see also* Hetty, Aunt)
Simon, Joseph, 9, 58, 139[1], 198[1], 244, 245[1], 245[2], 246[n]; —and Rosa, 245[2]
Simon, Rosa, 245[2], 246[n]
Simon, Shinah, 1
Smallie, writer, 102
Smith, Bishop, 245
Smith, Mrs. William Stephen, 385[2]
Smith, William Stephen, 285[2]
Smyrna, melons of, 382
South Carolina, 208, 229, 236, 419
Spain, 41[1]; Jews of, 276
Spark, Jared, 148[1], 200, 201
Spurzheim, 194, 195, 260, 261
St. Lawrence river, 378, 382, 383
St. Louis, 54, 218[1], 268, 301, 302[1], 302[3], 361, 363, 376[1], 379, 380, 399, 410, 411, 424[2]
Stark, Mr., 156, 157, 158
Stevens, John, 354
Stockton, Capt., 303
Sully, artist, 124, 126[3], 131, 132, 200, 209
Sully, Mrs., 161
Sulphur Springs, 102
Sunday School Union, 136
Swain, Panacea, 81, 82
Supreme Court, 72[1], 84[1]
Swallow Barn, 185

Tabernacles, Feast of, 244, 266, 268, 334
Tales of My Landlord, 140, 142
Taylor, General, 347, 349
Ten Lost Tribes of Israel, the, 274, 275
Tennessee, 210
Texas, 348, 360
The Backwoodsman, 11, 14
The Columbia Observer, newspaper, 77*n*
The Days of Bruce, 387
The Dutchman's Fireside, 122, 124, 126
The Great Western (ship), 252
Tilford, Major, 219, 287
Tilghman, Ben, 89, 90
Tisha b'Ab, 102[1]
Touro, Judah, 2[5]
Transylvania College, 120, 121
Transylvania University, 27, 30, 31, 34[1], 99, 104, 134[1], 194[1], 214[2], 235, 237
Treaty, the Spanish, 40, 41[1]
Trelawney, Edward John, 186
Trenton, Falls of, 242
Tressilian, character, in Scott's *Kenilworth,* 46
Trollope, Anthony, 212[1]

INDEX

Trollope, Mrs. Frances, 212[1]
Troy, New York, 1, 3

United States, 41[1], 57, 68, 114[1], 125, 194[1], 208, 211, 212[1], 240[2], 250, 267[2], 282[1], 334[3], 340, 342, 377, 379, 426, 435; Bank Bill of, 224, 225; Navy of, 115[1], 353[1], 371, 399[1], 431[1]; president of, 3; rabbis of, 366[1]; senate of, 152[1], 347, 349[1]; senator of, 98[1], 105, 107[1]
University of Pennsylvania, 14[1,3], 63[1], 93[1], 110[1], 153[1]
Urquharts, family, 101
Utica, New York, 242

Van Buren, President, 150, 232, 282[1]
Vaughan, John, 103, 133, 270
Venice, 281[1]
Vermont, 330
Vertner, Mrs., 273, 318, 397
Vertner, Rosa, 413
Vertners, the, 413
Victoria, Queen, 252
Vincennes, 15, 18, 19
Virginia, 30, 39, 185, 209, 240, 332, 350, 436
Virginia Springs, 389
Virginian, 31

Wahcoleet, 422
Walm, Wm., 82
Warfield, Mrs. E., 318
Warrenton, N. C., 142
Washington, D. C., 15, 17, 18, 27, 43[1], 44, 97, 114, *et passim*
Washington, George, 1, 2[3], 240, 279, 385[2]

Washington Globe, the (newspaper), 122, 125[2], 132[1]
Washington Hall, 199
Washington, Sparks', 200
Washington, Mrs., 200
Westchester, 338
West Indies, 87, 100
Westward Ho, 159
Wharton, F. I., 112
Wharton, Thomas I., 72, 256, 257
Wheeling, 166, 306, 307, 369
White House, the, 126[1]
White Sulphur Springs, 412
Wiconisco, 325
Wikoff, Harry, 80
Wilkesbarre, 273
Williams, Harry, 13, 24
Williamstown, 98[1]
Willing, Mary, 14
Willing, Mr., 136
Willington, 87
Willoughby, Lady Elizabeth, 314
Wilmington, 7
Wilson's Creek, 424
Wilson, Judge James, 84[1], 331[2]
Winter in the West, 200
Wise, Rev. Dr. Isaac M., 76[2]
Wolfe, Reverend Joseph, 244, 246
Woman's Mission, 269
Women and their Mothers, 283
Wood, Mrs., 285
Woodward, W. E., 201[2]
Wright, Julia, 229, 230

Yeatman, Mrs., 210
Yellow Springs, a watering place, 1
Young's *Night Thoughts*, 166

Zohar, the, 276[1]

Bar Mitzvah 75
Prayers for a
mixed marriage 76